A TREATISE ON WHITE MAGIC

OR

THE WAY OF THE DISCIPLE

BY
ALICE A. BAILEY

ISBN: 978-1-63923-527-8

Printed: October 2022

Cover Art By: Amit Paul

Published and Distributed By:
Lushena Books
607 Country Club Drive, Unit E
Bensenville, IL 60106
www.lushenabks.com

ISBN: 978-1-63923-527-8

RULES FOR MAGIC

RULE ONE
The Solar Angel collects himself, scatters not his force, but, in meditation deep, communicates with his reflection.

RULE TWO
When the shadow hath responded, in meditation deep the work proceedeth. The lower light is thrown upward; the greater light illuminates the three, and the work of the four proceedeth.

RULE THREE
The Energy circulates. The point of light, the product of the labours of the four, waxeth and groweth. The myriads gather round its glowing warmth until its light recedes. Its fire grows dim. Then shall the second sound go forth.

RULE FOUR
Sound, light, vibration, and the form blend and merge, and thus the work is one. It proceedeth under the law, and naught can hinder now the work from going forward. The man breathes deeply. He concentrates his forces, and drives the thought-form from him.

RULE FIVE
Three things engage the Solar Angel before the sheath of the one who thus creates, and steady contemplation. Thus are the heart, the throat, and eye, allied for triple service.

RULE SIX
The devas of the lower four feel the force when the eye opens; they are driven forth and lose their master.

RULE SEVEN
The dual forces of the plane whereon the vital power must be sought are seen; the two paths face the solar Angel; the poles vibrate. A choice confronts the one who meditates.

RULE EIGHT
The Agnisuryans respond to the sound. The waters ebb and flow. Let the magician guard himself from drowning at the point where land and water meet. The midway spot, which is neither dry nor wet, must provide the standing place whereon his feet are set. When water, land and air meet, there is the place for magic to be wrought.

RULE NINE
Condensation next ensues. The fire and waters meet, the form swells and grows. Let the magician set his form upon the proper path.

RULE TEN
As the waters bathe the form created, they are absorbed and used. The form increases in its strength; let the magician thus continue until the work suffices. Let the outer builders cease their labors then,

2

and let the inner workers enter on their cycle.

RULE ELEVEN
Three things the worker with the law must now accomplish. First, ascertain the formula which will confine the lives within the ensphering wall; next, pronounce the words which will tell them what to do and where to carry that which has been made; and finally, utter forth the mystic phrase which will save him from their work.

RULE TWELVE
The web pulsates. It contracts and expands. Let the magician seize the midway point and thus release those "prisoners of the planet" whose note is right and justly tuned to that which must be made.

RULE THIRTEEN
The magician must recognize the four; note in his work the shade of violet they evidence, and thus construct the shadow. When this is so, the shadow clothes itself, and the four become the seven.

RULE FOURTEEN
The sound swells out. The hour of danger to the soul courageous draweth near. The waters have not hurt the white creator and naught could drown nor drench him. Danger from fire and flame menaces now, and dimly yet the rising smoke is seen. Let him again, after the cycle of peace, call on the solar Angel.

RULE FIFTEEN
The fires approach the shadow, yet burn it not. The fire sheath is completed. Let the magician chant the words that blend the fire and water.

From "A TREATISE ON COSMIC FIRE"

INTRODUCTORY REMARKS

Man's Three Aspects

In the study of the ideas outlined in this book and their careful consideration certain basic concepts are borne in mind:

First, that the matter of prime importance to each student is not the fact of a particular teacher's personality but the measure of truth for which he stands, and the student's power to discriminate between truth, partial truth, and falsity.

Second, that with increased esoteric teaching comes increased exoteric responsibility. Let each student with clarity therefore take stock of himself, remembering that understanding comes through application of the measure of truth grasped to the immediate problem and environment, and that the consciousness expands through use of the truth imparted.

Third, that a dynamic adherence to the chosen path and a steady perseverance that overcomes and remains unmoved by aught that may eventuate, is a prime requisite and leads to the portal admitting to a kingdom, a dimension and a state of being which is inwardly or subjectively known. It is this state of realisation which produces changes in form and environment commensurate with its power.

These three suggestions will merit a close consideration by all, and their significance must be somewhat grasped before further real progress is possible. It is not my function to make individual and personal application of the teaching given. That must be done by each student for himself.

You have wisely guarded the teaching from the taint of superimposed authority, and there lies back of your books no esoteric principle of hierarchical authority or support, such as has produced the narrow limits of certain ecclesiastical bodies and groups, differing as widely as the Catholic Church, Christian Science, those who believe in the verbal inspiration of the Scriptures, and numerous (so-called) esoteric organisations. The curse of many groups has been the whispered word that "Those who know wish...." "The Master says...." "The Great Ones command..." and the group of silly sheep feebly and blindly tumble over themselves to obey. They think thereby, through their misplaced devotion, to contact certain authoritative personages, and to get into heaven by some short cut.

You have wisely guarded your books from the reaction accorded to those who claim to be masters, adepts and initiates. My anonymity and status must be preserved, and my rank be regarded as only that of a senior student and of an aspirant to that expansion of consciousness which is for me the next step forward. What I say of truth alone is of moment; the inspiration and help I can accord to any pilgrim on the path is alone vital; that which I have learned through experience is at the disposal of the earnest aspirant; and the wideness of the vision which I can impart (owing to my having climbed higher up the mountain than some) is my main contribution. Upon these points the students are at liberty to ponder, omitting idle speculation as to the exact details of unimportant personalities, and environing conditions.

Our theme is to be that of the Magic of the Soul, and the key thought, underlying all that may appear in this book, is to be found in the words of the *Bhagavad Gita* which runs as follows:

"Though I am Unborn, the Soul that passes not away, though I am the Lord of Beings, yet as Lord over My nature I become manifest, through the magical power of the Soul." Gita IV.6.

The statistical and the academic is a necessary basis and a preliminary step for most scientific study, but in this book we will centre our attention on the life aspect, and the practical application of truth to the daily life of the aspirant. Let us study how we can become practical magicians, and in what way we can best live the life of a spiritual man, and of an aspirant to accepted discipleship in our own peculiar times, state and environment.

To do this we will take the Fifteen Rules for Magic to be found in my earlier book, entitled *A Treatise on Cosmic Fire*. I will comment on them, dealing not with their cosmic significance or with solar and other correspondences and analogies, but applying them to the work of the aspirant, and giving practical suggestions for the better development of soul contact and soul manifestation. I shall take for granted certain knowledges and assume the students can follow and comprehend certain technical terms that I may be led to use. I am not dealing with babes but with matured men and women who have chosen a certain way and who are pledged to "walk in the light."

4

I seek in this book to do four things, and to make appeal to three types of people. It is based, as regards its teaching, upon four fundamental postulates. These are intended to:

1. Teach the laws of spiritual psychology as distinguished from mental and emotional psychology.
2. Make clear the nature of the soul of man and its systemic and cosmic relationships. This will include its group relationship as a preliminary step.
3. Demonstrate the relations between the self and the sheaths which that self may use, and thus clarify public thought as to the constitution of man.
4. Elucidate the problem of the supernormal powers, and give the rules for their safe and useful development.

We stand now towards the close of a great transition period and the subtler realms of life are closer than ever before; unusual phenomena and inexplicable happenings are commoner than at any time heretofore, whilst matters telepathic, psychic, and peculiar occupy the attention even of sceptics, scientists, and religionists. Reasons for the appearance of phenomena are being everywhere sought, and societies are formed for their investigation and demonstration. Many are likewise going astray in the effort to induce in themselves psychic conditions and the energy-producing factors which give rise to the manifestation of peculiar powers. This book will endeavor to fit the information given into the scheme of life as we today recognize it and will show how basically natural and true is all that is termed mysterious. All is under law, and the laws need elucidation now that man's development has reached the stage of a juster appreciation of their beauty and reality.

Three types of people will respond to this book. They are:

1. Those *open minded investigators* who are willing to accept its fundamentals as a working hypothesis until these are demonstrated to be erroneous. They will be frankly agnostic, but willing temporarily, in their search for truth, to try out the methods and follow the suggestions laid down for their consideration.
2. *Aspirants and disciples.* They will study this treatise in order to understand themselves better and because they seek to help their brother man. They will not accept its dicta blindly but will experiment, check and corroborate with care the stages and steps laid down for them in this section of the teachings of the Ageless Wisdom.
3. *Initiates.* These persons will arrive at a meaning which will not be apparent to those in the first group and which will only be suspected by the more advanced members of the second. Within themselves they know the truth of many of its statements and will realise the subjective working out of many of the laws. These laws of nature have effects in three distinct realms:
a. Physically, where they demonstrate as effects in the dense form.
b. Etherically, where they demonstrate as the energy lying back of those effects.
c. Mentally, where they concern the impulses which produce the other two.

The *Treatise on Cosmic Fire* dealt primarily with the solar system and only touched upon human aspects and correspondences insofar as they demonstrated the relation of the part to the whole, and of the unit to the totality.

The present book will deal more specifically with human development and unfoldment, elucidating the causes which are responsible for the present effects, and pointing to the future and its possibilities, and to the nature of the unfolding potentialities.

This book will be based also upon four fundamental postulates which must be admitted by the student of the succeeding pages as providing an hypothesis worthy of his consideration and trial. No true investigator of the Ageless Wisdom is asked to give blind adherence to any presentation of truth; he is asked, however, to have an open mind and seriously to weigh and consider the theories and ideals, the laws and the truths which have guided so many out of darkness into the light of knowledge and experience. The postulates might be enumerated as follows and are given in the order of their importance.

I. First, that there exists in our manifested universe the expression of an Energy or Life which is the responsible cause of the diverse forms and the vast hierarchy of sentient beings who compose the sum total of all that is. This is the so-called hylozoistic theory, though the term but serves to confuse. This great Life is the basis of Monism, and all enlightened men are Monists. "God is One" is the utterance of truth. One life pervades all forms and those forms are the expressions, in time and space, of the central universal energy. Life in manifestation produces existence and being. It is the root cause, therefore, of duality. This duality which is seen when objectivity is present and which disappears when the form aspect vanishes is covered by many terms, of which for the sake of clarity, the most usual might be here listed:

Spirit	Matter
Life --------------------	Form
Father------------------	Mother
Positive----------------	Negative
Darkness --------------	Light

Students must clearly have this essential unity in mind e'en when they talk (as they needs must) in finite terms of that duality which is everywhere, cyclically, apparent.

II. The second postulate grows out of the first and states that the one Life, manifesting through matter, produces a third factor which is consciousness. This consciousness, which is the result of the union of the two poles of spirit and matter is the soul of all things; it permeates all substance or objective energy; it underlies all forms, whether it be the form of that unit of energy which we call an atom, or the form of man, a planet, or a solar system. This is the *Theory of Self-determination* or the teaching that all the lives of which the one life is formed, in their sphere and in their state of being, become, so to speak, grounded in matter and assume forms whereby their peculiar specific state of consciousness may be realised and their vibration stabilised; thus they may know themselves as existences. Thus again the one life becomes a stabilised and conscious entity through the medium of the solar system, and is essentially, therefore the sum total of energies, of all states of consciousness, and of all forms in existence. The homogeneous becomes the heterogeneous, and yet remains a unity; the one manifests in diversity and yet is unchanged; the central unity is known in time and space as composite and differentiated and yet, when time and space are not (being but states of consciousness), only the unity will remain, and only spirit will persist, plus an increased vibratory action, plus capacity for an intensification of the light when again the cycle of manifestation returns.

Within the vibratory pulsation of the one manifesting Life all the lesser lives repeat the process of being,—Gods, angels, men, and the myriad lives which express themselves through the forms of the kingdoms of nature and the activities of the evolutionary process. All become self-centered and self-determined.

III. The third basic postulate is that the object for which life takes form and the purpose of manifested being is the unfoldment of consciousness, or the revelation of the soul. This might be called the *Theory of the Evolution of Light*. When it is realised that even the modern scientist is saying that light and matter are synonymous terms, thus echoing the teaching of the East, it becomes apparent that through the interplay of the poles, and through the friction of the pairs of opposites light flashes forth. The goal of evolution is found to be a gradual series of light demonstrations. Veiled and hidden by every form lies light. As evolution proceeds, matter becomes increasingly a better conductor of the light, thus demonstrating the accuracy of the statement of the Christ "I am the Light of the World".

IV. The fourth postulate consists of the statement that all lives manifest cyclically. This is the *Theory of Rebirth* or of re-incarnation, the demonstration of the law of periodicity.

Such are the great underlying truths which form the foundation of the Ageless Wisdom—the existence of life, and the development of consciousness through the cyclic taking of form.

In this book, however, the emphasis will be laid upon the little life; upon man "made in the image of God", who through the method of re-incarnation unfolds his consciousness until it flowers forth as the perfected soul, whose nature is light and whose realisation is that of a self-conscious identity. This developed unit has eventually to be merged, with full intelligent participation, in the greater consciousness of which it is a part.

Before we take up our subject it might be of value if we defined certain words which will be in constant use, so that we will know what we are talking about, and the significance of the terms we use.

1. *Occult.* This term concerns the hidden forces of being and those springs of conduct which produce the objective manifestation. The word "conduct" is used here deliberately, for all manifestation, in all the kingdoms of nature, is the expression of the life, purpose and type of activity of some being or existence, and thus is literally the conduct (or outer nature or quality) of a life. These springs of action lie hid in the purpose of any life, whether it be a solar life, a planetary entity, a man, or that Being who is the *sum total* of the states of consciousness and of the forms of any kingdom in nature.

2. *Laws.* A law presupposes a superior being who, gifted with purpose, and aided by intelligence, is so coordinating his forces that a plan is being sequentially and steadily matured. Through a clear knowledge of the goal, that entity sets in activity those steps and stages which when carried forward in order will bring the plan to perfection. The word "law", as usually understood, conveys the idea of subjection to an activity which is recognised as inexorable and undeviating, but which is not understood by the one who is subjected to it; it involves, from one standpoint, the attitude of the submersed unit in the group impulse and the inability of that unit to change the impulse or evade the issue; it inevitably brings about in the consciousness of the man who is considering these laws, a feeling of being a victim—of being driven forward like a leaf before the breeze towards an end about which speculation only is possible, and of being governed by a force which acts apparently with an unavoidable pressure and thus produces group results, at the expense of the unit. This attitude of mind is inevitable until the consciousness of man can be so expanded that he becomes aware of the greater issues. When, through contact with his own higher self, he participates in the knowledge of the objective, and when through climbing the mountain of vision his perspective changes and his horizon enlarges, he comes to the realisation that a law is but the spiritual impulse, incentive and life manifestation of that Being in which he lives and moves. He learns that that impulse demonstrates an intelligent purpose, wisely directed, and based on love. He then himself begins to wield the law or to

pass wisely, lovingly and intelligently through himself as much of that spiritual life impulse which his particular organism can respond to, transmit and utilise. He ceases to obstruct and begins to transfer. He brings to an end the cycle of the closed self-centered life, and opens the doors wide to spiritual energy. In so doing he finds that the law which he has hated and mistrusted is the vitalising, purifying agency which is sweeping him and all God's creatures on to a glorious consummation.

3. *Psychic.* There are two types of the above force in manifestation as far as the human kingdom is concerned, and these must be clearly grasped. There is the force which animates the subhuman kingdoms in nature,—the ensouling energy which, brought into conjunction with the energy of matter and self, produces all forms. The effect of this junction is to add to the embryo intelligence of substance itself a latent sentiency and responsiveness that produces that subjective something we call the animal soul. This exists in four degrees or states of sentient awareness:

a. The consciousness of the mineral kingdom.
b. The consciousness of the vegetable kingdom.
c. The consciousness of the animal kingdom.
d. The consciousness of the animal form through which the spiritual man functions, which after all is but a department of the former group in its highest presentation.

Secondly, there is that psychic force which is the result of the union of the spirit with sentient matter in the human kingdom and which produces a psychic centre which we call the soul of man. This psychic centre is a force centre, and the force of which it is the custodian or which it demonstrates, brings into play a responsiveness and an awareness which is that of the soul of the planetary life, a group consciousness which brings with it faculties and knowledge of a different order than that in the animal soul. These supersede eventually the powers of the animal soul which limit, distort, and imprison, and give man a range of contacts and a knowledge which is infallible, free from error, and which admits him to "the freedom of the heavens". The effect of the free play of the soul of man serves to demonstrate the fallibility and relative uselessness of the powers of the animal soul. All I desire to do here is to show the two senses in which the word "psychic" is used. Later we will deal with the growth and development of the lower psychic nature or the soul of the vehicles in which man functions in the three worlds, and then will seek to elucidate the true nature of the soul of man and of the powers which can be brought into play once a man can contact his own spiritual centre, the soul, and live in that soul consciousness.

4. *Unfoldment.* The life at the heart of the solar system is producing an evolutionary unfoldment of the energies of that universe which it is not possible for finite man as yet to vision. Similarly the centre of energy which we call the spiritual aspect in man is (through the utilisation of matter or substance) producing an evolutionary development of that which we call the soul, and which is the highest of the *form* manifestations—the human kingdom. Man is the highest product of existence in the three worlds. By man, I mean the spiritual man, a son of God in incarnation. The forms of all the kingdoms of nature—human, animal, vegetable and mineral—contribute to that manifestation. The energy of the third aspect of divinity tends to the revelation of the soul or the second aspect which in turn reveals the highest aspect. It must ever be remembered that *The Secret Doctrine* of H. P. Blavatsky expresses this with accuracy in the words "Life we look upon as the one form of existence, manifesting in what is called Matter; or what, incorrectly separating them, we name spirit, soul and matter in man. Matter is the vehicle for the manifestation of soul on this plane of existence, and soul is the vehicle on a higher plane for the manifestation of spirit, and these three are a trinity synthesized by life, which pervades them all." (*The Secret Doctrine.* Vol: I. p. 79. 80.)

Through the use of matter the soul unfolds and finds its climax in the soul of man, and this treatise will concern itself with the unfoldment of that soul and its discovery by man.

5. *Knowledge* might be divided into three categories:—First, there is *theoretical knowledge*. This includes all knowledge of which man is aware but which is accepted by him on the statements of other people, and by the specialists in the various branches of knowledge. It is founded on authoritative statements and has in it the element of trust in the writers and speakers, and in the trained intelligences of the workers in any of the many and varied fields of thought. The truths accepted as such have not been formulated or verified by the one who accepts them, lacking as he does the necessary training and equipment. The dicta of science, the theologies of religion, and the findings of the philosophers and thinkers everywhere colour the point of view and meet with a ready acquiescence from the untrained mind, and that is the average mind.

Then, secondly, we have *discriminative knowledge*, which has in it a selective quality and which posits the intelligent appreciation and practical application of the more specifically scientific method, and the utilisation of test, the elimination of that which cannot be proved, and the isolation of those factors which will bear investigation and are in conformity with what is understood as law. The rational, argumentative, scholastic, and concretising mind is brought into play with the result that much that is childish, impossible and unverifiable is rejected and a consequent clarifying of the fields of thought results. This discriminating and scientific process has enabled man to arrive at much truth in relation to the three worlds. The scientific method is, in relation to the mind of humanity, playing the same function as the occult method of meditation (in its first two stages of concentration and prolonged concentration or meditation) plays in relation to the individual. Through it right processes of thought are engendered, non-essentials and incorrect formulations of truth are ultimately eliminated or corrected, and the steady focussing of the attention either upon a seed thought, a scientific problem, a philosophy or a world situation results in an ultimate clarifying and the steady seeping in of right ideas and sound conclusions. The foremost thinkers in any of the great schools of thought are simply exponents of occult meditation and the brilliant discoveries of science, the correct interpretations of nature's laws, and the formulations of correct conclusions whether in the fields of science, of economics, of philosophy, psychology or elsewhere is but the registering by the mind (and subsequently by the brain) of the eternal verities, and the indication that the race is beginning also to bridge the gap between the objective and the subjective, between the world of form and the world of ideas.

This leads inevitably to the emergence of the third branch of *knowledge, the intuitive*. The intuition is in reality only the appreciation by the mind of some factor in creation, some law of manifestation and some aspect of truth, known by the soul, emanating from the world of ideas, and being of the nature of those energies which produce all that is known and seen. These truths are always present, and these laws are ever active, but only as the mind is trained and developed, focussed, and open-minded can they be recognized, later understood, and finally adjusted to the needs and demands of the cycle and time. Those who have thus trained the mind in the art of clear thinking, the focussing of the attention, and consequent receptivity to truth have always been with us, but hitherto have been few and far between. They are the outstanding minds of the ages. But now they are many and increasingly found. The minds of the race are in process of training and many are hovering on the borders of a new knowledge. The intuition which guides all advanced thinkers into the newer fields of learning is but the forerunner of that omniscience which characterises the soul. The truth about all things exists, and we call it omniscience, infallibility, the "correct knowledge" of the Hindu philosophy. When man

9

grasps a fragment of it and absorbs it into the racial consciousness we call it the formulation of a law, a discovery of one or other of nature's processes. Hitherto this has been a slow and piecemeal undertaking. Later, and before so very long, light will pour in, truth will be revealed and the race will enter upon its heritage—the heritage of the soul.

In some of our considerations, speculation must perforce enter in. Those who see a vision that is withheld from those lacking the necessary equipment for its apprehension are regarded as fanciful, and unreliable. When many see the vision, its possibility is admitted, but when humanity itself has the awakened and open eye, the vision is no longer emphasised but a fact is stated and a law enunciated. Such has been the history of the past and such will be the process in the future.

The past is purely speculative from the standpoint of the average man and the future is equally so, but he himself is the result of that past and the future will work out of the sum total of his present characteristics and qualities. If this is true of the individual it is then also equally true of mankind as a whole. That unit in nature, which we call the fourth or human kingdom, represents that which is the product of its physical heritage; its characteristics are the sum of its emotional and mental unfoldments and its assets are those which it has succeeded in accumulating during the cycles wherein it has been wrestling with its environment—the sum total of the other kingdoms in nature. Within the human kingdom lie potentialities and latencies, characteristics and assets which the future will reveal and which in their turn determine that future.

I have purposely chosen to begin with the undefinable and the unrecognised. The soul is as yet an unknown quantity. It has no real place in the theories of the academic and scientific investigators. It is unproven and regarded by even the more open-minded of the academicians as a possible hypothesis, but lacking demonstration. It is not accepted as a fact in the consciousness of the race. Only two groups of people accept it as a fact; one is the gullible, undeveloped, childlike person who, brought up on a scripture of the world, and being religiously inclined, accepts the postulates of religion—such as the soul, God and immortality—without questioning. The other is that small but steadily growing band of Knowers of God, and of reality, who know the soul to be a fact in their own experience but are unable to prove its existence satisfactorily to the man who admits only that which the concrete mind can grasp, analyse, criticise and test.

The ignorant and the wise meet on common ground as extremes always do. In between are those who are neither totally ignorant nor intuitively wise. They are the mass of the educated people who have knowledge but not understanding, and who have yet to learn the distinction between that which can be grasped by the rational mind, that which can be seen by the mind's eye, and that which only the higher or abstract mind can formulate and know. This ultimately merges in the intuition, which is the "knowing faculty" of the intelligent and practical mystic who—relegating the emotional and feeling nature to its own place—uses the mind as a focussing point and looks out through that lens upon the world of the soul.

MAN'S THREE ASPECTS

One of the main means whereby man arrives at an understanding of that great sum total we call the Macrocosm—God, functioning through a solar system—is by an understanding of himself, and the Delphic injunction "Man, know thyself" was an inspired utterance, intended to give man the clue to the mystery of deity. Through the Law of Analogy, or correspondences, the cosmic processes, and the nature of the cosmic principles are indicated in the functions, structure, and characteristics of a human being. They are indicated but not explained or elaborated. They serve simply as sign posts, directing man along the path whereon future sign posts may be found and more definite indications noted.

The comprehension of that triplicity of spirit, soul, and body lies as yet beyond man's achievement, but an idea as to their relationship and their general coordinated function may be indicated by a consideration of man from the physical side, and his objective functioning.

There are three aspects of man's organism which are symbols, and symbols only, of the three aspects of being.

1. The energy, or activating principle, which withdraws mysteriously at death, partially withdraws in the hours of sleep or of unconsciousness, and which seems to use the brain as its main seat of activity and from there to direct the functioning of the organism. This energy has a primary direct relation with the three parts of the organism which we call the brain, the heart, and the breathing apparatus. This is the microcosmic symbol of spirit.

2. The nervous system, with its complexities of nerves, nerve centres and that multiplicity of interrelated and sensitive parts which serve to coordinate the organism, to produce the sensitive response which exists between the many organs and parts which form the organism as a whole, and which serve also to make the man aware of, and sensitive to, his environment. This entire sensory apparatus is that which produces the organised awareness and coordinated sensitivity of the entire human being, first, within itself as a unit, and secondly, its responsiveness and sensitive reaction to the world within which it plays its part. This nervous structure, coordinating, correlating, and producing an outer and inner group activity demonstrates primarily through the three parts of the nervous system.

a. Cerebro-spinal system.
b. Sensory system of nerves.
c. Peripheral system of nerves.

It is closely associated with the energy aspect, being the apparatus utilised by that energy to vitalise the body, to produce its coordinated activity and functioning, and to bring about an intelligent rapport with the world in which it has to play its part. It lies back, if one might use such an expression, of the body-nature proper, back of the mass of the flesh and bone and muscle. It in its turn, is motivated by and controlled by two factors:

a. The sum total of the energy which is the individual quota of vital energy.
b. The energy of the environment in which the individual finds himself and within which he has to function and to play his part.

This coordinating nervous system, this network of interrelating and sensitive nerves is the symbol in man of the soul, and an outer and visible form of an inner spiritual reality.

3. There is finally what might be described as the body, the sum total of flesh, of muscle, and of bone which the man carries around, correlated by the nervous system and energised by what we vaguely call his "life".

In these three, the life, the nervous system and the body mass we find the reflection and the symbol of the greater whole, and by a close study of these, and a comprehension of their functions and group relation, we can arrive at an understanding of some of the laws and principles which direct the activities of "God in nature"—a phrase, sublimely true and equally finitely false.

The three aspects of divinity, the central energy, or spirit, the coordinating force or soul, and that which these two use and unify are in reality one vital principle manifesting in diversity. These are the Three in One, the One in Three, God in nature, and nature itself in God.

Carrying the concept, for the sake of illustration, into other realms of thought this trinity of aspects can be seen functioning in the religious world as the esoteric teaching, the fundamental symbology and doctrines of the great world religions and the exoteric organisations; in government it is the sum total of the will of the people whatever that will may be, the formulated laws, and the exoteric administration; in education it is the will to learn, the arts and sciences, and the great exoteric educational systems; in philosophy it is the urge to wisdom, the interrelated schools of thought, and the outer presentation of the teachings. Thus this eternal triplicity runs through every department of the manifested world, whether viewed as that which is tangible, or as that which is sensitive and coherent, or that which is energising. It is that intelligent activity which has been clumsily called "awareness"; it is the capacity of awareness itself, involving as it does sensitive response to environment, and the apparatus of that response, the divine duality of the soul; it is finally the sum total of that which is contacted and known; it is that of which the sensitive apparatus becomes aware. This, as we shall see later, is a gradually growing realisation, shifting ever into more esoteric and inner realms.

These three aspects are seen in man, the divine unit of life. First he recognises them in himself; then he sees them in every form in his environment, and finally he learns to relate these aspects of himself to the similar aspects in other forms of divine manifestation. Correct relation between forms will result in the harmonising and right adjustment of physical plane life. Correct response to one's environment will result in correct rapport with the soul aspect, hidden in every form, and will produce right relations between the various parts of the inner nervous structure to be found in every kingdom of nature, subhuman and superhuman. This is as yet practically unknown but is rapidly coming into recognition, and when it is proven and realised it will be discovered that therein lies the basis of brotherhood and of unity. As the liver, the heart, the lungs, the stomach, and other organs in the body are separate in existence and in function and yet are unified and brought into relation through the medium of the nervous system throughout the body, so will it be found that in the world such organisms as the kingdoms in nature have their separate life and functions yet are correlated and coordinated by a vast intricate sensory system which is sometimes called the soul of all things, the anima mundi, the underlying consciousness.

In dealing with the triplicities so often used when speaking of deity, such as spirit, soul, and body,—life, consciousness, and form,—it is of value to remember that they refer to differentiations of the one life, and that the more of these triplicities with which one can familiarise oneself the more one will be in rapport with a wider circle of men. But when one is dealing with things occult and subjective, and when the subject about which one writes deals with the undefinable, then difficulty is encountered. It is no difficult matter to describe a man's personal appearance, his clothing, his form, and the things with which he is surrounded. Language suffices satisfactorily to deal with the concrete and with the world of form. But when one endeavours to convey an idea of his quality, character, and nature one is immediately faced with the problem of the unknown, with that undefinable unseen part which we sense, but which remains in a large sense unrevealed, and unrealised even by the man himself. How then shall we describe him through the medium of language?

12

If this is so of man, how much greater is the difficulty when we seek through words to express that inexpressible sum total of which the terms spirit, soul, and body are regarded as the main component differentiations? How shall we define that undefinable life that men have (for the sake of understanding) limited and separated into a trinity of aspects, or persons, calling the whole by the name of God?

Yet where this differentiation of God into a trinity is universal and age-long in use, where every people—ancient and modern—employ the same triplicity of ideation to express an intuitive realisation, there is warrant for the usage. That some day we may think and express the truth differently may indeed be so, but for the average thinker of today the terms spirit, soul, and body stand for the aggregate of divine manifestation, both in the deity of the universe and in that lesser divinity, man himself. As this treatise is intended for the thinking human being and not for the crystallised theologians or the theoretically biassed scientists we will adhere to the well-used terminology and seek to understand what has lain back of the phrases in which man has sought to explain God Himself.

"God is Spirit, and they that worship Him must worship Him in Spirit and in Truth," states one of the scriptures of the world. "Man became a living soul," is to be found in another place in the same scripture. "I pray God your whole spirit and soul and body may be preserved blameless," said a great initiate of the White Lodge; and the greatest of them all yet present with us in physical form on earth, repeated the words of an earlier sage when He said: "I have said ye are Gods, and ye are all the children of the most High". In those words the triplicity of man, his divinity and his relationship to the life in Whom he lives and moves and has his being, is touched upon from the Christian standpoint, and all the great religions deal in analogous phrases with that relationship.

a. Spirit, Life, Energy.

The word spirit is applied to that undefinable, elusive, essential impulse or Life which is the cause of all manifestation. It is the breath of Life and is that rhythmic inflow of vital energy which manifests in its turn as the attractive force, as the consciousness, or soul, and is the sum total of atomic substance. It is the correspondence in the great Existence or Macrocosm of that which in the little existence or microcosm is the vital inspiring factor which we call the life of man; this is indicated by the breath in his body, which is abstracted or withdrawn when the life course is run.

What this something is, who shall say? We trace it back to the soul or consciousness aspect, and from the soul to the spirit (as we call the three aspects of the one breath) but what these words really signify, who has the courage to declare? We call this unknown something by differing names, according to our particular school of thought; we seek to express it in words, and end by call it Spirit, the One Life, the Monad, Energy. Again we must remember that understanding as to the nature of this one life is purely relative. Those who are engrossed in the form side of existence think in terms of physical vitality, of feeling, impulse, or of mental force and do not pass beyond that unified life-consciousness of which all the above are differentiations. Those again who are interested in the more metaphysical approach and in the soul-life more than in the form aspect express their concept in terms of soul manifestation and—passing beyond the personal selfish reactions of the body nature—think in terms of life, in terms of quality, of group will or power, group coordination or love-wisdom, and of group intelligence or knowledge, covering all by the generic term of brotherhood.

But even that is found to be separative, through the separation into larger units than the lower is capable of grasping. Therefore the initiate, especially after the third initiation, begins to think even more synthetically and to express truth to himself in terms of Spirit, Life, the One. These terms mean to him something significant, but something so far removed from the concept of ordinary thinking humanity that it is needless for me to enlarge further upon it.

This brings me to a point, that should be dealt with here, prior to any further expansion of our subject. In the *Treatise on Cosmic Fire* and in the above passage it frequently appears that teaching is carried forward to a certain point and then dropped with the statement that, owing to the point in evolution of the average man, his reaction to truth and the reaction of the disciple-student or the initiate will differ. This is necessarily so; each will read into the words his own state of consciousness; each will fail to interpret in terms of the more advanced reaction of those on a higher stage of the ladder of evolution. The average reader, however, objects to being forced to recognise wider points of view than his own, and the phraseology which says: "It is needless to enlarge on this for it would only be understood by the initiate", serves only to aggravate him, tends to make him believe that evasion is intended, and that the writer (having got out of his depth) is seeking to save his face by some such statement. Just as a scientific treatise would prove meaningless and a mere jumble of words to the average grammar school child, but would carry a clear definition and meaning to experts in the subject owing to training and mental development, so there are those to whom the subject of the soul and its nature as dealt with in such an instruction as this is as clear and lucid as current literature is to the average reader, and the best sellers, as you call them, to the general public. Equally, though fewer in number, there are those advanced souls to whom the spirit and its nature is also a rational and understandable subject, to be appreciated and comprehended through the medium of the soul and its powers just as it is possible to arrive at an understanding of the soul through the medium of the mind, correctly employed. On a lower level altogether, we know it is easy to understand the nature of the physical body through a study and right use of the desire nature. It is a form of pride, and a refusal to recognize one's temporary limitations that awakens in readers a dislike for phrases which aptly and truly say: "When you are further developed, you will understand the above." This should be made clear.

To the Master of the Wisdom, the nature of the spirit, or that positive centre of life which every form hides is no more a mystery than is the nature of the soul to the esoteric psychologist. The source of the one life, the plane, or state from which that life emanates is the great Hidden Mystery to the members of the hierarchy of adepts. The nature of spirit, its quality and type of cosmic energy, its rate of vibration and its basic cosmic differentiations are the study of initiates above the third degree and the subject of their investigations. They bring to that study a fully developed intuition, plus that mental interpretive capacity which their cycle of incarnation has developed. They employ the awakened and developed inner light of their souls to interpret and comprehend that life which (divorced from the world of form) persists on the higher levels of consciousness and penetrates into our solar system from some exterior centre of being. They throw this light (which is in them and which they manipulate and use) in two directions therefore, standing as they do in the midmost state and functioning as they choose to function on the plane of the intuition or of buddhi. They cast that light into the world of form and know all things, interpreting all with correctness; they cast that light into the formless realms of the higher three planes (formless from the standpoint of man in the three worlds below the intuitional plane) and seek to understand, through steady expansive growth, the nature and purpose of that which is neither body nor soul, neither force nor matter, but which is the cause of both in the universe.

Eventually, when the initiate has undergone the higher solar initiations and can function in the full consciousness of the monad, awareness of that which is divorced even from group form and from those nebulous sheaths which veil and hide the One, becomes possible. The highest types of consciousness

14

work from the plane of the monad as the initiate of lower degree works from the plane of the soul and uses the organs of perception (if such an unsatisfactory phrase is legitimate) and means of knowledge of which average man has no idea; they penetrate or include within their radius of awareness that sum total of life, consciousness and form which we designate God. These initiates of high degree then begin to be aware of a vibration, a revealing light, a note or directional indicating sound which emanates from outside our solar system altogether. The only way in which we can get an appreciation of the process followed in the expansion of the divine consciousness in man is to study the relation of the mind and the brain and note what follows when the brain becomes the intelligent instrument of the mind; then study the relation of the soul to the mind and what eventuates when man is directed by his soul and utilises the mind to control the physical plane activities through the medium of the brain. In these three—soul, mind and brain—we have the analogy and the clue to the understanding of spirit, soul and body, and their mutual functions. This was the subject matter of the book, *The Light of the Soul*. Upon the perfecting of the conditions dealt with in that book there follows still another expansion when the spirit aspect, man's emanating source of energy, begins to use the soul (via the intuition) and to impress upon the soul-consciousness those laws, knowledges, forces and inspirations which will make the soul the instrument of the spirit or monad, just as the personal man became, at an earlier stage (via the mind), the instrument of the soul. In that earlier stage the development was two-fold. As the soul assumed control, via the mind, so the brain became responsive to the soul. Man was awakened to a knowledge of himself as he really was and to the three worlds of his normal evolution; later he became group conscious and was no longer a separated individual. As the soul is brought under the dominance of the spirit, an analogous two stages are likewise seen:

First, the disciple becomes aware not only of his group and allied groups, but his consciousness is expanded until it might be called planetary consciousness.

Secondly, he begins to merge that planetary awareness into something more synthetic still, and gradually develops the consciousness of the greater life which includes the planetary life as man includes in his physical expression such living organisms as his heart or brain. When this takes place, he begins to comprehend the significance of spirit, the one life back of all forms, the central energy which is the cause of all manifestation.

The first reaction of the average student on reading the above is to think immediately of the body nature as it expresses some type or other of energy. Thus the duality is the thing noted, and that which employs the thing is present in his mind. Yet one of the main necessities before occult aspirants at this time is to endeavour to think in terms of the one reality which is energy itself and nothing else. Therefore, it is of value to emphasise in our discussion of this abstruse subject, the fact that spirit and energy are synonymous terms and are interchangeable. Only in the realisation of this can we arrive at the reconciliation of science and religion and at a true understanding of the world of active phenomena by which we are surrounded and in which we move.

The terms, organic and inorganic, are largely responsible for much of the confusion and the sharp differentiation existing in the minds of many people between body and spirit, between life and form, and have led to a refusal to admit the essential identity in nature of these two. The world in which we live is regarded by the majority as really solid and tangible, yet possessing some mysterious power (lying concealed within it) which produces movement, activity and change. This is of course putting it crudely, but it suffices to sum up the unintelligent attitude.

The orthodox scientist is largely occupied with structures and relationships, with the composition of forms and with the activity produced by the component form parts and their interrelations and dependencies. The chemicals and elements, and the functions and parts they play, and their mutual interactions as them compose all forms in all the kingdoms of nature, are the subject of their investigation. The nature of the atom, of the molecule, and the cell, their functions, the qualities of their force manifestations and the varying types of activity, the solving of the problem as to the character and nature of the energies—focalised or localised in the differing forms of the natural or material world—demand the consideration of the ablest minds in the world of thought. Yet, the questions, What is Life? or What is Energy? or What is the process of Becoming and the nature of Being? remain unanswered. The problem as to the Why and the Wherefore is regarded as fruitless and speculative and almost insoluble.

Nevertheless, through pure reason, and through the correct functioning of the intuition these problems can be solved and these questions answered. Their solution is one of the ordinary revelations and attainments of initiation. The only true biologists are initiates of the mysteries, for they have an understanding of life and its purpose and are so identified with the life principle that they think and speak in terms of energy and its effects, and all their activities in connection with the work of the planetary hierarchy are based on a few fundamental formulas which concern life as it makes itself felt through its three differentiations or aspects:—energy, force, matter.

It should be noted here, that only as a man understands himself can he arrive at an understanding of that which is the sum total that we call God. This is a truism and an occult platitude but when acted upon leads to a revelation which makes the present 'Unknown God' a recognised reality. Let me illustrate.

Man knows himself to be a living being and calls death that mysterious process wherein something which he commonly designates as the breath of life is withdrawn. On its withdrawal, the form disintegrates. The cohesive vitalising force is gone and this produces a falling apart into its essential elements of that which has hitherto been regarded as the body.

This life principle, this basic essential of Being, and this mysterious elusive factor is the correspondence in man of that which we call spirit or life in the macrocosm. Just as the life in man holds together, animates, vitalises and drives into activity the form and so makes of him a living being, so the life of God—as the Christian calls it,—performs the same purpose in the universe and produces that coherent, living, vital ensemble which we call a solar system.

This life principle in man manifests in a triple manner:

1. As the directional will, purpose, basic incentive. This is the dynamic energy which sets his being functioning, brings him into existence, fixes the term of his life, carries him through the years, long or short, and abstracts itself at the close of his life cycle. This is the spirit in man, manifesting as the will to live, to be, to act, to pursue, to evolve. In its lowest aspect this works through the mental body or nature, and in connection with the dense physical makes itself felt through the brain.

2. As the coherent force. It is that significant essential quality which makes each man different, which produces that complex manifestation of moods, desires, qualities, complexes, inhibitions, feelings, and characteristics which produce a man's peculiar psychology. This is the result of the interplay between the spirit or energy aspect and the matter or body nature. This is the distinctive subjective man, his colouring, or individual note; this it is which sets the rate of vibratory activity of his body, produces his particular type of form, is responsible for the condition and nature of his organs, his glands, and his outer aspects. This is the soul and—in its lowest aspect—is to be seen working through the emotional

or astral nature and, in connection with the dense physical body, through the heart.

3. As the activity of the atoms and cells of which the physical body is composed. It is the sum total of those little lives of which the human organs, comprising the entire man, are composed. These have a life of their own and a consciousness which is strictly individual and identified. This aspect of the life principle works through the etheric or vital body and, in connection with the solid mechanism of the tangible form, through the spleen.

Therefore let us remember that the definition of spirit is not possible of accomplishment, nor is the definition of God. When one says that spirit is the inexpressible, undefinable cause, the emanating energy, the one life and source of being, the totality of all forces, of all states of consciousness and of all forms, the aggregate of life and that which is actively manifested of that life, the self and the not-self, force, and all that force motivates, one is in reality evading the issue, attempting the impossible and hiding truth behind a form of words. This cannot however be avoided until such time as the soul-consciousness is touched and known and the formless One can be perceived through the clear light of the intuition.

One of the first lessons we need to learn is that our minds, being as yet unresponsive to the hidden intuitions, make it impossible for us to say with assurance that such a condition is this, that or the other; that, until we can function in our soul-consciousness, it is not for us to say what is or what is not; that until we have submitted ourselves to the needed training we are in no position to deny or affirm anything. Our attitude should be that of reasonable enquiry and our interest that of the investigating philosopher, willing to accept an hypothesis on the basis of its possibility, but being unwilling to acknowledge as proven truth anything until we know it for and in ourselves. I, an aspirant to the higher mysteries, and one who has searched into them for a longer period than has been possible as yet to many, may write of things as yet impossible of demonstration to you or to the public who may read these instructions. To me they may be and are truth and proven fact and for me that may suffice. For you they should be regarded as significant possibilities and hints as to the direction in which truth may be sought, but beyond that you should not permit yourself to go. The value of these instructions lies in their sum total and is to be found in the underlying structure or skeleton of coordinated and correlated statements which must be considered as a whole and not in detail and this for two reasons:

1. Language, as earlier said, hides truth and does not reveal it. If truth is recognised, it is because the investigating student has found a point of truth in himself which serves to illumine his steps as he slowly and gradually presses forward.

2. There are many types of minds, and it is not to be expected that the information given, for instance, in this Treatise will appeal to all. It should be remembered that all people are units of consciousness breathed forth on one of the seven emanations from God. Therefore, even their monads or spiritual aspects are inherently different just as in the prism (which is one) there are the seven differentiated colours. Even this is so only because of the nature and point of view and the perceiving apparatus of the man whose eye registers and differentiates the varying rates of vibratory light. These seven subsidiary groups again produce a varying outlook, mentality, and approach, all equally right, but all presenting a slightly different angle of vision. When the above realisation is coupled to such factors as the different points in evolution, varying nationalities and characteristics, the inherent distinctions brought about through the interplay between the physical body involved and the environment, it will be apparent that no approach to such abstruse subjects as the nature of spirit and soul could have a general definition and submit themselves to a universal terminology.

17

b. The Soul, the Mediator or Middle Principle.

There are two angles or points of view from which the nature of the soul must be grasped: one is the aspect of the soul in relation to the fourth kingdom in nature, i.e. the human, and the other that of the subhuman kingdoms in nature, which, it must be remembered, are reflections of the three higher.

It should be borne in mind that the soul of matter, the anima mundi, is the sentient factor in substance itself. It is the responsiveness of matter throughout the universe and that innate faculty in all forms, from the atom of the physicist, to the solar system of the astronomer, which produces the undeniable intelligent activity which all demonstrate. It can be called attractive energy, coherency, sentiency, aliveness, awareness or consciousness, but perhaps the most illuminating term is that the soul is the *quality* which every form manifests. It is that subtle something which distinguishes one element from another, one mineral from another. It is the intangible essential nature of the form which in the vegetable kingdom determines whether a rose or a cauliflower, an elm or a watercress shall come into being; it is a type of energy which distinguishes the varying species of the animal kingdom and makes one man different from another in his appearance, nature and character. The scientist has tabulated, investigated and analysed the forms; names have been selected and given to the elements, and the minerals, the forms of vegetable life and the varying species of animals; the structure of the forms and the history of their evolutionary progress have been studied and deductions and conclusions have been reached, but the solution of the problem of life itself still eludes the wisest, and until the understanding of the "web of life" or of the body of vitality which underlies every form and links every part of a form with every other part is recognised and known to be a fact in nature, the problem will remain unsolved.

The definition of the soul may be regarded as somewhat more feasible than that of spirit owing to the fact that there are many people who have experienced at sometime or another an illumination, an unfoldment, an uplifting, and a beatitude which has convinced them that there is a state of consciousness so far removed from that normally experienced as to bring them into a new state of being and a new level of awareness. It is something felt and experienced, and involves that psychic expansion which the mystic has registered down the ages, and which St. Paul referred to when he spoke of being "caught up to the third Heaven," and of hearing things there which it is not lawful for man to utter. When hearing and sight on those levels are both producing registered experience then we have the occultist plus the mystic.

1. The soul, macrocosmic and microcosmic, universal and human, is that entity which is brought into being when the spirit aspect and the matter aspect are related to each other.

a. The soul therefore is neither spirit nor matter but is the relation between them.
b. The soul is the mediator between this duality; it is the middle principle, the link between God and His form.
c. Therefore the soul is another name for the Christ principle, whether in nature or in man.

2. The soul is the attractive force of the created universe and (when functioning) holds all forms together so that the life of God may manifest or express itself through them.

a. Therefore the soul is the form-building aspect, and is that attractive factor in every form in the universe, in the planet, in the kingdoms of nature and in man (who sums up in himself all the aspects) which brings the form into being, which enables it to develop and grow so as to house more adequately

the indwelling life, and which drives all God's creatures forward along the path of evolution, through one kingdom after another, towards an eventual goal and a glorious consummation.
b. The soul is the force of evolution itself and this was in the mind of St. Paul when he spoke of the "Christ in you, the hope of glory."

3. This soul manifests differently in the various kingdoms of nature, but its function is ever the same, whether we are dealing with an atom of substance and its power to preserve its identity and form, and carry forward its activity along its own lines, or whether we deal with a form in one of the three kingdoms of nature, held coherently together, demonstrating characteristics, pursuing its own instinctual life and working as a whole towards something higher and better.

a. Therefore the soul is that which gives distinctive characteristics and differing form manifestations.
b. The soul plays upon matter, forcing it to assume certain shapes, to respond to certain vibrations and to build those specified phenomenal forms which we recognise in the world of the physical plane as mineral, vegetable, animal and human,—and for the initiate certain other forms as well.

4. The qualities, vibrations, colours, and characteristics in all the kingdoms of nature are soul qualities, as are the latent powers in any form seeking expression, and demonstrating potentiality. In their sum total at the close of the evolutionary period, they will reveal what is the nature of the divine life and of the world soul,—that oversoul which is revealing the character of God.

a. Therefore the soul, through these qualities and characteristics, manifests as conscious response to matter, for the qualities are brought into being through the interplay of the pairs of opposites, spirit and matter, and their effect upon each other. This is the basis of consciousness.
b. The soul is the conscious factor in all forms, the source of that awareness which all forms register and of that responsiveness to surrounding group conditions which the forms in every kingdom of nature demonstrate.
c. Therefore the soul might be defined as that significant aspect in every form (made through this union of spirit and matter) which feels, registers awareness, attracts and repels, responds or denies response and keeps all forms in a constant condition of vibratory activity.
d. The soul is the perceiving entity produced through the union of Father-Spirit and Mother-Matter. It is that which in the vegetable world, for instance, produces response to the sun's rays, and the unfolding of the bud; it is that in the animal kingdom which enables it to love its master, hunt its prey, and follow out its instinctual life; it is that in man which makes him aware of his environment and his group, which enables him to live his life in the three worlds of his normal evolution as the onlooker, the perceiver, the actor. This it is which enables him eventually to discover that this soul in him is dual and that part of him responds to the animal soul and part of him recognises his divine soul. The majority however, at this time will be found to be functioning fully as neither purely animal nor purely divine, but can be regarded as human souls.

5. The soul of the universe is—for the sake of clarity—capable of differentiation or rather (owing to the limitations of the form through which that soul has to function) capable of recognition at differing rates of vibration and stages of development. The soul nature in the universe therefore manifests in certain great states of awareness with many intermediate conditions, of which the major can be enumerated as follows:

a. Consciousness, or that state of awareness in matter itself, due to the fact that Mother-Matter has been fecundated by Father-Spirit and thus life and matter have been brought together. This type of consciousness concerns the atom, molecule and cell of which all forms are constructed. Thus the form of the solar system, of a planet, and of all that is found upon or within a planet is produced.

b. Intelligent sentient consciousness, i.e. that evidenced in the mineral and vegetable kingdoms. It is this which is responsible for the quality, shape, and colouring of the vegetable and mineral forms and for their specific natures.

c. Animal consciousness, the awareness of soul response of all forms in the animal kingdom, producing their distinctions, species and nature.

d. Human consciousness, or self-consciousness, towards which the development of the life, form and awareness in the other three kingdoms has gradually tended. This term concerns the individual consciousness of man; and in the early stages is more animal than divine, owing to the dominance of the animal body with its instincts and tendencies. H.P.B. defines man accurately as an "animal plus a God". Later it is more strictly human, neither purely animal nor entirely divine, but fluctuating between the two stages, thus making the human kingdom the great battleground between the pairs of opposites, between the urge or pull of spirit and the lure of matter or mother-nature, and between that called the lower self and the spiritual man.

e. Group consciousness, which is the consciousness of the great sum totals, is arrived at by man through the development, first of all, of his individual consciousness, the sum total of the lives of his animal, emotional and mental natures, plus the spark of divinity dwelling within the form which they make. Then comes awareness of his group, as specified for him in that group of disciples, working under some one Master who represents to him the Hierarchy. The Hierarchy might be defined as the sum total of those sons of men who are no longer centered in the individualised self-consciousness, but who have entered into a wider realisation, that of the planetary group life. There are stages in this realisation, mounting all the way from that tiny group recognition of the probationary disciple up to the completed group awareness of the life in Whom all forms have their being, the consciousness of the planetary Logos, that "Spirit before the Throne" Who manifests through the form of a planet, as man manifests through his form in the human kingdom.

The soul therefore may be regarded as the unified sentiency and the relative awareness of that which lies back of the form of a planet and of a solar system. These latter are the sum total of all forms, organic or inorganic, as the materialist differentiates them. The soul, though constituting one great total, is, however, limited in its expression by the nature and quality of the form in which it is found and there are consequently forms which are highly responsive to and expressive of the soul, and others which—owing to their density and the quality of the atoms of which they are composed—are incapable of recognising the higher aspects of the soul or of expressing more than its lower vibration, tone or color. The infinitely small is recognised, the infinitely vast is assumed; but it remains as yet a concept until such time as the consciousness of man is inclusive, as well as exclusive. This concept will be understood when the second aspect is contacted and men understand the nature of the soul. It must be also remembered that just as the basic triplicity of manifestation worked out symbolically in man as his quota of energy (physical energy), his nervous system and the body mass, so the soul can also be known as a triplicity, the higher correspondences of the lower.

There is first of all what might be called *the spiritual will*,—that quota of the universal will which any one soul can express, and which is adequate for the purpose of enabling the spiritual man to co-operate in the plan and purpose of the great life in which he has his being. There is also the second soul quality which is *spiritual love*, the quality of group consciousness, of inclusiveness, of mediatorship, of attraction and of unification. This is the paramount soul characteristic, for only the soul has it as the dynamic factor. The spirit, or monad is primarily the expression of will with love and intelligence as secondary principles, and the body nature, the personality, is paramountly distinguished by intelligence, but the soul has outstandingly the quality of love which demonstrates as wisdom also when the intelligence of the body nature is fused with the love of the soul. The following tabulation may make the thought clearer.

Monad ----------------------- *Will* ---------------- *Purpose*
1st Aspect ----------------- Will, enabling the Monad to participate in the universal purpose.
2nd Aspect ---------------- Love, the energy which is poured forth into the soul, making it what it is.
3rd Aspect----------------- Intelligence, transmitted via the soul and brought into manifestation through the medium of the body.

Soul -------------------------- *Love* --------------- *the Method*
1st Aspect ----------------- Will, held in abeyance but expressing itself through the mind aspect of the personality and through Kundalini, which when aroused correctly makes possible the final initiations into the consciousness of the Monad.
2nd Aspect --------------- Love, the dominating force of the soul life; through this possession and this type of energy, the soul can be en rapport with all souls. Through the emotional body, the soul can be in touch with all animal or subhuman souls, through its work on its own plane, with the meditating souls of all men; and through the principle of buddhi, with the second aspect of the Monad.
3rd Aspect----------------- Knowledge. This aspect is brought into touch with the intelligence of all cells in the threefold body mechanism.

By a close study of the above it becomes apparent in what way the soul acts as the mediator between the monad and the personality.

The personality hides within itself, as a casket hides the jewel, that point of soul light which we call the light in the head. This is found within the brain, and is only discovered and later used when the highest aspect of the personality, the mind, is developed and functioning. Then the union with the soul is made and the soul functions through the lower personal nature.

The soul hides within itself, as the "jewel in the lotus," that faculty of dynamic energy which is the manifested attribute of the monad, the will. When the soul has unfolded all its powers and has learnt to include within its consciousness all that is connoted by the "myriad forms that Being takes," then in turn a higher or more inclusive state becomes possible and soul life is superseded by monadic life. This involves an ability to know, to love, and to participate in the plans of a life which has the power to include within its radius of consciousness not only the sum total of the lives and consciousness of the life of the Logos of our planet, but all the lives and consciousnesses within our solar system. The nature of this awareness is only possible of comprehension by the man who has arrived at soul-knowledge. The great need at this time is for experts in the life of the soul and for a group of men and women who, undertaking the great experiment and transition, add their testimony to the truth of the statements of the mystics and occultists of the ages.

c. The Body, the Phenomenal Appearance.

Not much need be written here anent this, for the body nature and the form aspect have been the object of investigation and the subject of thought and discussion of thinking men for many centuries. Much at

21

which they have arrived is basically correct. The modern investigator will admit the Law of Analogy as the basis of his premises and recognise sometimes the Hermetic theory that "As above, so below" may throw much light on the present problems. The following postulates may serve to clarify:—

1. Man, in his body nature, is a sum total, a unity.

2. This sum total is subdivided into many parts and organisms.

3. Yet these many subdivisions function in a unified manner and the body is a correlated whole.

4. Each of its parts differs in form and in function but all are inter-dependent.

5. Each part and each organism is, in its turn, composed of molecules, cells, and atoms and these are held together in the form of the organism by the life of the sum total.

6. The sum total called man is roughly divided into five parts some of greater importance than others, but all completing that living organism we call a human being.

a. The head.
b. The upper torso, or that part which lies above the diaphragm.
c. The lower torso, or that part lying below the diaphragm.
d. The arms.
e. The legs.

7. These organisms serve varied purposes and upon their due functioning and proper adjustment the comfort of the whole depends.

8. Each of these has its own life which is the sumtotal of the life of its atomic structure and is also animated by the unified life of the whole, directed from the head by the intelligent will or energy of the spiritual man.

9. The important part of the body is that triple division, the head, upper and lower torso. A man can function and live without his arms and legs.

10. Each of these three parts is also triple from the physical side, making the analogy to the three parts of man's nature and the nine of perfected monadic life. There are other organs, but those enumerated are those which have an esoteric significance of greater value than the other parts.

a. Within the head are:
1. The five ventricles of the brain, or what we might call the brain as a unified organism.
2. The three glands, carotid, pineal and pituitary.
3. The two eyes.

b. within the upper body are:
1. The throat.
2. The lungs.
3. The heart.

c. Within the lower body are:
1. The spleen.
2. The stomach.
3. The sex organs.

11. The sum total of the body is also triple:

a. The skin and bony structure.
b. The vascular or blood system.
c. The three-fold nervous system.

12. Each of these triplicities corresponds to the three parts of man's nature:

a. Physical nature:—The skin and bony structure are the analogy to the dense and etheric body of man.
b. Soul nature:—The blood vessels and circulatory system are the analogy to that all pervading soul which penetrates to all parts of the solar system, as the blood goes to all parts of the body.
c. Spirit nature:—The nervous system, as it energises and acts throughout the physical man is the correspondence to the energy of spirit.

13. In the head we have the analogy to the spirit aspect, the directing will, the monad, the One:

a. The brain with its five ventricles is the analogy to the physical form which the spirit animates in connection with man, that fivefold sum total which is the medium through which the spirit on the physical plane has to express itself.
b. The three glands in the head are closely related to the soul or psychic nature (higher and lower).
c. The two eyes are the physical plane correspondences to the monad, who is will and love-wisdom, or atma-buddhi, according to the occult terminology.

14. In the upper body we have an analogy to the triple soul nature.

a. The throat, corresponding to the third creative aspect or the body nature, the active intelligence of the soul.
b. The heart, the love wisdom of the soul, the buddhi or Christ principle.
c. The lungs, the analogy for the breath of life, is the correspondence of spirit.

15. In the lower torso again we have this triple system carried out:

a. The sex organs, the creative aspect, the fashioner of the body.
b. The stomach, as the physical manifestation of the solar plexus is the analogy to the soul nature.
c. The spleen, the receiver of energy and therefore the physical plane expression of the centre which receives this energy is the analogy to the energising spirit.

The vital body is the expression of the soul energy and has the following function:

1. It unifies and links into one whole the sum total of all forms.

2. It gives to every form its particular quality, and this is due to:

a. The type of matter drawn into that particular part of the web of life.
b. The position in the body of the planetary Logos, for instance, of any specific form.
c. The particular kingdom in nature which is being vitalised.

3. It is the principle of integration and the cohesive force of manifestation, from the strictly physical sense.

4. This web of life is the subjective analogy to the nervous system, and beginners in the esoteric sciences can, if they remember this, picture to themselves a network of nerves and plexus running throughout the entire body, or the sum total of all forms, coordinating and linking, and producing an essential unity.

5. Within that unity is diversity. Just as the varied organs of the human body are inter-related by the ramification of the nervous system, so within the body of the planetary Logos are the various kingdoms in nature and the multiplicity of forms. Back of the objective universe is the subtler sensitive body— one organism, not many, one sentient, responsive, connected form.

6. This sensitive form is not only that which responds to the environment but is the transmitter (from inner sources) of certain types of energy, and the object of the Treatise might here be stated to be that of considering the various types of energy transmitted to the form in the human kingdom, the responsiveness of the form to the types of force, the effects of that force upon man, and his gradual responsiveness to force emanating:

a. From his environment, plus his own outer physical body.
b. From the emotional plane, or astral force.
c. The mental plane or thought currents.
d. Egoic force, a force only registered by man and of which the fourth kingdom in nature is the custodian and which has mysterious and peculiar effects.
e. The type of energy which produces the concretion of ideas on the physical plane.
f. Strictly spiritual energy, or force from the plane of the monad.

The different types of force can all be registered in the human kingdom. Some of them can be registered in the subhuman kingdoms, and the apparatus of the vital body in man is so constructed that through its three objective manifestations, the triple nervous system, through the seven major plexi, the lesser nerve ganglia, and the many thousands of nerves, the entire objective man can be responsive to:

a. The above mentioned types of force.
b. Energies generated in and emanating from any part of the planetary etheric web of life.
c. The solar web of life.
d. The constellations of the Zodiac which appear to have a real effect upon our planet and of which astrology is as yet the immature study.
e. Certain cosmic forces which, it will be recognised later, play upon and produce changes in our solar system and consequently upon our planet and upon all forms upon and within that planetary life. This has been touched upon in the *Treatise on Cosmic Fire.*

To all of these the planetary web of life is responsive, and, when astrologers work in the occult way and consider the planetary horoscope, they will arrive more quickly at an understanding of the zodiacal and cosmic influences.

24

The anima mundi is that which lies back of the web of life. The latter is but the physical symbol of that universal soul; it is the outer and visible sign of the inner reality, the concretion of the sensitive responsive entity which links spirit and matter together. This entity we call the Universal Soul, the middle principle from the standpoint of the planetary life. When we narrow the concept down to the human family, and consider the individual man, we call it the mediating principle, for the soul of mankind is not only an entity linking spirit and matter, and mediating between monad and personality, but the soul of humanity has a unique function to perform in mediating between the higher three kingdoms in nature and the lower three. The higher three are:

1. The Spiritual Hierarchy of our planet, nature spirits or angels and human spirits, who stand at a peculiar point on the ladder of evolution. Of these Sanat Kumara, embodying a principle of the planetary Logos is the highest, and an initiate of the first degree is the lowest, with corresponding entities in what we call the angel or deva kingdom.
2. The Hierarchy of Rays—certain groupings of the seven rays in relation to our planet.
3. A Hierarchy of Lives, gathered by an evolutionary process out of our planetary evolution and from four other planets, who embody in themselves the purpose and plan of the solar Logos in relation to the five planets involved.

In narrowing the concept down to the microcosm, the ego or soul acts verily as the middle principle connecting the Hierarchy of Monads with outer diversified forms which they use sequentially in the process of:

a. Gaining certain experiences, resulting in acquired attributes.
b. Working out certain effects, initiated in an earlier system.
c. Cooperating in the plan of the solar Logos in relation to His (if one may use a pronoun in speaking of a life which is an existence and yet is an extended concept) Karma—a point oft overlooked. This Karma of His must be worked out through the method of incarnation and the subsequent result of the incarnated energy upon the substance of the form. This is symbolised for us, if we could but grasp it, in the relation of the sun to the moon. "The Solar Lord with his warmth and light galvanises the moribund Lunar Lords into a spurious life. This is the great deception; and the Maya of His Presence." So runs the *Old Commentary* oft quoted by me in earlier books. The above concept has in it truth for the individual soul likewise.

This middle principle is in process of revelation now. The lower aspect is functioning. The higher remains unknown, but that which links them (and at the same time reveals the nature of the higher) is on the verge of discovery. The structure, the mechanism, is now ready and developed to its point of usefulness; the vital life that can guide and motivate the machine is likewise present, and man now can intelligently use and control, not only the machine, but the active principle.

The great symbol of the soul in man is his vital or etheric body and for the following reasons:

1. It is the physical correspondence to the inner light body we call the soul body, the spiritual body. It is called the "golden bowl" in the Bible and is distinguished by:

a. Its light quality.
b. Its rate of vibration, which synchronises always with the development of the soul.
c. Its coherent force, linking and connecting every part of the body structure.

2. It is the microcosmic "web of life" for it underlies every part of the physical structure and has three purposes:

a. To carry throughout the body the life principle, the energy which produces activity. This it does through the medium of the blood, and the focal point for this distribution is the heart. It is the conveyor of physical vitality.

b. To enable the soul, or human yet spiritual man to be en rapport with his environment. This is carried forward through the medium of the entire nervous system and the focal point of that activity is the brain. This is the seat of conscious receptivity.

c. To produce eventually, through life and consciousness, a radiant activity, or manifestation of glory which will make of each human being a centre of activity for the distribution of light and attractive energy to others in the human kingdom, and through the human kingdom, to the subhuman kingdoms. This is a part of the plan of the planetary Logos for the vitalising and renewing of the vibration of those forms which we designate subhuman.

3. This microcosmic symbol of the soul not only underlies the entire physical structure and thus is a symbol of the anima mundi, or the world soul, but is indivisible, coherent and a unified entity, thereby symbolising the unity and homogeneity of God. There are no separated organisms in it, but it is simply a body of freely flowing force, that force being a blend or unification of two types of energy in varying quantities, dynamic energy, and attractive or magnetic energy. These two types characterise the universal soul likewise—the force of will, and of love, or of atma and buddhi, and it is the play of these two forces on matter that attracts to the etheric body of all forms the needed physical atoms and that— having so attracted them—by the will force drives them into certain activities.

4. This coherent unified body of light and energy is the symbol of the soul in that it has within it seven focal points, wherein the condensation, if it must be so called, of the two blended energies is intensified. These correspond to the seven focal points in the solar system, wherein the Solar Logos, through the seven Planetary Logoi, focuses His energies. This will be later elaborated. The point to be noted here is simply the symbolic nature of the etheric or vital body, for it is by understanding the nature of the energies displayed and the unified nature of the form and work that some idea as to the work of the soul, the middle principle in nature, can be grasped.

5. The symbolism is also carried forward when one remembers that the etheric body links the purely physical, or dense body with the purely subtle, the astral or emotional body. In this is seen the reflection of the soul in man which links the three worlds (corresponding to the solid, liquid and gaseous aspects of the strictly physical body of man) to the higher planes in the solar system, linking thus the mental to the buddhic and the mind to the intuitional states of consciousness.

RULE ONE

The Solar Angel collects himself, scatters not his force but, in meditation deep, communicates with his reflection

Some Basic Assumptions.
The Way of the Disciple.

RULE ONE

SOME BASIC ASSUMPTIONS

We are entering upon a course of study wherein the entire tendency will be to throw the student back upon himself, and thus upon that larger self which has only, in most cases, made its presence felt at rare and highly emotional intervals. When the self is *known* and not simply felt and, when the realisation is mental as well as sensory, then truly can the aspirant be prepared for initiation.

I would like to point out that I am basing my words upon certain basic assumptions, which for the sake of clarity, I want briefly to state.

Firstly, that the student is sincere in his aspiration, and is determined to go forward no matter what may be the reaction of and upon the lower self. Only those who can clearly differentiate between the two aspects of their nature, the real self and the illusory self, can work intelligently. This has been well expressed in the *Yoga Sutras of Patanjali*.

"Experience (of the pairs of opposites) comes from the inability of the soul to distinguish between the personal self, and the purusa (or spirit). The objective forms exist for the use and experience of the spiritual man. By meditation upon this arises the intuitive perception of the spiritual man." Book III.35.

The forty-eighth Sutra in the same book gives a statement covering a later stage of this discriminative realisation. This discerning quality is fostered by a re-collected attitude of mind, and by careful attention to the method of a constant review of the life.

Secondly, I am acting upon the assumption that all have lived long enough and battled sufficiently with deterrent forces of life to have enabled them to develop a fairly true sense of values. I assume they are endeavouring to live as those who know something of the true eternal values of the soul. They are not to be kept back by any happenings to the personality or by the pressure of time and circumstance, by age or physical disability. They have wisely learnt that enthusiastic rushing forward and a violent energetic progress has its drawbacks, and that a steady, regular, persistent endeavour will carry them further in the long run. Spasmodic spurts of effort and temporary pressure peter out into disappointment and a weighty sense of failure. It is the tortoise and not the hare that arrives first at the goal, though both achieve eventually.

Thirdly, I assume that those who set themselves seriously to benefit by the instructions in this book are prepared to carry out the simple requirements, to read what is written thoughtfully, to attempt to organise their minds and adhere to their meditation work. The organising of the mind is an all-day affair, and the application of the mind to the thing in hand throughout the daily avocations, is the best way to make study and meditation periods fruitful and bring about fitness for the vocation of disciple.

With these assumptions clearly understood, my words are for those who are *seeking* to measure up to the need for trained servers. I say not, you note, those who measure up. Intention and effort are considered by us of prime importance, and are the two main requisites for all disciples, initiates and masters, plus the power of persistence.

In our consideration of these rules, I am not so much interested in their application to the magical work itself as in training the magician, and in developing him from the standpoint of his own character. Later we may get down to the application of knowledge to the outer manifestation of world forces, but now our objective is something different; I seek to interest the minds and brains (and therefore the lower self) of students in the higher self, thereby keying up their mental interest so that sufficient impetus is generated to enable them to go forward.

Also, let it not be forgotten that once the magic of the soul is grasped by the personality, that soul steadily dominates and can be trusted to carry forward the training of the man to fruition, unhampered (as you necessarily are) by thoughts of time and space, and by an ignorance of the past career of the soul concerned. It should always be borne in mind that, when dealing with individuals, the work required is twofold:

1. To teach them how to link up the personal lower self with the overshadowing soul so that in the physical brain there is an assured consciousness as to the reality of that divine fact. This knowledge renders the hitherto assumed reality of the three worlds futile to attract and hold, and is the first step, out of the fourth, into the fifth kingdom.

2. To give such practical instruction as will enable the aspirant to—

a. Understand his own nature. This involves some knowledge of the teaching of the past as to the constitution of man and an appreciation of the interpretations of modern Eastern and Western investigators.
b. Control the forces of his own nature and learn something of the forces with which he is surrounded.
c. Enable him so to unfold his latent powers that he can deal with his own specific problems, stand on his own feet, handle his own life, solve his own difficulties and become so strong and poised in spirit that he forces recognition of his fitness to be recognized as a worker in the plan of evolution, as a white magician, and as one of that band of consecrated disciples whom we call the "hierarchy of our planet".

Students of these matters are therefore begged to extend their concept of that hierarchy of souls so that they include all the exoteric fields of human life (political, social, economic, and religious). They are begged not to narrow down the concept as so many do, to only those who have brought their own little particular organisation into being, or to those who are working purely on the subjective side of life, and along what are reoognised by the conservative as the so-called religious or spiritual lines. All that tends to lift the status of humanity on any plane of manifestation is religious work and has a spiritual goal, for matter is but spirit on the lowest plane, and spirit, we are told, is but matter on the highest. All is spirit and these differentiations are but the products of the finite mind. Therefore, all workers and knowers of God in or out of fleshly bodies, and working in any field of divine manifestation form part of the planetary hierarchy and are integral units in that great cloud of witnesses who are the "onlookers and observers". They possess the power of spiritual insight or perception as well as objective or physical vision.

In studying Rule I we could summarize it simply yet profoundly under the following words:—

1. Egoic Communication.

2. Cyclic Meditation.
3. Coordination, or At-one-ment.

The rules start off in *A Treatise on Cosmic Fire* with a brief summary of the process and a statement as to the nature of the white magician.

I would like in this first consideration of our subject to enumerate briefly the facts given in the commentary so as to demonstrate to the aspirant how much is given him for his consideration and helping if he knows how to read and ponder upon that which he reads. The brief exegesis of Rule I gives the following statements:

1. The white magician is one who is in touch with his soul.

2. He is receptive to and aware of the purpose and the plan of his soul.

3. He is capable of receiving impressions from the realm of spirit and of registering them in his physical brain.
4. It is stated also that white magic—

a. Works from above downwards.
b. Is the result of solar vibration, and therefore of egoic energy.
c. Is not an effect of the vibration of the form side of life, being divorced from emotion and mental impulse.

5. The downflow of energy from the soul is the result of

a. Constant internal re-collectedness.
b. Concentrated one-pointed communication by the soul with the mind and the brain.
c. Steady meditation upon the plan of evolution.

6. The soul is, therefore, in deep meditation during the whole cycle of physical incarnation, which is all that concerns the student here.

7. This meditation is rhythmic and cyclic in nature as is all else in the cosmos. The soul breathes and its form lives thereby.

8. When the communication between the soul and its instrument is conscious and steady, the man becomes a white magician.

9. Therefore workers in white magic are invariably, and through the very nature of things, advanced human beings, for it takes many cycles of lives to train a magician.

10. The soul dominates its form through the medium of the sutratma or life thread, and (through it) vitalises its triple instrument (mental, emotional and physical) and thus sets up a communication with the brain. Through the brain, consciously controlled, the man is galvanised into intelligent activity on the physical plane.

The above is a brief analysis of the first rule for magic and I would like to suggest that in the future as the students meditate on the rules that they make such an analysis themselves. If they do this during their consideration of each rule they will approach the whole matter with greater interest and knowledge. They will also save themselves much looking back and reference.

It will be seen from a consideration of the above analysis that a very clear summation is given and that the student is started in his study of magic with a brief understanding of the past situation, his equipment and the method of approach. Let us realize from the start the simplicity of the idea intended to be conveyed by my remarks hitherto. Just as in the past the instrument and its relation to the outer world has been the paramount fact in the experience of the spiritual man, so now it is possible for a readjustment to take place wherein the outstanding fact will be the spiritual man, the solar angel or soul. It will also be realised that his relationship (through the form side) will be to the inner as well as the outer worlds. Man has included in his relation only the form side of the field of average human evolution.

He has used it and has been dominated by it. He has also suffered from it and consequently in time revolted, through utter satiety, from all that pertains to the material world. Dissatisfaction, disgust, distaste, and a deep fatigue are characteristic very frequently of those who are on the verge of discipleship. For what is a disciple? He is one who seeks to learn a new rhythm, to enter a new field of experience, and to follow the steps of that advanced humanity who have trodden ahead of him the path, leading from darkness to light, from the unreal to the real. He has tasted the joys of life in the world of illusion and has learnt their powerlessness to satisfy and hold him. Now he is in a state of transition between the new and the old states of being. He is vibrating between the condition of soul awareness and form awareness. He is "seeing double".

His spiritual perception grows slowly and surely as the brain becomes capable of illumination from the soul, via the mind. As the intuition develops, the radius of awareness grows and new fields of knowledge unfold.

The first field of knowledge receiving illumination might be described as comprising the totality of forms to be found in the three worlds of human endeavour, etheric, astral and mental. The would-be disciple, through this process, becomes aware of his lower nature and begins to realize the extent of his imprisonment and (as Patanjali puts it) "the modifications of the versatile psychic nature." The hindrances to achievement and the obstacles to progress are revealed to him and his problem becomes specific. Frequently then he reaches the position in which Arjuna found himself, confronted by enemies who are those of his own household, confused as to his duty and discouraged as he seeks to balance himself between the pairs of opposites. His prayer then should be the famous prayer of India, uttered by the heart, comprehended by the head, and supplemented by an ardent life of service to humanity.

"Unveil to us the face of the true spiritual sun,
Hidden by a disk of golden light,
That we may know the truth and do our whole duty
As we journey to Thy sacred feet."

As he perseveres and struggles, surmounts his problems and brings his desires and thoughts under control, the second field of knowledge is revealed—knowledge of the self in the spiritual body, knowledge of the ego as it expresses itself through the medium of the causal body, the Karana Sarira, and awareness of that source of spiritual energy which is the motivating impulse behind the lower manifestation. The "disk of golden light" is pierced; the true sun is seen; the path is found and the aspirant struggles forward into ever clearer light.

As the knowledge of the self and as the consciousness of that which the self sees, hears, knows and contacts is stabilized, the Master is found; his group of disciples is contacted; the plan for the immediate share of work he must assume is realized and gradually worked out on the physical plane. Thus the activity of the lower nature decreases, and the man little by little enters into conscious contact with his Master and his group. But this follows upon the "lighting of the lamp"—the aligning of the lower and higher and the downflow of illumination to the brain.

It is essential that these points should be grasped and studied by all aspirants so that they may take the needed steps and develop the desired awareness. Until this is done, the Master, no matter how willing He may be, is powerless, and can take no steps to admit a man to His group and thus take him into His auric influence, making him an outpost of His consciousness. Every step of the way has to be carried out by a man himself, and there is no short or easy road out of darkness into light.

THE WAY OF THE DISCIPLE

The white magician is ever one who, through conscious alignment with his ego, with his "angel", is receptive to his plans and purposes, and therefore capable of receiving the higher impression. We must remember that while magic works from above downwards, and is the result of solar vibration, and not the impulses emanating from one or the other of the lunar pitris, the downflow of the impressing energy from the solar pitri is the result of his internal recollectedness, the indrawing of his forces, prior to sending them concentratedly to his shadow, man, and his steady meditation upon the plan. It may be of use to the student if he here remembers that the ego (as well as the Logos) is in deep meditation during the whole cycle of physical incarnation. This meditation is cyclic in nature, the pitri involved sending out to his "reflection" rhythmic streams of energy, which streams are recognised by the man concerned as his "high impulses," his dreams and aspirations. Therefore, it will be apparent why workers in white magic are ever advanced and spiritual men, for the "reflection" is seldom responsive to the ego or the solar angel until many cycles of incarnation have transpired. The solar pitri communicates with his "shadow" or reflection by means of the sutratma, which passes down through the bodies to a point of entrance in the physical brain, if I might so express it, but the man, as yet, cannot focus or see clearly in any direction

If he looks backward he can see only the fogs and miasmas of the planes of illusion, and fails to be interested. If he looks forward he sees a distant light which attracts him, but he cannot as yet see that which the light reveals. If he looks around, he sees but shifting forms and the cinematograph of the form side of life. If he looks within, he sees the shadows cast by the light, and becomes aware of much impedimenta which must be discarded before the light he sees in the distance can be approached, and then enter within him. Then he can know himself as light itself, and walk in that light and transmit it likewise to others.

It is perhaps well to remember that the stage of discipleship is in many ways the most difficult part of the entire ladder of evolution. The solar angel is unceasingly in deep meditation. The impulses of energy, emanating from him are increasing in vibratory rate and are becoming more and more powerful. The energy is affecting more and more the forms through which the soul is seeking expression, and endeavouring to control.

This brings me to the consideration of the seventh point I made in my earlier analysis of Rule I. I said, "The soul's meditation is rhythmic and cyclic in its nature as is all else in the cosmos. The soul breathes and its form lives thereby". The rhythmic nature of the soul's meditation must not be overlooked in the life of the aspirant. There is an ebb and flow in all nature, and in the tides of the ocean we have a wonderful picturing of an eternal law. As the aspirant adjusts himself to the tides of the soul life he begins to realise that there is ever a flowing in, a vitalising and a stimulating which is followed by a flowing out as sure and as inevitable as the immutable laws of force. This ebb and flow can be seen functioning in the processes of death and incarnation. It can be seen also over the entire process of a man's lives, for some lives can be seen to be apparently static and uneventful, slow and inert from the angle of the soul's experience, whilst others are vibrant, full of experience and of growth. This should be remembered by all of you who are workers when you are seeking to help others to live rightly. Are they on the ebb or are they being subjected to the flow of the soul energy? Are they passing through a period of temporary quiescence, preparatory to greater impulse and effort, so that the work to be done must be that of strengthening and stabilising in order to enable them to "stand in spiritual being", or are they being subjected to a cyclic inflow of forces? In this case the worker must seek to aid in the direction and utilisation of the energy which (if misdirected) will eventuate in wrecked lives but which when wisely utilised will produce a full and fruitful service.

The above thoughts can also be applied by the student of humanity to the great racial cycles and much of interest will be discovered. Again, and of more vital importance to us, these cyclic impulses in the life of the disciple are of a greater frequency and speed and forcefulness than in the life of the average man. They alternate with a distressing rapidity. The hill and valley experience of the mystic is but one way of expressing this ebb and flow. Sometimes the disciple is walking in the sunlight and at other times in the dark; sometimes he knows the joy of full communion and again all seems dull and sterile; his service is on occasion a fruitful and satisfying experience and he seems to be able to really aid; at other times he feels that he has naught to offer and his service is arid and apparently without results. All is clear to him some days and he seems to stand on the mountain top looking out over a sunlit landscape, where all is clear to his vision. He knows and feels himself to be a son of God. Later, however, the clouds seem to descend and he is sure of nothing, and seems to know nothing. He walks in the sunlight and is almost overpowered by the brilliance and heat of the solar rays, and wonders how long this uneven experience and the violent alternation of these opposites is to go on.

Once however that he grasps the fact he is watching the effect of the cyclic impulses and the effect of the soul's meditation upon his form nature, the meaning becomes clearer and he realises that it is that form aspect which is failing in its response, and re-acting to energy with unevenness. He then learns that once he can live in the soul consciousness and attain that 'high altitude' (if I might so express it) at will, the fluctuations of the form life will not touch him. He then perceives the narrow-edged razor path which leads from the plane of physical life to the soul realm, and finds that when he can tread it with steadiness it leads him out of the ever changing world of the senses into the clear light of day and into the world of reality.

The form side of life then becomes to him simply a field for service and not a field of sensuous perception. Let the student ponder upon this last sentence. Let him aim to live as a soul. Then the cyclic impulses, emanating from the soul, are known to be impulses for which he himself is responsible and which he has sent forth; he then knows himself to be the initiating cause and is not subject to the effects.

Looked at from another angle we get two factors, the breath and the form which the breath energises and drives into activity. Upon careful study, it becomes apparent that we have, for aeons of time, identified ourselves with the form; we have emphasised the effects of the imparted activity but have not understood the nature of the breath, nor known the nature of the One who breathes. Now in our work we are concerning ourselves with that One Who, breathing rhythmically, will drive the form into right action and right control. This is our objective and our goal. A right understanding is necessary nevertheless if we are to appreciate intelligently our task and its effects.

Much more could be said on this rule but enough has been here given for the average applicant to discipleship to consider and upon which to base action. Most of us are average, are we not? If we regard ourselves otherwise, we divorce ourselves from others and become guilty of the sin of separateness—the one real sin.

An appreciation of the above thoughts should build in the aspirant a realisation of the value of his meditation work, whilst the idea of a cyclic response to soul impulse lies back of the activities of a morning meditation, a noonday recollection, and an evening review. A larger ebb and flow is also indicated in the two aspects of the full moon and the new moon. Let this be borne in mind.

May there be a full and steady play of cyclic force from the kingdom of spirit upon each one of us calling us forth into the realm of light, love and service and producing a cyclic response from each one! May there be a constant interchange between those who teach and the disciple who seeks instruction!

Much preliminary work will have to be done. The disciple on the physical plane and the inner teacher (whether one of the Great Ones or the "Master within the Heart") need to know each other somewhat, and to accustom themselves to each other's vibration. Teachers on the inner planes have much to contend with owing to the slowness of the mental processes of students in physical bodies. But confidence and trust will set up the right vibration which will produce eventually accurate work. Lack of faith, of calmness, of application, and the presence of emotional unrest will hinder. Long patience those on the inner side need in dealing with all who must, for lack of other and better material, be utilized. Some physical injudiciousness may make the physical body non-receptive; some worry or care may cause the astral body to vibrate to a rhythm impossible for the right reception of the inner purpose; some prejudice, some criticism, some pride, may be present that will make the mental vehicle of no use. Aspirants to this difficult work must watch themselves with infinite care, and keep the inner serenity and peace and a mental pliability that will tend to make them of some use in the guarding and guiding of humanity.

The following rules might therefore be given:

1. It is essential that there should be an endeavor to arrive at absolute purity of motive.

2. The ability to enter the silence of the high places will follow next. The stilling of the mind depends upon the law of rhythm. If you are vibrating in many directions and registering thoughts from all sides, this law will be unable to touch you. Balance and poise must be restored before equilibrium can be reached. The law of vibration and the study of atomic substance are closely intertwined. When more is known about these atoms and their action, reaction and inter-action, then people will control their bodies scientifically, synchronizing the laws of vibration and of rhythm. They are the same and yet unlike. They are phases of the law of gravitation. The earth is itself an entity which, by the force of will, holds all things to itself. This is an obscure matter, little has been learned about it as yet. The inbreathing and outbreathing of the entity of the earth affects vibration potently,—that is the vibration

of the physical plane matter. There is a connection also between this and the moon. Those members of humanity who are specially under lunar influence respond to this attraction more than any others, and they are difficult to use as transmitters. The silence that comes from the inner calm is the one to cultivate. Aspirants are urged to remember that the time will come when they too will form part of the group of teachers on the inner side of the veil. If then they have not learnt the silence that comes from strength and from knowledge, how will they bear the apparent lack of communication that they will then find exists between them and those on the outer side? Learn therefore, how to keep quiet or usefulness will be hampered by astral fretfulness when on the other side of death.

3. Remember always that lack of calm in the daily life prevents the teachers on egoic levels from reaching you. Endeavor therefore to remain quiescent as life unrolls, work, toil, strive, aspire, and hold the inner calm. Withdraw steadily into interior work and so cultivate a responsiveness with the higher planes. A perfect steadiness of inner poise is what the Masters need in those whom They seek to use. It is an inner poise that holds to the vision yet does its outer work on the physical plane with a concentrated physical brain attention which is in no way deviated by the inner receptiveness. It involves a dual activity.

4. Learn to control thought. It is necessary to guard what you think. These are days when the race as a whole is becoming sensitive and telepathic and responsive to thought interplay. The time is approaching when thought will become public property, and others will sense what you think. Thought has, therefore, to be carefully guarded. Those who are contacting the higher truths and becoming sensitive to the Universal Mind must protect some of their knowledge from the intrusion of other minds. Aspirants must learn to inhibit certain thoughts, and prevent certain knowledge from leaking out into the public consciousness when in contact with their fellow men.

It is of course of vital interest to appreciate the significance of the words "scatters not his force." There are so many lines of activity into which the soul-inspired disciple may throw himself. Assurance as to varying lines of activity is not easy to reach and every aspirant knows perplexity. Let us put the problem in the form of a question, relegating it to the plane of every-day endeavour, as we are not yet in a position to comprehend in what way a soul can "scatter its forces" on the higher planes.

What is the criterion whereby a man may know which out of several lines of activity is the right line to take? Is there, in other words, a revealing something which will enable a man unerringly to choose the right action and go the right way? The question has no reference to a choice existing between the path of spiritual endeavour and the way of the man of the world. It refers to right action when faced with a choice.

There is no question but that a man is faced, in his progress, with increasingly subtle distinctions. The crude discrimination between right and wrong which occupies the child soul is succeeded by the finer distinctions of right, or of more right, of high, or higher, and the moral or spiritual values have to be faced with the most meticulous spiritual perception. In the stress and toil of life and in the constant pressure on each one from those who constitute their group, the complexity of the problem is very great.

In solving such problems, certain broad discriminations can precede the more subtle and when these decisions have been made the more subtle can then take their place. The choice between selfish and unselfish action is the most obvious one to follow upon the choice between right and wrong, and is easily settled by the honest soul. A choice which involves discrimination between individual benefit and group responsibility rapidly eliminates other factors, and is easy to the man who shoulders his just responsibility. Note the use of the words "just responsibility." We are considering the normal, sane man and not the over-conscientious morbid fanatic. There follows next the distinction between the expedient, involving factors of physical plane relations of business and of finance, leading up to a consideration of the highest good for all parties concerned. But having through this triple eliminative process arrived at a certain position, cases arise where choice still remains in which neither common sense nor logical, discerning reason seem to help. The desire is only to do the right thing; the intent is to act in the highest possible way and to take that line of action which will produce the best good of the group apart from personal considerations altogether. Yet light upon the path, which must be trodden, is not seen; the door which should be entered is unrecognized and the man remains in the state of constant indecision. What, then, must be done? One of two things:

First the aspirant can follow his inclination and choose that line of action out of the residue of possible lines which seems to him the wisest and the best. This involves belief in the working of the law of Karma and also a demonstration of that firm decisiveness which is the best way in which his personality can learn to abide by the decisions of his own soul. It involves also the ability to go forward upon the grounds of the decision made, and so to abide by the results without forebodings or regrets.

Secondly, he can wait, resting back upon an inner sense of direction, knowing that in due time he will ascertain, through the closing of all doors but one, which is the way he should go. For there is only one open door through which such a man can go. Intuition is needed for its recognition. In the first case mistakes may be made, and the man thereby learns and is enriched; in the second case, mistakes are impossible and only right action can be taken.

It is obvious, therefore, that all resolves itself into an understanding of one's place upon the ladder of evolution. Only the highly advanced man can know the times and seasons and can adequately discern the subtle distinction between a psychic inclination and the intuition.

In considering these two ways of ultimate decision let not the man who should use his common sense and take a line of action based upon the use of the concrete mind, practice the higher method of waiting for a door to open. He is expecting too much in the place where he is. He has to learn through right decision and right use of the mind to solve his problems. Through this method he will grow, for the roots of intuitive knowledge are laid deep within the soul and the soul, therefore, must be contacted before the intuition can work. One hint only can here be given:—the intuition ever concerns itself with group activity and not with petty personal affairs. If you are still a man centered in the personality, recognize it, and with the equipment available, govern your actions. If you know yourself to be functioning as a soul and are lost in the interest of others, untrammeled by selfish desire, then your just obligation will be met, your responsibilities shouldered, your group work carried forward, and the way will unfold before you, whilst you do the next thing and fulfill the nest duty. Out of duty, perfectly performed, will emerge those larger duties which we call world work; out of the carrying of family responsibilities will come that strengthening of our shoulders which will enable us to carry those of the larger group. What, then, is the criterion?

For the high grade aspirant, let me repeat, the choice of action depends upon a sound use of the lower mind, the employment of a sane common-sense and the forgetfulness of selfish comfort and personal ambition. This leads to the fulfillment of duty. For the disciple there will be the automatic and necessary carrying forward of all the above, plus the use of the intuition which will reveal the moment when wider group responsibilities can be justly shouldered and carried simultaneously with those of the smaller group. Ponder on this. The intuition reveals not the way ambition can be fed, nor the manner in which desire for selfish advancement can be gratified.

RULE TWO

When the shadow hath responded, in meditation deep the work proceedeth. The lower light is thrown upward; the greater light illuminates the three, and the work of the four proceedeth.

The Hindrances to Occult Study.
The Overcoming of the Hindrances.

HINDRANCES TO OCCULT STUDY

This rule is one of the most difficult in the book and yet one of the most comprehensive. It will take us some time rightly to handle it. We have in it an interesting illustration of the microcosmic correspondence to the macrocosm. It can be elucidated in two ways in relation to the light it mentions.

Reference is made to the "greater light" which illuminates the three and, secondly, to the throwing upward of the "lower light".

The "greater light" is that of the soul, who is light itself illuminating the manifestation of the three-fold personality. Herein lies the correspondence to the macrocosm as it is symbolized for us in God, the manifesting light of the solar system. The solar system is three in one, or one in three, and the light of the Logos illuminates the whole. The "lower light" is that which is hidden within the human being on the physical plane. This light, at a certain stage of man's experience, is awakened throughout the physical body and blends eventually with the "greater light". The light and life of God Himself may emanate from the central Spiritual Sun, but it is only as the light within the solar system itself is awakened and aroused that there will come that eventual blazing forth which will typify the glory of the Sun shining in its strength. Similarly, the light of the soul may emanate from the Monad, but it is only as the light within the little system (directed by the soul) is awakened and aroused that there will come the eventual shining forth of a son of God.

In these instructions, however, we are dealing primarily with the microcosm and the light within it; we shall not enlarge upon the macrocosmic analogies.

In considering this second rule, we must note that a conscious relation has been established between the soul and its shadow, the man on the physical plane. *Both have been meditating*. Students would do well to note this and to remember that one of the objectives of the daily meditation is to enable the brain and mind to vibrate in unison with the soul as it seeks "in meditation deep" to communicate with its reflection.

The correspondence to this relation, or synchronizing vibration is interesting:

Soul ---------------- Man on the Physical Plane
Mind --------------- Brain
Pineal Gland ------ Pituitary Body

The relation also between the centers, and their synchronization is interesting and in it is epitomized the evolution of the race as well as the racial unit, man.

Head Center ------ Base of the Spine
Heart Center ------ Solar Plexus
Throat Center ----- Sacral Center

In the above lies a hint for the more advanced student (and he is the one who hesitates so to regard himself). It is also symbolized for us in the relation between the Eastern and the Western hemispheres and between those great bodies of truth which we call Religion and Science.

The life of meditation proceeds and the rapport between the soul and its triple instrument becomes steadily closer, and the resulting vibration more powerful. How many lives this will take depends upon various factors, which are too numerous to be mentioned here but which the student will find it useful to consider. Let him list the factors which he feels he needs to take into account as he seeks to decide his evolutionary standpoint.

The result of this response is a reorientation of the lower man in order to produce a synthesis of the Three and the One so that the work of the Four may proceed. Here you have the reflection consummated in the microcosm of that with which the Solar Logos started, the "Sacred Four" of the Cosmos; man in his turn becomes a "Sacred Four"—spirit and the three of manifestation.

Four words should be pondered upon here:

1. Communication
2. Response
3. Reorientation
4. Union

The *Old Commentary* expresses it in the following terms:

"When communion is established, words are forthwith used, and mantric law assumes its rightful place, provided that the One communicates the words and the three remain in silence.
"When response is recognized as emanating from the three, the One, in silence, listens. The roles are changed. A three-fold word issues from out the triple form. A turning round is caused. The eyes no longer look upon the world of form; they turn within, focus the light, and see, revealed, an inner world of being. With this the Manas stills itself, for eyes and mind are one.
"The heart no longer beats in tune with low desire, nor wastes its love upon the things that group and hide the Real. It beats with rhythm new; it pours its love upon the Real, and Maya fades away. Kama and heart are close allied; love and desire form one whole—one seen at night, the other in the light of day....

. . . .

37

"When fire and love and mind submit themselves, sounding the three-fold word, there comes response. "The One enunciates a word which drowns the triple sound. God speaks. A quivering and a shaking in the form responds. The new stands forth, a man remade; the form rebuilt; the house prepared. The fires unite, and great the light that shines: the three merge with the One and through the blaze a four-fold fire is seen."

In this pictorial writing which I have sought to convey in modern English, the sages of old embodied an idea. The *Old Commentary* from which these words are taken has no assignable date. Should I endeavor to tell you its age I have no means of proving the truth of my words and hence would be faced with credulity—a thing aspirants must avoid in their search for the essential and Real. I have sought in the above few phrases to give the gist of what is expressed in the Commentary, through the means of a few symbols and a cryptic text. These old Scriptures are not read in the way modern students read books. They are seen, touched and realized. The meaning is disclosed in a flash. Let me illustrate:—The words "the One enunciates the word which drowns the triple sound" are depicted by a shaft of light ending in a symbolic word in gold superimposed over three symbols in black, rose and green. Thus are the secrets guarded with care.

I felt it might be of interest to students to know this much about this ancient test book of the Adepts.

Our consideration of this rule will fall into two parts:

The relation between the soul and the personality. This will be handled particularly with reference to meditation in the daily life, more than from the theoretical and the academical.

The significance of the words, "the lower light is thrown upward." These deal with the centers and the Kundalini Fire.

I would like here to point out the advisability of each student arriving at an understanding of his etheric body, and this for certain reasons.

First, the etheric body is the next aspect of the world substance to be studied by scientists and investigators. This time will be hastened if thinking men and women can formulate intelligent ideas anent this interesting subject. We can aid in the revelation of the truth by our clear thinking and from the standpoint of the present pronouncements about the ether, scientists will eventually arrive at an understanding of etheric forms or bodies.

Secondly, the etheric body is composed of force currents, and in it are vital centers linked by lines of force with each other and with the nervous system of the physical man. Through these lines of force, it is connected also with the etheric body of the environing system. Note that in this lies the basis for a belief in immortality, for the law of brotherhood or unity and for astrological truth.

Thirdly, the need of realizing that the etheric body is vitalized and controlled by thought and can (through thought) be brought into full functioning activity. This is done by right thinking and not by breathing exercises and holding the nose. When this is grasped, much dangerous practice will be avoided and people will come into a normal and safe control of that most potent instrument, the vital body. That this end may rapidly be consummated is my earnest wish.

Occult study is of profound importance, and students of these sciences must bring to bear upon them, all that they have of mental application and concentrated attention. It involves also the steady working out of the truths learnt.

Occult study, as understood in the Occident, is intellectually investigated but not practically followed. Theoretically some glimmering of light may be appreciated by the man who aspires to the occult path, but the systematic working out of the laws involved has made small progress as yet.

Wherein lies the hindrance? It may be of value if we study three things:

1. The Occidental hindrances to correct occult study.
2. How these hindrances may be surmounted.
3. Certain things the aspirant may safely undertake in the equipping of himself for treading the occult path, for that is the stage, and for the majority, the only stage at present possible.

One of the main hindrances to the correct apprehension of the laws of occultism and their practical application lies in the fact of the comparative newness of the occident, and the rapid changes which have been the outstanding feature of European and American civilisation. The history of Europe dates back a bare three thousand years, and that of America, as we know, barely as many centuries. Occultism flourishes in a prepared atmosphere, in a highly magnetised environment, and in a settled condition which is the result of age-long work upon the mental plane.

This is one reason why India provides such an adequate school of endeavour. There knowledge of occultism dates back tens of thousands of years and time has set its mark even upon the physique of the people, providing them with bodies which offer not that resistance which occidental bodies so oft afford. The environment has been long permeated with the strong vibrations of the great Ones who reside within its borders and who, in Their passage to and fro, and through Their proximity, continuously magnetise the environing ether. This in itself affords another line of least resistance, for this etheric magnetisation affects the etheric bodies of the contacted population. These two facts, of time and of high vibration, result in that stability of rhythm which facilitates occult work, and offer a quiet field for mantric and ceremonial enterprise.

These conditions are not to be found in the West, where constant change in every branch of life is found, where frequent rapid shifting of the scene of action causes wide areas of disturbance which militate against any work of a magic nature. The amount of force required to effect certain results does not warrant their use, and time has been allowed to elapse in an effort to produce an equilibrising effect.

The climax of the disturbed condition has been passed, and a more stable state of affairs is gradually being brought about, and this may permit of definite occult work being attempted with success. The Master R. is working upon this problem, and likewise the Master of the English race,—not the Master who occupies Himself with the Labour Movement or the betterment of social conditions. They are aided by a disciple of rare capability in Sweden, and by an initiate in the southern part of Russia, who works much on the mental levels. Their aim is so to tap the resources of force stored up by the Nirmanakayas that its downflow may sweep out lower grade matter, and thus permit the free play of a higher vibration.

Another hindrance may be found in the strong development of the concrete mind. I would here impress upon you that this development must in no way be considered a detriment. All has been in due course of evolution, and later when the Orient and the Occident have reached a point of better understanding and interplay their interaction will be of mutual benefit; the East will profit from the mental stimulation afforded by the strong mental vibration of its Western brother, whilst the Occidental will gain much from the abstract reasoning of the Oriental, and, through the effort to grasp that which the first subrace of the Aryan root race so easily apprehended, he will contact his higher mind, and thus build with greater facility the bridge between the higher and the lower mind. The two types need each other, and their effect upon each other tends to eventual synthesis.

The concrete mind, in itself, offers opportunity for a treatise of great length, but here it will suffice to point out a few of the ways in which it hinders those races who so paramountly represent it.

a. By its intense activity and stimulated action it hinders the downflow of inspiration from on high. It acts as a dark curtain that shuts out the higher illumination. Only through steadiness and a stable restfulness can that illumination percolate, via the higher bodies, to the physical brain and so be available for practical service.

b. The wisdom of the Triad exists for the use of the personality, but is barred by the disquisitions of the lower mind. When the fire of mind burns too fiercely, it forms a current which counteracts the higher downflow, and forces the lower fire back into seclusion. Only when the three fires meet, through the regulation of the middle fire of mind, can a full light be achieved, and the whole body be full of light, the fire from above—the triadal light—the fire of the lower self,—kundalini—and the fire of mind,—cosmic manas—must meet upon the altar. In their union comes the burning away of all that hinders and the completed emancipation.

c. By discrimination—a faculty of the concrete mental body—the lower bodies are trained in the art of distinguishing illusion from the centre of reality, the real from the unreal, the self from the not-self. Then ensues, consequently, a period that must be surmounted wherein the attention of the Ego is centred necessarily on the lower self and its vehicles, and wherein, therefore, the vibrations of the Triad, the laws that deal with macrocosmic evolution, and the subjugation of fire for the use of the Divine, have temporarily to be in abeyance. When man quickly sees the truth in all that he contacts, and automatically chooses truth or the real, then he learns next the lesson of joyful action, and the path of bliss opens before him. When this is so, the path of occultism becomes possible for him, for the concrete mind has served its purpose, and has become his instrument and not his master, his interpreter and not his hinderer.

d. The concrete mind hinders in another and more unusual way, and one that is not realised by the student who attempts, at first, to tread the thorny road of occult development. When the concrete mind is rampant, and dominates the entire personality the aspirant cannot cooperate with these other lives and diverse evolutions until love supersedes concrete mind (even though he may, in theory, comprehend the laws that govern the evolution of the Logoic plan and the development of other solar entities besides his own Hierarchy). Mind separates; love attracts. Mind creates a barrier betwixt a man and every suppliant deva. Love breaks down every barrier, and fuses diverse groups in union. Mind repels by a powerful, strong vibration, casting off all that is contacted, as a wheel casts off all that hinders its whirling periphery. Love gathers all to itself, and carries all on with itself, welding separated units into a unified homogeneous whole. Mind repels through its own abundant heat, scorching and burning aught that approaches it. Love soothes and heals by the similarity of its heat to the heat in that which it contacts, and blends its warmth and flame with the warmth and flame of other evolving lives. Finally, mind disrupts and destroys whilst love produces coherence and heals.

Every change, in human life, is subject to immutable laws, if such a paradoxical statement may be permitted. In the attempt to find out those laws, in order to conform to them, the occultist begins to offset karma, and thus colours not the astral light. The only method whereby these laws can as yet be apprehended by the many who are interested is by a close study of the vicissitudes of daily existence, as spread over a long period of years. By the outstanding features of a cycle of ten years, for instance, as they are contrasted with the preceding or succeeding similar period a student can approximate the trend of affairs and guide himself thereby. When the point in evolution is reached where the student can contrast preceding lives, and gain knowledge of the basic colouring of his previous life cycle, then rapid progress in adjusting the life to law is made. When succeeding lives can be likewise apprehended by the student, and their colouring seen and known, then karma (as known in the three worlds) ceases, and the adept stands master of all causes and effects as they condition and regulate his lower vehicle.

He aspires to the occult path and considers changes and events in the light of all preceding events, and the longer and more accurate his memory the more he can dominate all possible situations.

Thus two of the hindrances will be found to be:

a. The comparative newness and change which is characteristic of the Occident.
b. The development of the concrete mind.

Our third hindrance grows out of the preceding one. It consists of the emphasis that has been laid in the West upon the material side of things. This has resulted in a three-fold condition of affairs. First, the world of spirit, or the formless abstract world of subjective consciousness is not recognised in a scientific sense. It is recognised innately by those of mystic temperament, and by those who are able to study the subjective history of men and races, but science recognises not this aspect of manifestation, nor do scientific men, as a whole, believe in a world of super-physical endeavour. All that in the earlier races held paramount place in the lives and thought of the peoples is now approached sceptically, and discussions are preceded by a question mark. But progress has been made and much has arisen out of the war. The question, for instance, is rapidly changing from the formula "Is there a life after death?" to the enquiry "Of what nature is the future life?" and this is a portent of much encouragement.

Secondly, the masses of the people are suffering from suppression and from the effects of inhibition. Science has said, There is no God and no spirit within man. Religion has said, There must be a God, but where may He be found? The masses say, We desire not a God constructed by the brains of theologians. Therefore the true inner comprehension finds no room for expansion, and the activity that should be finding its legitimate expression in the higher aspiration, turns itself to the deification of things,—things pertaining to flesh, connected with the emotions, or having a relation to the mind. The war, again, has accomplished much by relegating things to their just position, and, by the removal of possessions, many have learnt the value of essentials, and the necessity of eliminating that which is superfluous.

A third condition of affairs grows out of the above two. A right apprehension of the future does not exist. When the life of the spirit is negated, when the manifesting life concentrates itself on things concrete and apparent then the true goal of existence disappears, the true incentive to right living is lost, and the sarcastic words of the initiate, Paul, "Let us eat and drink for tomorrow we die" characterise the attitude of the majority of men.

41

Men deaden the inner voice that bears witness to the life hereafter, and they drown the words that echo in the silence by the noise and whirl of business, pleasure and excitement.

The whole secret of success in treading the occult path depends upon an attitude of mind; when the attitude is one of concrete materialism, of concentration upon form, and a desire for the things of the present moment, little progress can be made in apprehending the higher esoteric truth.

A fourth hindrance is found in the physical body, which has been built up by the aid of meat and fermented foods and drinks, and nurtured in an environment in which fresh air and sunlight are not paramount factors. I am here generalising, and speaking for the masses of men, and not for the would-be earnest occult student. For long centuries food that has been decomposing, and hence in a condition of fermentation, has been the basic food of the occidental races; and the result can be seen in bodies unfitted for any strain such as occultism imposes, and which form a barrier to the clear shining forth of the life within. When fresh fruit and vegetables, clear water, nuts and grains, cooked and uncooked, form the sole diet of the evolving sons of men, then will be built bodies fitted to be vehicles for highly evolved Egos. They patiently await the turning of the wheel, and the coming in of a cycle which will permit of their fulfilling their destiny. The time is not yet, and the work of elimination and adjustment must be slow and tedious.

THE OVERCOMING OF THE HINDRANCES

Certain paramount realisations must precede this work of removing hindrances, and they might be enumerated as follows:

a. A realisation that in obedience to the next duty and adherence to the highest known form of truth lies the path of further revelation.
b. A realisation that dispassion is the great thing to cultivate, and that a willingness to undergo joyously any amount of temporary inconvenience, pain or agony, must be developed, having in view the future glory which will blot out the clouds of the passing hour.
c. A realisation that synthesis is the method whereby comprehension is attained, and that, by blending the pairs of opposites, the middle path is gained that leads straight to the heart of the citadel.

With these three things paramountly controlling his views on life, the student may hope, by strenuous endeavour, to overcome the four hindrances which we have touched upon.

In taking up our consideration of the second Rule we will deal first with the relation of the soul to the personality, primarily from the standpoint of meditation. We are dealing therefore with "the greater light" and will take up later the "throwing upward of the lower light". This is in line also with the law of occult knowledge that one begins with universals.

It should be borne in mind that these rules are only for those whose personality is coordinated and whose minds are gradually being brought under control. The man therefore is utilising the lower mind, the reasoning mind, whilst the soul is utilising the higher or abstract mind. Both units are working with two aspects of the universal principle of mind, and on this ground their relation becomes possible. The man's work with his mind is to render it negative and receptive to the soul, and this is his positive occupation (note the use here of the word 'positive' in the attempt to make the mind receptive, for herein lies the clue to right action). The soul's work in meditation is to make the point of that meditation so positive that the lower mind can be impressed, and so the lower man can be brought into line with the Eternal Plan.

Thus, again, we have a relation established between a positive and a negative vibration, and the study of these relations carries much information to the student, and is part of the teaching given in preparation for the first initiation. A list of these related situations might here be given showing them in their progressive relation on the path of evolution.

1. The relation between male and female physical bodies, called by man, the sex relation, and deemed of such paramount importance at this time. In the vale of illusion, the symbol oft engrosses attention and that which it represents is forgotten. In the solving of this relationship will come racial initiation, and it is with this that the race is now engrossed.

2. The relation between the astral body and the physical, which, for the majority, is the control, by the positive astral nature, of the negative automatic physical. The physical body, the instrument of desire, is swayed and controlled by desire,—desire for physical life, and desire for the acquisition of the tangible.

3. The relation between the mind and the brain, which constitutes the problem of the more advanced men and races and of which the vast system of schools, colleges, and universities indicate the importance. Much progress in this relation has been made during the past fifty years, and the work of the psychologists marks its highest point. When this is understood, the mind will be regarded as the positive factor and the other two aspects of the form nature will respond receptively. They will be the automatons of the mind.

4. The relation between the soul and the personality, which is the problem engrossing the attention of aspirants now, for they are the pioneers of the human family, the pathfinders into the world of the soul. With this relation, the mystics and the occultists concern themselves.

5. The relation between the centres below the diaphragm and those above, or between:

a. The centre at the base of the spine and the thousand petalled lotus, the head centre. In this the four petals of the basic centre become the many, or the quaternary is lost in the universal.
b. The sacral centre and the throat. In this there comes a union between the twelve Creative Hierarchies and the quaternary, and the secret of the sixteen petals of the throat lotus is seen.
c. The solar plexus centre and the heart, in which the ten of the perfect man in this solar system is lost in the consummated twelve. As the twelve Creative Hierarchies (in their outer and creative aspect) are contacted by the man, who is the perfected quaternary from the standpoint of the form, so in the relation between the solar plexus and heart is the second aspect perfected; the love of the soul can express itself perfectly through the emotional nature.

6. The relation between the two head centres, or between the centre between the eyebrows and the centre above the head. This relation is set up and stabilised when soul and body are a functioning unit.

7. The relation between the pineal gland and the pituitary body as a result of the above.

8. The relation between the higher and the lower mind, involving steady and increasing soul contact. The meditative attitude of the soul is duplicated in the three bodies (or by the spiritual man) and the steady meditation of the soul goes on also on its own plane. It is with this and with its effects that we

are primarily concerned in this rule.

A later relationship, which in no way concerns us, is set up after the third initiation between the soul and the monad, and throughout the course of cosmic evolution these relationships will emerge. The race as a whole is, however, only concerned with the setting up of a relation between soul and body and beyond this there is no need to go.

As the man seeks to reach control of the mind, the soul in its turn becomes more actively aggressive. The work of the solar Angel has hitherto been largely in its own world and concerned with its relation to spirit, and with this the man, working through his cycles on the physical plane, has had no concern. The main expenditure of energy by the soul has been general, and outward-going into the fifth kingdom. Now the solar Angel approaches a time of crisis and of re-orientation. In the early history of humanity there was a great crisis which we call individualisation. At that time the solar Angels, in response to a demand or a pull from the race of animal-men (as a whole, note that), sent a portion of their energy, embodying the quality of mentalisation, to these animal-men. They fecundated, if I might so express it, the brain. Thus was humanity brought into being. This germ, however, carried within it two other potentialities, that of spiritual love and spiritual life. These must in due time make their appearance.

The flowering forth of the mind in men, which so distinguishes the present age, indicates to the solar Angel a second crisis, of which the first was but the symbol. That for which the solar Angel exists is making its presence felt within humanity, and another strong pull is being exerted upon the solar Angel which this time will produce a second fecundation. This will give to man those qualities which will enable him to transcend human limitations, and become a part of the fifth or spiritual Kingdom in nature. The first effort of the solar Angel turned animal-men into human beings; the second will turn human beings into spiritual entities, plus the gains of experience in the human family.

For this the solar Angel, the soul, is organising itself and re-orienting itself so that its power can be redirected into the world of men. Contact must be made by the soul between the lower aspect of its triple nature and the aspect which has already found lodgment in the brain of man. Intelligent activity and love wisdom must be united, and the union must take place on the physical plane. In order to do this the soul is entering into "meditation deep", in union with all other souls who may have brought their instrument into a responsive state. This is the basic group meditation, and when a man achieves what the oriental books call "samadhi", he has succeeded in participating, as a soul, in this group meditation, and enters upon that cycle of service which expresses itself through the planetary Hierarchy. The rational mind and the abstract mind function as a unit, and the motivating principle is love. The soul, expressing love and abstract intelligence, is at one with its expression on the physical plane through the brain, and, when this is the case, the lower man has synchronised his meditation with that of the soul.

This is the objective of our work. Let this not be forgotten, and let every effort be made to bring mind and brain into such a functioning condition that a man can slip out of his own meditation and (losing sight of his own thoughts) become the soul, the thinker in the kingdom of the soul.

It is perhaps a new thought to some that the soul is organising itself for effort, re-orienting its forces, and preparing for a fresh and powerful impulse, but so it is. All forms of life under the force of evolution pass from initiation to initiation and the soul is not exempt from the process. Just as the soul of animal-man became united with another divine principle, and so brought into being the fourth kingdom in nature, so the soul in humanity is seeking contact with another divine aspect. When that contact is made the Kingdom of God will come on earth; the physical plane will thereby be transformed and that peculiar period, presented symbolically under the term millennium, will come.

The Knowers of God in that era will preponderate over those who are simply aspiring to that knowledge, and their contact and the results of the force they transmit will be felt in all the kingdoms of nature. Dominion over all forms, and the power to act as transmitters of that spiritual energy we call love is the promised reward of the triumphant solar Angels, and the prized goal of their meditation work. The Sons of God will triumph on earth in full incarnated expression, and will bring light (therefore life) to all the manifested forms. This is the "life more abundant" of which the Christ speaks. This is the achievement of the true Nirvanee who, living in unbroken meditation in the spiritual realm yet can work on earth. The work of initiation is to enable a man to live ever at the centre, but to act as a distributor of divine energy in any direction and—after the later initiations—in all directions.

We will now, in our consideration of the next rule, take up the work of the "lesser light" of man on the physical plane. I, who have entered somewhat into an understanding of the life of the solar Angel, seek to assure my fellow pilgrims that the passing things of the senses are but trivial, and of no value compared to the rewards, here and in this life, to the man who seeks to merge his everyday consciousness with that of his own soul. He enters then into the community of souls, and stands not alone. The only lonely periods are the result of wrong orientation and the holding on to that which hides the vision, and fills the hands so full that they cannot grasp what has been called "the jewel in the lotus."

RULE THREE

The Energy circulates. The point of light, the product of the labours of the four, waxeth and groweth. The myriads gather round its glowing warmth until its light recedes. Its fire grows dim. Then shall the second sound go forth.

Soul Light and Body Light.
Principles and Personalities.

SOUL LIGHT AND BODY LIGHT

In these Rules for Magic, the laws of creative work are embodied and the means whereby man can function as an incarnated soul. They do not deal primarily with the rules governing man's development. Incidentally, of course, much may be learnt in this connection, for man grows through creative work and understanding, but this is not the primary objective of the teaching.

Through the gradually growing synthesis of the meditation process carried on by the soul on its own plane and that of the aspirant the man manifests (in the physical brain) a point of light which has been occultly lighted on the plane of the mind. Light ever signifies two things, energy and its manifestation in form of some kind, for light and matter are synonymous terms. The thought of the man and the idea

45

of the soul have found a point of rapport, and the germ of a thought form has come into being. This thought form, when completed, will embody as much of the great plan (on which the Hierarchy is working) as the man can vision, grasp, and embody on the mental plane. This, in the early stages of a man's aspiration, in his first steps along the Path of Discipleship, and for the first two initiations, is covered by the word "Service". He grasps, gropingly at first, the idea of the unity of the Life, and its manifestation as the Brotherhood existing between all forms of that divine Life. This subjective ideal gradually leads to an appreciation of the way in which this essential relationship can work out practically. This can be seen finding its expression in the great humanitarian efforts, in the organisations for the relief of human and animal suffering, and in world wide efforts for the betterment of the internal relations of nations, religions and groups.

Enough human units have now contacted the hierarchical plan so that it may be safely concluded that the collective brain of the human family (that entity which we call the fourth Kingdom of Nature) is susceptible to the vision, and has fashioned its lighted form on the mental plane. Later, the thought of service and of self will be found inadequate, and a more suitable form of expression will be found, but this suffices for the present.

This thought form, created by the aspirant, is brought into being by the focussed energies of the soul and the re-oriented forces of the personality. This is pictured as covering three stages.

1. The period wherein the aspirant struggles to achieve that inner quiet and directed attentiveness which will enable him to hear the Voice of the Silence. That voice expresses to him, through symbol and interpreted life experience the purposes and plans with which he may cooperate. According to his stage of development those plans will express either:

a. The already materialized plans, taking group form on the physical plane, with which he may cooperate and in whose interest he may submerge his own.
b. The plan, or fraction of a plan, which is his individual privilege to bring through into manifestation and thus cause to materialize as a group activity on the physical plane. It is the function of some aspirants to aid and help those groups which are already in functioning activity. It is the function of others to bring into being those forms of activity which are, as yet, on the subjective plane. Only those aspirants who are freed from personal ambition can truly cooperate in this second aspect of the work. Therefore "Kill out ambition."

2. The period wherein he habituates himself to the clear hearing and correct interpretation of the inner voice of the soul and broods reflectively upon the imparted message. During this period "the Energy circulates." A constant rhythmic response to the thought energy of the soul is set up, and, figuratively speaking, there is a steady flow of force between that centre of energy we call the soul on its own plane, and that centre of force which is a human being. The energy travels along the "thread" we call the sutratma and sets up a vibratory response between the brain and the soul.

An interesting angle of information might here be given, as it is my intent in these Instructions ever to link up the analogies between the different aspects of divinity, as they express themselves in man or in the macrocosm, the Heavenly Man.

The ancient yoga of Atlantean days (which has come down to us in the necessarily fragmentary teaching of the yoga of the centres) conveys to us the information that the reflection of the sutratma in the human organism is called the spinal cord, and expresses itself in three nerve channels. These three are called ida, pingala, and the central channel, the sushumna. When the negative and positive forces of the body, which express themselves via the ida and pingala nerve routes, are equilibrized, the forces can ascend and descend by the central channel to and from the brain, passing through the centres up the spine without hindrance. When this is the case we have perfected soul expression in the physical man.

This is in reality a correspondence to the sutratma as it links the physical man and the soul, for the sutratma in its turn expresses the positive energy of spirit, the negative energy of matter, and the equilibrized energy of the soul—the attainment of equilibrium being the present objective of humanity. During the period of the later initiations, the positive use of the spiritual energy supersedes the equilibrized use of soul force, but that is a later stage with which the aspirant need not as yet trouble himself. Let him find the "noble middle Path" between the pairs of opposites, and incidentally he will find that the forces he uses on the physical plane will employ the central nerve channel up the spine. This will occur as the transmission of light and truth to the physical brain, via the central channel of the linking sutratma, really works out into satisfactory usefulness. Those ideas and concepts (speaking in symbol) which come via the sutratmic negative channel are well meaning, but lack force and peter out into insignificance. They are emotionally coloured, and lack the organized form which pure mind can give. Those which come via the opposite channel (speaking figuratively) produce too rapid concretion, and are motivated by the personal ambition of a ruling mentality. The mind is ever egoistic, self-seeking, and expresses that personal ambition which carries within it the germ of its own destruction.

When, however, the sutratmic sushumna, the central nerve channel and its energy is employed, the soul, as a magnetic intelligent creator, transmits its energies. The plans can then mature according to divine purpose and proceed with their building activities "in the light". The point of egoic and lunar contact emits ever the point of light, as we have seen from our Rules for Magic, and that has its focus at the point in the sutratma which has its correspondence in the light in the head of the aspirant.

3. The period wherein he sounds the sacred Word and—blending it with the voice of the Ego or Soul—sets in motion mental matter for the building of his thought form. It is the man on the physical plane who now sounds the Word, and he does it in four ways:

a. He becomes the Word incarnated, and endeavours "to be what he is."
b. He sounds the Word within himself, seeking to do it as the soul. He visualizes himself as the soul breathing out energy through the medium of that Word through the entire system which his soul animates—his mental, emotional, vital, and physical instruments.
c. He sounds the Word literally on the physical plane, thus affecting the three grades of matter in his environment. All the time that he is thus occupied he is "holding the mind steady in the light", and is keeping his consciousness immovably in the realm of the soul.
d. Also he carries forward (and this is the most difficult stage) a paralleling activity of a steady visualization of the thought form through which he hopes to express that aspect of the plan which he has contacted, and which he hopes to bring into active being through his own life and in his own environment.

This is only truly possible when a steady rapport has been established between the soul and the brain. The process involves the capacity of the brain to register what the soul is visioning and becoming aware of in the Kingdom of the Soul. It involves also a paralleling activity in the mind, for the aspirant must interpret the vision and utilize the concrete intelligent faculty for the wise adaptation of time and of form to the true expression of that which has been learnt. This is by no means an easy thing to do, but the aspirant has eventually to learn to express himself in full consciousness in more than one way and that simultaneously. He begins to learn a triple activity in this manner. This the *Old Commentary* expresses as follows:

The Solar Orb shines forth in radiant splendor. The illuminated mind reflects the solar glory. The lunar orb rises from the centre to the summit, and is transformed into a radiant sun of light. When these three suns are one, Brahma breaks forth. A lighted world is born.

This literally means that when the soul (symbolized as the Solar Orb) the mind, and the light in the head form one unit, the creative power of the solar Angel can express itself in the three worlds, and can construct a form through which its energy can actively express itself. The lunar orb is a symbolic way of expressing the solar plexus which eventually must do two things:

1. Blend and fuse the energies of the lower two centres of force, and
2. Raise these fused energies and so, blending with the energies of the other and higher centres, reach the head.

All the above embodies a teaching and a theory. This has to be wrought out in the practical experiment and experience and conscious activity of the aspirant.

I would like also to point out the nature of the service humanity as a whole is rendering in the general plan of evolution. The rule under our consideration applies not only to the individual man but to the predestined activity of the fourth Kingdom in Nature. Through his meditation, discipline and service, man fans into radiant light, illuminating the three worlds, that point of light which flickered into being at the time of his individualization in past ages. This finds its reflection in the light in the head. Thus a rapport is set up, which permits not only of vibratory synchronization but of a radiation and display of magnetic force, permitting of its recognition in the three worlds of a man's immediate environment.

So it is with the human kingdom. As its illumination increases, as its light waxes more potent, its effect upon the sub-human kingdoms is analogous to that of the individual soul, its reflection, upon man in physical incarnation. I say analogous as a causative force, though not a correspondence in effects. Note this difference. Humanity is macrocosmic in relation to the sub-human states of consciousness, and this H. P. B. has well pointed out. The effect upon these lesser and more material states is primarily four-fold.

1. The stimulating of the spiritual aspect, expressing itself as the soul in all forms, such as the form of a mineral, a flower, or an animal. The positive aspect of energy in all these forms will wax stronger, producing radiation, for instance, increasingly in the mineral kingdom. In this lies a hint of the nature of the process that will set a term to our own planetary existence and eventually, to our solar system. In the vegetable kingdom, the effect will be the demonstration of increased beauty and diversity, and the evolution of new species with an objective impossible to explain to those not yet initiate. The production of nutritive forms which will serve the needs of the lesser devas and angels will be one of the results.

In the animal kingdom the effect will be the elimination of pain and suffering and a return to the ideal conditions of the Garden of Eden. When man functions as a soul, he heals; he stimulates and vitalizes; he transmits the spiritual forces of the universe, and all harmful emanations and all destructive forces find in the human kingdom a barrier. Evil and its effects are largely dependent upon humanity for a functioning channel. Humanity's function is to transmit and handle force. This is done in the early and ignorant stages destructively and with harmful results. Later when acting under the influence of the soul, force is rightly and wisely handled and good eventuates. True indeed it is that "the whole creation travaileth in pain until now, waiting for the manifestation of the sons of God."

2. The bringing of light. Humanity is the planetary light bearer, transmitting the light of knowledge, of wisdom, and of understanding, and this in the esoteric sense. These three aspects of light carry three aspects of soul energy to the soul in all forms, through the medium of the anima mundi, the world soul. Physically speaking, this can be realized if we can appreciate the difference between our planetary illumination today and that of five hundred years ago—our brilliantly lit cities, our rural districts, shining through the night with their lighted streets and homes; our airways, outlined with their search-lights and fields of blazing globes; our oceans, dotted with their lighted ships, and increasingly our lighted airships will be seen, darting through the skies.

These are but the result of man's growing illumination. His knowledge aspect of light has brought this into being. Who shall say what will eventuate when the wisdom aspect predominates? When these are welded by understanding, the soul will control in the three worlds and in all kingdoms of nature.

3. The transmission of energy. The clue to the significance of this can be grasped as a concept, though as yet it will fail of comprehension, in the realization that the human kingdom acts upon and affects the three sub-human kingdoms. The downpouring spiritual Triangle and the upraising matter Triangle meet point to point in humanity when the point of balance can be found. In man's achievement and spiritualization is the hope of the world. Mankind itself is the world Saviour, of which all world Saviours have been but the symbol and the guarantee.

4. The blending of the deva or angel evolution and the human. This is a mystery which will be solved as man arrives at the consciousness of his own solar Angel, only to discover that that too is also but a form of life which, having served its purpose, must be left behind. The angel or deva evolution is one of the great lines of force, contained in the divine expression and the solar Angels, the Agnishvattas of *The Secret Doctrine* and of *A Treatise on Cosmic Fire* belong—in their form aspect—to this line.

Thus humanity serves, and in the development of a conscious aptitude for service, in the growth of a conscious understanding of the individual part to be played in the working out of the plan and in the rendering of the personality subject to the soul, will come the steady progress of humanity towards its goal of world service.

May I speak a word here so as to make this consummation a practical goal in your life? Harmful magnetic conditions, as the result of man's wrong handling of force are the causes of evil in the world around us, including the three sub-human kingdoms. How can we, as individuals, change this? By the development in ourselves of Harmlessness. Therefore, study yourself from this angle. Study your daily conduct and words and thoughts so as to make them utterly harmless. Set yourself to think those thoughts about yourself and others which will be constructive and positive, and hence harmless in their effects. Study your emotional effect on others so that by no mood, no depression, and no emotional reaction can you harm a fellow-man. Remember in this connection, violent spiritual aspiration and enthusiasm, misplaced or misdirected, may quite easily harm a fellow-man, so look not only at your wrong tendencies but at the use of your virtues.

If harmlessness is the keynote of your life, you will do more to produce right harmonious conditions in your personality than any amount of discipline along other lines. The drastic purgation brought about by the attempt to be harmless will go far to eliminate wrong states of consciousness. See to it therefore, and bring this idea in your evening review.

I would like to urge each one who reads these pages to make a fresh beginning in spiritual living. I would say to him, forget all past achievements, realize fervour, and concentrate upon the Plan.

By this time some progress in group realization has surely been made, and less interest in the separated self has been gained. More faith in the Good Law which guides all creation to ultimate perfection has been visioned without doubt, and, through this vision, has come the capacity to take one's eyes off the affairs of individual experience, and fasten them on the working out of the purpose for the whole. This is the objective and the goal. Breadth of vision, inclusiveness of understanding and a widened horizon are the preliminary essentials to all work under the guidance of the hierarchy of adepts; the stabilizing of the consciousness in the one life, and the recognition of the basic unity of all creation has to be somewhat developed before any one can be trusted with certain knowledges and Words of Power and the manipulation of those forces which bring the subjective reality into outer manifestation.

Therefore, I say to you at this time, I—an older and perhaps more experienced disciple and worker in the great vineyard of the Lord—practice harmlessness with zest and understanding, for it is (if truly carried out) the destroyer of all limitation. Harmfulness is based on selfishness, and on an ego-centric attitude. It is the demonstration of forces concentrated for self-enforcement, self-aggrandisement, and self-gratification. Harmlessness is the expression of the life of the man who realizes himself to be everywhere, who lives consciously as a soul, whose nature is love, whose method is inclusiveness, and to whom all forms are alike in that they veil and hide the light, and are but externalizations of the one Infinite Being. This realization, let me remind you, will demonstrate in a true comprehension of a brother's need, divorced from sentiment and expediency. It will lead to that silence of the tongue which grows out of non-reference to the separate self. It will produce that instantaneous response to true need which characterizes the Great Ones who (passing beneath the outer appearance) see the inner cause which produces the conditions noted in the outer life, and so, from that point of wisdom, true help and guidance can be given. Harmlessness brings about in the life caution in judgment, reticence in speech, ability to refrain from impulsive action, and the demonstration of a non-critical spirit. So, free passage can be given to the forces of true love, and to those spiritual energies which seem to vitalize the personality, leading consequently to right action.

Let harmlessness, therefore, be the keynote of your life. An evening review should be carried forward entirely along this line; divide the review work in three parts and consider:

1. Harmlessness in thought. This will primarily result in the control of speech.
2. Harmlessness in emotional reaction. This will result in being a channel for the love aspect of the soul.
3. Harmlessness in act. This will produce poise, skill in action and the release of the creative will.

These three approaches to the subject should be studied from their effects upon one's own self and development, and from their effect upon those whom one contacts and upon one's environing associates.

May I interpolate here the remark that I make suggestions, based on experience in occult work. There is no obligation to obey. We seek to train intelligent servers of the race, and these are developed by self-initiated effort, freedom in action and discrimination in method and not by unquestioning obedience, negative acquiescence, and blind following. Let this not be forgotten. If any command may ever emanate from the subjective band of teachers of whom I am a humble member, let it be to follow the dictates of your own soul and the promptings of your higher self.

Before we proceed to an analysis of this Rule and of the previous one, for Rules II and III are the two halves of a whole, I would like to remind you that, in this series of meditations upon these ancient formulas, we are concerned with the magical work of the aspirant as a co-worker in the enterprises of the Great White Lodge. We are dealing with the methods of white magic. Let me remind you also, that the magical work of our planetary Hierarchy consists of tending the psyche in the world of forms, so that the unfolding flower of the soul may be nurtured and fostered in such wise that radiant glory, magnetic force and (ultimately) spiritual energy may be demonstrated through the medium of the form. Thus the power of the three Rays of divine Manifestation may be seen.

> First Ray ---------- Spiritual Energy
> Second Ray ------- Magnetic Force
> Third Ray -------- Radiant Glory

These rays likewise find their microcosmic reflections in the aura of perfected man.

> First Ray ---------- Monadic------- Spiritual Energy ----- Head Centre
> Second Ray ------- Egoic ---------- Magnetic Force ------ Heart Centre
> Third Ray -------- Personality ---- Radiant Glory ------- Solar Plexus

You inquire, Why do I not say the throat centre? Because the centres below the diaphragm symbolize primarily the personal lower self, and in their synthesising centre, the solar plexus, express the magnetic force of the matter aspect in man. The throat centre is swept into increasing creative activity as the personality vibrates to the soul.

Let us now consider the words at the end of the previous rule: *"The lower light is thrown upward and the greater light illuminates the three; the work of the four proceedeth."*

What of this lower light? The student should remember that for the present purposes he has three bodies of light to consider:

There is the radiant body of the soul itself, found on its own plane, and called, frequently, the Karana Sarira or the causal body.

There is the vital or etheric body, the vehicle of prana which is the body of golden light, or rather the flame coloured vehicle.

There is the body of "dark light", which is the occult way of referring to the hidden light of the physical body, and to the light latent in the atom itself.

These three types of energy are referred to in the *Old Commentary* under the following symbolic terms:

"When the radiant light of the Solar Angel is fused with the golden light of the cosmic intermediary, it awakens from darkness the rush light of anu, the speck."

The "cosmic intermediary" is the term given to the etheric body, which is part and parcel of the universal ether. It is through the etheric body that all the energies flow, whether emanating from the soul, or from the sun, or from a planet. Along those living lines of fiery essence pass all the contacts that do not emanate specifically from the tangible world.

The dark light of the tiny atoms of which the physical vehicle is constructed is responsive to the stimulation passing down from the soul into its vehicle, and, when the man is under control of the soul, there eventuates the shining forth of the light throughout the body. This shows as the radiance emanating from the bodies of adepts and saints, giving the effect of bright and shining light.

When the radiant light of the soul is blended with the magnetic light of the vital body, it stimulates the atoms of the physical body to such an extent that each atom becomes in turn a tiny radiant centre. This only becomes possible when the head, heart, the solar plexus and the centre at the base of the spine are connected in a peculiar fashion, which is one of the secrets of the first initiation. When these four are in close cooperation the "floor of the triangle" as it is symbolically called, is prepared for the magical work. In other words—these can be enumerated as follows:

a. The physical material form with its centre at the base of the spine.
b. The vital body working through the heart centre where the life principle has its seat. The activities of the body which are due to this stimulation are carried through the circulation of the blood.
c. The emotional body, working through the solar plexus centre.
d. The head centre, the direct agent of the soul and its interpreter, the mind. These four are in complete accord and alignment.

When this is the case, the work of initiation and its interludes of active discipleship become possible. Before this time the work cannot proceed. This is foreshadowed in the aspirant when there is enacted a symbolic happening in the light in the head which is the forerunner of the later stage of initiation.

In this stage, the soul light penetrates into the region of the pineal gland; there it produces an irradiation of the ethers of the head, of the vital airs; this produces a stimulation of the atoms of the brain so that their light is fused and blended with the other two, the etheric light and the soul light, and there is then produced that inner radiant sun of which the aspirant becomes conscious in his physical brain experience. Frequently students speak of a diffused light or glow, this is the light of the physical plane atoms of which the brain is composed; later they may speak of seeing what appears to be like a sun in the head. This is the contacting of the etheric light, plus the physical atomic light. Later they become aware of an intensely bright electric light; this is the soul light, plus the etheric and the atomic. When that is seen, they frequently become aware of a dark centre within the radiant sun. This is the entrance to the Path disclosed by the "shining of the light upon the door."

Students must remember that it is possible to have reached a high stage of spiritual consciousness without seeing any of this brain radiance. This is altogether in the nature of phenomena, and is largely determined by the calibre of the physical body, by past karma and achievement, and by the ability of the aspirant to bring down "power from on high", and to hold that energy steady in the brain centre whilst he himself in meditation is detached from the form aspect, and can look serenely at it.

When this has been accomplished (and it is not an objective to be worked for, but is simply an indication to be registered in the consciousness and then dismissed) the consequent stimulation produces a reaction of the physical body. The magnetic power of the light in the head, and the radiant force of the soul produce stimulation. The centres begin to vibrate, and their vibration awakens the atoms of the material body until eventually the powers of the vibrating etheric body have swung even the lowest centre into line with the highest. Thus the fires of the body (the sum total of the energy of the atoms) are swept into increased activity until such time as there is a rising up the spine of that fiery energy. This is brought about by the magnetic control of the soul, seated "on the throne between the eyebrows".

Here enters in the work of one of the means of yoga, abstraction or withdrawal. Where the three lights are blended, where the centres are aroused and the atoms are also vibrating, it becomes possible for the man to centre all three in the head at will. Then, by the act of the will and the knowledge of certain words of Power he can enter into samadhi and be withdrawn from his body, carrying the light with him. In this way the greater light (the three fused and blended) illuminates the three worlds of man's endeavours and "the light is thrown upward" and illuminates all the spheres of man's conscious and unconscious experience. This is spoken of in the occult writings of the Masters in these words:

"Then the Bull of God carries the light in his forehead, and his eye transmits the radiance; His head, with magnetic force, resembles the blazing sun, and from the lotus of the head, the path of light issues. It enters into the Greater Being, producing a living fire. The Bull of God sees the Solar Angel, and knows that Angel to be the light wherein he walks."

Then the work of the four proceeds. The four are at-one. The Solar Angel is identified with his instrument; the life of the sheaths is subordinated to the life of the inner divinity; the light of the sheaths is fused with the light of the soul. The head, the heart, and the base of the spine are geometrically aligned and certain developments then become possible.

In these two Rules, the foundation of the magical work of the soul has been laid down. Let us list, for the sake of clarity, the steps outlined:

1. The Solar Angel begins the work of initiating the Personality.
2. He withdraws his forces from soul enterprises in the spiritual Kingdom, and centres his attention on the work to be done.
3. He enters into deep meditation.
4. Magnetic rapport with the instrument in the three worlds is instituted.
5. The instrument, man, responds, and also enters into meditation.
6. The work proceeds in ordered stages and with cyclic activity.
7. The light of the soul is thrown downwards.
8. The light of the vital body and the physical form is synchronised with that of the head.
9. The centres swing into activity.
10. The light of the soul and the two other aspects of light are so intense that now all life in the three worlds is illumined.
11. Alignment is produced, the work of discipleship and of initiation becomes possible and proceeds according to the Law of Being.

PRINCIPLES AND PERSONALITIES

There is, however, a point which merits consideration and which could be approached in the form of a question. The student might well enquire into the matter as follows:

"Some people approach the problem of Being through mental appreciation; others through heart understanding; some are motivated through the head and others through the heart; some do things or avoid doing them because they know, rather than feel; some react to their surroundings mentally rather than emotionally.

"The point on which to seek illumination is whether the path for some is not to serve because they know rather than love God, Who, after all, is but their innermost selves. Is this not the path of the occultist and of the sage rather than of the mystic and the saint? When all is said and done, is it not a question, primarily, of the ray one is on and the Master under whom one serves one's apprenticeship? Is not true knowledge a species of intellectual love? If a poet can pen an ode to intellectual beauty why may not we express appreciation of a unity that is conceived of the head rather than of the heart? Hearts are well enough in their way but they are not suited to the world's rough usage.

"Can one do aught but accept his present limitation while seeking such transcendence as is his by the Divine Law of evolution? Is there not such a thing (by comparison) as a spiritual inferiority complex on the part of such as are sensible (and perhaps over-sensitive) of the fact that while their lives intellectually are replete with interest, the desert of their hearts has not yet been made to blossom like the rose?

"In other words, provided one repairs to his appointed station and there serves in his acceptance of Brotherhood in the Presence of Fatherhood, what difference does it make that the fundamental postulate is with him a thing of the head rather than of the heart?"

I would answer such a questioning as follows:

It is not a question of ray or even of the basic distinction between the occultist and the mystic. In the rounded-out individual both head and heart must function with equal power. In time and space, however, and during the process of evolution, individuals are distinguished by a predominating tendency in any one life; it is only because we do not see all the picture that we draw these temporary distinctions. In one life a man may be predominantly mental and for him the path of the Love of God would be unsuited. The Love of God is shed abroad in his heart and to a considerable degree his occult approach is based on the mystic perception of past lives. For him the problem is to know God, with the view of interpreting that knowledge in love to all. Responsible love, demonstrated in duty to group and family, is therefore for him the line of least resistance. Universal love, raying out to all nature and all forms of life, will follow on a more developed knowledge of God, but this will be part of his development in another life.

Students of human nature (and this all aspirants should be) would do well to bear in mind that there are temporary differences. People differ in:

a. Ray (which affects predominantly the magnetism of the life).
b. Approach to truth, either the occult or the mystic path having the stronger drawing power.
c. Polarisation, deciding the emotional, mental or physical intent of a life.
d. Status in evolution, leading to the diversities seen among men.
e. Astrological sign, determining the trend of any particular life.
f. Race, bringing the personality under the peculiar racial thought form.

The sub-ray on which a man is found, that minor ray which varies from incarnation to incarnation, largely gives him his coloring for this life. It is his secondary hue. Forget not, the primary ray of the Monad continues through the aeon. It changes not. It is one of the three primary rays that eventually synthesise the sons of men. The ray of the ego varies from round to round, and, in more evolved souls, from race to race, and comprises one of the five rays of our present evolution. It is the predominating ray to which a man's causal body vibrates. It may correspond to the ray of the monad, or it may be one of the complementary colours to the primary. The ray of the personality varies from life to life, till the gamut of the seven sub-rays of the Monadic ray has been passed through.

Therefore, in dealing with people whose monads are on a similar or complementary ray it will be found that they approach each other sympathetically. We must remember however that evolution must be far advanced for the ray of the monad to influence extensively. So the majority of cases come not under this category.

With average advanced men, who are struggling to approximate themselves to the ideal, similarity of the egoic ray will produce mutual comprehension, and friendship follows. It is easy for two people on the same egoic ray to comprehend each other's point of view, and they become great friends, with unshaken faith in each other, for each recognizes the other acting as he himself would act.

But when (added to the egoic similarity of ray) you have the same ray of personality, then you have one of those rare things a perfect friendship, a successful marriage, an unbreakable link between two. This is rare indeed.

When you have two people on the same personality ray but with the egoic ray dissimilar, you may have those brief and sudden friendships and affinities, that are as ephemeral as a butterfly. These things need bearing in mind and with their recognition comes the ability to be adaptable. Clarity of vision results in a circumspect attitude.

Another cause of difference can be due to the polarization of the bodies. Unless this too meets with recognition in dealing with people lack of comprehension ensues. When you use the term: "a man polarized in his astral body"—you really mean a man whose ego works principally through that vehicle. Polarity indicates the clarity of the channel. Let me illustrate. The ego of the average man has its home on the third sub-plane of the mental plane. If a man has an astral vehicle largely composed of third sub-plane astral matter, and a mental vehicle mostly on the fifth sub-plane, the ego will centre his endeavour on the astral body. If he has a mental body of fourth sub-plane matter and an astral body of fifth sub-plane, the polarization will be mental.

When you speak of the ego taking more or less control of a man you really mean that he has built into his bodies matter of the higher sub-planes.

The ego takes control with interest only when the man has almost entirely eliminated matter of the seventh, sixth, and fifth sub-planes from his vehicles. When he has built in a certain proportion of matter of the fourth sub-plane the ego extends his control; when there is a certain proportion of the third sub-plane, then the man is on the Path; when second sub-plane matter predominates then he takes initiation, and when he has matter only of atomic substance, he becomes a Master. Therefore, the sub-plane a man is on is of importance, and the recognition of his polarization elucidates life.

The third thing you need to remember is that even when these two points are admitted, the age of the soul's experience frequently causes lack of comprehension. The above two points do not carry us very far, for the capacity to sense a man's ray is not for this race as yet. Approximate supposition and the use of the intuition is all that is now possible. The little evolved cannot comprehend completely the much evolved, and in a lesser degree, the advanced ego comprehends not an initiate. The greater can apprehend the lesser but the reverse is not the case.

As regards the action of those whose point of attainment greatly transcends your own, I can only ask you to do three things:

a. Reserve judgment. Their vision is greater. Forget not that one of the greatest qualities members of the Lodge have achieved is their ability to view the destruction of form as unimportant. Their concern is with the evolving life.

b. Realize that all events are brought around by the Brothers with a wise purpose in view. Lesser grade initiates, though utterly free agents, fit into the plans of their superiors just as do you in your lesser way. They have their lessons to learn, and the rule of learning is that all experience has to be bought. Apprehension comes by the punishment that follows an ill-judged act. Their superiors stand by to turn to good account situations brought about by the errors of those inferior in point of development.

c. Remember also that the Law of Rebirth holds hidden the secret of the present crisis. Groups of egos come together to work out certain karma involved in past days. Men have erred grievously in the past. Punishment and transmutation are the natural working out. Violence and cruelty in the past will reap its heavy karma, but it lies in the hands of you all now to transmute the old mistakes.

Also bear in mind that principles are eternal, personalities temporal. Principles are to be viewed in the light of eternity; personalities from the standpoint of time. The trouble is that, in many situations, two principles are involved, one of which is secondary. The difficulty lies in the fact that (both being principles) both are right. It is a rule for safe guidance always to remember that usually basic principles (for their wise comprehension and fruitful working out) call for the play of the intuition whilst secondary principles are more purely mental. The methods hence necessarily differ. When holding to the basic principles, the wisest methods are silence and a joyful confidence that the Law works, an avoidance of all personality innuendo except wise and loving comment, and a determination to see all in the light of eternity and not of time, coupled with a constant endeavour to follow the law of love and see only the divine in your brothers, e'en if on an opposing side.

In secondary principles, which all opposing forces are at present emphasizing, the use of the lower mind involves the danger of criticism, the employment of methods sanctioned by time in the three worlds—methods involving personal attack, invective and the expenditure of force along destructive lines, and a spirit contrary to the law of the plane of unity. The term "opposing forces" is used rightly if you employ it only in a scientific sense and mean the contrasting pole that leads to equilibrium. Remember therefore, that opposing groups may be quite sincere, but the concrete mind acts in them as a barrier to the free play of the higher vision. Their sincerity is great but their point of attainment along some lines less than that of those who adhere to basic principles, seen in the light of the intuition.

A principle is that which embodies some aspect of the truth on which this system of ours is based; it is the seeping through to the consciousness of the man of a little of the idea on which our Logos bases all He does. The basis of all Logoic action is love in activity, and the fundamental idea on which He bases action connected with the human Hierarchy is the power of love to drive onward,—call it evolution, if you like, call it inherent urge, should you so prefer, but it is love causing motion and urging onward to completion. It is the driving of one and all to further expression. Hence, this principle should underlie all activity, and the government of the lesser organizations, if founded on love leading to activity, would lead to a divine urge in all its members, driving them likewise on to fullest expression, and thus tend to more adequate completeness and more satisfactory endeavour.

A principle, when really fundamental, appeals at once to the intuition and calls out an immediate reaction of assent from the man's higher Self. It makes little or no appeal to the personality. It embodies a conception of the ego in his relationship to others. A principle is that which governs always the action of the ego on his own plane, and it is only as we come more and more under the guidance of that ego that our personality conceives of, and responds to these ideas. This is a point to be borne in mind in all dealings with others and should modify judgments. To apprehend a principle justly marks a point in evolution.

A principle is that which ensouls a statement dealing with the highest good of the greatest number. That a man should love his wife is a statement of a principle governing the personality but it must later be transmuted into the greater principle that a man must love his fellow men. Principles are of three kinds and the higher must be reached via the lower:

(*a*) Principles governing the lower personal self, dealing with the actions or active life of that lower self. They embody the third aspect or the activity aspect of logoic manifestation and form the basis of later progress. They control the man during his little evolved state, and during his period of thoughtlessness and might be comprehended more easily if I were to say that they are embodied in the commonly accepted rules of decent living. Thou shalt not kill, thou shalt not steal, have to do with a man's active life, with the building up of character.

(*b*) Principles governing the higher self and dealing with the love or wisdom aspect. It is with these that we are now concerned and half the troubles in the world at present arise from the fact that these higher principles, having to do with love or wisdom in all their fullness, are only now beginning to be apprehended by the rank and file of mankind. In the quick recognition of their truthfulness and the attempt to make them facts, without previously adjusting the environment to those ideals, comes the frequent clashing and warfare between those actuated by the principles governing the personality and those governing the higher Self. Until more of the race are governed by the soul consciousness this warfare is inevitable and cannot be avoided. When the emotional plane is dominated by the intuitional, then will come universal comprehension.

The first set of principles is learnt by the man through grasping, and the subsequent disaster that results from that seizure. He stole, he suffered the penalty and he stole no more. The principle was wrought into him by pain and he learnt that only that which was his by right and not by seizure could be enjoyed. The world is learning this lesson in groups now, for, as its revolutionaries seize and unlawfully hold, they find the stolen property suffices not but brings sorrow. Thus in time they learn the principles.

The second set of principles is learnt through renunciation and service. A man looks away (having learnt first principles) from the things of the personality and in service learns the power of love in its occult significance. He spends and consequently receives; he lives the life of renunciation and the wealth of the heavens pours in on him; he gives all and is full to completeness; he asks nothing for himself and is the richest man on earth.

First principles deal with the differentiated unit and with evolution through heterogeneity. Principles such as the race is learning now have to do with groups; the question is not—"What will be best for the man?" but "What will be best for the many?" and only those who can think with vision of the many as one, can state these principles satisfactorily. They are the most important, for they are the basic principles of this love system. The trouble today is that men are confused. Certain first principles, the lower activity fundamentals are ingrained and inherent now, and a few of the higher egoic or love principles are seeping through into their bewildered brains causing an apparent momentary clashing of ideas. Therefore like Pilate they say: "What is truth?" If they will but remember that the higher principles deal with the good of the group and the lower with the good of the individual, mayhap clarity, will ensue. The lower activity of personal life, no matter how good or how worthy, must eventually be transcended by the higher love life that seeks the good of the group and not of the unit.

All that tends to synthesis and divine expression in collections of units is approaching closer to the ideal and approximating the higher principles. In thinking out these ideas may come some helpfulness. You have an illustration of what I say in the fact that many of the struggles that arise in organizations are based on the fact that some worthy people follow personalities, sacrificing themselves for a principle, yes, but a principle governing the personality life. Others, dimly glimpsing something higher and seeking the good of the groups and not of a person, stumble onto a higher principle, and in so doing bring in the force of the ego. They are working for others and aiming at the helping of their group. When egos and personalities clash, the victory of the higher is sure; the lower principle must give way to the higher. One is concentrated on what seems to him to be of paramount value, the fulfilling of the wish of the personal life, and (at this period) is only secondarily interested in the good of the many though he may have moments when he thinks that is his primary intent. The other cares naught for what becomes of the personal self and is only interested in the helping of the many. It boils down, to use an apt expression, to the question of selfish or unselfish motive, and, as you know, motives vary as time speeds by and the man nears the goal of the probationary path.

(c) Still higher principles are those comprehended by the Spirit and are only readily comprehended by the monadic consciousness. Only as the man transcends his active personal life and substitutes the life of love or wisdom as led by the ego can he begin to understand the scope of that life of love and know it as demonstrated power. Just as the personality deals with the principles governing the life of activity of the lower self, and the ego works with the law of love as demonstrated in group work, or love showing itself in the synthesis of the many into the few, so the Monad deals with the active life of love shown in power through the synthesis of the few into the one.

One deals with the life of the man on the physical plane, or in the three worlds, the second with his life on causal levels, and the last with his life after the attainment of the goal of present human endeavour. One deals with units, another with groups and the last with unity. One deals with differentiation at its most diverse point, the second with the many resolved into the egoic groups, whilst the third sees the differentiation resolved back into the seven, which marks unity for the human hierarchy.

All these factors and many others produce differences among human beings, and in sizing himself up a man must needs bring them into his consideration.

It should therefore be borne in mind that a disciple of any of the Masters will have his peculiar equipment, and his individual assets and deficiencies. He can nevertheless rest assured that, until the path of Knowledge has been added to the path of Love, he can never take the major initiations, for these are undergone on the higher levels of the mental plane. Until the path of light is united to the path of life the great transition from the fourth into the fifth kingdom cannot be taken. Certain expansions of consciousness are possible; initiations on the astral and lower mental planes can be taken; some of the vision can be seen, the sense of the Presence can be felt; the Beloved can be reached by love, and the bliss and the joy of this contact can carry with it its abiding joy, but that clear perception which comes from the experience undergone on the Mount of Illumination is a different thing to the joy experienced on the Mount of Blessing. The Heart leads in the one, the Head leads in

58

the other.

To answer categorically: The path of knowledge is that of the occultist and the sage; that of love is that of the mystic and the saint. The head or the heart approach is not dependent upon the ray, for both ways must be known; the mystic must become the occultist; the white occultist has been the saintly mystic. True knowledge is intelligent love, for it is the blending of the intellect and the devotion. Unity is sensed in the heart; its intelligent application to life has to be worked out through knowledge.

It is of prime value to recognize the tendency of the life purpose, and to know whether the head or the heart method is the objective of any specific life. A fine spiritual discrimination is needed here however, lest the glamour of illusion tempt to the path of inertia. Ponder these words with care, and see that the question is based on a true foundation and does not grow out of an inferiority complex, the consideration of a brother's enterprise and a consequent jealous tendency, or upon a placid complacency which negates activity.

As a general rule for the average aspirant to discipleship, it may be safely assumed that the past has seen much application of the heart way, and that in this incarnation the mental unfoldment is of prime importance.

An ancient Scripture says:

"Seek not, Oh twice-blessed One, to attain the spiritual essence before the mind absorbs. Not thus is wisdom sought. Only he who hath the mind in leash, and seeth the world as in a mirror can be safely trusted with the inner senses. Only he who knoweth the five senses to be illusion, and that naught remaineth save the two ahead, can be admitted into the secret of the Cruciform transposed.
"The path that is trodden by the Server is the path of fire that passeth through his heart and leadeth to the head. It is not on the path of pleasure, nor on the path of pain that liberation may be taken nor that wisdom cometh. It is by the transcendence of the two, by the blending of pain with pleasure, that the goal is reached, that goal that lieth ahead, like a point of light seen in the darkness of a winter's night. That point of light may call to mind the tiny candle in some attic drear, but—as the path that leadeth to that light is trodden through the blending of the pairs of opposites—that pin-point, cold and flickering, groweth with steady radiance till the warm light of some blazing lamp cometh to the mind of the wanderer by the way.
"Pass on, O Pilgrim, with steady perseverance. No candle is there nor earth lamp fed with oil. Ever the radiance groweth till the path ends within a blaze of glory, and the wanderer through the night becometh the child of the sun, and entereth within the portals of that radiant orb."

RULE FOUR

Sound, light, vibration, and the form blend and merge, and thus the work is one. It proceedeth under the law, and naught can hinder now the work from going forward. The man breathes deeply. He concentrates his forces, and drives the thought-form from him.

The Creative Work of Sound.
The Science of the Breath.

THE CREATIVE WORK OF SOUND

Before centering our attention upon this rule, it would be well to recollect certain things, so that our reflection on the rule may proceed with profit.

First, the rule we are at present considering concerns work on the mental plane, and before such work is possible it is important to have a developed mind, a well-nurtured intelligence, and also to have achieved some measure of mind control. These rules are not for beginners in the occult sciences; they are for those who are ready for magical work and for labour on the plane of mind. Love is the great unifier, the prime attractive impulse, cosmic and microcosmic, but the mind is the main creative factor and the utiliser of the energies of the cosmos. Love attracts, but the mind attracts, repels and co-ordinates, so that its potency is inconceivable. Is it not possible dimly to sense a state of affairs in mental realms analogous to that now seen in the emotional? Can we picture the condition of the world when the intellect is as potent and as compelling as is the emotional nature at this time? The race is progressing into an era wherein men will function as minds; when intelligence will be stronger than desire, and when thought powers will be used for appeal and for the guidance of the world, as now physical and emotional means are employed.

There lies in this thought a profoundly necessary incentive for a right understanding of the laws of thought, and a correct instruction to be given of the use of mental matter, and the building of that matter into thought forms.

These rules concern themselves with this information. The second necessary recollection is that the worker in magic and the potent entity wielding these forces must be the soul, the spiritual man, and this for the following reasons:

1. Only the soul has a direct and clear understanding of the creative purpose and of the plan.
2. Only the soul, whose nature is intelligent love can be trusted with the knowledge, the symbols and the formulas which are necessary to the correct conditioning of the magical work.
3. Only the soul has power to work in all three worlds at once, and yet remain detached, and therefore karmically free from the results of such work.
4. Only the soul is truly group-conscious and actuated by pure unselfish purpose.
5. Only the soul, with the open eye of vision, can see the end from the beginning, and can hold in steadiness the true picture of the ultimate consummation.

You ask, whether workers in black magic possess not an equal power? I answer, no. They can work in the three worlds, but they work from and in the plane of mind, and do not function, therefore, outside their field of endeavour, as does the soul. They can achieve, from their proximity and identification with their working materials, results more potent temporarily and more rapid in accomplishment than the worker in the White Brotherhood, but the results are ephemeral; they carry destruction and disaster in their wake, and the black magician is eventually submerged in the resulting cataclysm.

Let us therefore remember the necessity of a correct use of the mind, and (at the same time) let us ever hold a position beyond and detached from the creative work of our minds, desires and physical accomplishment.

Four words stand forth as one considers Rule IV. First, *sound*, the formula, or word of power which the soul communicates and so starts the work. This word is dual. It is sounded forth on the note to which the soul responds, his own peculiar note, blended with that of his personality. This chord of two notes is the producer of the resulting effects, and is more important than the set phrase composing the word of power.

Herein lies the problem—to sound these two notes synchronously and with the mind focussed. Herein lies a clue to the significance of the AUM or OM. In the early stages of meditation work, the word is sounded audibly, whilst later it is sounded inaudibly. This training in the sound of the AUM is an unconscious preparation for the dual work of spiritual creation; and facility comes as the attentive aspirant accustoms himself to hear within his brain the soundless sound of OM.

I would suggest here, that students accustom themselves to work in this manner, sounding the word audibly and with much frequency at the close of the morning meditation, but emphasizing in the early part that close attention to the inaudible hearing which will develop the sensitivity of the inner ear, the etheric ear. Later, when the personal note or sound is established and the inner sound is sensed, there can be definite practise in blending the two. This entails the closest attention and the power to perform two activities simultaneously, with the mental attitude of attention to both.

Students whose aspiration is keen and clear would do well to face the issue where the magical work is concerned, and study their aptitude in meditation and their willingness to proceed with stability and caution with the needed discipline. To facilitate this I would suggest that any who are deeply concerned in the work should study and answer the following questions in the light of their souls, and to their higher selves make reply.

1. Do you feel you have reached the stage wherein you can:

a. Eliminate the meditation form as you now have it.
b. Enter with relative facility into the state of contemplation.
c. Recognize the vibration of your own soul.

2. Does the Sacred Word mean anything to you, and could you formulate clearly the reason you sound it?

3. Are you anxious to proceed in this work because your personality aspires, or because your soul is beginning consciously to utilize its mechanism?

In connection with this last question, a close analysis is called for, and I conjure you to speak truth to yourself and thus clearly ascertain the true position. This question lies between a man's soul and himself.

I would like to interpolate here a few words in connection with myself. Students can side-track their energies in idle speculation as to my identity. Of what moment is it? My province in relation to the group is to give needed assistance to those who seek to fit themselves for active work as disciples. I am a disciple and, having progressed further along the Path of Return than the aspirants who study these instructions, know somewhat the pitfalls, understand what is needed, and can aid in the preparation for the momentous moment when they pass the portal. Is more necessary? Is not truth of

61

equal value if enunciated by an aspirant, a disciple or a Master, or e'en a Christ? Mayhap the nearer I am to you the greater may be my usefulness. My anonymity will not be broken and speculations as to my identity are fruitless waste of time. Suffice it that I am an Oriental, that I am on the Teaching Ray, and closely associated with the Master K. H., that part of my work is the steady search for aspirants of strong heart, fervent devotion and trained minds, and that I am a disciple, as are all from the humblest probationer up to the greatest of the Great Ones. One lesson all aspirants need to learn and to learn early and that is, that concentration upon the personality of the Teacher, hoping for personal contact with him, and constant visioning of that condition called "accepted chelaship" serves to postpone that contact and delay the acceptance. Seek to equip your instrument, learn to function in quietness, fulfill your obligations and do your duty, develop restraint of speech and that calm poise that comes from an unselfish life motive and forget the selfish satisfaction that might well up in the heart when recognition of faithfulness comes from the watching Hierarchy.

Give this Instruction careful consideration. These are days wherein many adjustments and changes are being wrought in the world of men. In the resulting confusion, individuals are appreciating the necessity for the uniting of their forces and for cooperation in their efforts, and the need for group work is more apparent than ever before. These are days, therefore, wherein quietness and confidence must be your strength, and wherein the only safeguard lies in a close searching of all underlying motives. As seen on the surface, many apparently diverse principles emerge and the surge of battle appears to go, first one way and then another. As seen on the inner side, the emerging factors are simpler. The contest leads primarily to a testing of motives, and through this testing it is made apparent (to the watching Guides) who, in every group, are capable of clear thinking, accurate discrimination, patient endurance, and an ability to proceed along the probationary path toward the portal of initiation, untrammelled and undisturbed in their inner life by the upheavals on the surface. Could you but see it, the unrest and difficulty everywhere is producing a good which far outweighs the seeming evil. Souls are finding themselves and learning dependence upon the inner Ruler. When all outward props fail and when all the apparent authorities differ in the solution proffered, then souls are thrown back upon themselves and learn to seek within. This inner contact with the higher self is becoming apparent in gradually unfolding degree, and leads to that self-reliance and inward calm which is based upon the rule of the inner God and which, therefore, makes a man an instrument for service in the world.

Several things are apparent at this juncture to the careful thoughtful student of men and of motives.

First: That idealism and the sensing of the plan for humanity have a close relationship. Idealism is analogous to the thought that precedes creation. The capacity for abstract thought and for concentration on the ideal is only now in process of development, for this capacity involves the utilization of certain atoms, the employment of matter of the higher sub-planes and the ability to synchronize one's vibrations with the Great Ones. Only a few people in the race are true idealists (though their numbers are increasing); the small minority only, employ the concrete mind; while the masses are swayed entirely by the emotions. The time is coming when the intuitional body (the buddhic vehicle) will be organized, utilizing the higher spiritual mind as its medium. When that organization is completed the lower concrete mind will be nothing but a transmitter or an interpreter. Even abstract or concrete thought will be superseded, and we shall have simply the inflow of the intuition, taking form through the medium of the mind stuff. We shall, therefore, have the apprehension of much that is now incomprehensible to our lower plane vision.

In all great movements you have some thought or aggregation of thoughts cast into the minds of the so-called idealists by the Great White Brotherhood. The idea is sounded forth by Them. They choose a man or a group of men and cast into their minds some idea. There it germinates and is embodied by them in other thoughts, not so pure or so wise but necessarily colored by the individuality of the thinker. These thought-forms are, in their turn, picked up by the concrete thinkers of the world who—grasping the main outline of the idea—crystallize it and build it into more definite shape, into one more easily apprehended by the general public. It has therefore now reached the lower levels of the mental plane, and a further development becomes possible. It is then seized upon as desirable by those who are focussed upon the astral plane; to them it makes an emotional appeal, becoming public opinion. It is now practically ready to take shape upon the physical plane, and we have the practical adaptation of an ideal to the needs of the physical life. It has been stepped down; it has lost much of its original beauty; it is not as pure and as lovely as when first conceived, and it is distorted from its original shape but it is, nevertheless, more adapted to public use and can be employed as a stepping-stone to higher things.

Secondly: In this sensing of the plan and its later materialization, human units are involved and men have perforce to be employed. A vision is given of tremendous possibilities and indications are also granted of the manner in which these possibilities may become facts, but beyond that the Great Ones do not go. The detail and the method of concretizing the ideal and the necessary work is left to the sons of men. To the disciple who is an organizer and transmitter of the Plan falls the work of filling in the details and of taking the necessary action. At this point it is wise for him to remember that he comes (with his little plans) under the same law as do the Great Ones in Their large endeavours, and that it is in his dealings with people and his manipulation of the human equation that the difficulties arise.

Units for work fall into three groups:

(a) Those who can sense the plan and are commissioned to work it out.
(b) Those who can be used but who are blind to the greater issues.
(c) Those who can sense nothing except those things which concern their own selfish interests.

The first group the Masters can contact. They work with these units of the human family and expect fair promise of average success. These both hear the sound, and vision the Plan. The second group have to be utilized as best may be, by the disciples of the world. The final group are frequently to be offset from the energy standpoint, and only used when necessary.

One of the primary conditions that a disciple has to cultivate, in order to sense the plan and be used by the Master, is solitude. In solitude the rose of the soul flourishes; in solitude the divine self can speak; in solitude the faculties and the graces of the higher self can take root and blossom in the personality. In solitude also the Master can approach and impress upon the quiescent soul the knowledge that He seeks to impart, the lesson that must be learnt, the method and plan for work that the disciple must grasp. In solitude the sound is heard. The Great Ones have to work through human instruments and the plan and the vision are much handicapped by failure on the part of these instruments.

Third: This brings me to the third point, the problems and the difficulties with which the Masters have to contend as They seek to further the plans of evolution through the medium of the sons of men. In conclave wise They make Their plans; with judgment, after due discussion, They apportion the tasks; then, to those who offer themselves for service and who have some measure of soul contact, They seek to transmit as much of the plan as possible. They impress the plan and some suggestion as to its scope upon the mind of some man or some woman upon the physical plane. If that mind is unstable or oversatisfied, if it is filled with pride, with despair, or with self-deprecation, the vision does not come through with clarity of outline; if the emotional body is vibrating violently with some rhythm set up by the personality, or if the physical vehicle is ailing and concentrated attention is therefore prevented, what will happen? The Master will turn sadly away, distressed to think of the opportunity for service that the worker has lost through his own fault, and He will seek someone else to fill the need,—someone perhaps not so fundamentally suitable, but the only one available on account of the failure of the first one approached.

It might incidentally be of value here to remind aspirants to service that much work done by many is the result of over-zealousness and is not a carrying forward of the Master's work. With wise discrimination He apportions the work and never lays upon one human being more than he can adequately accomplish. He can and does train His disciple so that it appears to the on-looking world as if he accomplishes miracles but forget not that the vast amount of work accomplished by one useful disciple only becomes possible when the control of all his three bodies is co-ordinated and his alignment accomplished. He who has a stable mental body that is strongly positive in reception from above, whilst negative to lower vibrations, he who has an astral body that is clear, uncoloured and still, he who also has a physical body with steady nerves and stable rhythm (it will be like a casket, beautiful, yet strong as steel) will serve as a vessel meet for the Master's use, a channel through which He can unhindered pour His blessing upon the world.

Fourth: It should be noted that even the Great Ones Themselves have to lay Their plans largely allowing for the lack of perception of those on the physical plane through whom They have to work. They are handicapped and dependent upon Their physical plane instruments and Their main trouble concerns the point of evolution reached by the mass of men in the Occident.

Remember that this point is indicative of the success of the evolutionary process and not of its failure but, because much yet remains to be done, the work of the Lodge is often hindered. The point reached at this time might be expressed as a swinging from the rank materialism of the past into a growing and profound realization of the unseen worlds without the balance that comes from self-acquired knowledge. The forces that have been set in motion by the thinkers—the scientists of the world, the truly advanced religious men, the Spiritualists, the Christian Scientists, the New Thought workers, the Theosophists and the modern philosophers and workers in other fields of human thought—are gradually and steadily affecting the subtler bodies of humanity and are bringing them to a point where they are beginning to realize three things:

a. The reality of the unseen worlds.
b. The terrific power of thought.
c. The need for scientific knowledge on these two matters.

Fifth: Certain dangers which aspirants must watch as they seek to be of use should here be mentioned:

They must guard against overemphasizing one aspect at the expense of another part of the plan or vision.

They must avoid unequal concentration of thought upon that part of the plan which appeals the most to them personally.

They must recognize the inability of the workers to continue to bring through the plans and to work together peacefully and steadily. Friction is oft unavoidable.

They must watch for the creeping in of self-interest and of ambition.

They must guard against fatigue, due to long effort in materializing the plan and the strain incident upon high endeavour.

They must develop the capacity to recognize those who are sent to help them in the work.

They must above all watch against failure to keep in touch with the higher self and with the Master.

Another point that has to be remembered is that the problem to be solved by all who are seeking to co-operate with the Great White Lodge has four objects in view.

First, that in the working out of the plan there is also the working out of karma. This karma is not merely individual nor purely national, but is part of the total working out of world karma.

Second. Another object is the preparing of an instrument for service in the inauguration of the New Age during the next two hundred years. The integration of a group of knowers and of mystics is going on steadily in all parts of the world and in all organizations. One group is being gathered but its members belong to many groups. To this group of knowers and mystics is given the opportunity of being the channel through which the Hierarchy can work, and through which the Great Ones can send Their illuminating thought. Through it also they can work for the uplift (in the occult sense) of humanity and thus aid evolution on every plane. According to the response of disciples, of mystics and of knowers everywhere, so will be the rapid coming in of the New Age.

I here seek to sound a word of warning: In the failure to respond, in the failure to adjust, construct and refine, in the failure to turn the inner ear to those voices on the subtler planes which utter "the Words of Reconstruction" may come the ultimate transference of the forces of reconstruction to other channels, the consequent withholding of opportunities and the ultimate discarding of the instrumentality of the group as a medium of service. I would like to emphasize the statement anent "the words of Reconstruction," begging all of you who earnestly desire to hear these words to study the Introduction to the book, *Light on the Path.* Let it be remembered that if the Great Ones have to change Their plans as to this integrating group of mystics, it will be changed by the mystics themselves—viewed as a group.

The third objective is the development of the intuition and discrimination of the disciples in the world, and their ability to sense the higher vision and to achieve at the cost of the lower, the consciousness of that higher plane. They will have to remember that the lower objective, owing to its proximity, will loom in many ways more attractive, and can only be transcended at infinite cost. Intuition must be developed in many people, and their sense of values adequately adjusted before this group, which must inaugurate the New Age, can measure up to the requirements.

Present day troubles are largely due to the lack of intuitive perception in the past and this fault lies primarily among the mystics of the world and not so much among the lower aspirants. The trouble has not lain in lack of idealism or even in a lack of intelligence and sincerity, it consists in the failure to sacrifice the personality at all times in order to make the intuitive realization demonstrate its realities. Compromise has been permitted and in the occult world compromise is forbidden. When indulged in, it leads to disaster and sweeps away eventually, in ruin and in storm, the personalities of those who so stoop. People have sought to adjust the truth to the hour instead of adjusting the hour to the truth, and in diplomacy they have endeavored to bring about as much of the reality as they deem wise. The Masters are looking out for those with clear vision, uncompromising adherence to the truth as sensed, and capacity to drive steadily forward toward the ideal. This entails the following factors:

1. A recognition of that ideal through meditation.
2. Its application to the present through one-pointedness.
3. Removal of the old and hindering thought-forms through self-sacrifice.
4. A refusal to compromise, through clear vision.
5. A discrimination that enables the disciple always to distinguish between the acts of an individual and the individual himself.
6. Realization that, in the occult work, it is not permitted to interfere with personal karma any more than it is permitted to shield from the consequences of action. This entails therefore a refusal to interfere in anyone's business—that is, as regards the personality life, and yet involves a refusal to shirk the business of the larger cause. It is essential that the workers learn to discriminate between the factors which make for personal liberty and those which militate against group liberty.

The fourth result to be brought about by the present opportunity to work is the bringing in the new cycle and the new group of participants. Workers in the new era will be drawn from all groups and the test of their choice depends largely upon the measure of impersonality with which they work and the strength of their inner contact with the soul. It is not easy for any of you, therefore, submerged as you are in the smoke and roar of battle, to judge results with accuracy or to judge people with perfect propriety. These things have to be dealt with on the inner planes and are noted by the watching guides of the race. I would like here briefly to point out a few of the things for which the Great Ones look.

They look to see whether the inner flame—the result of effort wisely to work and think and do—burns with increased brilliance; they note whether it remains hidden and dim through the whirl of astral currents and by thought forms of personal antagonism, ambition and envy. As a result of world work some will be drawn into closer connection with the work of the Hierarchy, and others will be temporarily set back. Capacity to dominate the astral and to work from mental levels will largely count.

They look to see who can struggle and contend for principle with personalities, and yet keep the link of love intact. This counts perhaps more than men realize and a man who can stand for principle and yet love all human beings—refusing compromise and yet refusing hate—has something rare to offer in these days and the Great Ones can use him. See to it, therefore, all of you who work, that with clear vision, upright purpose and firm undeviating action you forge ahead. See to it that you deal with patience and forbearance with those of your brothers who choose the lesser principle and the lesser right, who sacrifice the good of the group for their own personal ends or who use unworthy methods. Give to them love and care and a ready helping hand, for they will stumble on the way and sound the depth of the law. Stand ready then to lift them up and to offer to them opportunities for service, knowing that service is the great healer and teacher.

The Great Ones look to see the faculty of pliability and adaptability working out, that faculty of adaptation that is one of the fundamental laws of species which nature so wonderfully demonstrates. The transference of this law to the inner planes and its working out in the new cycle of effort must be undertaken. This law of adaptation involves the appreciation of the need, the recognition of the new force coming in with the new cycle and the consequent bringing together in wide synthesis of the need and of the force, regarding the personal self simply as a focal point for action and transmutation. It involves the transmutation of the five senses and their extension into the subtler planes so that sight, hearing, touch, taste and smell are welded into one synthetic cooperating whole, for use in the great work. On the physical plane, these tend to the unification of the personal life and to the adaptation of the physical world to the needs of the personal self. On the subtler planes they must be transmuted until they are adequate to the needs of the group of which the individual forms a fragmentary part. The ability to do this is one of the things that the Great Ones look for in those individuals whose privilege it may be to inaugurate the New Age.

Above all, They look for an enlarged channel from the soul to the physical brain, via the mind. Such an enlarged channel indicates that a man can be used. One might almost express it by saying that They look for the perfecting of the antaskarana, that channel of communication between the soul consciousness and the brain whose possessor is one whom the Masters can successfully use. They are guided in their choice of workers by a man's personally achieved capacity and by his own hard won ability. When there is capacity, ability, and faculty, then the Great Ones joyfully employ him. The wrong angle has been, at times, over-emphasized and the reverse of this taught. The Masters must not be sought because a man seeks capacity. They will be found when a man has capacity—capacity that makes him available for group work and that can be extended under careful instruction into the higher powers of the soul. Leadership in groups controlling the work of the New Age will grow out of the discipline of the individual, and leaders will be found among those who sense the inner issue. Leadership that endures does not come to those who strive for place and power nor for those who have their eyes only on outward conditions and overlook the underlying causes. Leadership does not come to those who place the personal self and its position and power before the good of the group. It comes enduringly to those who seek nothing for the separated self, to those who lose themselves in the good of the whole.

To resume our consideration of the AUM. The Sound or the Sacred Word when correctly used has various effects which might be touched upon here.

OM sounded forth, with intent thought behind it, acts as a disturber, a loosener of the coarse matter of the body of thought, of emotion, and of the physical body. When sounded forth with intense spiritual aspiration behind it, it acts as an attractive medium, and gathers in particles of pure matter to fill the places of those earlier thrown out. Students should strive to have these two activities in their minds as they use the Word in their meditation. This utilization of the Word is of practical value, and results in the building of good bodies for the use of the soul.

The use of the OM serves also to indicate to the workers on the universal planes, and to those in the outer world who are gifted with spiritual perception that a disciple is available for work and can be utilized actively in the needed places of the earth. This should be borne in mind by all aspirants and should serve as an incentive in making the outer phenomenal life coincide with the spiritual impulse.

The use of the Sacred Word has its place also in the magical work of the Hierarchy. Thought forms are created for the embodiment of ideas and these embodied forms are sent forth to contact the minds of the disciples who are responsible in the group of a Master for the carrying forward of the plan.

Through the cultivated receptivity of the developed and controlled mental body, aspirants become aware of the ideas which the Masters bring through from the plane of the Universal Mind, and hence are in a position to co-operate intelligently. They, in their turn, as this Rule seeks to indicate, create thought forms of those received ideas, and utilize them in their groups for the helping of the world. The main work of a disciple on the mental plane is to train himself to do four things:

1. To be receptive to the mind of the Master.
2. To cultivate a right intuitive understanding of the thoughts sent him by the Master.
3. To embody the ideas received in such form as will be suitable for those he is engaged in helping.
4. Through sound, light and vibration to make his thought form active (embodying as much of the universal thought as is desirable) so that other minds may contact it.

Thus are groups gathered, organized, taught and lifted, and thus the Hierarchy of Adepts can reach the world.

There are many other uses, of course, but if the students will ponder on these three they will make it possible for further uses to be imparted later.

May I add, that the sound is only truly potent when the disciple has learnt to subordinate the lesser sounds. Only as the sounds he sends forth normally into the three worlds are reduced in volume and in activity, as well as in quantity will it be possible for the Sound to be heard, and so to accomplish its purpose. Only as the multitude of spoken words is reduced, and silence in speech is cultivated, will it be possible for the Word to make its power felt on the physical plane. Only when the many voices of the lower nature and of our environment are silenced, will the "Voice that speaketh in the stillness" make its presence felt. Only when the sound of many waters dies away in the adjustment of the emotions will the clear note of the God of the waters be heard.

People seldom realize the potency of a word, yet it is stated, "In the beginning was the Word, and the Word was God. Without Him was not anything made that was made." When therefore we read those words our minds go back to the dawn of the creative process when, through the medium of sound, God spoke and the worlds were made.

It has been said that, "the chief agency by which Nature's wheel is moved in a phenomenal direction is sound," for the original sound or word sets in vibration the matter of which all forms are made and initiates that activity which characterizes even the atom of substance.

The literature and the scriptures of all the ancient nations and great religions bear testimony to the efficacy of sound in producing all that is tangible and visible. The Hindus say very beautifully that "the Great Singer built the worlds, and the Universe is His Song." This is another way of expressing the same idea. If this is realized and the science of this concept somewhat understood, the significance of our own words and the utterance of sound in speech, becomes almost a momentous happening.

Sound or speech and the use of words have been regarded by the ancient philosophers (and are increasingly so regarded by modern thinkers) as the highest agent used by man in moulding himself and his surroundings. Thought, speech and the resultant activity on the physical plane complete the triplicity which make a man what he is, and place him where he is.

The purpose of all speech is to clothe thought and thus make our thoughts available for others. When we speak we evoke a thought and make it present, and we bring that which is concealed within us into audible expression. Speech reveals, and right speech can create a form of beneficent purpose, just as wrong speech can produce a form which has a malignant objective. Without realizing this, however, ceaselessly and irresponsibly, day after day, we speak; we use words; we multiply sounds; and surround ourselves with form worlds of our own creation. Is it not essential, therefore, that before we speak we should think, thus remembering the injunction, "You must attain to knowledge, ere you can attain to speech"? Having thought, let us then choose the right words to express the right thought, attempting to give correct pronunciation, proper values, and true tonal quality to every word we utter.

Then will our spoken word create a thought form which will embody the idea we have in our minds. Then too will our words carry no discord, but will add their quota to that great harmonizing chord or unifying word which it is the function of mankind ultimately to utter. Wrong speech separates, and it is interesting to bear in mind that the word, the symbol of unity, is divine, whereas speech in its many diversifications is human.

As evolution proceeds, and the human family rises into its true position in the great plan of the universe, right and correct speech will be increasingly cultivated, because we shall think more before we utter words, or, as a great teacher has said, "through meditation we shall rectify the mistakes of wrong speech;" and the significance of word forms, true and correct sounds, and vocal quality will become ever more apparent.

The second word of importance in this fourth Rule is the word *light*. First the sound and then the first effect of sound, the pouring forth of light, causing the revelation of the thought form.

Light is known by what is revealed. The absence of light produces the fading away, into apparent non-existence, of the phenomenal world.

The thought form created by the Sound is intended to be a source of revelation. It must reveal truth, and bring an aspect of reality to the cognisance of the onlooker. Hence the second quality of the thought form in its highest use is that it brings light to those who need it, to those who walk in darkness.

I deal not here with light as the soul, cosmically or individually. I touch not upon light as the universal second aspect of divinity. I seek only in these Instructions to deal with that aspect of truth which will make the aspirant a practical worker, and so enable him to work with intelligence. His main work (and increasingly he will find this to be so) is to create thought-forms to carry revelation to thinking human beings. To do this he must work occultly, and through the sound of his breathed forth work, through the truth revealed in form, will he carry light and illumination into the dark places of the earth

Then he finally makes his thought form live through the power of his own assurance, spiritual understanding and vitality. Thus the significance of the third word, *vibration*, appears. His message is heard, for it is sounded forth; it carries illumination, for it conveys the Truth and reveals Reality; it is of vital import, for it vibrates with the life of its creator, and is held in being as long as his thought and sound and intelligence animate it. This is true of a message, of an organization, and of all forms of life, which are but the embodied ideas of a cosmic or a human creator.

Students would find it of value to take these three vital words and trace their relation to all embodied thought forms—a cosmos, a plane, a kingdom in nature, a race, a nation, a human being. Consider the diverse groups of creating agencies—solar Logoi, solar Angels, human beings, and others. Consider the spheres of the creative process and see how true the *Old Commentary* is when it says:

"The sound reverberated amidst varying wheels of uncreated matter; and lo, the sun and all the lesser wheels appeared. The light shone forth amidst the many wheels, and thus the many forms of God, the diverse aspects of his radiant robe blazed forth.

"The vibrant palpitating wheels turned over. Life, in its many stages and in its many grades commenced the process of unfolding, and lo, the law began to work. Forms arose, and disappeared, but life moved on. Kingdoms arose, holding their many forms which drew together, turned together, and later separated, but still the life moved on.

"Mankind, hiding the Son of God, the Word incarnate, broke forth into the light of revelation. Races appeared and disappeared. The forms, veiling the radiant soul, emerged, achieved their purpose and vanished into night, but lo, the life moved on, blended this time with light. Life merged with light, both blending to reveal a beauty and a power, an active liberating force, a wisdom and a love that we call a Son of God.

"Through the many Sons of God, who in their inmost centre are but one, God in his Fatherhood is known. Yet still that lighted life moved on to a dread point of power, of force creative, concerning which we say: It is the All, the Container of the Universe, the persistent centre of the Spheres, the One."

We have touched upon two words of significance in the fourth Rule,—sound and light,—and one paramount idea emerges. The soul is to be known as light, as the revealer, whilst the Spirit aspect will later be recognized as sound. Complete light and illumination is the right of the disciple who attains to the third initiation, whilst the true comprehension of the sound, of the triple AUM, the synthesizing factor in manifestation appears only to the one who stands master of the three worlds.

The word *vibration* must next engage our attention but it may not be dissociated from the next word in the sequence *form*. Vibration, the effect of divine activity, is two-fold. There is the first effect in which the vibration (issuing from the realm of subjectivity in response to sound and light) produces response in matter, and therefore attracts or calls together the atoms out of which molecules, cells, organisms and finally the integrated form can be built. This effected, the aspect of vibration is to be noted as a duality.

The form, through the medium of the five senses, becomes aware of the vibratory aspect of all forms in the environment wherein it, itself, is a functioning entity. Later, in time and space, that functioning form becomes increasingly aware of its own interior vibration, and by tracing back that vibration to its originating source becomes aware of the Self, and later of the Kingdom of the Self. Humanity as a whole is aware of its environment and, through the information conveyed by the sense of sight, hearing, touch, taste and smell, the phenomenal world, the outer garment of God, is known, and communication between the Self and what we call the natural world is set up. As the mind appropriates and synthesizes this knowledge, the dweller in the form passes through the following stages:

1. Vibration is registered, and the environment has its effect upon the form.

2. This effect is noted, but not understood. The man, under the slow and steady impact of this vibratory effect, slowly awakens to consciousness or awareness.

3. The environment begins to interest the man and he regards it as desirable. Steadily the attraction of the three worlds grows and holds the man in reiterated incarnation. (The word "re-iterated" is literally and more academically correct than the word "repeated." Each of us is really a re-iterated word,

sounding in time and space.)

4. Later, when the vibration of the environing forms of the natural world becomes monotonous through constant impact over many lives, the man begins to turn a deaf ear and an un-seeing eye upon the familiar phenomenal world of desire. He becomes insensitive to its vibratory impact and increasingly aware of the vibration of the Self.

5. Later, on the Path of Probation and of Discipleship, this subtler vibratory activity exerts an increasing allure. The outer world ceases to attract. The inner world of the self assumes paramount place in the desire nature.

6. Little by little, using the language of modern psychology, within the outer form, which is the response apparatus for the process of becoming aware of the phenomenal world, the disciple builds a new subtler response apparatus whereby the subjective worlds can be known.

When this stage is reached there ensues a steady turning away from vibratory contact with the outer worlds of form, and an atrophying of desire in that direction. All seems arid and undesirable, and all fails to satisfy the ardent and aspiring soul. The difficult process of re-orientation toward a new world, a new state of being and a new condition of awareness is set up, and because the inner subtle response apparatus is only in an embryonic condition there is a devastating sense of loss, a groping in the dark, and a period of spiritual wrestling and exploration that tests the endurance and steadfastness of purpose of the aspirant to the very limits.

But (and this is the encouraging point to be remembered) all "*proceedeth under the law and naught can hinder the work from going forward.*" Note these words in Rule IV. There comes a stage when a man is verily and indeed "founded on the rock," and though he may experience the alternation of light and shade, though the waves of the purifying waters may roll over him, and threaten to sweep him off his feet, and though he may feel himself deaf and dumb and blind, naught can ultimately defeat the purpose of the soul. All that is lacking is the developed spiritual body which is equipped to respond to the vibration of the inner spiritual world. It exists in embryo, and the secret of its use lies in the attitude of the brain to the functions of the etheric body, as it exists as an intermediary between the brain, nervous system and the mind, or between the soul, mind and the brain. This cannot be elaborated here but the hint can be given for the reflection of the keen aspirant.

We have therefore the following stages dealt with in Rule IV and pointed out with lucid clarity, yet with that parsimony of phrase which distinguishes all occult and symbolic writings:

1. The integration of the form, as the result of the activity of the soul, through the use of

a. Sound,
b. Light,
c. Vibration.

2. The development of a response apparatus for use in the phenomenal world.

3. The eventual turning away from the phenomenal world, as the result of use and consequent satiety, and the gradual use of the subtler response apparatus.

4. The response apparatus of the soul—mind, etheric body, brain and nervous system—is re-oriented, and the man becomes aware of the kingdom of the soul, another kingdom in nature.

5. The turning away from the kingdom of the world to the kingdom of the soul becomes an esoteric habit, and in this thought lies hid the secret of esoteric psychology. The man is stabilized in the spiritual life. Naught can now hinder.

THE SCIENCE OF THE BREATH

Now we come to the significant words in Rule IV. "The man breathes deeply." This is a phrase covering many aspects of rhythmic living. It is the magical formula for the science of pranayama. It covers the art of the creative life. It sweeps a man into tune with the pulsating life of God Himself, and this through detachment and re-orientation.

It is notably interesting as a demonstration of the succinctness and inclusiveness of occult phrases as in Rule IV. The art of breathing is dealt with in three phases, and these I commend to each of you for the most careful consideration.

There is first the aspect of *Inhalation.* "The man breathes deeply." From the very depths of his being he draws the breath. In the process of phenomenal living, he draws the very breath of life from the soul. This is the first stage. In the process of detaching himself from phenomenal living, he draws from the depths of his being and experiences the life, that it may be rendered again back to the source from whence it came. In the occult life of the disciple, as he develops a new and subtler use of his response apparatus, he practices the science of the breath, and discovers that through deep breathing (including the three stages of the deep, middle, and top breath) he can bring into activity, in the world of esoteric experiences, his vital body with its force centres. Thus the three aspects of "deep breathing" cover the entire soul experience, and the relationship to the three types of breath, touched upon above, can be worked out by the interested aspirant.

Next we read "he concentrates his forces." Here we have the stage indicated which can be called *retention of the breath.* It is a holding of all the forces of the life steadily in the place of silence, and when this can be done with ease and with forgetfulness of process through familiarity and experience, then the man can see and hear and know in a realm other than the phenomenal world. In the higher sense this is the stage of contemplation, that "lull between two activities" as it has been so aptly called. The soul, the breath, the life has withdrawn out of the three worlds, and in the "secret place of the most high" is at rest and at peace, contemplating the beatific vision. In the life of the active disciple it produces those interludes which every disciple knows, when (through detachment and the capacity to withdraw) he is held by nothing in the world of form. As he is but wrestling toward perfection and has not yet attained, these interludes of silence, withdrawingness, and of detachment are frequently difficult and dark. All is silence and he stands appalled by the unknown, and by the apparently empty stillness in which he finds himself. This is called, in advanced cases, "the dark night of the soul"—the moment before the dawn, the hour before the light streams forth.

In the science of Pranayama it is the moment following upon inhalation wherein all the forces of the body have (through the medium of the breath) been carried upward to the head and concentrated there, prior to the stage of breathing forth. This moment of retention, when properly carried forward, produces an interlude of intense concentration and it is in this moment that the aspirant must seize opportunity. Herein lies a hint.

72

Then comes the process of *exhalation*. We read in Rule IV "he drives the thought-form from him." This is ever the result of the final stage of the science of the breath. The form, vitalized by the one who breathes in correct rhythm, is sent forth to do its work and fulfil its mission. Study this idea with care, for it holds the secret of creative work.

In the experience of the soul, the form for manifestation in the three worlds is created through intense meditation, which is ever the paralleling activity of breathing. Then by an act of the will, resulting in a "breathing forth", and engendered or arrived at dynamically in the interlude of contemplation or retention of the breath, the created form is sent forth into the phenomenal world, to serve as a channel of experience, a medium of expression and a response apparatus in the three worlds of human living.

In the life of the disciple, through meditation and discipline he learns to reach high moments of interlude whenever he concentrates his forces on the plane of soul life, and then again by an act of his will, he breathes forth his spiritual purposes, plans and life into the world of experience. The thought form that he has constructed as to the part he has to play, and the concentration of energy which he has succeeded in bringing about become effective. The energy needed for the next step is breathed forth by the soul and passes down into the vital body, thus galvanizing the physical instrument with the needed constructive activity. That aspect of the plan which he has appreciated in contemplation, and that part of the general purpose of the Hierarchy in which his soul feels called upon to co-operate is breathed forth simultaneously, via the mind into the brain, and thus "he drives the thought forms from him."

Finally, in the science of Pranayama, this stage covers that exhaling breath which, when carried forward with thought and conscious purpose behind it, serves to vitalize the centres and fill each of them with dynamic life. More need not be said here.

Thus, in this science of "breathing deeply" we have the whole process of creative work and of the evolutionary unfoldment of God in nature covered. It is the process whereby the Life, the One Existence, has brought the phenomenal world into being, and Rule IV is a digest of the Creation. It is equally the formula under which the individual soul works as it centres its forces for manifestation in the three worlds of human experience.

The right use of the Life-Breath is the whole art at which the aspirant, the disciple, and the initiate work, bearing in mind however that the science of the physical breath is the least important aspect and follows sequentially upon the right use of energy, which is the word we apply to the divine breath or life.

Finally, in the mental life of the disciple, and in the great work of learning to be a conscious creator in mental matter and so produce results in the phenomenal world, this fourth Rule holds the instructions upon which the work is based. It embodies the science of the entire magical work.

Therefore, this Rule warrants the closest consideration and study. Rightly understood and rightly studied it would lead each aspirant out of the phenomenal world into the kingdom of the soul. Its instructions, if carried out, would lead the soul back again into the phenomenal world as the creating force in soul magic and as the manipulator and dominating factor of, and through, the medium of the form.

In the training of the occidental student, blind unquestioning obedience is never asked. Suggestions are made as to method and as to a technique which has proved effective for thousands of years and with many disciples. Some rules as to breathing, as to helpful process and as to practical living on the physical plane will be imparted, but in the training of the new type of disciple during the coming age, it is the will of the watching Gurus and Rishis that they be left freer than has heretofore been the case. This may mean a slightly slower development at the beginning but will result, it is hoped, in a more rapid unfoldment during the later stages upon the Path of Initiation.

Therefore, students are urged to go forward during their period of training with courage and with joy, knowing that they are members of a band of disciples, knowing that they are not alone but that the strength of the band is theirs, the knowledge of the band is theirs too as they develop the capacity to apprehend it,—and knowing also that the love and wisdom and understanding of the watching Elder Brothers are back of every aspiring Son of God, e'en though apparently (and wisely) he is left to wrestle through to the light in the strength of his own omnipotent soul.

RULE FIVE

Three things engage the Solar Angel before the sheath created passes downward; the condition of the waters, the safety of the one who thus creates, and steady contemplation. Thus are the heart, the throat, and eye, allied for triple service.

The Soul and its Thought-forms.
Heart, Throat and Eye.
The Awakening of the Centres.

THE SOUL AND ITS THOUGHT-FORMS

We have been dealing with the processes of creation as they concern:

1. The Creator of a solar system or a planetary scheme.
2. The Ego, as it creates its body of manifestation. It should here be remembered that the entire human family has been brought into manifestation by a paralleling group of egos.
3. Man, as he creates those thought-forms by which he expresses himself, through which he works, and by which he is surrounded. It should also here be borne in mind that this definite creative work is only possible to those who function on mental levels—the thinkers of the world and the disciples of the Masters.

In every case, as we have seen, the objective form has been the result of meditation on the part of the creating agency, of response from the material acted upon by the force generated in meditation, thus producing the building of the form, and its utilization through sound. This is succeeded by the stage wherein the form is seen objectively and becomes a vibrant living entity. Thus is "the Word made Flesh," and thus do all forms—universes, men, and ensouled thoughts—come into being.

This fifth rule touches upon three factors which engage the attention of the creating agent before the physical form emerges into view on the exterior plane. These three are:

1. The condition of the waters.
2. The safety of the one who thus creates.
3. Steady contemplation.

We will deal briefly with these three and then we will consider the three factors which the disciple needs to relate if he ever aims to become an active and potent co-operator with the Hierarchy. These are the Eye, the Heart, the Throat. The interpretation and significance of these rules can be carried forward along several lines. For our purposes, the one followed will be that relating to the disciple and his work, and will deal with his training in the magical work of the ego, as that ego occupies and employs a physical form. These teachings are intended to be practical; they will emphasize the training and discipline of the disciple, and, scattered throughout, will be found those hints and esoteric suggestions which, when followed, will lead the aspirant on to experiment and to experience of truth. Those who are not true aspirants will fail to recognize the hints and thus will be preserved from danger and premature experience.

Let us therefore take up the three factors which engage our attention, and let us consider them from the standpoint of the human being who is creating thought-forms, and not primarily from the standpoint of a solar Creator or of an ego, preparing to take incarnation through the medium of form. Two collateral thoughts are here of value. One is that the process of creating thought-forms is part of the work done by every aspirant in the daily meditation process. If the student would remember that every time he sits down to his morning meditation he is learning to build and vitalize thought-forms, his work might assume greater interest. The tendency of most aspirants is to be occupied with their deficiencies in the work of meditation and their inability to control their minds, whereas both those aspects of their endeavour would be aided if they were to be occupied by the profoundly engrossing work of thought-form building.

A secondary and less important thought is that as egos, preparing to take human bodies, are deeply engaged in meditation work, it is highly improbable that they can be reached by the ordinary medium in the ordinary seance. At the most, only those who have passed over quite recently can be thus contacted, and they are, in most cases, in a condition of deep abstraction of a different kind. There is no time or purpose in enlarging upon this theme here but it is of interest to those investigating these matters.

1. *The Condition of the Waters*

The creating agency, man, has through the incentives of a co-ordinating purpose, intent meditation, and creative activity built the thought-form which he is ensouling with his own vitality and directing with his will. The time has come for that thought-form to be sent upon its mission and to carry out the purpose of its being. As we saw in the earlier rule, the form is "driven" from its creator by the power of the expulsive breath. This is a symbolic statement but, at the same time, an experimental fact in the magical work. In the disciple's work, there is often failure owing to his inability to understand both the esoteric and the literal significance of this expulsive breath as he carries forward his meditation work. This expulsive breath is the result of a preceding period of rhythmic breathing, paralleled by concentrated meditation work, then a definite focussing of the attention and the breath, as the purpose of the created form is mentally defined, and finally, the vitalizing of the thought-form, by its creator, and its consequent energizing into independent life and activity.

The first hindrance to the potency of the work comes through the failure of the disciple to carry on these activities simultaneously. The second cause of failure lies in his neglecting to consider the condition of the waters or the state of the emotional substance into which this mental form must go and so gather to itself the matter of the astral plane which will enable it to become a functioning entity on that plane. If it cannot do this, it becomes simply and eventually a dead form on the plane of mind, for it will lack that motivating power of desire which is necessary to carry it forward to completion on the physical plane.

It is interesting to remember this: If a thought-form is sent forth into the emotional world to gather to itself a body of desire (the impelling force which produces all objectivity) and is immersed in a "condition of the waters" which can best be described as purely selfish, all that occurs is as follows: It is lost, by being drawn into the astral body of the disciple, which is the focal point for all astral energy employed by the disciple. It is swept into a vortex of which the individual astral body is the centre and loses its separate existence. The simile of the whirlpool is of value here. The thinker is like a man throwing a toy boat from the shore into a stream of water. If he throws it into a whirlpool, it is sucked in time into the central vortex and so disappears. Many forms, thus constructed by an aspirant in his meditation work are lost and fail in their objective because of the chaotic and whirling state of the aspirant's emotional body. Thus good intentions come to naught; thus good purpose and planned work for the Master fail to materialize because, as the thought-form passes downward on to the plane of desire and emotion, it contacts only the seething waters of fear, of suspicion, of hatred, of vicious or purely physical desire. These being more potent than the little form, drown it, and it passes out of sight and out of existence, and the man becomes conscious of another abortive effort.

Or again, the "condition of the waters" is not that of a self-engendered whirlpool, but is more allied to that of a pool, stirred into a frothy and boiling surge, through the activities of others. There are many disciples who have achieved a fair measure of self-control and of personal disinterestedness. They are not the victims of personality desire and aims, and are comparatively free from the whirlpool of selfish tendencies. But their astral bodies are again and again swept into a state of agitation by the group for, and in which, they work. They are elated or depressed, satisfied or dissatisfied by the results they achieve or fail to achieve; this achievement or lack of achievement and the steadiness or disloyalties of their fellow servers produce agitation and emotional upset, and on this powerful reaction their thought-forms, constructed so diligently and prayerfully, come to naught. Their "skill in action" is lost, because they are tied to the desired result and so their labour produces nothing.

There are many other "conditions of the waters" which each aspirant can for himself supply. There is one more however upon which I would like to touch. The emotional body of the disciple which must feed and nurture the baby thought-form (with its mental nucleus) is necessarily part of the planetary emotional form and hence vibrates in unison with that form. This should also be carefully considered, for the emotional body is thrown into a state of activity by the general astral condition and must be handled wisely from this angle.

At this time there are three qualities predominating in the planetary form—fear, expectancy and a climaxing desire (in the human family) for material possession. Note the word "climaxing". The summation of human desire for material happiness has been reached, and the peak of that desire has been passed; thus mankind has achieved and surmounted much. But the rhythm of the ages is strong.

These three qualities have to be grasped and discounted by the aspirant as he seeks to serve from mental levels. In the place of fear he must substitute that peace which is the prerogative of those who live always in the Light of the Eternal; in the place of questioning expectancy he must substitute that placid, yet active, assurance of the ultimate objective which comes from a vision of the Plan and his contact with other disciples and later with the Master. Desire for material possession must be superseded by aspiration for those possessions which are the joy of the soul—wisdom, love and power to serve. Peace, assurance and right aspiration! These three words, when understood and experienced in the life of every day, will bring about that right "condition of the waters" which will ensure the survival of every thought-form, rightly engendered in meditation by the man, functioning as a soul.

2. The Safety of the One Who Thus Creates

It might be said here with emphasis, even if it is a recognized truism, that people are frequently slain (in the occult and therefore in the more important sense) by their own thought-forms. Thought creation, through concentration and meditation, is a potently dangerous matter. This must never be forgotten. There are forms of thought, unencumbered by much desire matter, which, failing to pass downward, poison the man on mental levels. This they do in two ways:

1. By growing so potent on the mental plane that the man falls a victim to the thing he has created. This is the "idée fixe" of the psychiatrist; the obsession which drives to lunacy; the one-pointed line of thought which eventually terrorises its creator.
2. By multiplying so fast that the mental aura of the man becomes like unto a thick and dense cloud, through which the light of the soul must fail to penetrate, and through which the love of human beings, the lovely and beautiful and comforting activities of nature and of life in the three worlds equally fail to pierce. The man is smothered, is suffocated by his own thought-forms, and succumbs to the miasma which he himself has engendered.

Or again, there are lines of thought which draw forth from the emotional body a reaction of a poisonous nature. A certain line of thought is followed by a human being in relation to his brethren. It breeds hatred, jealousy and envy, and works through into manifestation in such a manner that it produces those physical plane activities which cause the death of their creator. This may be literal as in the case of murder, which is in many cases the result of crystallised intent, or it may result in disease. Pure thought, right motive and loving desire are the true correctives of disease, and where the desire for these (which does animate many) is raised to constructive thinking there will be the gradual elimination of disease. As yet, though many desire, few think. Let it never be forgotten that the Great Ones do not look for those who only desire and aspire. They look for those who blend with their desire the determination to learn to use their mental bodies and become creators, and who will work constructively towards these ends.

Thus it will be seen why, in all systems of true occult training, the emphasis is laid on right thinking, loving desire, and pure, clean living. Only thus can the creative work be carried forward with safety, and only thus can the thought-form pass downward into objectivity, and be a constructive agent on the plane of human existence.

3. Steady Contemplation

You will note here that the word 'meditation' is not used. The thought is a different one. The meditation process, involving the use of thought and the mental building of the form so that it can be completed and rounded out and in line with the thought-form of the disciple's group of co-disciples, and therefore with the Plan, has been completed to the best of the man's ability. Now he must, with steadiness, contemplate that which he has created, and with equal steadiness inspire it with needed life, so that it can fulfill its function.

He ceases to reason, to think, to formulate, and to build in mental matter. He simply pours his life into the form and sends it forth to carry out his will. Just as long as he can contemplate and hold steady, so will his creation fulfill his intention and act as his agent.

Just so long as he can focus his attention on the ideal for which he created his thought-form and can link the form and the ideal together in one steady vision, just so long will it serve his purpose and express his ideal. Herein lies the secret of all successful co-operation with the Plan.

We will now study for a while the words "heart, throat, and eye," for they have a peculiar significance. These three form the apparatus to be employed by all disciples during the world cycle which is so rapidly coming.

That there is not as yet a very large body of disciples in incarnation at this time, and that the apparatus with many who are functioning on the level of discipleship is but in embryo, is profoundly true. It should be remembered however, that the world cycle has only just been inaugurated and will cover a vast period of time. There are only about four hundred accepted disciples in the world at this time— that is, men and women who really know they are disciples and know what their work is and are doing it. There are nevertheless many hundreds (out of the present generation of young people) who stand on the verge of acceptance, and thousands are upon the probationary path.

In all truly esoteric groups, there should be forming a group in which an intellectual understanding of this mechanism of heart, throat, and eye, will be found. It should be constituted of those who are submitting themselves to a discipline and a training which will make its use a demonstrated fact in nature to them. I would call attention to those words, and request their careful study.

A mechanism in the natural body comes into use in two ways: First, its use is involuntary, and there is no comprehension of how, or why, or when, the apparatus is used. An animal employs a mechanism, analogous in many respects to that employed by man. He sees, and hears and functions organically along similar lines to the human, but lacks the mental understanding and the linking of cause and effect which are characteristic of the higher kingdom in nature.

A similar state of affairs exists in the early stages of the path of discipleship, and the final stages of the probationary path. The disciple becomes aware of capacities and powers which are not as yet intelligently under his control. He experiences flashes of insight, and of knowledge which seem unaccountable and of no immediate value. He contacts vibrations and the phenomena of other realms but remains unaware of the process whereby he has done so, and is incompetent either to renew or recall the experience. Within his etheric body, he senses active forces. Sometimes he can localise them, and in any case he admits theoretically that there is awakening into conscious activity, a sevenfold structure, which is symbolic in form, and potent when employed. He cannot as yet control it and he is quite incapable of calling it into intelligent co-operation with his purposes and ideas, no matter how hard he tries. All that he can do is to register such phenomena and keep a record of these experiences, bearing always in mind that in the early stages of his unfoldment only the coarsest and most material of the vibrations will be registered on his brain consciousness. He simply has to wait and to bring his mind to bear upon the purifying of his vehicles and the elimination of all that he recognises

78

as liable to distort his vision. This period may be long or short according as the aspirant is entering into the subjective consciousness for the first time or is taking up the thread of an older or partially achieved undertaking.

I would like here, to make perfectly clear to all true and earnest aspirants that, in the training to be given during the next few decades, the unfoldment of astral vision and hearing will be entirely ruled out, or (if it exists) will eventually have to be overcome. The true disciple has endeavoured to centre himself on the mental plane with the object in view of transferring his consciousness higher still, into the wider and inclusive awareness of the soul.

His aim is to include the higher, and there is no need for him, at this stage, to regain that astral facility which was the possession, as you well know, of the little evolved races of the earth, and of many of the higher animals. Later on, when adeptship has been reached, he can function on the astral plane should he so choose, but it should be remembered, that the Master works with the soul aspect of humanity (and of all forms) and does not work with their astral bodies. This has been oft forgotten by teachers both in the East and in the West.

In working with souls the true technique of evolution is carried forward, for it is the soul within the forms in every kingdom in nature which is responsible for the developing work of, and within, the form. May I say therefore to students that their main objective is to become aware of the soul, to cultivate soul consciousness, and to learn to live and work as souls. Until such time as their use of their apparatus becomes voluntary they would be well advised to train their minds, study the laws governing manifestation, and learn to include all that which we now cover by the word 'higher'—a misnomer, but it must suffice.

Second, when the use of the subjective instrument becomes *voluntary* and a man knows how it should be employed, when he is using it, and can discontinue its use or resume it at will, then his whole status changes and his usefulness increases. Through the use of the mind, humanity has become aware of the purposes and employment of the physical apparatus. Now through the use of a still higher faculty, which is a characteristic of the soul, he enters into voluntary and intelligent control of his instrument and learns to understand the purposes for which it exists. This higher faculty is the *intuition*.

May I add with emphasis that only as the man becomes intuitive does he become of use in a Master's group and I commend to all aspirants that they most carefully study the meaning and significance of the intuition. When it is beginning to function, then the disciple can pass from the stage of probation to that of acceptance in a Master's group.

You might ask here how this can be known or ascertained by the probationer.

A great deal of training is given to a probationer without his really recognising it consciously. Fault tendencies are indicated to him as he seeks with sincerity to train himself for service, and the analysis of motive when truthfully undertaken, serves amazingly to lift the would-be disciple out of the astral or emotional world into that of the mind. It is in the mental world that the Masters are first contacted, and there They must be sought.

But the time has come when the Light in the head is not only present but can be somewhat used. The karma of the aspirant is such that it becomes possible for him, through strenuously applied effort, to handle his life in such a way that he can not only fulfill his karma and carry out his obligations, but has sufficient determination to enable him to handle the problems and obligations of discipleship also. His service to others is carried out with the right motive, and is beginning to count and make its power felt, and he is losing sight of his own interests in those of others. When this occurs certain esoteric happenings take place.

The Master confers with some of His senior disciples as to the advisability of admitting the aspirant within the group aura, and of blending his vibration with that of the group. Then, if decision is arrived at, for the space of two years a senior disciple acts as the intermediary betwixt the Master and the newly accepted aspirant. He works with the new disciple, stepping down (if I so might express it) the vibration of the Master so as to accustom the disciple's bodies to the higher increased rate. He impresses the disciple's mind, via his Ego, with the group plans and ideals, and he watches his reaction to life's occurrences and opportunities. He practically assumes, pro tem, the duties and position of Master.

All this time the aspirant remains in ignorance of what has happened and is unaware of his subjective contacts. He, however, recognizes in himself three things:

Increased mental activity. This at first will give him much trouble, and he will feel as if he were losing in mind control instead of gaining it, but this is only a temporary condition and gradually he will assume command.

Increased responsiveness to ideas and increased capacity to vision the plan of the Hierarchy. This will make him, in the early stages, fanatical to a degree. He will be continually swept off his feet with new ideals, new isms, new modes of living, new dreams for race betterment. He will take up one cult after another as they seem to make possible the coming millennium. But after a time he regains his poise, and purpose assumes control of his life. He works at his own job, and carries forward his contribution to the activity of the whole, to the best of his ability.

Increased psychic sensitiveness. This is both an indication of growth and at the same time a test. He is apt to be taken in by the allurements of the psychic powers; he will be tempted to side-track his efforts from specialised service to the race into the exploitation of the psychic powers, and their use for self assertion. The aspirant has to grow in all parts of his nature, but until he can function as the soul, the psyche, consciously and with the use of cooperative intelligence, the lower powers must be quiescent. They can only be safely used by advanced disciples and initiates. They are weapons and instruments of service to be then used in the three worlds by those who are still tied by the Law of Rebirth to those worlds. Those who have passed through the great Liberation and have "occultly crossed the bridge" have no need to employ the powers inherent in the lower sheaths. They can use the infallible knowledge of the intuition, and the illumination of the principle of Light.

There is much misapprehension in people's minds as to how a Master lets an accepted disciple become aware that he is accepted. An impression is abroad that he is told so and that an interview is accorded wherein the Master accepts him and starts him to work. Such is not the case. The occult law holds good in discipleship as in initiation, and the man goes forward blindly. He hopes, but he does not know; he expects that it may be so, but no tangible assurance is given; from a study of himself and of the requirements he arrives at the conclusion that perhaps he has reached the status of accepted disciple. He therefore acts on that assumption and with care he watches his acts, guards his words, and controls his thoughts so that no overt act, unnecessary word or unkind thought will break the rhythm which he believes has been set up. He proceeds with his work but intensifies his meditation; he searches his motives; he seeks to equip his mental body; he sets before himself the ideal of service and seeks ever to serve; and then (when he is so engrossed in the work on hand that he has forgotten himself), suddenly one day he sees the One Who has for so long seen him.

This may come in two ways: in full waking consciousness or by the registering of the interview on the physical brain as it has been participated in during the hours of sleep.

But accompanying this recognition of the event by the disciples will come certain other recognitions.

1. The event is recognised as fact past all controversy. No doubt remains in the disciple's mind.

2. There is recognised an inhibition on the disciple's part to mention the happening to any one. Months or years may slip away before the disciple will mention it, and then only to those who are also recognised as disciples or to some fellow worker, also under *the same group influence*, whose right it is to know and whose right is sanctioned by the Master of the group.

3. Certain factors, governing the Master's relation to the disciple, are gradually recognised and begin increasingly to govern the disciple's life.

a. He recognises that his points of contact with his Master are governed by group emergency and need, and deal with his group service. It gradually dawns on him that his Master is only interested in him insofar as his ego can be used in service, through the personality on the physical plane. He begins to realise that his Master works with his soul and that it is his ego, therefore, which is en rapport with the Master and not the personal self. His problem, therefore, becomes increasingly clear and this is the problem of all disciples. It is to keep the channel of communication open between the soul and the brain, via the mind, so that when the Master seeks to communicate, He can do so at once and easily. Sometimes a Master has to wait weeks before He can get His disciple's ear, for the channel upward is closed and the soul is not en rapport with the brain. This is especially true of the early stages of discipleship.

b. He finds that it is *he* who shuts the door in the majority of cases through lower psychism, physical disability, and lack of mind control, and he therefore discovers that he has to work constantly and ceaselessly with his lower self.

c. He finds that one of the first things he has to do is to learn to discriminate between:

His own soul's vibration.
The vibration of the group of disciples with whom he is associated.
The vibration of the Master.

All three are different and it is easy to confuse them, especially at first. It is a safe rule for aspirants to assume when they contact a high vibration and stimulus, that it is their own soul contacting them, the Master in the heart, and not run off with the idea (so flattering to their pride and personality) that the Master is endeavouring to reach them.

d. He finds also that it is not the habit of the Masters to flatter or to make promises to their disciples. They are too busy and too wise, nor do They trouble Themselves to tell Their disciples that they are destined for high office, or that they are Their intermediaries and that the Hierarchy is depending upon them. Ambition, love of power, and the self-sufficiency which characterises many mental types test out the struggling aspirant, and he gets from his personality all that he needs in that line. These qualities delude him and lead him astray, forcing him onto a pedestal from which eventually he must descend. The Masters say nothing to feed pride in Their disciples, nor do They speak words to them which could foster in Their chelas the spirit of separateness.

e. The disciple soon finds also that the Masters are not easily accessible. They are busy men, ill able to spare even a few moments in which to communicate with the disciple, and only in emergencies, in the case of a beginner on the Path of Discipleship, do the Masters expend the necessary energy with which to get en rapport. With old and tried disciples, the contacts are more frequent, being more easily achieved and bearing more rapid results. It should be remembered, however, that the newer the disciple the more he demands attention and considers he should have it. The old and more experienced servers seek to fulfil their obligations and carry forward their work with as little contact with the Masters as possible. They seek to save the Master's time and frequently consider an interview with the Master as demonstrating failure on their part, and producing, therefore, regret that they have had to take the Master's precious time, and force Him to use His energy in order to safeguard the work from error and the disciple perhaps from harm. The aim of every high disciple is to carry out his work and be en rapport with the spiritual force centre which is his group, and thus in steady touch with the Master, without interviews and phenomenal contacts. Many only expect to contact their Master once a year, usually at the time of the full moon in May.

f. He finds also that the relationship between Master and disciple is governed by law and that there are definite stages of contact and grades in the desired rapport. These can be enumerated, but cannot be enlarged upon.

1. The stage wherein a disciple is contacted by the Master through another chela on the physical plane. This is the stage of "Little Chelaship".

2. The stage wherein a higher disciple directs the chela from the egoic level. This is the stage called a "Chela in the Light".

3. The stage wherein, according to necessity, the Master contacts the chela through:

a. A vivid dream experience.
b. A symbolic teaching.
c. A using of a thought form of the Master.
d. A contact in meditation.
e. A definite, remembered interview in the Master's Ashram.

This is definitely the stage of Accepted Disciple.

4. The stage wherein, having shown his wisdom in work, and his appreciation of the Master's problem, the disciple is taught how (in emergencies) to attract the Master's attention and thus draw on His strength and knowledge and advice. This is an instantaneous happening, and practically takes none of the Master's time. This stage has the peculiar name of "a chela on the Thread, or Sutratma."

5. The stage wherein he is permitted to know the method whereby he may set up a vibration and a call which will entitle him to an interview with the Master. This is only permitted to those trusted chelas

who can be depended upon not to use the knowledge for anything except the need of the work; no personality reason or distress would prompt them to use it. At this stage the disciple is called "one within the aura."

6. The stage wherein the disciple can get his Master's ear at any time. He is in close touch always. This is the stage wherein a chela is being definitely prepared for an immediate initiation or, having taken initiation, is being given specialised work to do in collaboration with his ———. At this stage he is described as "one within his Master's heart."

There is a later stage of a still closer identification, where there is a blending of the Lights, but there is no adequate paraphrase of the terms used to cover the name. The six stages above mentioned have been paraphrased for occidental understanding and must in no way be considered as translations of the ancient terms.

Such are some of the teachings concerning disciples and their recognitions and it is valuable for aspirants to ponder them. It should be realised that though good character, high ethics, sound morality and spiritual aspiration are basic and unalterable requirements, yet more is needed if the right to enter the Master's Ashram is to be granted.

To be admitted to the privilege of being an outpost of His consciousness requires an unselfishness and a self-surrender for which few are prepared; to be drawn within His aura so that the disciple's aura forms an integral part of the group aura presupposes a purity which few can cultivate; to have the ear of the Master and to earn the right to contact Him at will necessitates a sensitiveness and a fine discrimination which few would care to purchase at the price. Yet a door stands wide open to all who care to come, and no earnest, sincere soul, who meets the requirements, ever receives a rebuff.

There is no question at this time that those who are in any way advanced in evolution are having that evolution hastened as never before in the history of the world. The crisis is so grave and the need of the world so great, that those who can contact the inner side of life, who can even in a small way sense the vibrations of the senior disciples and the Elder Brothers of the race, and who can bring down the ideals, as known on the higher planes, are being very carefully, forcefully, yet strenuously trained. It is necessary that they should be enabled to act accurately and adequately as transmitters and interpreters.

I would like to point out certain factors and methods which should be borne in mind in connection with inspirational writing and mediumship, and which have a bearing on the writing of such books as *The Secret Doctrine*, the Scriptures of the world and those transmitted volumes which potently affect the thought of the race. The interpretation of the process arises from many causes; the status of the writers can be overestimated or not sufficiently appreciated; the terms used by the transmitter being dependent upon his educational status may also be incorrect or give rise to misinterpretation. It is necessary, therefore, that some understanding of the process should be found.

Some transmitters work entirely on astral levels and their work is necessarily part of the great illusion. They are unconscious mediums and are unable to check the source from whence the teachings come; if they claim to know that source, they are frequently in error. Some receive teaching from discarnate entities of no higher evolution, and frequently of lower, than themselves. Some are simply abstracting the content of their own subconsciousnesses, and hence we have the beautiful platitudes, couched in Christian phraseology, and tinctured by the mystical writings of the past, which litter the desks of disciples, working consciously on the physical plane.

Some work only on mental levels, learning, through telepathy, that which the Elder Brothers of the race and their own souls have to impart. They tap the sources of knowledge stored in the egoic consciousness. They become aware of the knowledge stored up in the brains of disciples on the same ray as themselves. Some of them, being outposts of the Master's consciousness, become also cognizant of His thought. Some use several of the methods, either consciously or unconsciously. When they work consciously, it is then possible for them to correlate the teaching given and, under the Law of Correspondences and through the use of symbols (which they see through mental clairvoyance), to ascertain the accuracy of their teaching. Those who work unconsciously (I refer not to astral psychics), can use only trust and discrimination until they are further evolved. They must accept nothing that contradicts facts imparted through the Lodge's great Messengers, and they must be ready to superimpose upon the modicum of knowledge which they possess a further structure of greater extent.

Each generation now should produce its seers. I like the word spelt "see-ers", for to see is to know. The fault of all of you is that you see not; you perceive an angle, a point of vision, a partial aspect of the great fabric of truth, but all that lies hidden behind is occult to your three dimensional vision. It is necessary for those who want to act as true transmitters and intermediaries between the Knowers of the race and the "little ones" that they keep their eyes on the horizon and seek thus to extend their vision; that they hold steadily the inner realization that they already have and seek to increase its scope; that they hold on to the truth that all things are headed towards the revelation, and that the form matters not. They must seek pre-eminently to be dependable instruments, unswayed by passing storms. They must endeavor to remain free from depression, no matter what occurs; liberated from discouragement; with a keen sense of proportion; a right judgment in all things; a regulated life; a disciplined physical body and a whole-hearted devotion to humanity. Where these qualities are present, the Masters can begin to use Their destined workers; where they are absent, other instruments must be found.

Some people learn at night and regularly bring over into their physical brain consciousness the facts they need to know and the teachings they should transmit. Many methods are tried, suited to the nature of the aspirant or chela. Some have brains that act telepathically as transmitters. I deal with safer and rarer methods which utilize the mental vehicle as the intermediary between the soul and the brain, or between the teacher and the disciple. Methods of communication on the astral level, such as the ouija board, the planchette pencil, automatic writing, the direct voice and statements made by the temporarily obsessed medium are not utilized as a rule by chelas, though the direct voice has had its use at times. The higher mental methods are more advanced and surer—even if rarer.

The true transmitters from the higher egoic levels to the physical plane proceed in one or other of the following ways:

1. They write from personal knowledge, and therefore employ their concrete minds at the task of stating this knowledge in terms that will reveal the truth to those that have the eyes to see, and yet will conceal that which is dangerous from the curious and the blind. This is a hard task to accomplish, for the concrete mind expresses the abstract most inadequately and, in the task of embodying the truth in words, much of the true significance is lost.

2. They write because they are inspired. Because of their physical equipment, their purity of life, their singleness of purpose, their devotion to humanity and the very karma of service itself, they have developed the capacity to touch the higher sources from which pure truth, or symbolic truth, flows. They can tap thought currents that have been set in motion by that great band of Contemplators, called

Nirmanakayas, or those definite, specialized thought currents originated by one of the great staff of teachers. Their brains, being receptive transmitters, enable them to express these contacted thoughts on paper—the accuracy of the transmission being dependent upon the receptivity of the instrument (that is, the mind and the brain) of the transmitter. In these cases, the form of words and the sentences are largely left to the writer. Therefore, the appropriateness of the terms used and the correctness of the phraseology will depend upon his mental equipment, his educational advantages, the extent of his vocabulary and his inherent capacity to understand the nature and quality of the imparted thought and ideas.

3. They write because of the development of the inner hearing. Their work is largely stenographic, yet is also partially dependent upon their standard of development and their education. A certain definite unfoldment of the centres, coupled with karmic availability, constitutes the basis of choice by the teacher on the subtler planes who seeks to impart a definite instruction and a specialized line of thought. The responsibility as to accuracy is therefore divided between the one who imparts the teaching and the transmitting agent. The physical plane agent must be carefully chosen and the accuracy of the imparted information, as expressed on the physical plane, will depend upon his willingness to be used, his positive mental polarization, and his freedom from astralism. To this must be added the fact that the better educated a man may be, the wider his range of knowledge and scope of world interests, the easier it will be for the teacher on the inner side to render, through his agency, the knowledge to be imparted. Frequently the dictated data may be entirely foreign to the receiver. He *must* have a certain amount, therefore, of education, and be himself a profound seeker of truth before he will be chosen to be the recipient of teachings that are intended for the general public or for esoteric use. Above everything else, he must have learnt through meditation to focus himself on the mental plane. Similarity of vibration and of interests hold the clue to the choice of a transmitter. Note that I say; similarity of vibration and of interests and not equality of vibration and of interests.

This form of work might be divided into three methods: There is first the higher clairaudience that speaks directly from mind to mind. This is not exactly telepathy but a form of direct hearing. The teacher will speak to the disciple as person to person. A conversation is therefore carried on entirely on mental levels with the higher faculties as the focusing point. The use of the head centres is involved and they must both be vivified before this method can be employed. In the astral body the centres corresponding to the physical have to be awakened before astral psychism is possible. The work that I refer to here involves a corresponding vivification in the mental body counterparts.

Secondly, we have telepathic communication. This is the registry in the physical brain consciousness of information imparted:

a. Direct from Master to pupil; from disciple to disciple; from student to student.
b. From Master or disciple to the ego and thence to the personality, via the atomic sub-planes. You will note therefore that only those in whose bodies atomic sub-plane matter is found can work this way. Safety and accuracy lie in this equipment.
c. From ego to ego via the causal body and transmitted direct according to the preceding method or stored up to work through gradually and at need.

Thirdly, we have inspiration. This involves another aspect of development. Inspiration is analogous to mediumship, but is entirely egoic. It utilizes the mind as the medium of transmission to the brain of that which the soul knows. Mediumship usually describes the process when confined entirely to the astral levels. On the egoic plane this involves inspiration. Ponder on this explanation for it explains much. Mediumship is dangerous. Why is this so? Because the mental body is not involved and so the soul is not in control. The medium is an unconscious instrument, he is not himself the controlling factor; he is controlled. Frequently also the discarnate entities who employ this method of communication, utilizing the brain or voice apparatus of the medium, are not highly evolved, and are quite incapable of employing mental plane methods.

Some people combine the method of inspiration and of receiving instruction along various lines and, when this is the case, great accuracy of transmission is found. Occasionally again, as in the case of H. P. B. you have deep knowledge, ability to be inspired and mental clairaudience combined. When this is the case you have a rare and useful instrument for the aiding of humanity.

Inspiration originates on the higher levels; it presupposes a very high point in evolution, for it involves the egoic consciousness and necessitates the use of atomic matter, thus opening up a wide range of communicators. It spells safety. It should be remembered that the soul is always good; it may lack knowledge in the three worlds and in this way be deficient; but it harbors no evil. Inspiration is always safe, whereas mediumship is always to be avoided. Inspiration may involve telepathy, for the person inspiring may do three things:

a. He may use the brain of the appointed channel, throwing thoughts into it.
b. He may occupy his disciple's body, the latter standing aside, consciously, in his subtler bodies, but surrendering his physical body.
c. A third method is one of a temporary fusing, if I might so call it,—an intermingling when the user and the used alternate or supplement, as needed, to do the appointed work. I cannot explain more clearly.

4. They write what they see. This method is not of such a high order. You will note that in the first case you have wisdom or availability on buddhic or intuitional levels; in the second case you have transmission from the causal body, from the higher mental levels; in the third case you have sufficient development to enable the aspirant to receive dictation. In the fourth case, you have the ability to read in the astral light but frequently no ability to differentiate between that which is past, that which is, and that which will be. Therefore you have illusion and inaccuracy. This is a method, however, sometimes used but—unless directly used under stimulation applied by a Master—it is liable to be most misleading, as is its corollary, astral clairaudience. It is the method of mental clairvoyance, and requires a trained interpreting mind, which is rare indeed to find.

In all these cases that I have cited error may creep in owing to physical limitation and the handicap of words, but in the case of those who write from personal knowledge the errors in expression will be of no real moment; whilst in the second and third cases the errors will be dependent upon the point in evolution of the transmitting agent. If, however, he couples intelligence, devotion and service, with his capacity to receive and hear, he will soon correct the errors himself and his understanding will grow.

Later two new methods will be employed which will facilitate the transmission of truth from the inner side to the outer plane. Precipitated writing will be given to those who can be trusted, but the time is not yet for its general use. It will be necessary to wait until the work of the esoteric schools has reached a more definite phase of development. Conditions as yet are not appropriate, but humanity is urged to be ready and open-minded and prepared for this development. Later will come the power to materialize thought-forms. People will come into incarnation who will have the ability temporarily to create and vitalize these thought-forms, and so enable the general public to see them. The time, however, is not yet. There is too much fear, and not enough experience of truth in the world. More knowledge must be acquired as to the nature of thought and of matter, and this must be followed experimentally by those with acute trained minds, a high rate of vibration, and bodies built of the finest matter. The attainment of this will involve discipline, pain, self-abnegation and abstinence. See you to it.

The group of Teachers with whom the average aspirants and probationary disciples may be in touch on the mental plane are but men of like passions but with a longer experience upon the path and a wiser control of themselves. They do not work with aspirants because They personally like or care for them, but because the need is great and They seek those whom They can train. The attitude of mind that They look for is that of teachableness and the ability to record and refrain from questioning until more is known. Then the aspirant is urged to question everything. May I remind you of the words of one Teacher who said, "Know us for sane and balanced men who teach as we taught on earth, not flattering our pupils but disciplining them. We lead them on, not forcing them forward by feeding their ambitions by promises of power, but giving them information and leading them to use it in their work, knowing that right use of knowledge leads to experience and achievement of the goal."

How often does one find a student more occupied with the Master and what He will do than he is with his own side of the question! And yet the fitting of himself for service and the equipping of himself for useful cooperation is, or should be, his main preoccupation.

Inquiry about the Master is more interesting than inquiry about the needed qualifications for discipleship. Interest for the data available in relation to the Adepts is more potent than the steadfast investigation into limitations and disabilities which should engross the aspirant's attention. Curiosity as to the habits and methods of specific Masters and Their ways of handling Their disciples is more prone to be displayed than patient application to right habits and ways of work in the life of the would-be disciple. All these matters are side issues and only handicap and limit, and one of the first things we advise one who would enter into communication with the Masters is to take his eyes off those things which concern him not, focus his attention on the needed steps and stages which should demonstrate in his life, and eliminate those wasted moments, moods and thought periods which so often occupy the major part of his thought life.

When a Master seeks to find those fitted to be instructed and taught by Him, He looks for three things first of all. Unless these are present, no amount of devotion or aspiration, and no purity of life and mode of living suffices. It is essential that all aspirants should grasp these three factors and so save themselves much distress of mind and wasted motion.

1. The Master looks for the light in the head.
2. He investigates the karma of the aspirant.
3. He notes his service in the world.

Unless there is indication that the man is what is termed esoterically "a lighted lamp" it is useless for the Master to waste His time. The light in the head, when present, is indicative of:

a. The functioning to a greater or less extent of the pineal gland, which is (as is well known) the seat of the soul and the organ of spiritual perception. It is in this gland that the first physiological changes take place incident upon soul contact and this contact is brought about through definite work along meditation lines, mind control, and the inflow of spiritual force.

b. The aligning of the man on the physical plane with his ego, soul or higher self, on the mental plane and the subordination of the physical plane life and nature to the impress and control of the soul. This is covered sufficiently in the first two or three chapters of *Letters on Occult Meditation* and these should be studied by aspirants.

c. The downflow of force via the sutratma, magnetic cord, or thread from the soul to the brain via the mind body. The whole secret of spiritual vision, correct perception and right contact lies in the proper appreciation of the above statement, and therefore the *Yoga Sutras of Patanjali* are ever the text-book of disciples, initiates and adepts, for therein are found those rules and methods which bring the mind under control, stabilize the astral body and so develop and strengthen the thread soul that it can and does become a veritable channel of communication between the man and his ego. The light of illumination streams down into the brain cavity and throws into objectivity three fields of knowledge. This is often forgotten and hence the undue distress and premature interpretations of the partially illuminated disciple or probationer.

The light first throws into relief and brings into the foreground of consciousness those thought-forms and entities which depict the lower life, and which (in their aggregate) form the Dweller on the Threshold.

Thus the first thing of which the aspirant becomes aware is that which he knows to be undesirable and the revelation of his own unworthiness and limitations, and the undesirable constituents of his own aura burst on his vision. The darkness which is in him is intensified by the light which glimmers faintly from the centre of his being and frequently he despairs of himself and descends into the depths of depression. All mystics bear witness to this and it is a period which must be lived through until the pure light of day drives all shadows and darkness away and little by little the life is brightened and lightened until the sun in the head is shining in all its glory.

d. Finally, the light in the head is indicative of the finding of the Path and there remains then for the man to study and understand the techniques whereby the light is centralized, intensified, entered and eventually becomes that magnetic line (like unto a spider's thread) which can be followed back until the source of the lower manifestation is reached and the soul consciousness is entered. The above language is symbolic and yet vitally accurate but is expressed thus in order to convey information to those who know, and protect those who as yet know not.

"The path of the just is as a shining Light" and yet at the same time a man has to become that path itself. He enters the light and becomes the light and functions then as a lamp set in a dark place, carrying illumination to others and lighting the way before them.

The next point that a Master has to consider before admitting a man into His group is whether or no such a step is karmically possible or whether there exist in a man's record those conditions which negate his admission in this life.

There are three main factors to be considered separately and in their relation to each other.

First, are there such karmic obligations in a man's present life as would render it impossible for him to function as a disciple? In this connection it must be carefully borne in mind that a man can become a disciple and merit the attention of a Master only when his life counts for something in the world of men, when he is an influence in his sphere, and when he is moulding and acting upon the minds and hearts of other men.

Until that is the case it is waste of a Master's time to personally deal with him, for he can be adequately helped in other ways and has, for instance, much knowledge from books and teachers which is as yet theory and not practice, and much experience to pass through under the guidance of his own ego, the Master in his heart. When a man is a disciple he is one because he can be used for working out the plan of the Hierarchy, and can be influenced to materialize those endeavours which are planned to enable humanity to make the needed forward steps. This involves (in his physical plane life) time, and thought, right circumstance, and other considerations and it is quite possible for a man to have reached the stage *from the character standpoint*, where he merits the recognition of a Master, and yet have obligations and duties to work through which would handicap him for active service in some particular life. This the Master has to consider and this a man's own ego also considers.

The result quite frequently at this time is that (perhaps unconsciously to the physical brain) a man will shoulder a great amount of experience, and undertake the working out of an abnormal amount of responsibility in one particular life, in order to free himself for service and chelaship in a later life. He works then at the equipping of himself for the next life, and at the patient performance of duty in his home, his circle of friends, and his business. He realises that from the egoic standpoint one life is but a short matter and soon gone and that by study, intelligent activity, loving service, and patient endurance, he is working out those conditions which are preventing his prompt acceptance in a Master's group.

A Master also studies the condition of an aspirant's physical body and of the subtler bodies to see whether in them are to be found states of consciousness which would hinder usefulness and act as obstacles. These conditions are likewise karmic and must be adjusted before his admission among other chelas becomes possible. A sick physical body, an astral body prone to moods, emotions and psychic delusions, and a mental body uncontrolled or ill-equipped are all dangerous to the student unless straightened out and perfected. A chela is subjected constantly to the play of force coming to him from three main sources:

1. His own ego,
2. His Master,
3. The group of co-disciples,

and unless he is strong, purified and controlled, these forces will serve but to stimulate undesirable conditions, to foster that which should be eliminated and to bring to the surface all the hidden weaknesses. That this has to be done inevitably is so, but much must be done along this line before admission into a group of disciples; otherwise much of the Master's valuable time will perforce be given to the elimination and nullifying of the effects of the chela's violent reactions on other chelas in the same group. It is better to wait and work gradually and intelligently oneself than force one's way unprepared into lines of forces before one can handle either them or their consequences.

Another factor that an adept has to consider is whether there are in incarnation those chelas with whom a man has to work and who are karmically linked to him by ancient ties and old familiarity in similar work.

Sometimes it may be deemed wiser for a man to wait a little while before being permitted to step off the physical path until a life comes in which his own co-workers, keyed to his vibration, and accustomed to work with him, are also in physical bodies, for a Master's group is entered in service to be rendered and specific work to be done, and not because a man is to receive a cultural training which will make him an adept some day. Chelas train themselves and when ready for any work a Master uses them. They develop themselves and work out their own salvation and as step by step is taken their particular Master lays more and more responsibility upon them. He will train them in service technique, and in vibratory response to the Plan, but they learn to control themselves and to fit themselves for service.

There are other karmic factors to be considered by a Master but these are the three paramount ones and of the most importance for aspirants to consider now. They are specified so that no true and earnest worker need be depressed and discouraged if he has no conscious link with the Master and is unaware of any affiliation with an esoteric group of chelas. It may not be because he is not fit. It may simply be because his ego has chosen this life to clear the decks for later action, to eliminate hindrances in one or other, or all of the three lower bodies, or to wait for that time when his admission may count the most.

The third factor, that of service, for which the Master looks is one upon which the aspirant has the least to say and may very probably misinterpret. Spiritual ambition, the desire to function as the centre of a group, the longing to hear oneself speaking, teaching, lecturing, or writing are often wrongly interpreted by the aspirant as service. The Master looks not at a worker's worldly force or status, not at the numbers of people who are gathered around his personality but at the motives which prompt his activity and at the effect of his influence upon his fellowmen. True service is the spontaneous outflow of a loving heart and an intelligent mind; it is the result of being in the right place and staying there; it is produced by the inevitable inflow of spiritual force and not by strenuous physical plane activity; it is the effect of a man's being what he truly is, a divine Son of God, and not by the studied effect of his words or deeds. A true server gathers around him those whom it is his duty to serve and aid by the force of his life and his spiritualised personality, and not by his claims or loud speaking. In self-forgetfulness he serves; in self-abnegation he walks the earth, and he gives no thought to the magnitude or the reverse of his accomplishment and has no pre-conceived ideas as to his own value or usefulness. He lives, serves, works and influences, asking nothing for the separated self.

When a Master sees this manifestation in a man's life, as the result of the awakening of the inner light and the adjustment of his karmic obligations, then He sounds out a note and waits to see if the man recognises his own group note. On this recognition, he is admitted into his own group of co-workers, and can stand in the presence of his Master.

HEART, THROAT AND EYE

Later, when the knowledge here conveyed is assimilated, the aspirant will come to an understanding of the true meaning of the heart, the throat, and the eye—which it is the effect of the Guides of the race to stimulate into functioning activity at this time. We will therefore consider now:

1. The heart centre, the throat centre, and the centre between the eyes.
2. Their awakening and co-ordination.
3. To what uses they will be put in the coming world cycle.

This subject is of vital importance to the modern aspirant, for the mechanism of the heart, the throat, and the eye—constituting part of the inner structure which he must learn to use—has to be mastered and consciously employed by him before any true creative work is possible. When I use the words 'creative work' I am speaking esoterically and am not referring to the valuable work done by the artists of the world in their many lines of expression. Their efforts, to the seer, are indicative of an inner stirring, of an inner co-ordination and a motivated activity which will lead to true esoteric endeavour and to creative work on the subtler planes.

I am assuming in the student an elementary knowledge of the vital body and of its force centres and I am assuming that these seven centres or lotuses have, theoretically, a place in his imagination. I use the word imagination with purposeful intent, for until there is knowledge and clear vision, imaginative assumption is a potent factor in bringing about the activity of the centres.

Let us, for the sake of clarity, list these lotuses with their petal numbers, and their location. Their colours are immaterial at present from the standpoint of the student, for much that has been given out is erroneous or in the nature of a blind, and in any case, the esoteric colours are widely different from the exoteric.

1. The base of the spine ------------------------ 4 petals.
2. The sacral centre ----------------------------- 6 petals.
3. The solar plexus centre ---------------------- 10 petals.
             Diaphragm.
4. Heart centre --------------------------------- 12 petals.
5. Throat centre -------------------------------- 16 petals.
6. Centre between the eyebrows-------------- 2 petals.
7. Head centre --------------------------------- 1000 petals.

Next, let the student remember two important facts, which may be regarded as elementary and preliminary but which nevertheless have to be worked out into conscious realisation and become part of the purposed intent of the aspirant's training. It is easy to generalise. It is difficult to realise. It is simple to grasp the informative intellectual data regarding the centres of force; it is most difficult to bring about the rearrangement of the forces flowing through these vortices, and to learn to function consciously through the higher centres, subordinating the lower ones. This has to be done also without laying the emphasis upon the form aspect as is the case in many practices used to vitalise the centres. The two facts of importance are:

1. The three centres below the diaphragm,

a. Base of spine,
b. Sacral centre,
c. Solar plexus centre,

which are, at present, the most potent in average humanity and the most 'alive', require to be re-organised, re-oriented, and to be brought from a state of positivity into that of negativity.

Equally, the four centres above the diaphragm,

a. The heart centre,
b. The throat centre,
c. The centre between the eyebrows,
d. The head centre,

must be awakened and brought from a state of negativity into that of positivity.

This has to be brought about in two ways. First, by the transference of the positive energy of the lower centres into that of the higher, and secondly by the awakening of the head centre by the demonstration of the activity of the will. The first effect is produced by character building, and by the purification of the bodies, as used by the soul in the three worlds. The second is the result of meditation and the development of organised purpose, imposed by the will upon the daily life. Character building, clean living, controlled emotional reactions, and right thinking are the platitudes of all religious systems and have lost weight from our very familiarity with them. It is not easy to remember that as we live purely and rightly, we are verily and indeed working with forces, subjecting energies to our needs, subordinating elemental lives to the requirements of spiritual being, and bringing into activity a mechanism and a vital structure which has hitherto been only latent and quiescent. Nevertheless, it remains a fact that when the energies, latent at the base of the spine, are carried to the head and are brought (via the solar plexus, that clearing house of energy, and the medulla oblongata) to the centre between the eyebrows, then the personality, the matter aspect, reaches its apotheosis and the Virgin Mary—in the individual sense, which is a finite parallel of an infinite Reality—is "carried up into Heaven" there to sit by the side of her son, the Christ, the soul.

When the energies of the sacral centre, focussed hitherto on the work of physical creation and generation and therefore the source of physical sex life and interest, are sublimated, re-oriented and carried up to the throat centre, then the aspirant becomes a conscious creative force in the higher worlds; he enters within the veil, and begins to create the pattern of things which will bring about eventually the new heavens and the new earth.

When the energies of the solar plexus—expressions hitherto of the potent desire nature, feeding the emotional life of the personality—are equally transmuted and re-oriented, then they are carried to the heart centre and there is brought about as a result a realisation of group consciousness, of group love, and group purpose which makes the aspirant a server of humanity and a fit associate of the Elder Brethren of the race.

When these three transfers have been consummated then an activity transpires in the head centre, the ultimate governing factor, and by an act of the will of the indwelling ruling soul, certain happenings take place which we can consider later in our studies.

2. The second fact to bear in mind is that as these changes and re-orientations take place, the disciple begins to awaken psychologically to new states of consciousness, to new states of existence, and to new states of being. It will be apparent therefore how necessary it is to go slowly in these matters, so that the mental apprehension and ability to reason logically and sanely may parallel the growth of the intuition and of spiritual perception. Many schools are simply forcing schools, prematurely developing the higher faculties and leading the aspirant (if I might express it in mystical language) directly out of the realm of feeling and of desire into that of the intuition, but leaving the intellectual faculties and the mental apparatus totally undeveloped and latent. When this is the case then—again speaking mystically—an hiatus or a gap occurs, in part of the equipment which the soul must perforce use in the three worlds of its endeavour. The interpreting, organising, understanding mind is unable to play its part. Where there is lack of understanding and of mental ability, there is danger of misapprehension, of credulity and of wrong interpretation of the phenomena of other states of being. A sense of values will be lacking, and the aspirant will over-estimate the non-essentials and fail to grasp the value of the

spiritual realities.

Energy may pour into the force centres in these cases, but because there is no directing intelligence it will run riot and we then have those sad cases which strew the path of occult endeavour and have brought the work of the Lodge into disrepute—cases of over-emphasized personalities, of superstitious devotees, of credulous followers of leaders, of fanatical unbalanced idealists, and of those warped minds which arrogate to themselves powers which are not theirs. Men and women become swayed by astralism and wander in the vale of illusion regarding themselves as different from other men, placing themselves upon a pedestal far above average humanity. They fall consciously into the sin of separateness. Add to the above category, the cases of sex perversion, brought about by over-stimulation of the sacral centre, the cases of neuroticism and over-sensitivity and emotionalism, brought about by the premature vitalisation of the solar plexus centre, and lastly the cases of insanity, brought about by over-stimulation of the brain cells through unwise meditation work, and it will become increasingly clear why it is deemed necessary to proceed slowly and to develop the mental processes as well as the spiritual nature.

The average student starts with the knowledge that he has centres, and with a desire for purity of character. He is assured by those who know that, as he strives, meditates, studies and serves, certain changes will take place within him, and that there will arise from the depths of his being, an awakening which will be dynamic. He is told that there will follow a breathing forth, a stirring and a vitalising which will bring his subjective spiritual life into prominence. This subjective life expresses itself as spiritual energy, through the medium of the energy or vital body and the energy thus expressed will change his life focus and interests, and produce a magnetic and dynamic effect which will attract and lift humanity. This energy is sevenfold in nature and utilises seven focal points in the etheric body as its agents.

It is not possible for the aspirant to work with and utilise all these seven types of energy intelligently in the early stages of the path of Discipleship. The emphasis, for training purposes, is laid upon only three of them. These are:

1. *That of Will, strength or power*, through the medium of the head centre. This is the energy of the spiritual man, and comes directly from the Monad, via the soul. Up to the third initiation however, all that the disciple needs to grasp is that the will aspect of the soul should control the personality, via the mental body to the head centre. When this is the case the thousand-petalled lotus begins to function. The line of this stream of force is:

> *Monad.*
> Atma. Spiritual will.
> The inner circle of petals in the egoic lotus, the will petals.
> The mental body.
> The head centre in the etheric body.
> The nervous system and brain.

2. *That of Love-Wisdom*, through the medium of the heart centre. This centre, when awakened, leads to that expansion of consciousness which initiates a man into his group life. He loses the sense of separateness, and finally emerges into the full light of realisation—a realisation of unity with his own indwelling God, with all humanity, with all souls in all forms of nature, and so with the Oversoul. This force stream comes likewise from the Monad, via the soul, and its line is as follows:

Monad.
Buddhi. Spiritual love. The intuition.
The second circle of petals in the egoic lotus, the love petals.
The astral body.
The heart centre.
The blood stream.

In the little evolved man, this force stream simply passes through the heart centre direct to the solar plexus and expends its two aspects of vital life and of soul quality, one energising the blood stream and the other awakening the solar plexus centre. This then becomes the dominant factor in the energy life of the man, and the force through which his desire nature expresses itself, until such time as the aspirant brings about the needed transmutation and re-orientation of his emotional desire nature. Then the heart awakens into activity and the life of the solar plexus centre becomes subordinated to that of the heart. This is brought about by the development of group interests, by the cultivation of inclusiveness and the steady loss of interest in the personality, and in things separative and selfish.

3. *That of active intelligence*, or the energy which animates the form aspect, and which creates forms in line with the subjective purposes of the presiding intelligence—God or man, human or divine. This also proceeds from the third aspect of the Monad, and the line of its contact is:

Monad.
Manas. Spiritual intelligence. The higher mind.
The third or outer circle of petals in the egoic lotus, the knowledge petals.
The etheric body as a whole, as it pervades the dense physical body.
The throat centre.
The cells of the body.

In the little evolved man, as in the case of the second aspect and its unfoldment, the energy simply passes through the throat centre and goes directly to the sacral centre, and thus brings into activity the generative processes and creative faculties, utilised in the reproductive work and sex life of the race.

This is a broad and general outline of the three main streams of force or divine energy and their direction.

The relationship of the head centre to the base of the spine, where lies the sleeping fire, will not be considered here, nor will the function of the solar plexus centre as a clearing-house for the lower energies be touched upon. I am anxious for the students simply to grasp the general idea and the skeleton of the teaching.

Every human being in the course of time works his way back on the Path of Return to one of the three major rays. All have eventually to express intelligent creative faculty, to be animated by divine love, and to bring into functioning activity the Will, as it works out divine purpose and plan.

The first centre which the aspirant seeks consciously to energise and on which he concentrates during the early stages of his novitiate, is the heart centre. He has to learn to be group conscious, to be sensitive to group ideals, and to be inclusive in his plans and concepts; he has to learn to love collectively and purely, and not be actuated by personality attraction, and the motive of reward. Until

94

there is this awakening in the heart, he cannot be trusted to wield the creative powers of the throat centre, for they would be subordinated to self-aggrandisement and ambitions of various kinds.

Here it should be noted that none of these unfoldments can ever be approached from the standpoint of complete static passivity or from the angle of an entirely new undertaking. We are in process of evolution. Certain aspects of our force centres are already awakened, and functioning in relation to the form aspect, but are not yet expressing soul qualities. We have behind us a long and fruitful past. We are none of us purely selfish or separative. Human society is now cohesive and inter-dependent. Humanity, as a whole, has already done much in bringing the heart centre into partial activity, and in awakening some of the more important aspects of the throat centre.

The problem with many aspirants today is that of the solar plexus, for it is wide open, actively functioning and almost fully awakened. The work of transmutation is however going on simultaneously, leading—as one might naturally suppose—to a good deal of difficulty and to chaotic conditions. The heart centre is also beginning to vibrate, but is not yet awakened; the throat centre is frequently prematurely awakened, through the transfer of energy from the sacral centre. This is due to several causes—sometimes to spiritual purpose and intent, but more frequently to a negation of the normal sex life, owing to economic conditions, or to a lack of physical vitality, which predisposes to celibacy. This lack of vital force is in its turn due to many factors, but primarily to a long heredity, producing a degeneracy of the physical body, or to enforced celibacy in past lives; this enforced celibacy was very often the result of monasticism and the living of the mystical life. When this creative awakening finds expression through any of the arts—literature, painting, music,—or in group organization and executive work there is no harm wrought, for the energy finds a normal creative outlet. These points should he remembered by the aspirant. He is facing a most complex problem. He enters blindly into a situation which is the result of a long evolutionary process and to which he has not the key. Especially in the early stages and prior to the first initiation is this the case, for he has no knowledge of the history of the past, nor any prevision as to the future. He has simply to take his equipment and his opportunity and do the best he can, guided by the age-old rules of Raja Yoga, and the light of his own soul.

As the heart centre is awakened and the throat centre swings into creative work, a definite relation is set up and there is an interplay of energy between the two. This activity in its turn brings about a response from that aspect of the thousand petalled lotus (a synthetic lotus) through which the energy always animating the heart and throat centres normally passes. This responsive activity and inter-action brings about two results, and these should be most carefully noted.

First, the light in the head makes its appearance. A sparking (if I might so express it) is set up between the higher positive over-shadowing energy as it is centralised within the form of the thousand-petalled lotus, and the steadily heightening vibration of the heart and throat centres or lotuses. These two lower centres in their turn are responding to the energies being lifted and raised from the centres below the diaphragm.

Secondly, the centre between the eyebrows also begins to make its presence felt, and this significant two-petalled lotus begins to vibrate. It symbolises the work of at-one-ing the soul and the body, the subjective and the objective. In some occult books it is called the lotus with the ninety-six petals, but this is only a differentiation dealing with the energies focussed in the two petals. It will be noted that the sum total of the force petals in the centres (excluding the two head centres) amount in all to forty-eight petals. These energies in their two aspects of physical vital energy and soul qualities make up the ninety-six aspects or vibrations of the two petals of the Ajna or eyebrow centre. It must be remembered also that the word 'petal' only symbolises an expression of force and its apparent effect in matter.

The five centres with their forty-eight petals are synthesised therefore into the two-petalled lotus, and then we have forty-eight plus two equals fifty, the number of the perfected personality, for five is the number of man and ten is that of perfection. Symbolically also, if the sum total of the forty-eight petals of the five centres is added to the ninety-six petals of the centre between the eyebrows, the number one hundred and forty-four appears. This number signifies the completed work of the twelve creative Hierarchies, twelve times twelve, and thus the bringing together of the subjective soul and the objective body in perfect union and at-one-ment. This is the consummation. To these figures, one hundred and forty-four add that of the number one thousand (the number of the petals in the lotus of the head centre) and you have the number of the saved in the Book of Revelations, the one hundred and forty-four thousand who can stand before God, for the three ciphers which are found indicate the personality. When man has completed within himself the great work, when the number one hundred and forty-four thousand is seen as symbolising his point of attainment, then he can stand before God—standing now not only before the Angel of the Presence, but before the very Presence Itself.

THE AWAKENING OF THE CENTRES

The question now arises: How can this awakening and co-ordination be brought about? What steps must be taken in order to produce this vitalisation and the eventual synthetic activity of the three centres? Faced with these questions, the true teacher finds a difficulty. It is not easy to make clear the esoteric and paralleling activities which are the result of character building. So oft the aspirant is anxious to be told some new thing and when he is told some old truth—so old and so familiar that it fails to call forth a registering response—he feels that the teacher has failed him and so succumbs to a sense of futility and depression. However, this must be met and the questions must be answered. I will state therefore the necessary requirements as succinctly as possible, giving them in their sequential order and according to their importance from the standpoint of the average aspirant. Let us then enumerate them in tabulated form, and then we will deal briefly with each point afterwards.

1. Character building, the first and essential requisite.
2. Right motive.
3. Service.
4. Meditation.
5. A technical study of the science of the centres.
6. Breathing exercises.
7. Learning the technique of the Will.
8. The development of the power to employ time.
9. The arousing of the Kundalini fire.

This last and ninth point will not be considered at this stage of our training. The reason is obvious. Most aspirants are at the stage of the third and fourth points and are just beginning to work at the fifth and sixth. Let us touch briefly upon each of these necessary steps, and let me enjoin upon you the need there is to realise in some measure the responsibility entailed by knowledge. Do you appreciate the fact that if you were making full use of each piece of information given in the course of the training, and making it a fact in your experience, and were living out in your daily life the teaching so steadily imparted, you would be standing ere now before the Portal of Initiation? Do you realise that truth has to be wrought out in the texture of daily living before new truth can be safely imparted?

1. *Character building.* These nine points are to be studied from their force aspect, and not from their ethical or spiritual import. It is the "world of force into which the initiate enters," and it is the training he receives as an aspirant that makes such a step possible. Each of us enters life with a certain equipment—the product of past lives of endeavour and of experience. That equipment has in it certain deficiencies or lacks, and is seldom of a balanced nature. One man is too mental. Another is too psychic. A third is primarily physical, and still another is too mystical. One man is sensitive, irritable, and impressionable. Another is the reverse of all these qualities. One person is centred in his animal nature, or is strictly material in his outlook on life, whilst another is visionary and free from the sins of the flesh. The diversities among men are innumerable, but in each life there is a predominant trend towards which all the energies of his nature turn. Perhaps he is swayed strongly by his physical forces and lives consequently the life of an animal. Or he is swayed by astral energy and lives a potently emotional and psychic life. Perhaps—like so many—he is swayed by three types of energy, physical, emotional and an occasional flow of soul energy. The point to be remembered is that the bodies in which we, as souls, are functioning, constitute primarily energy bodies. They are composed of energy units, atoms in a state of constant flux and movement and find their place in an environment of a similar nature. Acting as the positive nucleus in these energy bodies, and at present, in the majority of cases relatively static, is the soul. It exerts as yet little pressure upon its sheaths and identifies itself with them, thus temporarily negating its own intrinsic life.

The day comes, however, when the soul awakens to the need of dominating the situation and of asserting its own authority. Then the man (spasmodically at the beginning) takes stock of the situation. He has to discover first which type of energy preponderates and is the motivating force in his daily experience. Having discovered this, he begins to re-organize, to re-orient and to re-build his bodies. The whole of this teaching can be summed up in two words: Vice and Virtue.

Vice is the energy of the sheaths, individual or synthesised in the personality, as it controls the life activities and subordinates the soul to the sheaths and to the impulses and tendencies of the lower self.

Virtue is the calling in of new energies and of a new vibratory rhythm so that the soul becomes the positive controlling factor and the soul forces supersede those of the bodies. This process is that of character building. Let me illustrate! A man is the victim of an irritable and nervous disposition. We say to him that he needs to be calm and peaceful and to cultivate detachment and so gain control of himself. We teach him that in place of a cross disposition there should be sweetness and calm. This sounds a platitude and most uninteresting. Yet what is really being stated is that in place of the restless self-centered emotional nature and the activity of the solar plexus centre (carrying the powerful forces of the astral plane) there should be imposed the steady detached and harmonising rhythm of the soul, the higher self. This work of imposing the higher vibration on the lower is character building, the first pre-requisite upon the Path of Probation. On reading this the earnest student can begin to sum up his energy assets; he can tabulate the forces which he feels control his life, and thus arrive at a reasonable and truthful understanding of the forces which require to be subordinated and those which require to be strengthened. Then in the light of true knowledge, let him go forward upon the path of his destiny.

2. *Right Motive.* The Master of the Wisdom, we are told, is the "rare efflorescence of a generation of enquirers." The question which the seeker now asks and which he only has the right to answer is: What is the motive governing my aspiration and my endeavour? Why do I seek to build upon a true foundation? Why do I so diligently invoke my soul?

97

The development of right motive is a progressive effort, and constantly one shifts the focus of one's incentive when one discovers himself, as the Light shines ever more steadily upon one's way, and constantly a newer and higher motive emerges. Again, let me illustrate: An aspirant in the early stages is practically always a devotee. To measure up to the standard set by a loved friend and teacher, he struggles and strives and gains ground. Later, this object of his devotion and ardent effort is superseded by devotion to one of the Great Ones, the Elder Brothers of the race. He bends all his powers and the forces of his nature to Their service. This incentive is, in its turn, surely and steadily superseded by a vital love for humanity, and love of one individual (be he ever so perfect) is lost sight of in love for the whole brotherhood of men. Unceasingly, as the soul takes more and more control of its instrument and the soul nature steadily manifests, this too is superseded by love of the ideal, of the Plan, and of the purposes underlying the universe itself. The man comes to know himself as naught but a channel through which spiritual agencies can work, and realises himself as a corporate part of the One Life. Then he sees even humanity as relative and fractional, and becomes immersed in the great Will.

3. *Service.* A study of right motive leads naturally to right service, and often parallels in its objective form, the motivating consciousness. From service to an individual as an expression of love, to the family, or to the nation, there grows service to a member of the Hierarchy, to a Master's group and thence service to humanity. Eventually there is developed a consciousness of and service of the Plan, and a consecration to the underlying purpose of the great Existence Who has brought all into being for the fulfillment of some specific objective.

4. *Meditation.* Upon this matter we will not enlarge as it has formed the basis of much of the teaching in my other books and many of you are working steadily upon the work of meditation. I have placed it fourth upon the list, for meditation is dangerous and unprofitable to the man who enters upon it without the basis of a good character and of clean living. Meditation then becomes only a medium for the bringing in of energies which but serve to stimulate the undesirable aspects of his life, just as the fertilising of a garden full of weeds will produce a stupendous crop of them, and so crush out the weak and tiny flowers. Meditation is dangerous where there is wrong motive, such as desire for personal growth and for spiritual powers, for it produces, under these conditions only a strengthening of the shadows in the vale of illusion and brings to full growth the serpent of pride, lurking in the valley of selfish desire. Meditation is dangerous when the desire to serve is lacking. Service is another word for the utilisation of soul force for the good of the group. Where this impulse is lacking, energy may pour into the bodies, but—lacking use and finding no outlet—will tend to over-stimulate the centres, and produce conditions disastrous to the neophyte. Assimilation and elimination are laws of the soul life as well as of the physical life, and when this simple law is disregarded serious consequences will follow as inevitably as in the physical body.

5. *Study of the centres.* This we are now beginning. It is a study as yet in its infancy in the West, and little applied in the East. Our approach will be somewhat new, for though we will accustom ourselves to the names, locations and relationships of the centres *we shall do no meditation work upon them.* Eventually we shall arrive at an appreciation of their vibration, of their tone and colours and of the astrological significances. We shall not work with the centres down the spinal column, nor aim at their conscious utilisation as does the clairvoyant and clairaudient person. All the work done by students must be done entirely in the head and from the head. There is the seat of the Will, or Spirit aspect, working through the soul. There also is the synthetic expression of the personality, and in the understanding of the relation of the two head centres and their mutual interplay will come gradually the domination of the personality by the soul. This will lead to the consequent and subsequent guided

activity of the five other centres. The work in these five centres will eventually be as automatic as the present functioning of the heart and the lungs in the physical body.

The presiding Intelligence, the Self, "seated on the throne between the eyebrows" and guided by the Light in the head will be awake to the interests of the soul and as alert as is the 'I' consciousness of the average self-centered man. By the rhythm of his divine life and by his conscious cooperation with the Plan, and functioning through the use of the Will, must the disciple in incarnation act as the agent of his soul in the three worlds.

6. *Breathing Exercises.* Little by little as progress is made will the needed instruction be imparted. Let me point out however that no breathing exercises can be safely used where there is no attempt to impose rhythm upon the life of every day. The two activities must go hand in hand.

The effect of breathing exercises is varied:

a. There is an oxygenating effect. The blood stream is purified and pressure is relieved. A symbolism underlies this:—for as the blood is oxygenated so is the life of the man in the three worlds permeated by spiritual energy.
b. There is the imposition of a peculiar rhythm, brought about by the particular spacing and time limit of the breaths—inhalation, retention, and exhalation—and this will vary according to the counts.
c. There is a subtle effect of prana (which is the subjective element underlying the air breathed in and out) which affects most potently the body of prana, the vital or etheric body. Students should remember that subtle effects are more powerful than the physical effects. They produce results in two directions; on the physical body and on the etheric body. The entire vital body assumes a particular rhythm according to the breathing exercises. This kept up for a long period of time will have a shattering or a cohesive effect upon the physical body, and devitalise or vitalise the etheric body correspondingly.
d. There is the effect upon the centres, which is most effectual and which follows the trend of the aspirant's thought. If, for instance, a man thinks upon the solar plexus, that centre will inevitably be vitalised and his emotional nature be strengthened. Hence the need for students to hold their meditation *steady in the head* and so awaken the head centre.

Let no one doubt the effect of breathing exercises upon the vital body. As surely as eating and drinking build or destroy the physical body, and aid or hinder its right functioning, so do breathing exercises produce potent effects, if rightly used over a long enough period of time.

And what shall I say about the last three requirements? Nothing much, for the time is not yet ripe for their correct understanding. Step by step must the aspirant proceed and his theory must not persistently run ahead of his experience. Perhaps I can give the clue to each of these three through the formulation of a simple rule for daily living. This will be grasped by those for whom it is intended and will not work harm to the unevolved. This rule, when followed will bring about, gently and subjectively, the necessary conditions for the manifestation of the requirement.

Learn to use the will through the development of steady purpose and the organising of the daily life, so that that purpose may reach fulfillment.

Learn to do something else with time besides organise it and use it. Learn to do several things simultaneously, and utilise therefore all the three bodies synchronously. Let me illustrate:—When you are practicing your daily breathing exercise keep your count with accuracy, listen attentively for the sound that "soundeth in the silence" of the interlude. At the same time think of yourself as the soul, the imposer of rhythm, and the voice that speaks. This is something which can be acquired by practice by each of you.

Discover the serpent of illusion by the help of the serpent of wisdom and then will the sleeping serpent mount upwards to the place of meeting.

RULE SIX

The devas of the lower four feel the force when the eye opens; they are driven forth and lose their master.

The Work of the Eye

THE WORK OF THE EYE

We have for consideration now one of the simplest of the Rules for Magic yet at the same time one of the most practical, and one upon which the entire success of all magical work depends.

I would like to point out to the investigating aspirant that the key to the situation depicted in the rule lies in the word *contemplation* found in the preceding one. Let us therefore study that word with care and seek its accurate definition.

To contemplate involves steady vision, one-pointedly directed towards a specific objective. The soul or solar angel might be regarded as gazing in three directions.

1. Towards the Light Supernal, towards that central Life or Energy which holds hid within Itself the purpose and plan towards which all Being tends. I know not how to express this more clearly. What that directive force may be, what is the secret of Being Itself is only revealed during the more advanced initiations, and is only finally grasped when the causal body itself, the karana sarira, disintegrates and the final limitation slips away. With this direction of the solar Angel's vision we need not concern ourselves.

2. Over the kingdom wherein the solar Angel reigns supreme, over the world of souls, or egoic impulses, of hierarchical work and of pure thought. This is the Kingdom of God, the world of heavenly Being. It is the state whereof disciples are becoming increasingly aware, wherein initiates work, and from which the Masters in Their graded ranks direct the evolutionary process of the planet. These two directions in which the soul looks constitute the world of its spiritual experience and the object of its aspiration. Let it not be forgotten that the spiritual man, the solar Angel, has also his goal of endeavour, and that his becomes the predominant impulse once the subjugation of the vehicle in the three worlds is brought about. Just as the fully intelligent human being can only begin consciously to function as a soul and to contact the kingdom of the soul, so only the fully active and dominant soul, in

which the buddhic principle is potentially controlling, can begin to contact the state of pure Being in which the monad or spirit eternally rests.

The development of the intellect in man marks his fitness for the work of treading the Path, back to full soul consciousness. The development of the buddhic or wisdom-love aspect in the solar Angel demonstrates his fitness for further progression in the awareness of the state of pure Being.

3. The third direction in which the soul looks and wherein he exercises the faculty of contemplative vision is towards his reflection in the three worlds. The object of the long struggle between the higher and the lower man has been to make the lower responsive to and sensitively aware of the forces emanating from the soul as the soul "contemplates" his triple instrument.

There is an interesting relation between these three "directions of contemplation" and the awakening in the three major centres. This cannot be more than hinted at owing to the abstruseness of the subject. So many factors govern this awakening, and each aspirant has to determine for himself the order and mode of his awakening.

The centre between the eyebrows, commonly called the third eye has a unique and peculiar function. As I have pointed out elsewhere, students must not confound the pineal gland with the third eye. They are related, but not the same. In *The Secret Doctrine* they are apparently regarded as the same, and the casual reader can easily confound them but they are by no means identical. This H. P. B. knew, but the apparent confusion was permitted until more of the etheric nature of forms was known. The third eye manifests as a result of the vibratory interaction between the forces of the soul, working through the pineal gland, and the forces of the personality, working through the pituitary body. These negative and positive forces interact, and when potent enough produce the light in the head. Just as the physical eye came into being in response to the light of the sun so the spiritual eye equally comes into being in response to the light of the spiritual sun. As the aspirant develops he becomes aware of the light. I refer to the light in all forms, veiled by all sheaths and expressions of the divine life, and not just to the light within the aspirant himself. As his awareness of this light increases so does the apparatus of vision develop, and the mechanism whereby he can see things in the spiritual light comes into being in the etheric body.

This is the eye of Shiva, for it is only fully utilized in the magical work when the monadic aspect, the will aspect, is controlling.

By means of the third eye the soul accomplishes three activities:

1. *It is the eye of vision.* By its means, the spiritual man sees behind the forms of all aspects of divine expression. He becomes aware of the light of the world, and contacts the soul within all forms. Just as the physical eye registers forms, so does the spiritual eye register the illumination within those forms which "illumination" indicates a specific state of being. It opens up the world of radiance.

2. *It is the controlling factor of the magical work.* All white magical work is carried forward with a definitely constructive purpose, made possible through the use of the intelligent will. In other words, the soul knows the plan, and when the alignment is right and the attitude correct, the will aspect of the divine man can function and bring about results in the three worlds. The organ used is the third eye. The analogy to this can be seen in the often noticed power of the human eye as it controls other human beings and animals by a look, and through steady gazing can act magnetically. Force flows through the

focused human eye. Force flows through the focused third eye.

3. *It has a destructive aspect* and the energy flowing through the third eye can have a disintegrating and destroying effect. It can, through its focused attention, directed by the intelligent will, drive out physical matter. It is the agent of the soul in the purificatory work.

It should be noted here that in each of the subtle bodies in the three worlds there is a corresponding point of focus, and the centre between the eyebrows is but the physical counterpart (for etheric matter is physical) of inner correspondences.

Through this point of focus the soul looks out upon, or contemplates the mental plane, including the mental mechanism. Similarly on the emotional plane, the soul is brought into a state of awareness or vision of its emotional sheath and the world of astral phenomena, and the physical parallel exists for the etheric body.

It is this third work of the soul that is touched upon here, the destructive work of getting rid of the old forms, of shaking out of the bodies matter of an undesirable nature and of breaking down the barriers and limitations to true soul activity.

These three activities of the soul, through the medium of the third eye, are the correspondences to the three aspects, and students would find it of interest to work these out.

The seeing of the light within all forms through the agency of the third eye (brought into being through the realization of the light in the head, the spiritual light) is but the correspondence to the physical eye, revealing forms in the light of the physical sun. This corresponds to the personality.

The aspect of control through magnetic energy and the attractive force in the spiritual eye, which is the dominant factor in magical work, is the correspondence to the soul. In a most mysterious sense, the soul is the eye of the monad, enabling the monad, which is pure Being, to work, to contact, to know, and to see.

The aspect of destruction is the correspondence to the monad or will aspect; in the last analysis it is the monad that brings about the final abstraction, destroys all forms, withdraws itself from manifestation and ends the cycle of creative work.

Bringing these concepts down to practical expression in relation to the Rule under consideration, it can be noted that all these three activities are dealt with in this Rule. The third eye opens as the result of conscious development, right alignment and the inflow of soul life. Then its magnetic controlling force makes itself felt, controlling the lives of the lower bodies, driving forth the lower four elementals (of earth, water, fire, air) and forcing the lunar lords to abdicate. The personality, which has hitherto been the master, no longer can control, and the soul comes into full domination in the three worlds.

The elemental of earth, who is the sum total of the many lives which form the physical body, is controlled and feels the eye of the Master (the one Master in the head) upon it. The gross elements constituting that body are "driven forth" and better and more adequate atoms or lives are built in.

The elemental of the astral or body of water undergoes a similar activity plus a stabilising effect which brings to an end the restlessness and fluidic tempestuousness which have hitherto characterised it.

Through the controlling magnetic power of the spiritual eye, the soul rebuilds the astral body and holds it steady and coherent through its focused attention.

Again, an analogous process goes forward in the mental body. Old forms disappear before the clear light in which the spiritual man is working and as the Old Commentary puts it:

"One glance the soul doth cast upon the forms of mind. A ray of light streams out and darkness disappears; distortions and evil forms fade out, and all the little fires die out; the lesser lights are no more seen.
"The eye through light awakens into life the needed modes of Being. To the disciple this will carry knowledge. To the ignorant no sense is seen for a sense lacks."

The elemental of the air symbolically understood is that substratum of energy which works through the forms of the etheric body, which is dealt with through the breath, and handled through the science of pranayama. This elemental form is the intricate etheric structure, the nadis and centres, and all advanced students know well how these are controlled by the focused attention of the soul in contemplation, acting through the head centre, focused in the region of the third eye and swept into right and specific activity by an act of the will. In the above sentence I have concentrated the formula for all magical work on the physical plane. It is through the etheric body and the force, directed through one or other of the centres, that the soul carries on the work in magic.

It is through the intense focusing of intention in the head and the turning of the attention through the third eye towards the centre to be used that the force finds its correct outlet. That force is made potent by the energising, directed intelligent will. Study these points, for in them you will find the clue to the magical work in your own life reconstruction, to the magical work of human reconstruction which certain adepts are carrying on, and to the magical work of the evolution of the divine plan which is the motivating power of the occult Hierarchy.

RULE SEVEN

The dual forces on the plane (whereon the vital power must be sought) are seen; the two paths face the solar Angel; the poles vibrate. A choice confronts the one who meditates.

The Battleground of the Astral Plane.
The two Paths.

THE BATTLEGROUND OF THE ASTRAL PLANE

We must start our study and consideration of the seventh Rule for Magic. We have completed the first six Rules which deal specifically with work on the mental plane, and hence have a practical value only for those who are beginning to utilize the power of the mind in the magical work of creation.

It is interesting to note in this connection that, as humanity enters into its heritage of mind, there appears simultaneously a growing tendency towards magical work. Schools of affirmation are cropping up on all sides, whose announced intent is to create those natural conditions wherein a man may have what he deems to be admirable and advisable. Books on the subject of the creative mind are flooding the markets, and discussions on the force back of the creative arts are deemed of vital interest. Psychologists are giving the entire matter much consideration, and though at present the ideal is viewed almost entirely in terms of the physical plane, yet the sum total indicates a vibratory activity in the world soul, as it expresses itself through humanity, and issues forth from the mental realm. The pioneers of the race, and the foremost thinkers and creative workers of humanity are but the sensitives who respond most readily to the mental impulses. They are in the minority as yet, and most people respond to the forces and vibrations emanating from the plane of the emotions and of desire. More and more however are awakening, and the significance of the six first Rules of Magic will become increasingly apparent.

These fifteen rules are divided into:

Six rules on the mental plane.
Five rules on the desire or astral plane.
Four rules on the physical plane.

The main thought to be held clearly in the mind is that they confine themselves to the use of energy in the three worlds, and that this energy is either consciously manipulated by the governing soul or is swept into activity by the force inherent in the matter of the three worlds, independently of the soul. When this is the case, the man is a victim of his own form energies and the matter aspect of all manifestation. In the other case, he is the intelligent ruler, controller of his own destinies, and swings the lower energies into forms and activities through the power of his mind impulses, and the focussed attention of his own soul. In the six rules already considered one or two thoughts most clearly emerge and might be summed up in the following terms:

Rule 1—Recollection, resulting in concentration.
Rule 2—Response, resulting in an interaction between higher and lower.
Rule 3—Radiation, resulting in a sounding forth.
Rule 4—Respiration, resulting in creative work.
Rule 5—Re-union, resulting in the at-one-ment.
Rule 6—Re-orientation, resulting in a clear vision of the Plan.

Students would do well to consider these relationships, and to work out the underlying synthesis.

In the words of this rule the astral plane, with its function and problem, is ably synthesized. Note the terms used in the description given in a few short phrases:

1. The plane of dual forces.
2. The plane of the two paths.
3. The plane whereon the vital power is sought.
4. The plane of the vibrating poles.
5. The plane whereon a choice is made.

One of the most vital things every aspirant has to do is to learn to understand the astral plane, to comprehend its nature and to learn both to stand free from it and then to work on it. In this instruction,

I seek to give some clear teaching on this plane, for the moment a man can "see" on the astral plane, and can achieve equilibrium and hold steady in the midst of its vibrating forces, that moment he is ready for initiation.

First, let us gather together some of the terms which are used to describe this sphere of divine Being wherewith a man has first to identify himself, penetrate to the centre, pierce through its veiled illusion, and eventually stand poised, untouched, detached, uninfluenced and free.

The term "astral" so often used is in reality a misnomer. H. P. B. was basically right when she used the term in connection with the etheric or vital planes of the physical plane. When contact is made with the etheric world, the first impression given is always of a starry light, of brilliance, of scintillation. Gradually, however, the word became identified with Kama or desire, and so was used for the plane of emotional reaction.

It is interesting to note this for it is in itself an instance of the effect of the astral plane upon the human brain, which in its uninformed condition reverses the reality and sees things in an upside down state. The appearance of the astral plane when first definitely *seen* by the "opened eye" of the aspirant is one of dense fog, confusion, changing forms, interpenetrating and intermingling colours, and is of such a kaleidoscopic appearance that the hopelessness of the enterprise seems overwhelming. It is not light, or starry or clear. It is apparently impenetrable disorder, for it is the meeting ground of forces. Because the forces in the aspirant's own body are equally in disorder, he blends in with the surrounding chaos to such an extent that it is at first almost impossible for the onlooking soul to dissociate its own astral mechanism from the astral mechanism of humanity as a whole, and from the astral mechanism of the world.

One of the first things then that the aspirant has to learn is to dissociate his own aura in the emotional sense from that of his surroundings and much time is expended in learning to do this. It is for this reason that one of the first qualifications of discipleship is *discrimination*, for it is through the use of the mind, as analyzer and separator, that the astral body is brought under control.

Secondly, the astral plane is the plane of illusion, of glamour, and of a distorted presentation of reality. The reason for this is that every individual in the world is busy working in astral matter, and the potency of human desire and of world desire produces that constant "out-picturing" and form building which leads to the most concrete effects of astral matter. Individual desire, national desire, racial desire, the desire of humanity as a whole, plus the instinctual desire of all subhuman lives causes a constant changing and shifting of the substance of the plane; there is a building of the temporary forms, some of rare beauty, some of no beauty, and a vitalising by the astral energy of its creator. Add to these forms that persistent and steadily growing scenario we call the "akashic records" which concern the emotional history of the past, add the activities of the discarnate lives which are passing through the astral plane, either out of or towards incarnation, add the potent desire, purified and intelligent, of all superhuman Lives, including those of the occult planetary Hierarchy, and the sum total of forces present is stupendous. All play upon, around and through every human being, and according to the calibre of his physical body, and the condition of his centres will be his response. Through this illusory panorama, the aspirant has to make his way, finding the clue or thread which will lead him out of the maze, and holding fast to each tiny fragment of reality as it presents itself to him, learning to distinguish truth from glamour, the permanent from the impermanent and the certainty from the unreal. As the *Old Commentary* puts it:

"Let the disciple seize hold of the tail of the serpent of wisdom, and having with firmness grasped it, let him follow it into the deepest centre of the Hall of Wisdom. Let him not be betrayed into the trap set for him by the serpent of illusion, but let him shut his eyes to the colourful tracery upon its back, and his ears to the melody of its voice. Let him discern the jewel, set in the forehead of the serpent whose tail he holds, and by its radiance traverse the miry halls of maya."

No glamour, no illusion can long hold the man who has set himself the task of treading the razor-edged Path which leads through the wilderness, through the thick-set forest, through the deep waters of sorrow and distress, through the valley of sacrifice and over the mountains of vision to the gate of Deliverance. He may travel sometimes in the dark (and the illusion of darkness is very real); he may travel sometimes in a light so dazzling and bewildering that he can scarcely see the way ahead; he may know what it is to falter on the Path, and to drop under the fatigue of service and of strife; he may be temporarily sidetracked and wander down the by-paths of ambition, of self-interest and of material enchantment, but the lapse will be but brief. Nothing in heaven or hell, on earth or elsewhere can prevent the progress of the man who has awakened to the illusion, who has glimpsed the reality beyond the glamour of the astral plane, and who has heard, even if only once, the clarion call of his own soul.

The astral plane is also the Kurukshetra, both of humanity as a whole and of the individual human unit. It is the battle-ground whereon must be found the Waterloo of every aspirant. In some one life, there comes an emotional crisis in which decisive action is taken, and the disciple proves his control of his emotional nature. This may take the form of some great and vital test, covering a brief time but calling forth every resource of wisdom and of purity that the disciple possesses, or it may be a long and protracted emotional strain, carried over many years of living. But in the attaining of success and in the achievement of clear vision and right discernment (through right discrimination) the disciple testifies to his fitness for the second initiation.

I would like to point out that it is this test and crisis through which humanity is now passing, and which began in those conditions which culminated in the world war and the present world strain. The first initiation of humanity, as an entity, took place when individualization became possible, and the soul was born in the body of humanity. This was preceded by a period of fearful stress and strain, dimly sensed by the pioneers into the human kingdom from the ranks of the animal-men. Should this crisis be successfully passed, the second initiation of humanity will be the result—the passing through the baptism and the entering of the stream. So the world war and its resulting effects constitute the Kurukshetra of the world Arjuna, and the outcome is still in the balance. Let this not be forgotten. There is however no cause for pessimism. The outcome of good is inevitable. It is however a question of a slow or a rapid realization and liberation from the great world illusion, and to this end every aspirant is begged to work strenuously and to lend his aid. Every man who liberates himself, who sees clearly, and who releases himself from the glamour of illusion aids in the Great Work.

Again, the astral plane is that whereon the pairs of opposites act and interact, and whereon the pull of the great dualities is most potently felt. Primarily, the interaction is between the soul and its vehicle, matter, but there are many lesser dualities which play their part and are more easily recognized by the average man.

Light and darkness interact, as do pleasure and pain; good and evil meet and form the playground of the Gods, and poverty and riches are offset one against the other. The entire modern economic situation is of an astral nature; it is the outcome of desire and the result of a certain selfish use of the forces of matter. Heat and cold, as we understand the term, in a most peculiar manner are the result of the interplay of the pairs of opposites, and an interesting line of occult study concerns itself with the effects of racial emotions on climatic conditions. We most truly make our climate in one significant sense. When desire has burnt itself out, planetary life comes to an end, as climatic conditions will negate form-life as we understand it.

In relation to the human unit, the secret of liberation lies in the balancing of the forces and the equilibrising of the pairs of opposites. The Path is the narrow line between these pairs which the aspirant finds and treads, turning neither to the right nor to the left.

It must be remembered always that when the pairs of opposites are discerned, when a man balances the forces of his own nature, when he has found the Path and become the Path, then he can work with the world forces, can preserve the balance and the equilibrium of the energies of the three worlds and so become a co-worker with the Masters of the Wisdom. Let us pray and hope that this may be the practical outcome of our understanding of the nature of the battleground of the astral plane.

THE TWO PATHS

Passing from our consideration of the nature of the astral plane we will deal with its functions and the relation of the disciple to its activities. Let us remember certain things about it. First, it is pre-eminently the battle-ground, and on it is fought the warfare which eventuates in the final release of the imprisoned soul. It is useful to have in mind the outstanding characteristics of the three planes and the three bodies which function on them.

The *physical* plane is the plane of active experience in and through matter. It is the plane of externalisation and, according to the condition and point of development of the inner man, so will be the outer form and its activities.

The *astral* plane is the plane whereon the man passes through three stages of consciousness:

a. He gains, through his sensory apparatus, consciousness in the world of forms, and develops ability to re-act to those forms with wisdom and intelligence. This consciousness he shares with the animal world, though he goes far beyond them in some respects, owing to his possession of a correlating and co-ordinating mind.
b. Sensitivity, or awareness of moods, emotions and feelings, desires and aspirations which have their roots within him in the principle of self-consciousness, or in the ahamkara principle, as the occultist (who loves difficult phrases) is apt to call it. This he shares in common with his fellow-men.

c. Spiritual awareness or sensitiveness to the spiritual world, and the feeling aspect of the higher consciousness. This has its roots in the soul, presupposes the dominance of the mental nature, and is that faculty which constitutes him a mystic. This awareness he shares in common with all disciples and it is the reward of the gained victories of his astral plane experience.

The *mental* plane comes next. In it the right use of the intellect is the outstanding achievement. This is also characterised by three stages:

a. The stage wherein the mind is the receiver of impressions from the outer world, via the five senses and the brain. This is a negative condition, and, in it, the "modifications of the thinking principle" are brought about through the impacts of the external world, and the re-actions of the astral world.

b. The stage wherein the mind initiates its own activities, and wherein the intellect is a dominating factor. Though thrown into activity by the factors enumerated above, it is responsive also to the thought currents of the mental plane as well, and becomes exceedingly active as the result of these two contacts. Out of these a third activity supervenes wherein the reasoning principle acts upon the information gained in these two ways, sets its own streams of thoughts, and formulates its own thought forms, as well as registering those of others.

c. The stage wherein the soul, through concentration and meditation succeeds in imposing its ideas and impressions upon the mind held "steady in the light" and so enables the mental body to respond to impressions and contacts emanating from the subjective and spiritual worlds.

Yet the battle, par excellence, is fought out in the astral body, and only reaches its most intense point and its potent fierceness when there is a good physical instrument and a well-equipped mentality. The greater the sensitivity of the astral body, the greater its reactions to the physical world and to the mental condition and hence the fact emerges that disciples and the more highly evolved people in the world have a more potent astral body and work under greater emotional strain than the less highly evolved and the liberated sons of God.

Students are therefore begged to deal drastically and potently with their emotional natures, remembering that victory descends from above and cannot be worked up to from below. The soul *must* govern and its instrument in the warfare is the consecrated mind.

It is interesting to note the occult sequence in the description given of this plane in the rule under consideration.

It is first of all the plane of dual forces. The first thing the aspirant becomes aware of is duality. The little evolved man is aware of synthesis, but it is the synthesis of his material nature. The highly spiritual man is aware also of synthesis but it is that in his soul, whose consciousness is that of unity. But in between is the wretched aspirant, conscious of duality above all else and pulled hither and thither between the two. His first step has, for its objective, to make him aware of the pairs of opposites and of the necessity to choose between them. Through the light, which he has discovered in himself, he becomes aware of the dark. Through the good which attracts him, he sees the evil which is for him the line of least resistance. Through the activity of pain, he can visualize and become aware of pleasure, and heaven and hell become to him realities. Through the activity of the attractive life of his soul, he realizes the attraction of matter and of form, and is forced to recognize the urge and pull of both of them. He learns to feel himself as "pendant 'twixt the two great forces", and, once the dualities are grasped, it dawns on him slowly and surely that the deciding factor in the struggle is his divine will, in contradistinction to his selfish will. Thus the dual forces play their part until they are seen as two great streams of divine energy, pulling in opposite directions, and he becomes then aware of the two paths, mentioned in our rule. One path leads back into the dreary land of rebirth, and the other leads through the golden gate to the city of free souls. One is therefore involutionary and involves him in deepest matter; the other leads him out of the body nature, and makes him eventually aware of his spiritual body, through which he can function in the kingdom of the soul. One path, later on (when he is a true and pledged chela) is known to him as the left hand path and the other the path of right activity. On one path, he becomes proficient in black magic, which is only the developed powers of the personality, subordinated to the selfish purposes of a man whose motives are those of self interest and worldly ambition. These confine him to the three worlds and shut the door which opens on to life. On the other path, he subordinates his personality and exercises the magic of the White Brotherhood, working always in the light of the soul with the soul in all forms, and laying no emphasis upon the ambitions of the personal self. Clear discrimination of these two paths reveals what is called in some occult books that "narrow razor-edged Path" which lies between the two. This is the "noble middle Path" of the Buddha and marks the fine line of demarcation between the pairs of opposites, and between the two streams which he has learnt to recognize—one going up unto the gates of heaven, and the other passing down into the nethermost hell.

By the exercise of the two main weapons of the aspirant, discrimination and dispassion, he gains that quality which is called in this rule "the vital power". Just as the eye is the instrument of choice in choosing the way of travel on the physical plane and has besides a potency all its own whereby it attracts and develops its own sign language, so a vital power is felt in the aspirant. This eventually brings the third eye into activity, and so there is gained a potency and a clear vision which make right choice and quick progress upon the way a steady progression. We are told that power is grown or developed in silence, and only he who can find a centre of peace within his head, where the paths of the bodily forces and the spiritual inflowing tides meet, can rightly practice true discrimination and that dispassion which bring the controlled astral and mental bodies under the guidance of the soul.

Then he can understand the significance of "the vibrating poles", and achieve that point of equilibrium which is the result of their interaction and vibration.

The sensing of the dual forces and the clear discrimination of the two paths leads to the development of the vital power. This vital power demonstrates its first activity in enabling the aspirant to achieve a point of balance and so stand on that pinnacle of achievement whereon "a choice is made".

What is that choice? For the aspirant, it is that between rapid and slow progress. For the disciple, accepted and loyal, it is the choice between methods of service. For the initiate it oft lies betwixt spiritual advancement and the arduous work of staying with the group and working out the plan. For the Master it is the choice between the seven Paths, and it will therefore be apparent how much more strenuous and difficult is his problem.

All however prepares the aspirant for right choice through right discrimination leading to right action, and made possible through practiced dispassion. In this sentence is summed up the technique of the warrior upon the battle-field of the desire plane.

It should here be noted that in the steadily developing power of choice, and the loyally fought battle of the astral plane, the consciousness in the man shifts stage by stage. First, it is the battered earth-weary aspirant who has to struggle with desire, with glamour, with ambition and with his sensitive emotional body. He thinks the battle is stupendous but from the wider angle it is relatively small—yet all that he can stand.

Later, it is the experienced probationary disciple who wrestles in the vale of illusion, and deals not alone with his own nature but with the forces of that vale also, recognising its dual nature. Then, the disciple comes forth to battle and faces with courage (and often with clear vision) the forces arrayed against him. They involve not only those in his own nature and in those aspects of the astral plane to which he naturally re-acts, but also involve the forces of illusion arrayed against the group of disciples to which he belongs. Let all disciples take note of this and have it in mind in these difficult and strenuous days. Such disciples are in conscious contact at times with their soul forces and for them there is no defeat nor turning back. They are the tried warriors, scarred and tired, yet knowing that triumphant victory lies ahead, for the soul is omnipotent. Accepted disciples, who battle all the above enumerated factors, plus the black forces arrayed against the Elder Brothers, can call upon the spiritual energies of their group and at rare and indicated moments upon the Master under whom they work. Thus the work and labour expands; thus the responsibility and struggle steadily increases; yet at the same time there is also a steadily growing reception of potencies which can be contacted and utilized and which when correctly contacted insure victory at the end.

The phrase "the one who meditates" relates to the soul. Arjuna, the aspiring disciple, resigns the struggle and hands the weapons and the reins of government to Krishna, the soul, and is rewarded at last by understanding and by a vision of the divine form which veils the Son of God Who is Himself.

When this battle has been fought and won the disciple steps into the ranks of the white magicians of our planet and can wield forces, cooperate with the plan, command the elementals, and bring order out of chaos. He is no longer immersed in the world illusion but has risen above it. He can no longer be held down by the chains of his own past habits and his karma. He has gained the vital power and stands forth an Elder Brother.

Such is the path ahead of each and all who dare to tread it. Such is the opportunity offered to all students who have made their choice with dispassion and are prompted by love and the desire to serve.

RULE EIGHT

The Agnisuryans respond to the sound. The waters ebb and flow. Let the magician guard himself from drowning, at the point where land and water meet. The midway spot, which is neither dry nor wet, must provide the standing place whereon his feet are set. When water, land and air meet there is the place for magic to be wrought.

Types of Astral Force.
Cyclic Ebb and Flow.

TYPES OF ASTRAL FORCE

It would be advisable for the student to read with care the commentary on this rule as given in the *Treatise on Cosmic Fire*. It will be noted how extremely abstruse it is and how full of almost blind occult information. This should however be studied. The word "astral plane" should also be looked up and a general idea gained as to its nature and its function as the battle-ground of the senses, and as the place from which magic is wrought. The intelligent and constructive desire of the white magician, acting under the instruction of his own soul and therefore occupied with group work, is the motivating power back of all magical phenomena. This magical work is begun in the magician's own life, extends to the world of the astral plane and from thence (when potent there) can begin to demonstrate on the physical plane and on the higher planes eventually.

We shall, therefore, take a good deal of time over this rule for it covers the immediate work and activity of the intelligent aspirant. It is the most important in the book from the standpoint of the average student. It cannot be understood where there is no soul contact, nor can the magical force of the soul work out in manifestation upon the physical plane until the meaning of its esoteric phrases has been somewhat wrought out in the inner experience of the magician.

Most true aspirants are now at the midway spot, and can either drown (and so make no further progress this life), stand and so hold the ground gained, or become true practicing magicians, efficient in white magic, which is based on love, animated by wisdom and intelligently applied to forms.

We will, therefore, divide this rule into several parts, the more easily to study it and take them up step by step, so as to grasp their application to the average life of the probationary disciple, and to gain a wise understanding of their wide implications.

These three divisions are:

1. The response of the astral elementals and the consequent ebb and flow of the waters.
2. The dangers of the midway spot, its nature and the opportunity it affords.
3. The place where magic is wrought.

We will study now the first point which is summed up for us in the words:

"The Agnisuryans respond to the sound.
The waters ebb and flow."

The situation might be stated in the following terse statements. The rules already studied convey the truth anent the magician.

1. The soul has communicated with his instrument in the three worlds.

2. The man on the physical plane recognises the contact, and the light in the head shines forth, sometimes recognised and sometimes unrecognised by the aspirant.

3. The soul sounds forth its note. A thought-form is created in consonance with the *united* meditation of the soul and the man, his instrument.

4. This thought-form, embodying the will of the ego or soul, cooperating with the personality, takes to itself a triple form, constituted of the matter of all three planes, and vitalized through the activity and by the emanations from the heart, throat and ajna centres of the white magician—the soul in conjunction with its instrument.

5. The personality sheaths, each with its own individual life, feel they are losing their power and the battle between the forces of matter and the force of the soul is violently renewed.

6. This battle must be fought out on the astral plane and will decide three things:

a. Whether the soul will, in any one life (for some life holds the critical stage), be the dominant factor and the personality from henceforth be the servant of the soul.
b. Whether the astral plane is no longer the plane of illusion, but can become the field of service.
c. Whether the man can become an active co-operator with the Hierarchy, able to create and to wield

mental matter, and so work out the purposes of the Universal Mind, which are prompted by boundless and infinite love, and are the expression of the One Life.

This is the crux of the entire situation, and when the man has mastered the forces opposed to him, he is ready for the second initiation which marks the release of the soul from the prison of the astral body. Henceforth the soul will use the astral body, and mould desire into line with divine purpose.

It is of value for the student to know where he stands and what his particular problem is. The average man is learning the control of the physical body and the organizing of his physical plane life. The student on the probationary path is learning a similar lesson in relation to his astral body, its focus, its desires and its work. The student on the path of accepted discipleship has to demonstrate this control and begin to discipline the mind nature and so function consciously in the mental body. The work of the initiate and the adept grows out of these achievements and they need not be dealt with here.

The battle is spread over quite a series of lives, but in some one life it becomes critical; the final stand is made and Arjuna triumphs in the fight, but only by letting Krishna assume the reins of control, by learning mind control and by the revelation of the form of God. By distinguishing between the soul and the form, and by a vision of the perfection of the glory which can radiate from the forms "indwelt by God", he learns to choose the Way of light and to see his form and all forms as custodians of the light. So he buckles down to the work of making the astral body simply a reflector of that light and by the quelling of desire, through the subjugation of the "Agnisuryans" who constitute his astral body and are the living substance of the astral plane, he learns to function as an adept on that plane, to pierce through its illusion and to see life *true*.

Speaking symbolically the substance of the astral plane is animated by three types of divine force, which, when brought together, produce the great Illusion. These are:

First, the force of selfish desire. This involutionary energy plays a big part in bringing about evolution, for selfishness is the nursery of infant souls. Hence the aspirant refuses to be held by it.

Second, the force of fear. This is the product of ignorance, and in its initial stages it is not the product of wrong thinking. It is basically instinctual and is found dominating in the non-mental animal kingdom as well as in the human kingdom. But in the human, its power is increased potently through the powers of the mind, and through *memory* of past pain and grievance and through anticipation of those we foresee, the power of fear is enormously aggravated by the thought-form we ourselves have built of our own individual fears and phobias. This thought form grows in power as we pay attention to it, for "energy follows thought" till we become dominated by it. Second ray people are peculiarly a prey to this. For the majority of them it constitutes the "dweller on the threshold", just as ambition and love of power, backed by frantic desire and unscrupulousness form the "Dweller" for the first ray types. The crystallized thought form of intellectual achievement for selfish ends, and the use of knowledge for personality objectives stand before the portal of the path in the case of the third ray person, and unless broken up and destroyed will dominate him and turn him into a black magician.

You oft have been told that fear is an illusion. Yet this statement does not help. It is a generalisation that one can admit, yet which remains profoundly difficult to apply individually. The fears to which aspirants are subject (note the mode of wording this) are seldom of a selfish nature except insofar as suffering has caused them to recoil from a further continuation of untoward happenings. Their fears are wrapt in seeming love around their loved ones. Yet should each disciple ask himself a most practical question: How many of the torturing hours have been expended on realities and on tangible happenings, and how many on illusory premonitions and on doubts and questionings, based on that which has never happened? I would like to point out to my brothers that they need to do two things: To meditate on *truth in daily life*, using the concept of *truth practised and lived by* as their seed thought in meditation; to this end I would suggest that they memorise and use at all times when swept by illusory fears and needless foreboding the following formula or prayer:

"Let reality govern my every thought, and truth be the master of my life."

Let each say this to himself as constantly as need requires, forcing his mind to focus attention upon the significance of these spoken words.

I would suggest also sound common sense and the cultivation of an attitude of mind which refuses to permit *time* for illusory fears to grow.

Fear is the main obstacle frequently to a very vital step forward which could be taken in this life, but may have to be delayed to another if due opportunity is not taken and the will nature powerfully excited.

The first ray aspirant who fails to overcome his Dweller may become a "destroyer of souls", as it is called, and be condemned (until he learns his lesson) to work in the forces of matter, and with the forms which hold all souls in prison. This is the occult significance of the misunderstood words, death and destruction. Of this type, the Devil is the great prototype.

The second ray aspirant who builds his Dweller and permits its steady and increasing control becomes a "deluder of souls". He is the true Anti-Christ, and through false teaching and the working of so-called miracles, through hypnotism and mass suggestion he draws a veil over the world and forces men to walk in the great illusion. It is interesting to note that the work of the Devil, the imprisoner of souls, is beginning to lose its power, for the race is on the verge of understanding that true death is immersion in form, and that matter is but a part of the divine whole. The thought form of this "Dweller on the Threshold" which humanity has built for millions of years is on the verge of destruction. But the work of Anti-Christ is only rising now to its height, and the delusion of riches, of possession, of false teaching will increasingly hold sway but the term of the delusion will be shorter than the term of destruction, for all these factors function under their own cycles and have their own ebb and flow.

The third ray person who also fails to shatter his "Dweller" becomes what is called a "manipulator of souls" and uses the mind to destroy the real and to put a veil between the man and reality. It must be remembered that none of these names and these activities refer to the soul on its own plane but only to human souls in incarnation on the physical plane. This must be stressed, for on its own plane the souls of all men stand free from illusion, and neither can be destroyed, deluded nor manipulated. It is only "the souls in prison" who are subject to the activities of the forces of evil and only for a term. The first group works through governments, through politics, and the interplay between nations and is relatively small in number. The second ray group who delude and deceive, work through religious agencies, through mass psychology, and the misuse and misapplication of devotion and of the arts. They are largest in number. The third group work primarily through commercial relations in the business world, and through the use of money, the concretisation of prana or universal energy, and the outer symbol of the universal flux and flow. These thoughts are suggestive but not vital, dealing as they do with the cosmic tendencies.

Thirdly, the force of sex attraction. This is a pull from the physical plane and the swinging back of a type of involutionary energy on to the path of return. Cosmically speaking, it manifests as the attractive force between spirit and matter; spiritually speaking, it is demonstrated as the activity of the soul, as it seeks to draw the lower self into full realisation. Physically speaking, it is the urge which tends to unite male and female for the purpose of procreation. When man was purely animal, no sin was involved. When to this urge was added emotional desire, then sin crept in, and the purpose for which the urge manifested was perverted into the satisfaction of desire. Now that the race is more mental, and the force of mind is making itself felt in the human body, an even more serious situation is apparent, which can only be safely worked out when the soul assumes control of its triple instrument.

Humanity is now at the midway point as this rule shows. Man is swept by selfish desire and by ambition, for all of us have first ray qualities. He is racked by fear—his own, family fears, national fears and racial, for all of us swing to the rhythm of the second ray. He is dominated by sex and by money which is another manifestation of the energy of matter and hence has a triple problem with which he is well equipped to deal through the medium of his triple vehicle and the triple potencies of his divine soul. Let us close the instruction on that note—well equipped to deal. We can overcome mental inertia and begin to function as souls in command of our environment. The soul is omniscient and omnipotent.

CYCLIC EBB AND FLOW

Let us consider now the words "the ebb and flow of the waters."

In the understanding of the law of cycles, we gain knowledge of the underlying laws of evolution and come to a realization of the rhythmic work of creation. Incidentally also we gain poise as we study our own life impulses, for they also have their ebb and flow, and alternate between periods of light and periods of darkness.

We have with us always that symbolic daily occurrence wherein the part of the world in which we live swings out into the clear light of the sun, and later returns into the healing dark of the night. Our very familiarity with the phenomenon causes us to lose sight of its symbolic significance and to forget that under the great law, periods of light and dark, of good and evil, of submergence and emergence, of progress into illumination and apparent betrayal into darkness, characterize the growth of all forms, distinguish the development of races and nations, and constitute the problem of the aspirant who has built for himself a picture of walking in a constant illumined condition and of leaving all dark places behind.

In these Instructions, it is not possible for me to deal with the ebb and flow of the divine life as it manifests in the various kingdoms in nature and through the evolutionary growth of humanity, through experience in races, nations and families. I seek, however, to elaborate somewhat the cyclic experience of a soul in incarnation, indicating the apparent ebb and flow of its unfoldment.

The outstanding cycle for every soul is that of its forthgoing into incarnation and its return or flowing back into the centre from whence it came. According to the point of view will be the understanding of this ebb and flow. Souls might esoterically be regarded as those "seeking the light of experience" and therefore turned towards physical expression, and those "seeking the light of understanding", and therefore retreating from the realm of human undertaking to forge their way inward into the soul consciousness, and so become "dwellers in the light eternal". Without appreciating the significance of the terms, the psychologists have sensed these cycles and call certain types, extraverts, and others, introverts. These mark an ebb and flow in individual experience and are the tiny life correspondences to the great soul cycles. This passing into, and passing out of, the web of incarnated existence are the major cycles of any individual soul, and a study of the types of pralaya dealt with in *The Secret Doctrine* and *A Treatise on Cosmic Fire* would be found of real value by the student.

There is also an ebb and flow in soul experience on any one plane and this, in the early stages of development, will cover many lives. They are usually quite extreme in their expression. A study of the racial ebb and flow will make this clearer. In Lemurian days the "flow", or the outward going cycle, spent itself on the physical plane and the ebb carried the life aspect right back to the soul itself, and there was no secondary ebb and flow on the astral or mental planes.

Later, the tide broke on the shores of the astral plane, though including the physical in less degree. The flow directed its attention to the emotional life, and the drift back to the centre took no account of the mental life at all. This was at its height for humanity in Atlantean days and is true also of many today. Now the ebb and flow is increasingly inclusive, and the mental experience has its place so that all three aspects are swept by the life of the soul; all are included in the outgoing energy of the incarnating soul, and for many lives and series of lives this cyclic force spends itself. Within the aspirant there arises an understanding of what is going on and he awakens to the desire to control consciously this ebb and flow or (to put it in simple words) to turn the forces of the outgoing energy in any direction he chooses, or to withdraw to his centre at will. He seeks to arrest this process of being swept out into incarnation without having any conscious purpose, and refuses to see the tide of his life beat out on emotional or mental spheres of existence, and then again see that life withdrawn without his conscious volition. He stands at the midway point and wants to control his own cycles, the "ebb and flow" as he himself may determine it. With conscious purpose he longs to walk in the dark places of incarnated existence and with equally conscious purpose he seeks to withdraw into his own centre. Hence he becomes an aspirant.

The life of the aspirant begins to repeat earlier cycles. He is assailed by a sudden stimulation of the physical nature and violently swept by ancient desires and lusts. This may be succeeded by a cycle wherein the physical body is conscious of the flowing away from it of vital energy and is devitalised, because not the subject of attention. This accounts for much of the sickness and lack of vitality of many of our most cherished servers. The same process can affect the emotional body, and periods of exaltation and of highest aspiration alternate with periods of the deepest depression and lack of interest. The flow may pass on to the mental body and produce a cycle of intense mental activity. Constant study, much thought, keen investigation and a steady intellectual urge will characterize the mind of the aspirant. To this may succeed a cycle wherein all study is distasteful, and the mind seems to lie entirely fallow and inert. It is an effort to think, and the futility of phases of thought assail the mind. The aspirant decides that *to be* is better far than *to do*. "Can these dry bones live?" he asks, and has no desire to see them revitalised.

All true seekers after truth are conscious of this unstable experience and frequently regard it as a sin or as a condition to be strenuously fought. Then is the time to appreciate that "the midway spot which is neither dry nor wet must provide the standing place whereon his feet are set."

This is a symbolic way of saying that he needs to realize two things:

1. That states of feeling are quite immaterial and are no indication of the state of the soul. The aspirant must centre himself in the soul consciousness, refuse to be influenced by the alternating conditions to which he seems subjected, and simply "stand in spiritual being" and then "having done all, stand."

2. That the achievement of equilibrium is only possible where alternation has been the rule, and that the cyclic ebb and flow will continue just as long as the soul's attention fluctuates between one or other aspect of the form and the true spiritual man.

The ideal is to achieve such a condition of conscious control that at will a man may be focussed in his soul consciousness or focussed in his form aspect,—each act of focussed attention being brought about through a realised and specific objective, necessitating such a focussing.

Later when the words of the great Christian teacher have significance, he will be able to say "whether in the body or out of the body" is a matter of no moment. The act of service to be rendered will determine the point where the self is concentrated, but it will be the same self, whether freed temporarily from the form consciousness or immersed in the form in order to function in different aspects of the divine whole. The spiritual man seeks for the furthering of the plan and to identify himself with the divine mind in nature. Withdrawing to the midway spot, he endeavours to realize his divinity and then, having done so, he focusses himself in his mental form which puts him en rapport with the Universal Mind. He endures limitation so that thereby he may know and serve. He seeks to reach the hearts of men and to carry to them "inspiration" from the depths of the heart of spiritual being. Again he asserts the fact of his divinity and then, through a temporary identification with his body of sensory perception, of feeling, and of emotion, he finds himself at-one with the sensitive apparatus of divine manifestation which carries the love of God to all forms on the physical plane.

Again he seeks to aid in the materialising of the divine plan on the physical plane. He knows that all forms are the product of energy rightly used and directed. With full knowledge of his divine Sonship and a potent mind realisation of all that that term conveys, he focusses his forces in the vital body and becomes a focal point for the transmission of divine energy and hence a builder in union with the building energies of the Cosmos. He carries the energy of illumined thought and sanctified desire down into the body of ether, and so works with intelligent devotion.

You ask for a clearer definition of the "midway" spot.

For the *probationer* it is the emotional plane, the Kurukshetra, or the plane of illusion, where land (physical nature) and water (emotional nature) meet.

For the *disciple* it is the mental plane where form and soul make contact and the great transition becomes possible. For the advanced disciple and the initiate, the midway spot is the causal body, the karana sarira, the spiritual body of the soul, standing as the intermediary between Spirit and matter, Life and form, the monad and the personality.

This can also be discussed and understood in terms of the centres.

As every student knows, there are two centres in the head. One centre is between the eyebrows and has the pituitary body as its objective manifestation. The other is in the region at the top of the head and has the pineal gland as its concrete aspect. The pure mystic has his consciousness centred in the top of the head, almost entirely in the etheric body. The advanced worldly man is centred in the pituitary region. When, through occult unfoldment and esoteric knowledge, the relation between the personality and the soul is established there is a midway spot in the centre of the head in the magnetic field which is called the "light in the head", and it is here that the aspirant takes his stand. This is the spot of vital import. It is neither land or physical, nor water or emotional. It might be regarded as the vital or etheric body which has become the field of conscious service, of directed control, and of force utilisation towards specific ends.

Here the magician takes his stand and through the medium of his force or energy body performs the magical creative work.

One point is rather abstrusely dealt with in this rule, but it clarifies, if the words are studied with care. At the close of the rule we are told that when "water, land and air meet" there is the place for the working of magic. Curiously in these phrases the idea of location is omitted and only the time equation considered.

Air is the symbol of the buddhic vehicle, of the plane of spiritual love, and when the three above enumerated (in their energy aspects) meet, it is indicative of a focussing in the soul consciousness and a centralisation of the man in the spiritual body. From that point of power, outside of form, from the central sphere of unification and from the focussed point within that circle of consciousness, the spiritual man projects his consciousness into the midway spot within the brain cavity where the magical work must, in relation to the physical plane, be carried out. This ability to project the consciousness from the plane of soul realisation into that of creative magical work on the etheric subplanes is gradually made possible as the student in his meditation work develops facility in focussing his attention in one or other of the centres in the body. This is accomplished through the medium of the force centres in the etheric body. He gradually gains that plasticity and that fluidity of the self-directed consciousness which will enable him to play on the centres, as a musician utilises the seven notes of music. When this has been achieved he can begin to train himself in wider and more extended focussings and must learn to withdraw his consciousness, not only to the brain, but to the soul on its own plane and thence re-direct his energies in the performance of the magical work of the soul.

The fundamental secret of the cycles lies in this withdrawal and the subsequent re-focussing of attention and it must be remembered in this connection that the basic law underlying all magical work is that "energy follows thought". If aspirants would remember this they would live through their periods of aridity with greater ease and would be conscious of the underlying purpose.

It might here be asked what are the dangers of this midway spot?

The dangers of too violent fluctuation between land and water, or between the emotional response to life and truth or life on the physical plane. Some aspirants are too emotional in their reactions; others too materialistic. The effect of this is felt in the midway spot and produces a violent instability. This instability has a direct effect on the solar plexus centre which was the "midway spot" in early Atlantean times, and is still the midway point in the transmutation processes of the aspiring personality. It transmutes and transmits the energies of the sacral centre and of the centre at the base of the spine, and is the clearing house for all energies focussed in the centres below the diaphragm.

The dangers incident to a premature and uncontrolled pouring in of pure spiritual energy to the mechanism of the personality. That vital spiritual force enters through the cranial aperture, and pours into the head centres. From them will follow the line of least resistance which is determined by the daily trend of the aspirant's thought life.

Another and rather potent danger is the result, literally, of the bringing together of the land and water. It demonstrates as the pouring into the brain consciousness (the land aspect) of the knowledges of the astral plane. One of the first things an aspirant becomes aware of is a tendency to the lower psychism. It is a reaction from the solar plexus centre. But this midway point can be utilised as a "jumping off place" into the world of astral phenomena. This will produce "death by drowning", for the aspirant's spiritual life can be swamped and entirely submerged in the interests of the lower psychical experiences. It is here that many worthy aspirants go astray—temporarily it may be, but the times are so critical that it is a matter to be deplored if any time is lost in futile experimentation and the retracing of any path chosen.

A clue to the significance of these words is to be found in the recognition of the following occult fact. The place where water and land meet is the solar plexus centre. The place where water, land and air meet is in the head. Land is the symbol of the physical plane life, and of the exoteric form. Water is the symbol of the emotional nature. It is from the great centre of the personality life, the solar plexus, that the life is usually ruled and government administered. When the centre of direction lies below the diaphragm there is no magic possible. The animal soul controls and the spiritual soul is perforce quiescent. Air is the symbol of the higher life in which the Christ principle dominates, in which freedom is experienced and the soul comes to full expression. It is the symbol of the buddhic plane, as water is of the emotional. When the life of the personality is carried up into Heaven, and the life of the soul comes down on to earth, there is the place of meeting, and there the work of transcendental magic becomes possible.

This meeting place is the place of fire, the plane of mind. Fire is the symbol of the intellect and all magical work is an intelligent process, carried out in the strength of the soul, and by the use of the mind. To make itself felt on the physical plane, a brain is required which is receptive to higher impulses and which can be impressed by the soul utilizing the "chitta" or mental substance in order to create the needed thought forms, and so express the ideas and purposes of the intelligent loving soul. These are recognized by the brain and are photographed upon the "vital airs" found in the brain cavity. When these vital airs can be sensed by the magician in meditation, and the thought-forms imprinted on this miniature reflection of the astral light, then the real potency in magic can begin to make itself felt. The brain has "heard" occultly the injunctions and instructions of the mind as it relays the behests of the soul. The vital airs are swept into form-making activity just as their higher correspondence, the "modifications of the thinking principle, the mind stuff" (as Patanjali calls it), are thrown into an analogous form-making activity. These can then be seen interiorly by the man who is seeking to perform the magical work and much of his success is dependent upon his ability to register impressions exactly, and to see with clarity the *forms* of the process in magic which he is seeking to demonstrate as magical work in the outer world.

It might therefore be said that there are three stages in the form-making process. First, the soul or spiritual man, centered in the soul consciousness and functioning in "the secret place of the Most High", visualizes the work to be done. This is not a sequential act, but the *finished* completed work of magic is visioned by a process that does not involve the time element or spatial concepts at all. Secondly, the mind responds to the soul (calling attention to the work to be performed), and is swept into thought-form making activity by this impression. According to the lucidity and illumination of the mind-stuff so will be the response to the impression. If the mind is a true reflector and receiver of soul impress, the corresponding thought-form will be true to its prototype. If it is not true (as is usually the case in the early stages of the work) then the thought-form created will be distorted and incorrect, unbalanced and "out of drawing".

It is in meditation that this work of accurate reception and correct building is learnt and hence the emphasis laid in all true schools of esoteric training upon a focussed mind, a capacity to visualize, an ability to build thought-forms, and an accurate grasp of egoic intent. Hence also the need of the magician beginning the practical work of magic with himself as the subject of the magical experiment. He begins to grasp the vision of the spiritual man, as *he is in essence*. He realizes the virtues and reactions which that spiritual man would evidence in physical plane life. He builds a thought-form of himself as the ideal man, the true server, the perfect master. He gradually coordinates his forces so that power to be these things in external reality begins to take shape so that all men can see. He creates a pattern in his mind which hews as true as he can make it to the prototype, and which serves to model the lower man and force conformity to the ideal. As he perfects his technique he finds a transmuting, transforming power at work upon the energies which constitute his lower nature, until all is subordinated and he becomes in practical manifestation what he is esoterically and essentially. As this takes place, he begins to be interested in the magical work in which it is the function of all true souls to participate.

Then the third aspect of the form-making process can manifest. The brain is synchronized with the mind, and the mind with the soul, and the plan is sensed. The vital airs in the head can be modified and respond to the force of the building magical work. A thought-form exists then as the result of the previous two activities, but it exists in the place of the brain activity and becomes a focussing centre for the soul, and a point through which energy can flow for the performance of the magical work.

This magical work, carried out under the direction of the soul (inspiring the mind which in its turn impresses the brain), leads then (as the result of this triple coordinated activity) to the creation of a focussing centre, or form, within the head of the magician. The energy which flows through this focal point acts through three distributing agents, and hence all three are involved in all magical work.

1. The right eye, through which the vital energy of the spirit can express itself.
2. The throat centre, through which the Word, the second aspect or the soul expresses itself.
3. The hands, through which the creative energy of the third aspect works.

"The White Magician" works "with the eyes open, the voice proclaiming and the hands conferring."

These points are or technical interest to the experienced worker in magic, but of symbolic interest only to the aspirants for whom these letters are intended.

That the inner vision may be ours, the eye see clearly the glory of the Lord, and the voice speak only in benediction, and the hands be used only in helpfulness, may well be the prayer of each of us.

RULE NINE

Condensation next ensues. The fire and waters meet, the form swells and grows. Let the magician get his form upon the proper path.

The Necessity for Purity.
Fundamental Forms.

THE NECESSITY FOR PURITY

Rule number nine is found on page 1017 in *A Treatise on Cosmic Fire*, and the comment given in the Treatise is noticeably brief:

"The rule is very briefly summed up in the injunction: Let desire and mind be so pure and so equally apportioned and the created form so justly balanced that it cannot be attracted towards the destructive or 'left-hand' path."

The reasons for this brevity may be stated to be due to the extreme simplicity of this rule in the consciousness of the man who knows, and its extreme complexity from the standpoint of the casual reader. Only the simplest and most practical of its significances is there given but perhaps a few of the deeper meanings can be imparted.

It is interesting to note that as progress is made upon the path, the forms in which truth can be given become more and more simple, whilst the meaning grasped becomes more and more wide and inclusive, and hence involves (on analysis) more and more complexity. Finally, resort is had to symbols and the cosmic plan is grasped through the presentation of geometrical forms to the inner eye of the aspirant.

The cardinal point emphasized in this rule is *purity* and, in the last analysis, purity is largely a question of motive. If the incentive to action of any kind in the three worlds is based on personality desire and brought about by the applied use of the mind, then impurity characterizes that action. If the impulse emanates from the Dweller in the form, it is then subordinated and controlled by the Dweller to the desired end. Then the characteristic is purity within the group limitations, for absolute purity only exists when entire freedom from control has been brought about. The soul is group conscious and group controlled, and (until the causal body has been overcome and liberation from its control achieved) the real significance of purity will not be comprehended. Suffice it to say that there is a close connotation between impurity and limitation of any kind, physical, emotional and mental.

But absolute purity need not here be considered by the aspirant. No one in the esoteric groups of the world has yet achieved the fifth initiation, wherein the meaning will enter the consciousness in a blaze of intensest realisation. For the majority, physical and emotional purity are the objectives, and primarily therefore liberation from emotional control and desire. Hence the constant, e'en though badly worded injunction in many of the esoteric books "Kill out desire". Perhaps a more just rendering for the immediate present would be "re-orient desire" or "re-direct desire", for a constant process of re-orientation of the entire desire nature so that it eventually becomes a habitual state of mind is the clue to all the transmutation processes, and to effective magical work.

As progress on the Path is made the thought processes of the aspirant become more potent, and the thought-forms—created with definite purpose and in the meditation work—become more effective in the bringing about of results. It will be apparent therefore that in magical work (which has ever to be wrought out on the physical plane) there will always exist the tendency towards the "left-hand path" until soul consciousness is permanently established, and purity of motive has become a habit of the mind.

May I remind all who read that the establishing and stabilizing of right habits is, for the aspirant to discipleship, a prime requisite. Those who are working in the field of planetary evolution are looking for dependable instruments, and this cannot be too emphatically impressed upon all of you. People whose emotional moods and feelings run riot or who lack physical control cannot be counted upon in an emergency by Those who are seeking helpers. People whose minds are clouded or whose inability to hold the mind "steady in the light" is inherent, are unsuitable workers in the high places of world endeavour. This remark need deter no one in these groups from pushing forward, for the recognition of a defect is a preliminary step towards its overcoming. These groups are in training and this must be borne in mind or else discouragement is apt to ensue when the ideal is enunciated. World need and opportunity go hand in hand at this time. The Great Ones, Who stand as a wall between humanity and planetary Karma are, we are told, hard pressed at this time, and I assure you that this is but an inadequate statement of the case.

The thoughts of men since the middle of the Atlantean period have steadily been attracted toward the destructive or left-hand path, because selfishness has been the motive, and self-interest the dominant factor. Part of the work of the Christ when He came 2000 years ago was to offset this tendency by the inculcation, through example and precept, of sacrifice and unselfishness, and the martyr spirit (tinctured as it oft was by hysteria and a heavenly self-interest) was one of the results of this endeavour. Seen from the standpoint of the Hierarchy, the effort has been successful, for the Christian spirit stands for re-orientation to heavenly things. Hence purity of motive and the instinct for service, which latter keynote is new from the standpoint of the past eternities.

In spite of this, however, the tendency to selfish interest is the most potent factor in the world at this time, and hence the critical situation existing between the Hierarchy of Light and the hierarchy controlling the left-hand path, or the path of control by form and desire.

Let there be no discouragement, however, for the spiritual thought, resulting in magical work, of one brother of pure intent is of far greater potency than that of many brothers who follow the tendencies of the personality. Though every true aspirant as he grasps the magnitude of the Plan and surveys the forces arrayed against him may be overcome by the apparent futility of his effort and the seeming smallness of the part he plays, let him remember that there is a steadily growing group of those similar to him and that this is a group effort. Under the Law the Great Ones work through Their disciples in all countries and never before have there been so many endeavouring to fit themselves for this function of being "Transmitters of the Purpose," and never before has there existed such a strong inner integrity and subjective relation between workers in all fields in all parts of the world. For the first time in history is there a coherent group for the Masters to use. Heretofore, there have been lonely isolated workers or tiny detached groups, and this has greatly hampered the work. Now this is changed.

I want to charge you all to realize this and to work to substantiate this group integrity and to develop the power to recognize all such workers everywhere under any name or organization and to cooperate with them when so recognized. This is no easy thing to do. It presupposes the following:

1. An inner sensitiveness to the Plan.
2. An ability to recognize principles, governing conduct and administration.

3. A capacity to overlook the non-essentials and to emphasize the essentials.
4. A submergence of personal ambition and interest in the furthering of the group ideals and
5. A steady preservation of the inner contact through meditation and the overlooking and non-emphasis of personality reactions.

These are basic pre-requisites and should receive the attention of workers and students in all groups.

It would be of value if each student would link up every day at five o'clock by an act of the will with this rapidly integrating group of servers, mystics and brothers. To this end it might be wise to commit to memory the following brief dedication to be said silently at that hour with the attention focussed in the head:

"May the Power of the one Life pour through the group of all true servers.
"May the Love of the One Soul characterize the lives of all who seek to aid the Great Ones.
"May I fulfil my part in the One work through self-forgetfulness, harmlessness and right speech."

Then carry the thought forward from the rapidly forming group of world-servers to the Great Ones who stand back of our world evolution.

This can be done in a few seconds of time wherever one may be and in whatever company, and will not only aid in the magical work of the forces of light, but will serve to stabilize the individual, to increase his group consciousness, and to teach him the process of carrying forward interior subjective activities in the face of and in spite of outer exoteric functioning.

FUNDAMENTAL FORMS

The simplicity of this Rule nine is such that in a few words the entire process of creative evolution is summarized. On the mental plane an idea takes form. On the desire plane sentient energy pervades that form. Under the evolutionary process the form "swells and grows". Through the right direction of the form and its orientation in the needed direction, the purpose of the thinker is fulfilled.

All life is vibration and the result of vibration is form, dense or subtle, and ever subtler as ascension takes place. As the pulsating life progresses its rate of vibration changes, and in this changing of vibration lies hid the secret of form-shattering and form-building. Forms are of four kinds in this era of the fourth round:

1. *The Form of the Personality*, that vehicle of physical, astral and mental matter that provides the means of contact in the three worlds. It is built in each life, the key of the vibration being set up in the life preceding the present. That form proves adequate for the average man and serves him till death. The man who is entering on the occult path starts with the vehicle provided, but during incarnation builds for himself ever a newer and better vehicle, and the more progressed he is the more consciously he works. Hence eventuates that constant turmoil and frequent ill-health of the beginner in the occult life. He senses the law, he realises the need of raising his key, and frequently he begins with mistakes. He starts to build anew his physical body by diet and discipline, instead of working from the inner outward. In the careful discipline of the mind and the manipulation of thought-matter and in transmutation of emotion comes the working out on the physical plane. Add to the two above, physical plane purity as to food and manner of life, and in seven years time the man has built for himself three new bodies around the permanent atoms.

2. *The Form of the Environment.* This is really the evolutionary working out of the involutionary group soul. It relates to our contacts, not just exterior, but on the inner planes as well. In similarity of vibration comes coherency. When therefore a man raises his vibration and builds anew from om the beginning, and alters consequently his key, it results in dissonance in his surroundings and subsequent discord. Therefore—under the law—there comes always to the striver after the Mysteries and the manipulator of the law, a period of *aloneness* and of sorrow when no man stands by and isolation is his lot. In lesser degree this comes to all, and to the arhat (or initiate of the fourth degree) this complete isolation is a characteristic feature. He stands midway between life in the three worlds and that in the world of adepts. His vibration does not synchronise, prior to initiation with the vibrations of either group. Under the law he is alone, But this is only temporary. When the environment satisfies then is the moment of anxiety; it indicates stagnation. The application of the law causes primary disruption.

3. *The Form of the Devotee.* Yes, I mean just that word, for it expresses an abstract idea. Each person of every degree has his devotion, that for which he lives, that for which—in ignorance, in knowledge or in wisdom—he wields as much of the law as he can grasp. Purely physical may that devotion be, centred in flesh, in lust for gold, in possessions concrete. He bends all his energies to the search for the satisfaction of that concrete form and therein learns. Purely astral may be the aim of the devotee—love of wife or child, or family, pride of race, love of popularity, or lust of some kind—to them he devotes the whole of his energy, using the physical body to fulfil the desire of the astral.

Higher still may be the form of his devotion,—love of art, or science or philosophy, the life religious, scientific, or artistic—to them he consecrates his energies, physical, astral and mental, and always the form is that of devotion. Always the vibration measures up to the goal, finds that goal, passes it and disintegrates. Pain enters into all shattering of the form, and changing of the key. Many lives, for millennia of years, are spent under the lower vibrations. As evolution progresses, more rapid is the development, and the key changes from life to life, whereas in the earlier stages one key or tone might be sounded for several lives in their entirety. As a man nears the Path, the Probationary Path becomes strewn with many shattered forms, and from lesser cycle to lesser cycle he changes the key, often in one life heightening his vibration several times. See therefore how the life of all aspirants, if progressing with the desired rapidity, is one of constant movement, constant changes and differentiations, and continuous building and breaking, planning and seeing those plans disrupted. It is a life of ceaseless suffering, of frequent clashing with the environing circumstances, of numerous friendships made and transferred, of mutation ceaseless and consequent agony. Ideals are transcended only to be found to be stations on the road to higher; visions are seen, only to be replaced by others; dreams are dreamt only to be realized and discarded; friends are made, to be loved and left behind, and to follow later and more slowly the footsteps of the striving aspirant; and all the time the fourth form is being built.

4. *The Form of the Causal Body.* This is the vehicle of the higher consciousness, the temple of the indwelling God, which seems of a beauty so rare and of a stability of so sure a nature that, when the final shattering comes of even that masterpiece of many lives, bitter indeed is the cup to drink, and unutterably bereft seems the unit of consciousness. Conscious then only of the innate Divine Spirit, conscious only of the Truth of the Godhead, realizing profoundly and to the depths of his being the ephemeral nature of the form and of all forms, standing alone in the vortex of initiatory rites, bereft of all on which he may have leant (be it friend, Master, doctrine or environment), well may the Initiate cry out: "I am that I am, and there is naught else." Well may he then figuratively place his hand in that of his Father in Heaven, and hold the other out in blessing on the world of men, for only the hands that

123

have let slip all within the three worlds are free to carry the ultimate blessing to struggling humanity. Then he builds for himself a form such as he desires,—a new form that is no longer subject to shattering, but suffices for his need, to be discarded or used as occasion warrants.

In these days you will need to ponder on this matter of the form, for with the entering in of a new ray, and the commencement of a new era comes ever a period of much disruption until the forms that be have adapted themselves to the newer vibration. In that adaptation those who have cultivated pliability and adaptability, or who have that for their personality ray, progress with less disruption than those more crystallized and fixed.

Particularly now should pliability and responsiveness of form be aimed at, for when He Whom we all adore comes, think you His vibration will not cause disruption if crystallization is present? It was so before; it will be so again.

Cultivate responsiveness to the Great Ones, aim at mental expansion and keep learning. Think whenever possible in terms abstract or numerical, and by loving all, work at the plasticity of the astral body. In love of all that breathes comes capacity to vibrate universally, and in that astral pliability will come responsiveness to the vibration of the Great Lord.

This summation of process and of the forms is equally true of God and His cosmic creative work; of the soul, as it builds its instrument for expression, either unconsciously in the early stages or consciously in the later; of the disciple, as he seeks to express his realization of the work through group work and the organization of his life; and of perfected man, as he learns, through experience, to centre his forces on the mental plane and from there accomplish his purpose in generating and producing those thought-forms which mould the minds of men, and embody in themselves that aspect of the Universal Mind which is needed for the right production of that immediate fraction of the Plan which his age and generation require.

All these various applications of the rule could be elucidated and enlarged upon. Our problem, however, must be kept clearly in mind. We are conscious souls, or in process of becoming conscious. We are beginning, through our meditation work and our application to study, to work on mental levels. We are creating forms continuously, pervading them with energy and sending them out to fulfill their function in line with our realized subjective purpose.

The emphasis should be laid upon the word *realized* in the above paragraph. According to the clarity of vision and the depth of the inner realization so will be the adequacy of the created form, and so will be the strength of the life which will enable it to perform its intended function.

Up to the present time the majority of aspirants in the world express the results of little and weak thought, but rapid action. The goal for students should at this time be rapid concentrated thought and slow action. That slow action however will be potent in result; there will be no lost motion, no delayed reactions, and no tendency towards hesitation. The attention of the thinker being focussed on the mental plane, the progress of his manifested thought will be sure and inevitable. When the idea is clearly grasped, the attention closely focussed, and the energy or life aspect steadily applied, the result will be irresistible appearance and potent action on the physical plane.

This thought must be borne in mind if the dangers of the left hand path are to be avoided. Let me here make some statements in brief tabulated form, which will produce a truer understanding of the words "left hand path". We are dealing here primarily with those thought-forms which man creates:

1. The left hand path concerns the matter aspect and the life poured into the form serves only to vitalize the atoms in substance. The potency of the love aspect—as wielded by the soul—is lacking.

2. The form created is constituted of mental matter, of astral matter and of physical substance. It lacks the soul contribution. Its purpose is in line with the development of form, but not in line with soul expression.

3. The left hand path, therefore, is the path of progress for substance or matter. It is not the path of progress for the soul aspect. It is the "way of the Holy Ghost" but not the way of the Son of God. I express this truth in these words as it serves peculiarly to make the distinction clear and yet preserves the integrity of substance-matter and their Unity within the One Life.

4. All forms created at every stage are either confined to the left hand path or embrace it and yet go beyond it, and follow the right hand way. This sentence provides food for thought and its meaning is difficult to gather. It should be borne in mind that all forms, whether they follow the right or left hand way are alike up to a certain point; they travel the same progressive stages and at one time in their career they appear uniform and alike. Only when their purpose appears does the distinction become apparent, and hence the training of the aspirant in right motive as a preparatory step to true occult work.

The question might be asked: What is meant by occult work?

True occult work involves:

1. The contacting of the Plan.
2. Right desire to co-operate with the Plan.
3. The work of thought-form building and the confining of the attention of the creator of these thought-forms to the mental plane. This is of so potent a nature that the thought-forms created have a life cycle of their own and never fail to manifest and perform their work.
4. The direction of the thought-form from the mental plane and the confining of the attention to that specific enterprise, knowing that right thought and right orientation lead to correct functioning and the sure avoidance of the left hand path.

This is a lesson little appreciated by aspirants. They engage in emotional desire for the appearance of their thought-form and the manifestation of the idea. They spend much time following the orthodox methods of work and in physical plane activities. They wear themselves out by identifying themselves with the form they have created instead of remaining detached from it, and acting solely as the directing agents. Learn to work on the plane of mind. Build there your form, remembering that if you submerge yourself in the form for which you are responsible it may obsess and dominate you and then the form will be the dominant factor and not the purpose of its existence. When the form controls then comes the danger that it may be turned in the wrong direction and find its way on to the left hand path and so increase the power of matter and its hold over sentient souls.

It might be briefly added that anything that tends to increase the power of matter and add to the potent energy of form-substance produces a tendency to the left hand path and a gradual attraction away from the Plan and the Purpose which it veils and hides.

All work and all created thought-forms (whether they materialize as an organization, a religion, a school of thought, a book or a life work of any kind) which express spiritual ideals and lay the emphasis upon the life-aspect come under the category of white magic. They then form part of the stream of life which we call the right hand Path, because it leads humanity out of form into life, and away from matter into consciousness.

In an ashram of one of the Great Ones not long ago, a disciple asked his master to express this truth to him in such a way that though the words might be few yet the import would be worthy of continuous consideration. His master made this reply:

"Only the Sons of Men know the distinction between the magic of the right and left hand ways and when they have achieved, these two ways will disappear. When the Sons of Men know the distinction which exists between matter and substance, the lesson of this epoch will be grasped. Other lessons will be left but this one passes. Matter and substance together work out the way of darkness. Substance and purpose blended indicate the way of light."

RULE TEN

As the waters bathe the form created, they are absorbed and used. The form increases in its strength; let the magician thus continue until the work suffices. Let the outer builders cease their labours then, and let the inner workers enter on their cycle.

Thought-Form Building.
The Centres, Energies, and Rays.
Astral Energy and Fear.
The Right Use of Energy.
The Present Age and the Future.
The Founding of the Hierarchy.
The New Group of World Servers.
Astrology and the Energies.

THOUGHT-FORM BUILDING

In Rule Ten two facts about the form are stated, which are true of all forms, and three strong injunctions are given in the following terms:

The facts are:

1. The form absorbs and uses the waters in which it is immersed.
2. As a result it grows in strength.

The three injunctions are:

126

1. Let the magician go on building his form until its adequate potency is assured.
2. Then let the "outer builders" cease from labour.
3. Let the "inner builders" enter on their cycle.

We have seen how, in the process of thought-form building, the time came when the form had to be oriented in the right direction and set upon the proper path in order to carry out its creator's will and purpose. This takes place fairly early in the work and after the process of orientation the work of building proceeds, for the thought-form is not yet ready for an independent life. There is a true analogy between the gestation period of an infant and that of a thought-form. The importance of the right placement of the child within the womb is never overlooked by a good physician, and where there is analogously a wrong position upon the path to be followed into manifested existence, death and trouble oft ensue. The analogy is close—as you well know. Birth is preceded by the "breaking of the waters" (in medical parlance), and before the thought-form brings about the desired results on the physical plane there comes too a similar reaction; the waters of desire become so potent as to cause precipitation, and the consequent appearance of the desired form of expression.

Let us take the facts and analogies as they stand and study them from the standpoint both of the macrocosm and the microcosm.

We note that the form absorbs and uses the substance wherein it is immersed. Our solar system is one of many, and not the greatest. It constitutes a fragment of a greater whole. This greater whole, formed of seven parts (or seven solar systems), is itself immersed in the waters of space, is born of desire and, therefore, a child of necessity. It draws its life from its surroundings. Streaming into our solar system from all sides are force currents, emanating from what *A Treatise on Cosmic Fire* calls the "One about Whom naught may be said". These currents embody His will and desire, express His love or attractive capacity, and manifest as that great thought-form we call our system.

In parentheses, it is well to note that this Existence is termed "the One about Whom naught may be said", not because of secrecy or mystery, but because all formulation of ideas about His life and purpose are impossible until one has completed the term of evolution in our solar system. Note, I say, our solar system, not just our planetary existence. Speculation about the Existence who, through His life, informs seven solar systems is wasted energy. On our planet, only such great lives as the Buddha, the Kumaras and the planetary Logos, are beginning to sense the dynamic impulse of the greater Whole, and even they are only sensitive to it but are, as yet, utterly unable to conceive of its trend, for it lies beyond mind and love and will. It brings into play factors for which we have no terms and tendencies which are as yet not even remotely visioned on our planet.

We have generated a term we call the ether. Occultly speaking, this is the modern way of expressing "the waters of space", which are the waters of desire, in which we are immersed. It is in constant ebb and flux, and is the stream of life, constituted of forty-nine types of energy, which pours through the cosmic egoic lotus, and (radiating forth from it) feeds with its measure of sustenance the form—solar, planetary, or human—for which it is responsible. This is dealt with in *A Treatise on Cosmic Fire*.

Man is immersed in forces which are to him as the waters of space are to our solar system. He finds himself, as does our sun and its attendant planets, forming part of a whole, and just as our system is but one of seven systems, drawn together to form the body, or manifested expression of a life, so is the human kingdom of which he is an infinitesimal part, one of seven kingdoms. These are the correspondences in the life of the planetary Logos to the seven solar systems. When he begins to sense the life of the solar Logos as it expresses itself through the seven planetary schemes we will have touched the consciousness of the planetary Logos of our special scheme, who is sensing somewhat the united vibrations of the lives of the seven solar Logoi.

Bringing the analogy down closer still, the human kingdom itself is an analogous state of consciousness to the human unit through its subjective force existence, and from the standpoint of consciousness provides "the waters of space" in which a human being thrives and grows. Again, we are met in the fourth kingdom with expressions of the same seven forces, and as man awakens to a recognition of the seven rays or types, and begins to work consciously with them, he is taking the first step towards transcending them and controlling them within his field of operation. This is now taking place. Knowledge of the seven ray types is beginning to permeate among the thinkers of the race and this knowledge was in past aeons the prerogative of the initiates of the time. Held latent in the astrological presentation is that information which will lead disciples to realization, and which will put them en rapport with the seven planetary schemes. Real developments in astrology may not be looked for, however, until the New Age is really with us and the new orientation achieved.

The form of humanity is completed. Its right placement within the womb of matter is the objective of the Hierarchy, with all the consequent implications. Note these words. The need at this time is terrific, and the soul is at the birthing in humanity as a whole. Cosmically speaking, if right direction of the forces of the human kingdom is now achieved, there will be manifested on the earth a humanity which will manifest a purpose, a beauty and a form which will be full expressions of an inner spiritual reality and in line with egoic purpose. Other eventualities can be sensed as sadly possible but these we will not consider for it is the hope and the belief of the watching Brothers that men will transcend all undesirable eventualities and make the goal. One word here, and one hint. The Hierarchy of the planet constitutes symbolically the head centre of humanity and their forces constitute the brain forces. On the physical plane are a large band of aspirants, probationary disciples and accepted disciples who are seeking to be responsive to the "head centre", some consciously, others unconsciously. They are gathered from all fields of expression but are all creative in some way or other. They in their turn constitute what might be symbolically called the "pineal gland" of humanity. As in individual man this is usually dormant and asleep, so, in humanity, this group of cells within the brain of the body corporate is dormant, but thrilling to the vibrations of the head centre—the occult Hierarchy. Some of the cells are awake. Let them intensify their endeavour and so awaken others. The pioneers of the human family, the scientists, thinkers and artists constitute the pituitary body. They express the concrete mind but lack that intuitive perception and idealism which would place them (symbolically speaking) in the pineal gland; they are nevertheless brilliant, expressive and investigating. The objective of the Hierarchy (again symbolically speaking) is to make the pineal gland so potent and, therefore, so attractive that the pituitary body of cell lives may be stimulated and thus a close interplay be brought about. This will lead to such potent action that there will be a streaming forth of new cells to the pineal gland and at the same time such a strong reaction set up that the entire body will be affected, resulting in the streaming upward of many stimulated lives to take the places of those who are finding their way into the centre of hierarchical endeavour.

The "waters of space", in which this re-orientation and reversal of tendencies is progressing, are in a state of violent turmoil. The vortex of conflicting desire in which men find themselves is now chaotic and so potent that these waters are stirred to the very depths. Students of modern history and of social order are faced with an unprecedented condition, corresponding in the corporate body of humanity to that upheaval in the life of an individual aspirant which always precedes the passing onto the Path of Discipleship. Hence there is no cause for depression or undue anxiety, but only ardent desire that the transition may be made in due time and order and be neither too rapid—hence destructive to all right ties and affiliations—nor too prolonged and so strain beyond endurance the sorely tried fabric of humanity. All new manifestations in all kingdoms in all ages must come slowly, and therefore safely, to the birthing. All new forms, if they are ultimately to carry weight and gather adequate momentum to carry them through their life cycle, must be built in silent subjectivity, in order that the building may be strong and sure and the inner contact with the creator (human or divine) and true conformity to the pattern may be substantial and unbreakable. This is true of a universe, a kingdom in nature, or a thought-form created by a human thinker.

In all form-building the technique of construction remains basically the same, and the rules and realizations may be summed up in the following aphoristic phrases.

Let the creator know himself to be the builder, and not the building.

Let him desist from dealing with the raw material on the physical plane, and let him study the pattern and the blue prints, acting as the agent of the Divine Mind.

Let him use two energies and work with three laws. These are the dynamic energy of purpose, conforming to the Plan, and the magnetic energy of desire, drawing the builders to the centre of endeavour.

Let these three laws hold sway, the law of synthetic limitation, of vibratory interplay, and of active precipitation. The one concerns the life, the second concerns the building, and the third produces manifested existence.

Let him deal first with the outer builders, sending his call to the periphery of his circle of influence.

Let him set the waters of living substance in motion by his idea and impulse, bending the builders to his purpose and plan.

Let him build with judgment and with skill, preserving always the "stool of the director" and coming not down into close contact with his thought-form.

Let him project, in time and space, his form through visualization, meditation and skill in action, and so produce that which his will commands, his love desires, and his need creates.

Let him withdraw the builders of the outer form, and let the inner builders of dynamic force push it forth into manifestation. Through the eye of the creator are these inner builders brought to functioning, directed action. Through the word of the creator were the outer builders guided. Through the ear of the creator the volume of the greater Word vibrates through the waters of space.

Let him remember the order of creative work. The waters of space respond to the word. The builders build. The cycle of creation ends and the form is adequate in manifestation. The cycle of performance succeeds and depends for its duration on the potency of the inner builders, who constitute the subjective form and transmit the vitalising life.

Let him remember that the cessation of the form ensues when purpose is achieved, or when impotency of will produces failure of functioning in the cycle of performance.

Students would do well to study these cycles of creative building, of performance and of subsequent disintegration. They are true of a solar system, of a human being, and of the thought-forms of a creative thinker. The secret of all beauty lies in the right functioning of these cycles. The secret of all success on the physical plane lies in right understanding of law and of order. For the aspirant the goal of his endeavour is the correct building of forms in mental matter remembering that "as a man thinketh so is he"; that for him the control of mental substance and its use in clear thinking is an essential to progress.

This will demonstrate in organization of the outer life, in creative work of some kind—a book written, a picture painted, a home functioning rhythmically, a business run along sound and true lines, a life salvaged, and the outer dharma carried out with precision, whilst the inner adjustments proceed in the silence of the heart.

For the disciple, the work extends. For him there has to be realization of the group plan and purpose and not simply of his own individual spiritual problem. There has to be conformity to the purpose for his immediate cycle and life period; the subordinating of his personal dharma and ideas to the need and service of that cycle. For him there has to be that attainment of knowledge, of strength, and of coordination between the personal self and the soul which will result in ability to build organized forms and groups on the physical plane and to hold them coherently together. This he does, not through the force of his own character and equipment but because that character and equipment enable him to act as a transmitter of the greater life energies and to serve as an efficient cooperator with a plan of which he can only vision a fragment. He works, however, faithfully at the building of his aspect of the great plan and finds one day when the building is completed and he sees the whole, that he has built true to design and in conformity with the blue prints as they have been carried in the minds of the architects (the Elder Brothers) who—in Their turn—are in touch with the Mind of the one Existence.

The practical application of these truths is of utmost importance. There is no life so circumscribed and no person so situated who cannot begin to work intelligently and to build thought-forms under law and with understanding. There is no day in any man's life, particularly if he is an aspirant or a disciple, when a man cannot work in mental matter, control his use of thought, watch the effect of his mental processes on those he contacts, and so handle his "chitta" or mind-stuff (as Patanjali calls it) that he becomes more and more useful.

THE CENTRES, ENERGIES AND RAYS

There are two connections in which this Rule Ten can be studied and thereby results of practical value can be achieved. We can study it from the standpoint of the work which the soul does in relation to its instrument, the human being, and we can also study it from the standpoint of organisation work and of that form-building which the disciple does in relation to his service for the Hierarchy.

Back of the outer form of a human being, responsible for its creation, its maintenance and its use, lies, we know, the soul. Back of all activity for the furthering of human evolution as well as of other evolutionary processes stands the Hierarchy. Both represent centres of energy; both work under Law creatively; both proceed from subjective activity to objective manifestation and both are responsive (in the great sequence of graded lives) to vitalisation and stimulation from higher centres of energy. Some of the factors that the disciple has to learn to recognize as his particular series of lives unfolds falls into two main groups, each of them bringing his form aspect under seven types of energy, or influences.

There is first the group of forces which concerns purely the form side, that are the work of the outer Builders, and which are the predominant factors right up to the stage of the Probationary Path. These are the forces inherent in matter itself; they deal with the body nature and might be listed as follows:

1. Physical forces. These are due to the life of the cells which constitute the body. This cell life is responsive to the cell life of the environment. Never let it be forgotten that the occultist always sees the correlation between the factors in himself and the corresponding factors in his surroundings. We live in a world of forms. These forms are made up of lives and these lives have their own emanatory and contributory influence. They fall in their turn into three main groups:

a. Those emanations, which issuing from the cells themselves and dependent upon their quality, produce a good or a bad effect, are coarsening or refining in their influence, and raise or lower the physical vibration of the united cell body. Thus, as we well know, the physical effect of a coarse brutal animal natured man will be different to that of the refined beautifying results of contact with an older soul, functioning in a body, cultured, clean, disciplined and purified.

b. Those emanations, of a purely physical kind which are responsible for that chemical affinity between one animal body and another which produces the coming together of the sexes. It is an aspect of animal magnetism and is the response of the cells to the call of other cells, acting under the Law of Attraction and Repulsion. It is shared by man with the animals, and is instinctive and free from all mental reactions.

c. Those forces or emanations, which are the response of the cells to harmonious rhythms and therefore dependent upon the cell having in itself something of that to which it responds. These emanations are little understood as yet, but will increasingly come to the fore as the race progresses. This type of force is that mysterious something which enables the physical body to recognise as harmonious or congenial a physical surrounding or environment, for instance. It is that undefinable reaction which results in two human beings (apart from all sex attraction, for people of the same sex experience it with each other) having a harmonious effect physically upon each other. This is, on the outer plane, the esoteric basis for all group relation, and it is the understanding of these emanations that enables the isolation and segregation of races to be carried forward under the great evolutionary plan.

These three might be described as the *quality* of the cell forces operating entirely on the physical plane which produce a peculiar type of physical body, the *magnetic attraction* between two physical bodies, and the *racial types*. These three factors guide the Manu of the race as He builds a new race and impresses the outer Builders with His ideas. They also guide a Master of the Wisdom as He builds His physical body at will for the carrying forward of His work in any time or place. These emanations should, in measure, be understood somewhat by all those engaged in forming organisations and groups for active service in the world. What, should the disciple ask himself, should be the vibratory quality of the cells of that body, of the individuals who compose it? What should be the quality of its attractive force, and of the magnetic effect it is to have in the world? What does the group possess through the medium of its corporate units which will put it en rapport with other groups and so make it harmonious in its relations with them? These questions warrant careful attention and should be considered by all group builders.

2. Vital forces. These are often regarded by the materialists as intangible and therefore not material at all. But the occultist regards the etheric medium as a form or aspect of matter and as relatively tangible as the outer objective form. To him the ether of space, which term necessarily includes the etheric form of all bodies, the astral or emotional sentient body and the mental body, constituted of mind-stuff, are all of them material and are the substance of the form side of life. As the basis of correct understanding, it should be noted that the cell life to which we have above referred is coordinated, influenced and vitalised by the blood stream, that intricate system which interpenetrates every part of the body, is responsible for its welfare and demonstrates in a manner not yet truly comprehended the fact that the "blood is the life". The blood is an aspect of energy, as is the sap in the vegetable kingdom.

The sympathetic nervous system, that marvellous apparatus of sensation, is closely related to the emotional or astral body. The contact is made via the solar plexus, just as the vitality, governing the quality of the blood stream, makes its contact via the heart. In the heart is the centre of physical plane existence. The cerebrospinal system works in close relation to the chitta or mind stuff. Therefore we have the following to consider:

1. Cell life-------------Blood stream----------------------- Heart centre -----------Thymus gland.
2. Sensory life---------Sympathetic nervous system----- Solar plexus centre ---Pancreas.
3. Mental life----------Cerebro-spinal system ------------ Ajna centre ------------Pituitary body.
4. Vital life-------------Seven centres ---------------------- --------------------------Spleen.

This, as you see, governs the manifestations of the quaternary, but there are other aspects of humanity which manifest through the objective form and which complete the entire man and make the seven of his manifold objective existence.

5. Self-conscious------upper brain ------------ Head centre ------------------------Pineal gland.
6. Self-expression-----lower brain ------------ Throat centre -----------------------Thyroid.
7. Self-perpetuation---sex organs ------------- Sacral centre-----------------------Reproductive organs.
8. Self-assertion-------entire man ------------- Centre at base of spine ------------Adrenals.

You will notice that eight factors are here enumerated, and it is here that many of the schools go astray. The heading 'vital life' is a comprehensive one, but it must be remembered that it relates entirely to the physical vitalisation of man through the lowest aspect of the centres. This vital life of the universe of matter enters into the human organism through the spleen.

The centres have three main functions:

First, to vitalise the physical body.
Second, to bring about the development of self-consciousness in man.
Third, to transmit spiritual energy and sweep the entire man into a state of spiritual being.

The vitality aspect is shared by man with the animals and with all created forms, and his capacity to move freely in a three dimensional world is the outstanding achievement of that aspect. The self-consciousness aspect is the prerogative of the human family. When man has evolved, when all parts of his nervous system, his endocrine system, and his centres are coordinated and working in harmonious rhythm then the highest aspect (the spiritual) makes its presence felt. The spiritual energy and not just the consciousness or sentient energy pours through Man, the instrument of divine Life, and the custodian of forces, to be held and used for the other and lower kingdoms in nature.

The above enumeration might therefore be arranged in the following order. The table gives man as he is intended to be and not as he now is in the course of his evolutionary progress.

1. Self-assertion (full development)..the coordinated quaternary..Centre at base of spine...Adrenals.
2. Self-expression (creative work)..Lower brain....Throat centre...Thyroid.
3. Self-conscious life (personality)..Upper Brain..Head centre.....Pineal gland.
4. Self-perpetuation..Sex organs..Sacral centre..Sex glands.
5. Mental life...Cerebro-spinal system..Ajna centre....Pituitary.
6. Sensory life...Sympathetic nervous system...Solar plexus..Pancreas.
7. Cell life........Blood stream...Heart centre..Heart.

The eighth point, the vital life, functioning through the seven centres and a whole system of lesser chakras and the nadis (which underlie the nerves and are the cause of their existence as the centres are of the glands) is the medium of many forces and energies—some purely physical, others related to the Anima Mundi, the World Soul, and others unknown as yet, because they will only make their presence felt later in the evolutionary programme. They will then express divinity, the energy of the Father or the highest aspect.

It should be noted that the above tabulation pictures the second ray unfoldment, and also that the self referred to is the self-realisation of the spiritual man. The lowest aspect of the vital life of God is the perpetuation of the species, and this is the result of the livingness of the incarnated Life; and the next is simply expressive of the stage when the "I" consciousness is dominant and has reached its consummation in the completed personality. Then comes the expression of the indwelling self, hidden by the personality, through its creative activity of a non-physical character. Finally, we have the assertion or full manifestation of the divine nature. This, curiously enough, can only occur when the lower spinal centre is aroused, when the energy of the material nature is carried by an act of the will up into Heaven, and when therefore the entire nature—material, sensitive or psychic, and the existence aspect—are unified and realised. Meditate upon these words, for they connote the consummation as far as humanity is concerned.

The occult aphorism: *"To will, to know, to dare, and to be silent"*, has a special significance not hitherto revealed and at which it is only possible for me to hint. Those of you who have the inner knowledge will comprehend at once.

To Will. These words relate to the ultimate achievement, when, by an act of the combined will of the soul and of the lower man, unification and realisation are brought about. It concerns the centre at the base of the spine.
To Know. These words concern the Ajna centre, the centre between the eyebrows. A hint lies in the words 'Let the Mother know the Father'. It has relation to the marriage in the Heavens.
To Dare. These words give the clue to the subordination of the personality, and have a close connection with the solar plexus, the great clearing house of desire and of the astral forces, and also the main centre of the transmutative work.
To Be Silent. This phrase relates to the transmutation of the lower creative energy into the higher creative life. The sacral centre has to relapse into silence.

It will be seen then that for the disciple the following centres are of paramount importance:

1. The ajna centre, through which the purified personality expresses itself.
2. The centre at the base of the spine, which is the centre through which complete and utter control and coordination is achieved, through the arousing of the purifying agency of fire.
3. The sacral centre, wherein the basic force of our particular solar system, the force of attraction of form to form is transmuted, and the attractive force of the soul takes the place of the reproductive creative material activity.
4. The solar plexus centre which, situated in the centre of the body and being the organ of the astral body and of the lower psychism, gathers together all lower forces and redirects them under the impulse of the soul to their higher repositories.

I realise that the teaching given here is both deep and abstruse, but it is needed for the few, and their numbers will increase as time elapses.

The complexity of the subject is also increased by the fact that each ray holds within its teaching a different approach and a different method for those souls who are found responsive to its peculiar impulse.

I give here the seven keys for each of the ray methods. These can be studied in relation to the above tabulations and in connection with the four words we have been considering. We must remember that 'To Will' is the prerogative of Spirit, 'To Know' is the function of the Soul, 'To Dare' is the duty of the personality, and 'To Be Silent' is the ultimate dharma or destiny of the matter aspect, of the animal nature in its interplay with the soul.

First Ray:—"Let the Forces come together. Let them mount to the High Place, and from that lofty eminence, let the soul look out upon a world destroyed. Then let the word go forth: 'I still persist!'"

Second Ray:—"Let all the life be drawn to the Centre, and enter thus into the Heart of Love Divine. Then from that point of sentient Life, let the soul realise the consciousness of God. Let the word go forth, reverberating through the silence: 'Naught is but Me!'"

Third Ray:—"Let the Army of the Lord, responsive to the word, cease their activities. Let knowledge end in wisdom. Let the point vibrating become the point quiescent, and all lines gather into One. Let the soul realise the One in Many and let the word go forth in perfect understanding: 'I am the Worker and the Work, the One that Is.'"

Fourth Ray:—"Let the outer glory pass away and the beauty of the inner Light reveal the One. Let dissonance give place to harmony, and from the centre of the hidden Light, let the soul speak: Let the word roll forth: 'Beauty and glory veil me not. I stand revealed. I am.'"

Fifth Ray:—"Let the three forms of energy electric pass upward to the Place of Power. Let the forces of the head and heart and all the nether aspects blend. Then let the soul look out upon an inner world of light divine. Let the Word triumphant go forth: 'I mastered energy for I am energy Itself. The Master and the mastered are but One.'"

Sixth Ray:—"Let all desire cease. Let aspiration end. The search is over. Let the soul realise that it has reached the goal, and from that gateway to eternal Life and cosmic Peace, let the word sound: 'I am the seeker and the sought. I rest!'"

Seventh Ray:—"Let the builders cease their work. The Temple is completed. Let the soul enter into its heritage and from the Holy Place command all work to end. Then in the silence subsequent, let him chant forth the Word: 'The creative work is over. I, the Creator, Am. Naught else remains but Me.'"

The vital forces, which are simply the passing through the outer sheath of the constantly moving ether of space, are of many kinds. One of the concepts, lying back of the astrological theories, is that the etheric body of any form constitutes part of the etheric body of the solar system, and is therefore the medium for the transmission of solar energies, of planetary forces, and of extra-solar or cosmic impulses, esoterically called 'breaths'. These forces and energies of the cosmic rays are constantly circulating and following definite paths through the ether of space in all parts, and are therefore constantly passing through the etheric bodies of every exoteric form. This is a basic truth and must be carefully borne in mind, for its implications are many and varied; but all lead back to the idea of unity, and of the Oneness of all manifestation, only to be known and realised on the subjective side.

The second basic idea is that the response of the etheric vehicle of all forms and its capacity to appropriate, to utilise, and to transmit are dependent upon the condition of the centres, of the chakras, as they are called in the East. These include not only the well known seven major centres but numbers of lesser vortices of force, as yet unnamed and unknown in the occident. It is dependent also upon the quality of the etheric vehicle, upon its aliveness, and also upon the interlacing network in which the centres have their place, and which in its entirety is called 'the web' or the 'golden bowl'. If this is clear of impediments and of sediment, and if its channels are not clogged then the circulating rays, energies and forces can find an easy medium and can circulate unimpeded throughout the entire body. They can then utilise those centres which are responsive to their vibrations, and can be passed on and through to forms in other or the same kingdoms in nature. Here lies the secret of all scientific and occult healing. Healers are experimenting with the etheric body and yet little real knowledge is theirs. They know little or nothing of the centres in their own body through which the magnetic or other currents must flow; they are unaware of the condition of the etheric centres of those they seek to heal and of the nature of the forces they wish to employ. All they can do is to discipline their lives, and so control their appetites that they build a clean body and provide clear channels for the passage of forces from and through themselves to others.

The third concept to be noted is that forms are, as yet primarily responsive to the forces which reach them from other forms on the planet, to the seven basic types of energies emanating from the seven planets, and also to the life-giving solar ray. All forms in all the four kingdoms respond to these many forces, to these seven energies and to the one ray. The human family are responsive also to other energies and to solar rays,—all however coloured by the force generated within the solar ring-pass-not.

The work of the occultist and of the aspirant is to arrive at an understanding of these forces and so learn their nature and their use, their potency and vibratory rate. He has also to learn to recognise their source and be able to differentiate between forces, energies and rays. For the beginner a clear distinction can be made between forces and energies by appreciating the fact that personalities affect us through the forces emanating from their form aspect, but that these same personalities, purified and aligned, can be transmitters of the energies of the soul.

Broadly speaking, the work of the human kingdom is to transmit energy to the lower kingdoms in Nature, whilst the work of the Hierarchy, in its relation to the human kingdom, is to transmit energies from the spiritual realm, from other planetary centres, and from the solar system. These energies when stepped down for transmission differentiate into forces.

Students must not get confused by the complexity of the subject. They must learn certain large generalisations, and remember that as the omniscience of the soul is tapped, the more detailed knowledge will gradually fall into place.

The other types of energy which concern the first two main groups with which the aspirant has to deal are related entirely to the form side. The third and succeeding groups are:

3. Astral energy.
4. The energy of the lower concrete mind, of the chitta, the mind-stuff.
5. The energy of the Personality.
6. Planetary energy.
7. Solar energy, or the Life Breath.

These can be subdivided as follows:

3. *Astral Energy.* Emanating from:

a. A man's own astral or sentient body.

b. The human family as a whole.
c. The astral plane in the large sense.
d. The 'heart of the Sun'

4. *Mental Energy*. Emanating from:

a. The individual chitta or mind-stuff.
b. The mentality of:
1. The human family as a whole.
2. The particular race to which a man belongs.
c. The mental plane as a whole.
d. The Universal Mind.

5. *Personality Energy*. Emanating from:

a. The coordinated form of man.
b. Advanced human beings who are dominant personalities.
c. Groups, i.e.
1. The Hierarchy of the Planet. Subjective.
2. The integrating group of Mystics. Objective.

6. *Planetary Energy*. Emanating from:

a. The seven planets. This is the basis of astrological practice.
b. The Earth.
c. The Moon.

7. *Solar Energy*. Emanating from:

a. The physical Sun.
b. The Sun, acting as a transmitter of cosmic Rays.

ASTRAL ENERGY AND FEAR

The subject now to be considered is of most practical application for it concerns the astral body—the body in which a man is pre-eminently polarised and of which he is more potently conscious than of any other body. The etheric body is really below the threshold of consciousness. Human beings remain unaware of the passage of forces through this vehicle and the nearest they get to the recognition of it is when they speak in terms of vitality or lack of vitality. The physical body makes its presence felt when something goes wrong or through the gratification of one or other of the appetites. The situation is however different in connection with the astral body for there is the vehicle of experience for the majority, and few there are who do not pass the greater part of their conscious life, recording the reactions of that body and vibrating between the two poles of happiness and misery, of satisfaction or non-satisfaction, of assurance or doubt, of courage or of fear. This really means that the inherent force and life of the emotional sentient vehicle govern the life-expression and mould the experience of the incarnated soul. Therefore, it is of value to us to understand something of what those forces are, where they come from, and how they act and react on the man. There lies his battleground and there also lies his field of victory.

To begin with, it is advisable to bear in mind that all astral energy is part of the astral energy of the solar system and that therefore:

1. The sentient body of a human being is an atom of substance in the sentient body of the planetary Logos.
2. The sentient body (a term I much prefer to the term astral, and which I shall continue to use) of the planetary Logos is an aspect—not an atom—of the sentient body of the solar Logos.
3. This in its turn is influenced by, and is a channel for sentient forces, emanating from vast centres of energy outside our solar system altogether.

If this is borne in mind it becomes apparent that man, being but a tiny fragment of a vaster whole which in its turn is incorporated into a still vaster vehicle, is the meeting ground of forces greater and more diversified than his brain is capable of recognizing. Hence the complexity of his problem and hence all the possibilities growing out of those expansions of consciousness which we call initiation. Every stream of energy pouring through his body of desire and of sentient reaction, is but a pathway leading him to wider and every widening contacts and realisations. Here also lies the safeguard for the majority of human beings, in the fact that they possess as yet an apparatus inadequate for the registering and recording of those infinite possibilities which these avenues of realisation offer. Until the mental apparatus is sufficiently awakened and controlled it would not be possible for man to interpret rightly and utilise correctly the information which his body of sensitive response could, but fortunately does not yet, convey to him.

Apart from the constant circulation through his astral body of planetary and solar and cosmic energies, every human being has appropriated, out of the greater Whole, enough of the astral energy wherewith to construct his own individual and separate astral body, responsive to his peculiar note, coloured by his peculiar quality, and limiting him or not according to his point on the ladder of evolution.

This constitutes his astral ring-pass-not, defining the limits of his emotional response to life experience, embodying in its quality the range of his desire life, but being at the same time capable of tremendous expansion, development, adjustment and control under the impulse of the mental body and of the soul. It is subject also to vibratory activity as the result of the interplay between it and the physical plane life experience, and thus the great wheel of experience is set in motion and will persist until the four Noble Truths of the Buddha are understood and realised.

This astral body has in it the counterparts of the etheric or laya centres, and through them stream the forces and energies, earlier dealt with, into the etheric body. These centres carry energies from the seven planets and from the sun to every part of the astral organism, thus putting man en rapport with all parts of the solar system. This results in the fixation of a man's life destiny, until such a time as the man awakens to his immortal heritage and so becomes sensitive to forces that are as yet—for the many—unrecognised. These emanate from the form. This is the reason why a horoscope is frequently quite accurate in its delineation for the unevolved and for the unawakened, but is quite in error and at fault in the case of the highly evolved man. Man is, en masse, what his desire body makes him. Later, "as a man thinketh so is he". The astral body, with its longings, appetites, moods, feelings, and cravings moulds the physical body through the attractive forces which flow through it, and so guides the man on unerringly to the fulfilment of his desires. If the cravings of the sentient nature are dominantly animal in their objective we shall have the man with strong appetites, living a life given over to the effort to satisfy them. If the craving is for comfort and for happiness, we shall have the man with a sensuous, beauty-loving and pleasure-loving disposition, governed practically entirely by selfish effort. So it is through all the many grades of desire, good, bad, and ordinary, until that re-orientation takes place which so refocusses the astral energies that they are turned in a different direction. Desire becomes aspiration. Thus liberation from the wheel of birth is brought about and a man is freed from the necessity to reincarnate. Then the horoscope as now understood proves futile, untrue and useless and the term sometimes used, but wrongly, 'the horoscope of the ego or the soul' means nothing. The soul has no individual destiny, but is submerged into the One. Its destiny is the destiny of the group, and of the Whole; its desire is the working out of the great Plan, and its will is the glorification of the incarnated Logos.

I would like to suggest to students that they procure if possible *The Science of the Emotions* by Bhagavan Das. It is an able treatise on the astral and sentient body, and deals with the factors that most nearly concern the aspirant as he faces the problem of understanding and of controlling his emotional nature, of mastering the technique of development, and of reorienting it to wider experience and of preparing it for the tests and expansions of the second major initiation—the baptism and the final entering of the stream. Metaphorically speaking, the experience that lies ahead upon the Path is covered in the following esoteric phrases:

"When the stream enters the River of Life, its passage can be traced for a short moment and then is lost. When the currents of the sentient life meet where the river passes round the mountain's massive foot, then one vast stream is seen which floweth north."

The symbology of this is apparent, and can be also used to depict the flow of the two currents—Ida and Pingala—and their blending in the river of energy that mounts to the head. There is the meeting place, and there the sacrifice, enacted upon the mount of Golgotha (the place of the skull).

In considering the sentient body of a human being I will probably help the most if I deal with it in terms of its moods and ordinary expressions, for it is only in dealing with its effects and in seeking to master them that man arrives at knowledge of himself and so becomes a Master. The most ordinary manifestations of astral activity are:

I. Fear.
II. Depression or its opposite pole, hilarity.
III. Desire for the satisfaction of the animal appetites.
IV. Desire for happiness.
V. Desire for liberation. Aspiration.

In these five are summed up practically most of the sentient experiences of man and we will consider each one from the following angles:

1. The cause.
2. The effect.
3. The method of direction.

You will note that I say 'method of direction' not method of control. Aspirants must learn that they are working with, and in, forces, and that right and wrong activity on the physical plane is due simply to a right or wrong direction of the force currents and not to anything inherently wrong or right in the energies themselves.

I. *Fear.* This is one of the most usual of the manifestations of astral energy, and is put first because it constitutes, for the vast majority, the Dweller on the Threshold and also in the last analysis is the basic astral evil. Every human being knows fear and the range of the fear vibrations extends from the instinctual fears of the savage man based on his ignorance of the laws and forces of nature, and on his terror of the dark and the unknown, to the fears so prevalent today of loss of friends and loved ones, of health, of money, of popularity and on to the final fears of the aspirant—the fear of failure, the fear which has its roots in doubt, the fear of ultimate negation or of annihilation, the fear of death (which he shares equally with all humanity) the fear of the great illusion of the astral plane, of the phantasmagoria of life itself, and also fear of loneliness on the Path, even to the very fear of Fear itself. This list could be largely extended but suffices to indicate the prevalence of fears of all kinds. They dominate most situations and darken many happy moments. They reduce man to a timid and frightened atom of sentient life, standing afraid before the stupendousness of the problems of existence, aware of his insufficiency as a man to cope with all situations and unable to leave his fears and questionings behind and step into his heritage of freedom and of life. Often he is so ridden by fear that he becomes afraid of his very reason. The picture cannot be too blackly coloured, for fear is the dominant astral energy at this time and sensitive humanity succumbs all too easily to it.

You ask: What are the basic causes of fear? To that question, if carried far enough back into the esoteric history of the solar system there is no intelligible answer to be given. Only the advanced initiate can comprehend. Fear has its roots in the warp and woof of matter itself, and is par excellence, a formulation or effect of the mind principle, and a result of mental activity. The fact that birds and animals know fear puts the whole subject upon a wider footing than if it were simply a human failing and the result of the activity of the functioning of the human mind. It is not incident upon a man's possessing a reasoning mind; if he used his reason in the correct way he could eliminate fear. It lies in what is called cosmic Evil—a high sounding phrase, conveying little. It is inherent in the fact of matter itself and in the play of the pairs of opposites—soul and matter. The sentient souls of animals and of men are subconsciously aware of factors such as:

1. The vastness and therefore the sensed oppression of the Whole.
2. The pressure of all other lives and existences.
3. The working of inexorable Law.
4. The sense of imprisonment, of limitation, and of consequent inadequacy.

In these factors, growing out of the manifested process itself and persisting and growing in potency during the ages, are found the causes of all modern fear and the basis of all terror, above all that which is purely psychological and not just the instinctual fear of the animal.

To concretise the matter more clearly would not help. Of what use is it to be told that fear is a quality of evil (or of matter) which colours fundamentally or characterises the astral or sentient body of our planetary Logos? What have you gained if I outlined to you the problem of the great Life in Whom we live and move and have our being as He, on His Own cosmic plane, seeks liberation and faces His Own peculiar trials and tests? How can words adequate be found to convey a cosmic struggle between Lives so impersonal and exalted in consciousness that the words his, or he or tests prove simply laughable and convey no possible aspect of truth or reality whatsoever? Cosmic evil, cosmic progression, or cosmic problems can well be left to that distant time when aspirants have taken the third initiation, have lost all sense of separateness, and—being identified with the Life Aspect and not with the form side— can therefore enter somewhat into the state of consciousness of our planetary Logos, sense His destiny, and vision fleetingly the wonder of the consummation.

Let us confine our attention therefore to man and more particularly to average man, and see whence come the waves of fear which sweep him so constantly off his feet.

1. *The Fear of Death* is based upon:

a. A terror of the final rending processes in the act of death itself.
b. Horror of the unknown and the indefinable.
c. Doubt as to final immortality.
d. Unhappiness at leaving loved ones behind or of being left behind.
e. Ancient reactions to past violent deaths, lying deep in the subconsciousness.
f. Clinging to form life, because primarily identified with it in consciousness.
g. Old erroneous teaching as to Heaven and Hell, both equally unpleasant in prospect to certain types.

I speak about Death as one who knows the matter from both the outer world experience and the inner life expression:—There is no death. There is, as you know, entrance into fuller life. There is freedom from the handicaps of the fleshly vehicle. The rending process so such dreaded does not exist, except in the cases of violent and of sudden death and then the only true disagreeables are an instant and overwhelming sense of imminent peril and destruction, and something closely approaching an electric shock. No more. For the unevolved, death is literally a sleep and a forgetting, for the mind is not sufficiently awakened to react, and the storehouse of memory is as yet practically empty. For the average good citizen, death is a continuance of the living process in his consciousness and a carrying forward of the interests and tendencies of the life. His consciousness and his sense of awareness are the same and unaltered. He does not sense much difference, is well taken care of, and oft is unaware that he has passed through the episode of death. For the wicked and cruelly selfish, for the criminal and for those few who live for the material side only, there eventuates that condition which we call 'earth-bound'. The links they have forged with earth and the earthward bias of all their desires force them to remain close to the earth and their last setting in the earth environment. They seek desperately and by every possible means to re-contact it and to re-enter. In a few cases, great personal love for those left behind or the non-fulfilment of a recognised and urgent duty holds the good and beautiful in a somewhat similar condition. For the aspirant, death is an immediate entrance into a sphere of service and of expression to which he is well accustomed and which he at once recognises as not new. In his sleeping hours he has developed a field of active service and of learning. He now simply functions in it for the entire twenty-four hours (talking in terms of physical plane time) instead of for his usual few hours of earthly sleep.

As time progresses and before the close of the next century death will be finally seen to be non-existent in the sense in which it is now understood. Continuity of consciousness will be so widely developed and so many of the highest types of men will function simultaneously in the two worlds that the old fear will go and the intercourse between the astral plane and the physical plane will be so firmly established and so scientifically controlled that the work of the trance mediums will rightly and mercifully come to an end. The ordinary common trance mediumship and materialisations under controls and Indian guides are just as much perversions of the intercourse between the two planes as are sex perversions and the distortions of the true relationship and intercourse between the sexes. I refer not here to the work of clairvoyants, no matter how poor, nor to the taking possession of the body by entities of high calibre, but of the unpleasant phenomena of the materialisation seance, of ectoplasm, and the blind unintelligent work done by old Atlantean degenerates and earthbound souls, the average

Indian chief and guide. There is nothing to be learned from them and much to be avoided. The reign of the fear of death is well-nigh ended and we shall soon enter upon a period of knowledge and of certainty which will cut away the ground from under all our fears. In dealing with the fear of death, there is little to be done except to raise the whole subject onto a more scientific level, and—in this scientific sense—teach people to die. There is a technique of dying just as there is of living, but this technique has been lost very largely in the West and is almost lost except in a few centres of Knowers in the East. More of this can perhaps be dealt with later but the thought of the needed approach to this subject can rest in the minds of the students who read this and perhaps as they study and read and think, material of interest will come their way which could be gradually assembled and published.

2. *Fear of the Future.* This is a fear that will as yet show a growing tendency to develop and will cause much distress in the world before it is obliterated. It grows out of three human capacities:

a. Instinctive psychological thought habits, which have their roots deep in the animal nature and hark back to the primal instinct of self-preservation. Savage races however, have little of this. That forward looking anticipatory state of mind is predominantly a human characteristic and is that germ of the imaginative faculty, linked to the mental processes, which will eventually merge into that intuitive meditation, plus visualisation, which is the true basis of all creative work. But at present it is a menace and a hindrance. Ancient suffering, dire memories, haunting miseries, deep-seated in the subconscious rise to the surface frequently and cause a condition of fear and of distress which no amount of reasoning seems able to quiet. Facilities of communication put even the most unimportant en rapport with the tragedies, pains and sufferings of his brother thousands of miles away. The economic catastrophe of the present time has brought about a condition of mass terror, and the more sensitive the individual the more he will react to this state of mind. Fear of the future is therefore a distressing blend of instinctual memory and anticipatory imagination, and few there are who escape this menace. Worry and anxiety are the lot of every man and cannot and will not be offset and overcome by any lesser factor than the soul itself.

b. The flashes of prevision emanating from the soul who is dwelling in the consciousness of the Eternal Now. When contact with the soul is firmly established and the consciousness of the Knower is stabilised in the brain then prevision will carry with it no terror. The picture will then be seen as a whole, and not as a passing and fragmentary glimpse as is now the case. So again, the remedy remains the same: the establishing of such close relations between the soul and the brain, via the trained and controlled mind, that cause and effect will be seen as one, and right steps can be taken to handle situations correctly and to the best advantage. Prevision seldom takes the form of forecasting happiness, and the reason is not far to seek. The race is at a point where the prodigal son is conscious of the husks and of the futility of earthly life. He is ready for a careful consideration of the Buddha's message, and he is ready because he has been devoured for centuries by war and famine, by desire and by the economic struggle. The vista he sees before him appears black and forbidding and full of cataclysmic disaster.

Yet if men carried the concept of brotherhood with all its implications into the life and work of every day, into all intercourse whether between the capitalist and the labourer, the politician and the people, between nation and nation, or between race and race, there would emerge that peace on earth which nothing could upset or overturn. So simple a rule, and yet utterly beyond the mental grasp of the majority!

c. A mass of individual distress and fear can be taken on by an individual and yet have nothing to do with him whatsoever. It is quite possible for a man to tune in on the fears of other people whilst he himself has literally nothing to fear of any kind. He can so identify himself with their forebodings of future disaster that he interprets them in terms of his own coming experience. He is unable to dissociate himself from their reactions and absorbs so much of the poison in their emotional and mental auras that he is swept into a very vortex of terror and of fear. Yet, if he did but know it, the future holds for him no hidden catastrophes. He is simply deluded, but the effect on his astral body and upon his solar plexus is identically the same. This is painfully the case now that there are so many thousands of sensitive aspiring souls, inexperienced in the handling of the world karma, wide open to the suffering of others and unable to distinguish between their own destiny in the immediate future and the destiny of others in their environment.

It is possible also for the more advanced aspirant and those upon the Path of Discipleship to contact ancient vibrations of evil and misery on the astral plane—evil long past and gone; it is possible for them to read a tiny fragment of the akashic records which concerns coming distress to an individual or a group, which they themselves may never see and yet nevertheless appropriate the conveyed information to themselves and suffer consequently.

3. *Fear of Physical Pain.* Some people have this fear as the underlying cause of all their anxieties, little though they may recognise it. It is really a result of the other three classes of fears; of the strain which they put upon their astral body, and the tension caused by the use of the imaginative faculty and the reasoning tension in the physical nervous system. This system becomes very much over-sensitised and capable of the most acute physical suffering. Ills and ails which would seem of no vital importance to the ordinary and more phlegmatic types are aggravated into a condition of real agony. This should be recognised by those who care for the sick and steps should be taken to minimise the physical condition through the use of sedatives and of anesthetics so that undue strain should not be put on an already overworked nervous system.

You ask me whether I am endorsing the use of ether and chloroform in operations, and of sedative drugs. Not basically, but most certainly temporarily. When man's contact with his soul is firmly established, and when he has developed the faculty of passing in and out of his physical body at will, these helps will no longer be needed. They may be regarded in the meantime as emergency measures, necessitated by world karma and the point of evolution of the race. I am not of course referring to the use of narcotics and of drugs by hysterical and unbalanced people, but to the judicious use of ameliorants of pain under the wise guidance of the physician.

4. *Fear of Failure.* This affects many people along many lines. The fear that one may fail to make good, the fear that we may not gain the love and admiration of those we love, the fear that others despise us or look down upon us, the fear that one may fail to see and grasp opportunity, these are all aspects of the fear complex which colours the lives of so many worthy people. This can be based upon an environment which is uncongenial and unappreciative, on an equipment which seems inadequate to its task, and in many cases has its roots in the fact that a man is a disciple, or a really big soul ready to tread the Probationary Path.

He has had a touch of soul contact; he has seen the vision and the possibility; he looks at his personality and ranges it up alongside the work to be done, and the quality of the people with whom that has brought him into contact. The result is an inferiority complex of a most powerful kind, because fed by real streams of force from above. Energy, we know, follows thought and is tinctured by the quality of that thought. The man turns a critical and disgusted eye upon his personality and by so doing feeds the

142

very things which he deplores and thus renders himself still more inadequate to the task. It is a vicious circle of effort and must be offset by a complete realisation of the truth contained in the words: "As a man thinketh, so is he." As he dwells upon the nature of his omniscient soul, he becomes like that soul. His thought is focussed in the soul consciousness and he becomes that soul in manifestation through the medium of the personality.

This is but a brief summation of the major fears which afflict humanity and serves only to open up the subject and give opportunity for a few practical suggestions.

II. *Depression or its polar opposite, hilarity.* When we touch on the subject of depression we are dealing with something so widespread that few escape its attacks. It is like a miasma, a fog which environs the man and makes it impossible for him to see clearly, walk surely, and cognise Reality. It is part of the great astral illusion and, if this is grasped, it will become apparent why depression exists, for the cause of it is either astral or physical and incident to a world situation or a personal situation. We might therefore study depression in individuals and look at its causes. It is caused by:

1. The world glamour. This sweeps an isolated unit, otherwise free from individual conditions producing depression, into the depths of a world reaction. This world glamour with its devitalising and depressing results has its roots in various factors which we have only the time to briefly indicate:

a. Astrological factors, either affecting the planetary chart and hence individuals, or primarily racial. These two factors are oft overlooked.
b. The path of the sun in the heavens. The southern path tends to a lowered vibratory influence and aspirants should bear this in mind in autumn and the early winter months.
c. The dark half of the moon, the period towards the end of the waning moon, and the early new moon. This, as you well know, affects the meditation work.
d. Psychological factors and mass inhibitions due undoubtedly to forces external to the planet and to plans, obscure in their intent to ordinary humanity. These forces, playing upon the human race, affect the most sensitive; they in their turn affect their environment and gradually a momentum is established which sweeps through a race or a nation, through a period or a cycle of years, and produces conditions of profound depression and of mutual distrust. It causes a sad self-absorption and this we term a panic or a wave of unrest. The fact that the working out may be military, economic, social or political, that it may take the form of a war, of a religious inquisition, of financial stringency or international distrust is incidental. The causes lie back in the blue prints of the evolutionary process and are governed—even if unrealised—by the good Law.

2. Astral polarisation. Just as long as a man identifies himself with his emotional body, just as long as he interprets life in terms of his moods and feelings, just as long as he reacts to desire, just so long will he have his moments of despair, of darkness, of doubt, of dire distress, and of depression. They are due to delusion, to the glamour of the astral plane, which distorts, reverses and deceives. There is no need to dwell on this. If there is one factor aspirants recognise it is the need of freeing themselves from the Great Illusion. Arjuna knew this, yet succumbed to despair. Yet in his hour of need, Krishna failed him not, but laid down in the *Gita* the simple rules whereby depression and doubt can be overcome. They may be briefly summarised as follows:

a. Know thyself to be the undying One.
b. Control thy mind, for through that mind the undying One can be known.
c. Learn that the form is but the veil which hides the splendour of Divinity.

d. Realise that the One Life pervades all forms so that there is no death, no distress, no separation.
e. Detach thyself therefore from the form side and come to Me, so dwelling in the place where Light and Life are found. Thus illusion ends.

It is his astral polarisation which lays a man open to his many emotional reactions and to waves of mass feeling of any kind. This is the cause of his being swept into that vortex of uncontrolled energy and misdirected emotional force which eventuates in a world war, a financial panic, a religious revival, or a lynching. It is this also that raises him to the heights of hilarity and of spurious happiness in which the "light deceptive" of the astral plane uncovers to him false sources of amusement, or the mass hilarity—owing to his sensitivity—sweeps him into that hysterical condition which finds its vent in unrestrained merriment and which is the opposite pole of unrestrained weeping. I refer not here to true merriment nor the proper sense of humour, but to those hysterical outbreaks of hilarity which are so common among the rank and file of humanity and lead to reactions of fatigue.

3. A devitalised condition of the physical body. This is due to various causes, such as:

a. A depleted etheric or vital body.
b. Physical disease, either inherent or brought over from another life, accidental, or due to wrong emotional reactions, or produced as the result of group karma, such as an epidemic.
c. Atmospheric. This is sometimes overlooked, but the condition of the atmosphere, the nature of the climate, the density, humidity or dryness, the heat or cold have a definite effect upon the psychological outlook.

You will find, if you study, that all subsidiary and temporary causes of depression and its opposite can be grouped under one of these three heads, and when one has ascertained the cause, the cures will become apparent.

I have dealt somewhat at length with the two first manifestations of astral force—Fear—fear of death, of the future, of suffering, of failure, and the many lesser fears to which humanity is subject—and Depression—because these two fears constitute for man the Dweller on the Threshold in this age and cycle. Both of them indicate sentient reaction to psychological factors and cannot be dealt with by the use of another factor such as courage. They must be met by the omniscience of the soul working through the mind,—not by its omnipotence. In this is to be found an occult hint. I shall not deal with the other factors listed, such as desire for happiness, for the satisfaction of the animal appetites, and for liberation, for these do not constitute for the majority such a problem as the first two. One could write at length on the manifestation and the cause of all these, but when fear and depression are overcome, the race will enter into its heritage of happiness, of true satisfaction (of which the cravings above indicated are but the symbols) and of liberation. Let us deal with the basic evils first. Once they have been dominated all that remains is right orientation and polarisation in the soul.

We will next consider the overcoming of wrong vibration in the astral body and the use of astral energy in the right direction.

We have been dealing at length with the subject of the astral or sentient body, and have considered the various wrong ways in which it makes its presence felt. Humanity vibrates primarily in one or other of these ways, and the sentient body of the average human being is scarcely ever free from some mood, some fear, some excitement. This has provided a condition whereby the solar plexus centre is abnormally developed. In the bulk of humanity the sacral centre and the solar plexus govern the life, and that is why desire for material living and for the sex life are so closely blended. The solar plexus in the animal is the brain and governs all the instinctual reactions, but is not so closely allied with the purely sex expression as it is in the human being. When the brain is becoming sensitive to the awakening mind and is not so entirely occupied with the mechanism which registers sensory impression, we shall have the orientation which will eventually raise the consciousness into those centres which lie above the diaphragm. The solar plexus will then again be relegated to its old function as a directing agent of the purely instinctual animal life. For the advanced pupil in the world, the solar plexus is largely the organ of psychic sensitivity and will remain so until the higher psychic powers supersede the lower and man functions as a soul. Then the sensory life will drop below the threshold of consciousness.

THE RIGHT USE OF ENERGY

In considering the overcoming of wrong vibration and the right direction of astral energy it might be of value here if we were very briefly to list the major energies which impress the human organism and circulate through the sentient body of man.

1. Energies passing and repassing through the sentient body of the planet itself. This is, in other words, the astral body of the spirit of the earth. This entity is *not* the planetary Logos, but a being of great power on the involutionary arc, who holds the same relation to the planetary Logos as the astral elemental does to the human being. Facts about this life will be found in the *Treatise on Cosmic Fire*. Its life is the aggregate of a vast number of lives, and those lunar pitris or lesser builders who constitute the sentient life of the personality aspect of the planetary Logos—a more potent force for good and also for evil, as we use the word "evil". Evil, per se, is non-existent, as is good in the sense of the pairs of opposites. Only in time and in space are there varying states of consciousness, producing differing outer effects. The energy of this involutionary life has a potent effect on that other tiny involutionary life which constitutes our astral elemental. The fact that protects from complete sensitive identification with this greater life is man's individuality and the potency of his rapidly coordinating personality.

Man is an individual. He is the result of other factors and the combination of these factors constitutes his protection from complete absorption in the planetary sentient life, as is the case with the animals. At death, man's astral body disintegrates and then its particles again constitute undifferentiated fragments of the great whole.

2. Certain astral energies, emanating from some planetary forms which as yet exist not in the form of physical planets, nor yet in the etheric realm, but which are enclosed within the ring-pass-not of our solar system. They represent, in the planetary sense, two groups of lives:—First, those astral shells of decaying and disintegrating planets which are to be seen by the initiate, still revolving around our sun, but which are nevertheless fast disappearing. Our moon will join their number when the complete disintegration of the outer form has taken place. Second, the astral forms of those lesser solar lives on the evolutionary arc who are taking form slowly but have not yet taken an etheric body, and will never in this world period take a physical body. These two groups are the planetary correspondences to the re-incarnating types of men, and to those who have passed over and are slowly shedding their bodies, prior to eventual rebirth, or who have completely vacated their shells.

There are two of these astral forms in close proximity to our Earth, which are rapidly "decomposing", if I may so term it, and yet have a very potent influence. On account of this close relation, they produce two types of desire or of astral tendency among men. One produces much of that instinctual tendency to cruelty which one sees in children and in certain types of men, and the other has an effect upon the sex life and produces some of those tendencies to perversions which cause so much difficulty now. Sadistic tendencies and sex perversions find much strengthening influence from these dying astral emanations. In ancient days they were still more potent, being closer to our earth than now; hence the ritualistic cruelties and the horrors, for instance, of Sodom and Gomorrah. Their power is rapidly declining and it should be remembered that they would have no power at all were there not in humanity itself certain instincts upon which these energies can work. It should also be remembered that in Lemurian times their influence was constructive, for in those days, the lesson of sex and the intelligent registering of pain had a place in the schemes of those who were endeavouring to lead animal man into human consciousness—not into soul consciousness or even into self-consciousness in those very early times.

Close to our earth, on the road to rebirth, is a great Life in process of taking etheric form. This Life, being on the evolutionary arc and not constituting the life of a decaying shell, is having a real effect in the inauguration of the New Age. This effect is twofold:—through the emanations from the astral body of this great Life the work of breaking down the separative wall of individualism which demonstrates in man as selfishness and in nations as nationalism is carried forward. Through this rapidly integrating etheric body this Life is bringing the etheric body of our planet into a state of increased rapid vibration. Reference will be found in the *Treatise on Cosmic Fire* to an avatar from Sirius who comes to bring about certain planetary effects. This Life is not that avatar but is in the nature of a forerunner—of a St. John the Baptist, who "baptiseth with water (astral emanations) and the Holy Ghost". More information along these lines is not possible, but mention is made of it, as the energies coming from these two factors must be borne in mind.

3. Astral energies emanating from the new sign of the zodiac into which we are now entering, the sign Aquarius. This sign, that of the water-carrier, is a living sign and an emotional sign. It will (through the effect of its potent force) stimulate the astral bodies of men into a new coherency, into a brotherhood of humanity which will ignore all racial and national differences and will carry the life of men forward into synthesis and unity. This means a tide of unifying life of such power that one cannot now vision it, but which—in a thousand years—will have welded all mankind into a perfect brotherhood. Its emotional effect will be to "purify" the astral bodies of men so that the material world ceases to hold such potent allure, and may in its later stages bring about a state of exaggeration as potent in the line of sentiency as that which we have undergone in the line of materiality! The final stages of all signs produce over-development of the factor on which they most potently work. At present the effect of this sign is constructive among the pioneers of the race, and destructive among the rank and file of humanity. Facts about the coming Aquarian age can be searched for in the current books on the subject and it profits not for me to enlarge upon them here.

4. Faint emanations from the sacred "heart of the sun", unrecognized by the masses but instantly calling forth response from the mystics of the race who are asserting increasingly a group integrity of a very real moment and interest. These emanations are too high to be sensed by humanity at large, but the mystics react and are drawn together by the sensing of the new vibration. Their work is then to step down the vibration so that its effects can be sensed in time by the foremost of the race. The work of this group of mystics must therefore inevitably grow, for the "heart of the solar Logos" beats now in closer rhythm with this planet than has heretofore been the case (this not being a sacred planet.) The love and thought of that divine Life is turned towards this "little daughter of a long lost son", as our planet is sometimes called in the occult books of the Great Ones.

5. Another mass emanation which sweeps the astral body of man into strenuous activity is the impulsive desire of the astral body of the fourth or human kingdom, viewing it as a whole, or as the expression of a life. This sentient body of humanity responds in an unrealised manner to all the four above types of astral energy and according to the calibre of the individual astral body, and according to the stage of development so will come response. It is in this fact that the roots of mass psychology and of mob rule lie. Also the roots of public opinion, so-called, are to be found here, but it will be long before the psychologists of the academic schools will recognize these four factors. It is with this type of sentient response that the leaders of men seek to work, moulding the thoughts of men in order to awaken desire for this, that and the other. They work with this type of sentient matter without the least understanding of the situation, and without any comprehension of the factors with which they are dealing; they work magnetically if on the second ray, and with the inspiring of fear through destruction if on the first ray. If on the third ray, they use the Law of Expediency. Thus all three work with the astral bodies of men, and their capacity to succeed is dependent largely upon their own type of astral body, and its power to attract others who are sufficiently developed to respond with adequate sentiency and then to carry forward the good work. The man in the street is therefore the victim of the astral potency of those who drive him either for their own ends or for the good of his soul—for it works in both directions.

6. The astral life, or sensitive emanations of a man's surrounding family or friends. They affect him far more than he may credit, or he may affect them, according to which side is positive and which is negative. Everyone we meet, or contact, every person with whom we live or daily consort has an effect upon us, either for good or evil. They either stir up our emotional nature in a good and high sense, and so aid its work of re-orientation, or they lower its standard so that progress is hindered and the work of drawing downwards towards materiality is carried forward. This we know well, and it is unnecessary for me to enlarge upon it here.

7. The emotional (astral sentient) equipment with which a man enters into life, which he utilises, and which he builds as life progresses. Many a man is the victim of an emotional body which he has himself constructed as he responded to the energies of the groups enumerated above. The astral body reacts to all emanations of a sensitive character in three ways:

a. *Emotional.* The astral body is swept into response of some kind to the emanations of the astral bodies—group bodies or individual—of those surrounding him. This phrase warrants careful study.
b. *Sensitive.* There is always a registering of all impressions by the sensitive astral body, even if emotional response lacks, and disciples have to learn to distinguish carefully between the two. Sometimes when emotional reaction lacks, as generally understood, there is nevertheless a registering of the originating cause which sought to bring about an effect on the emotional body.
c. *Simple reaction.* The registering or the refusal to register or respond to an impact, to an emotional impression. This can be either good or bad.

In all three cases, one or other of the pairs of opposites is chosen and the choice depends upon the quality of the astral mechanism of the man concerned. A fourth method involves complete detachment from the emotional body altogether, and a complete capacity to isolate oneself from any sensory impression at will—in order to serve with greater efficiency and to love with greater intelligence. Forget not that in the last analysis, love and emotion are *not* the same.

The practical question now arises: How is one to overcome the wrong vibration?

First:—It is necessary that one recognises what wrong vibration is, and that one is able to register reaction. A vibration, an impulse, an emotion, a desire originate in a lower aspect of the form side. They differ from an emanation coming from the soul. The two impacts upon the sentient body must be recognised as different. The question has to be asked: Is this reaction a response to personality life or is it a response to the soul consciousness? Does this impulse which seeks to sweep my sentient body into activity come from the divine Life within me or is it coming from the form aspect in any of its manifestations? Does it cause my astral body to become active in such a way that those who are en rapport with me are hurt thereby or helped? Are they hindered or aided?

A close study of one's emotional reactions brings one to the consideration of that basic characteristic which cannot be over-emphasized in view of the world's present condition. *Harmlessness.* I tell you that the achieving of harmlessness in the positive sense (not in the negative) means the attainment of that step which leads definitely to the Portal of Initiation. When first mentioned, it sounds of small moment, and to bring the whole subject of initiation into such small account that it becomes unimportant. But let him who so thinks practice that positive harmlessness which works out in right thought (because based on intelligent love), right speech (because governed by self-control), and right action (because founded on an understanding of the Law), and he will find that the attempt will call forth all the resources of his being and take much time to achieve. It is not the harmlessness that comes from weakness and sentimental loving disposition, which dislikes trouble because it upsets the settled harmony of life and leads to consequent discomfort. It is not the harmlessness of the little evolved negative impotent man or woman, who has not the power to hurt because possessing so little equipment wherewith damage can be done.

It is the harmlessness that springs from true understanding and control of the personality by the soul, that leads inevitably to spiritual expression in every-day life. It emanates from a capacity to enter into the consciousness and to penetrate into the realisation of one's brother, and when this has been accomplished—all is forgiven and all is lost sight of in the desire to aid and to help.

Response to wrong vibration will not be basically prevented by the methods of either "building a shell", or by "insulation" through the power of mantrams and visualisation. These two methods are temporary expedients by which those who as yet have somewhat to learn seek to protect themselves. The building of a shell leads to separativeness, as you well know, and necessitates the eventual overcoming of the habit of shell-building, and a shattering and consuming of the shells already built. This latter can be more easily done than the overcoming of the habit. Automatically the building process goes on until finally the aspirant has built so many ramparts around himself that he can neither get out nor can any contacts be made with him. The process of insulation, which is a more advanced practice and calls for more magical knowledge, consists of the emanating of certain energies of the vital body in a particular direction, which serve to keep other energies at a distance through what is called impact. Through this impact upon approaching energies, they are reversed and sent in another direction. But those energies must go somewhere, and should they damage another person, is not the one who reversed their direction through a desire to protect himself responsible?

The practice of *harmlessness* is the best and easiest way for the aspirant to work. There is then nothing in him which is inimical to any life in any form, and he therefore attracts to himself only that which is beneficent. He uses the beneficent forces thus attracted for the helping of other beings. This has to be the first step, and the discipline it entails and the constant supervision of all the activities on the three planes of human evolution and of all reactions bring the emotional body under the dominance of the illumined mind. They also bring about the understanding of one's fellow men.

There is secondly, a later stage wherein the disciple learns to absorb and transmute the wrong vibrations and the energies which are destructive. He has no shells nor barriers. He does not insulate himself nor isolate himself from his brothers. Through harmlessness he has learnt to neutralise all evil emanations. Now he acts with a positiveness of a new kind. Definitely and with full awareness of what he is doing, he gathers into himself all the evil emanations (destructive energies, and wrong forces) and he breaks them up into their component parts and returns them whence they came, neutralised, impotent and harmless, yet intact in nature. You say that this is a hard teaching and conveys but little to the average aspirant? Such is ever the way in esoteric teaching, but those who know will understand and for them I speak.

Another method is still more advanced and is utilised by the initiate. Through a knowledge of the law and of certain Words of Power he can command the energies to reverse themselves and to return to their originating centre. But with this method we have nothing to do. There must as yet be much practice in harmlessness and a close watch kept upon its application in the daily life.

The right direction of astral energy can be summed up in its three aspects from the ancient Book of Rules, given to chelas of the entering degrees. All true esoteric schools begin with the control of the astral body and, the chela had to memorise and practice these three rules after he had made some real growth in the manifestation of harmlessness.

Rule I. Enter thy brother's heart and see his woe. Then speak. Let the words spoken convey to him the potent force he needs to loose his chains. Yet loose them not thyself. Thine is the work to speak with understanding. The force received by him will aid him in his work.
Rule II. Enter thy brother's mind and read his thoughts, but only when thy thoughts are pure. Then think. Let the thoughts thus created enter thy brother's mind and blend with his. Yet keep detached thyself, for none have the right to sway a brother's mind. The only right there is, will make him say: "He loves. He standeth by. He knows. He thinks with me and I am strong to do the right." Learn thus to speak. Learn thus to think.
Rule III. Blend with thy brother's soul and know him as he is. Only upon the plane of soul can this be done. Elsewhere the blending feeds the fuel of his lower life. Then focus on the plan. Thus will he see the part that he and you and all men play. Thus will he enter into life and know the work accomplished.

A note, appended to these three rules says:

"These three energies—of speech, of thought, and of purpose—when wielded with understanding by the chela and blended with the awakening forces of his brother whom he seeks to aid, are the three energies with which all adepts work."

It is almost impossible to translate these ancient formulas into adequate terms, but the above rough paraphrase will convey the idea to the illumined; these rules sum up the few thoughts which the average aspirant needs to grasp about the right direction of energy, and for which he is ready.

THE PRESENT AND THE FUTURE

Thus we have seen the place that the tiny sentient unit, employed by an individual human being, plays in relation to the Great Whole. We have noted the various forms which astral evolution assumes. We

149

have also recorded some of the sources from which astral energy comes. We have found that each of us is immersed in a sea of sentient forces which have their effect upon us because—under the Law—we have appropriated for our own use a portion of that universal energy, through the medium of which we are en rapport with the whole. One of the types of astral energy upon which we did not touch emanates, we are told, from the "Heart of the Sun". I cannot, however, touch upon it at length owing to the inability of the human brain to understand it or the human heart to appropriate it until such time as the heart centre is opened and functioning. This stream of living energy can nevertheless be sensed in a large way, though not as yet appropriated in its pure essence. We call it the "love of God". It is indeed that free flowing, outgoing, magnetically attractive force which leads each pilgrim home to the Father's House. It is that force which stirs in the heart of humanity and finds expression through the medium of world avatars, through the mystical yearning found in every human being, through all movements that have for their objective the welfare of humanity, through philanthropic and educational tendencies of every kind, and (in the natural world so-called) through the instinct of protective motherhood. But it is essentially a group sentiency, and only in the coming Aquarian Age will its true nature find correct understanding and right appropriation. I touch on it here as it is one of the factors to be considered. Only those, however, whose "hearts are opened and lifted up unto the Lord" will know whereof I speak.

It is needless for us to concern ourselves with that which lies far ahead of the race. Immediate problems call for attention—problems which are personal or racial and which all concern the control of the astral vehicle. Opportunity is offered to demonstrate in chaos the potentialities of the ego or soul, and its capacity to control and dominate in its little sphere of influence. Therein lies for all aspirants at this time the peculiar effort of the coming days, and I would—for your guidance—make certain suggestions to be followed by you or not as deemed wise.

We must remember that every aspirant is a focal point of energy and should be, in his place, a conscious focal point. In the midst of the whirl and storm he should make his presence felt. The Law of action and re-action works here, and often the Great Ones (foreseeing the need of just such points of inner contact in periods of world unrest, such as the present) gather into certain localities those who are aspirants to service. They act as a balance and aid the general plan, and at the same time they themselves learn much needed lessons.

The effort on the part of all aspirants should not be to resist and repel the pressure or to fight and ward off. Such a method centres the attention upon the not-self and leads to added chaos. The effort should be along the lines of an endeavour to make contact with the higher self, and keep it stable and steady, and to be in such direct alignment that the force and power of the soul may be poured upon and through the lower threefold nature. This pouring through will bring about a steady radiation which will affect the surroundings exactly in proportion to the extent of the inner contact, and in direct relation to the clarity of the channel linking the physical brain to the causal body. The aspirant should also strive after that self-forgetfulness which merges itself in the good of those contacted. This self-forgetfulness refers to the lower self. Self-recollectedness and self-forgetfulness should be companions.

The man who aims at providing a point of contact, between conditions of chaos and Those Who work for constructive ends and order, should likewise use that most necessary factor of *common-sense* in all that he does. This involves always obedience to the law of economy of force, due to discrimination, and a true sense of values. Where these are present, time will be economised, strength will be husbanded, energy will be wisely distributed, excessive zeal will be eliminated, and the Great Ones will be able to depend upon an aspirant's sagacity and thus find a helper.

All occult training has in view the development of the aspirant so that he may indeed be a focal point of spiritual energy. It should be remembered, however, that under the law, this training will be cyclic, and will have its ebb and flow, as all else in nature. Times of activity succeed times of pralaya, and periods of registered contact alternate with periods of apparent silence. Note here the choice of words. This alternation is due to the imposition of the Law of Periodicity and if the student develops as desired, each pralayic period is succeeded by one of greater activity, and of more potent achievement. Rhythm, ebb and flow, and the measured beat of the pulsating life are ever the law of the universe, and in learning to respond to time vibration of the high Places this rhythmic periodicity must be borne in mind. The same law governs a human being, a planet, a solar system—all centres or focal points of energy in some greater Life. If such work as you are doing is to succeed (and it is largely the work of developing the ability to touch certain currents on mental levels—currents which emanate from the higher self, from your egoic group, or from the Master) definite planned conditions must be provided. Certain factors must be present. If they do not exist, then the currents are (if I may so express it) deflected, and contact fails of accomplishment. If occupation with mundane affairs is necessitated—and such periods come in every life cycle—then the attention should be concentrated on these details, and the higher contact may be then temporarily unrealised. Such attention to affairs on the physical plane is not necessarily loss of time, for it may be as much a part of the plan at that particular time as any other kind of service. Full expression and consciousness on each and every plane is the objective, remembering that each plane with its varying states of consciousness is equally a part of the divine Life. What is lacking as yet with the majority of aspirants is a synthetic consciousness and the capacity to hold and register continuity.

If emotional or mental chaos exists, then again the currents are deflected and the brain makes no record of that which may be inwardly seen and heard. If fatigue is present and the physical body is in need of rest, then likewise the inner fails to be recorded. It is the centres in the etheric vehicle which are vitalised and become active in this work of contact and consequent transmission of energy; if therefore the vitality is low and the pranic fluids are not assimilated, then the whole vibratory contact is lowered and the centre fails to register vibration and response. When again the stimulation is adequate and the other conditions are resolved into the necessary quietude, then again the currents may be encountered, response follows and a fresh cycle of receptivity eventuates. I have entered thus into explanation as I have seen many questioning, and am anxious that the process followed may be somewhat clarified. It is wise that all who work should have a clear understanding of that work and should—along lines so closely affecting their power to serve   be fully aware of each step taken.

As regards the problems occupying the attention of all of you who are living in this time of world unrest and upheaval, I have a word of cheer to give you. Though, to you, the whole situation may have seemed clouded and the horizon darkened by storms, bear in mind that when the disturbance is general, as now, and the whole area involved, then the end is near. In nature, a general electric storm serves to clear the atmosphere, and ushers in a period of sunshine and more grateful living conditions. We have had the electrical storm of the world war, and the period of gradual dispersion of the clouds has been with us, with the thunder rumbling round, and sudden sharp storms of wind and rain upsetting the hopefulness of those desiring sunshine. Those who with patience carry on the work, who keep the inner calm and surety who lose sight of the foreground of personalities, and bear only in mind the formless forces that are at work through all forms and seasons, will see order brought out of chaos, construction out of past destruction and present adjustments; they will see the setting loose of fresh life forces, hitherto shut out by the crystallising shells built by man. So hold the inner vision steadily and have that long patience which endures through the lesser cycle, because the key to the greater cycle has been held with firmness.

It might be of value to touch briefly upon certain main lines of thought which are emerging at the present time and which are the outgrowth of the past and the promise of the future.

The thoughts of men have ever been religious. There has never been a time when religion or the thoughts of men about God, about the infinite, and about the Life which has brought all into being has not been present. Even the most ignorant of savage races have recognized a Power and have attempted to define their relationship to that Power in terms of fear, of sacrifice or of propitiation. From the rudiments of nature worship, from the fetichism and degraded idol worship of primitive man we have built up a structure of truth which though as yet imperfect and inadequate, does verily lay the foundation of the future Temple of Truth where the light of the Lord will be seen and which will prove adequate as an expression of Reality.

Out of the darkness of time there have emerged the great religions. These religions though diverse in their theologies and forms of worship, though characterized by distinctions of organization and ceremonial, and though differing in their methods of application of truth, are united in three basic aspects:

1. In their teaching as to the nature of God and of man.
2. In their symbolism.
3. In certain fundamental doctrines.

When men recognize this and succeed in isolating that inner significant structure of truth which is the same in all climes and in all races, then there will emerge the universal religion, the One Church, and that unified though not uniform approach to God, which will demonstrate the truth of St. Paul's words "One Lord, one faith, one baptism, one God and Father of all, who is above all and through all and in you all." Theologies will disappear into the knowledge of God; doctrines and dogmas will no longer be regarded as necessary, for faith will be based on experience, and authority will give place to personal appreciation of Reality. The power of the Church over the group will be supplanted by the power of the awakened soul in men; the age of miracles and the disputations as to the why and how of those miracles with the consequent scepticism or agnosticism will give way to the understanding of the laws of nature which control the superhuman realm and the supernatural stage of the evolutionary process. Man will enter into his divine heritage and know himself as the Son of the Father, with all the divine characteristics, powers and capacities which are his because of his divine endowment. But in the meantime what have we? A breaking away from old established tradition, a revolt from authority, whether of the Church, of dogma, doctrine or theology; a tendency towards self-determination and an overthrowing of the old standards, and of old barriers of thought and the divisions existing between races and faiths.

Hence we are passing through an intermediate stage of change and of questioning, of rebellion and consequent apparent license. The methods of science,—investigation and analysis, comparison and deduction,—are being applied to religious belief. The history of religions, the foundations of doctrine, the origin of ideas and the growth of the God idea are being subjected to research and study. This leads to much disputation; to the rejection of old established ideas as to God, the soul, man and his destiny. Schools of thought have ever existed differing in their ideas and methods and the six Schools of Indian Philosophy have embodied in themselves practically all the basic speculations of man as to the why and wherefore of manifestation. Little which is new has been added by the occident to these six speculative schools, though the western mind, with its genius for scientific techniques and method, has elaborated the ideas and differentiated the six theories into a multiplicity of lesser propositions. Out of the medley of ideas, theories, speculations, religions, churches, cults, sects and organizations, two main lines of thought are emerging—one doomed eventually to die out, the other to strengthen and grow until it, in its turn, gives birth to that (for us) ultimate formulation of truth which will suffice for the next age and carry man to a high pinnacle of the Temple to the Mount of Initiation. These two lines are:

1. Those who look back to the past, who hang on to the old ways, the ancient theologies, and the reactionary rejection methods of finding truth. These are the people who recognize authority, whether that of a prophet, a bible or a theology. These are those who prefer obedience to imposed authority to the self-imposed guidance of an enlightened soul. These are the followers of a Church and a government, who are distinguished by a pure devotion and love, but refuse recognition to the divine intelligence with which they are gifted. Their devotion, their love of God, their strict but misguided conscience, their intolerance mark them out as devotees, but they are blinded by their own devotion and their growth is limited by their fanaticism. They belong mostly to the older generation and the hope for them lies in their devotion and the fact that evolution itself will carry them forward into the second group.

To this first group is committed the work of crystallization which will result in the complete destruction of the old form; to them is given the task of defining the old truths so that the mind of the race will be clarified, that non-essentials and essentials will be recognized for what they are, and fundamental ideas so contrasted with the formulation of dogmas that that which is basic will be seen and the secondary and unimportant beliefs therefore rejected, for only the basic and causative will be of value in the coming age.

2. The second group is as yet a very small minority, but a steadily growing one. It is that inner group of lovers of God, the intellectual mystics, the knowers of reality who belong to no one religion or organization, but who regard themselves as members of the Church universal and as "members one of another". They are gathered out of every nation, race and people; they are of every color and school of thought, yet they speak the same language, learn by the same symbols, tread the same path, have rejected the same non-essentials, and have isolated the same body of essential beliefs. They recognize each other; they accord equal devotion to the spiritual leaders of all races, and use each other's Bibles with equal freedom. They form the subjective background of the new world; they constitute the spiritual nucleus of the coming world religion; they are the unifying principle which will eventually save the world.

In the past we have had world Saviours—Sons of God who have enunciated a world message and brought an increase of light to the peoples. Now, in the fullness of time, and through the work of evolution there is emerging a group who perhaps will bring salvation to the world, and who—embodying the group ideas and demonstrating the group nature, manifesting in a small way the true significance of the body of Christ, and giving to the world a picture of the true nature of a spiritual organism—will so stimulate and energize the thoughts and souls of men that the new age will be ushered in by an outpouring of the love, knowledge and harmony of God Himself.

Religions in the past have been founded by a great soul, by an Avatar, by an outstanding spiritual personality, and the stamp of their lives and words and teaching has been set upon the race and has persisted for many centuries. What will be the effect of the message of a group Avatar? What will be the potency of the work of a group of knowers of God, enunciating truth and banded together subjectively in the great work of saving the world? What will be the effect of the mission of a group of world Saviours, not as Christs, but all knowers of God in some degree, who supplement each other's efforts, reinforce each other's message, and constitute an organism through which the spiritual energy and principle of spiritual life can make their presence felt in the world?

Such a body now exists with its members in every land. Relatively they are few and far between, but steadily their numbers are increasing and increasingly their message will be felt. In them is rested a spirit of construction; they are the builders of the new age; to them is given the work of preserving the spirit of truth, and the reorganizing of the thoughts of men so that the racial mind is controlled and brought into that meditative and reflective condition which will permit it to recognize the next unfoldment of divinity.

Connected with these two groups, the reactionary doctrinaires and the subjective band of mystics, is the majority of the new generation of young people who are part of neither band and whose ideas are largely disorganized by the recognition of both. This majority do not belong to the past and refuse to accept the authority of that past. They do not belong to the inner group of Knowers who are working at the task of swinging the thoughts of men into right channels, for they hare not reached as yet the point of knowledge. They only recognize two things: their need for freedom, and an intense eagerness for knowledge. They despise the tradition of the past; they reject the old formulations of truth ; and because as yet they stand on no sure ground but are only in the position of seekers and enquirers, we have our present state of world upheaval, of apparent license and disruption. It should not be forgotten that this world state is therefore the result of the clashing of the three types of force prevalent in the world of today.

1. That emanating from the holders with the old tradition, who, emphasizing the forms and the past produce the destruction of those forms.

2. That emanating from the inner group of mystics, who, under the guidance of the planetary Hierarchy are building the new form.

3. That emanating from the masses who belong to neither group and who are wielding force as yet blindly and often unwisely until such time comes when they recognize those constructive channels into which it can wisely be poured.

Hence the problem of this transition period and hence the necessity for the giving out of teaching which will enable the seeking aspirant and enquirer to find himself. Hence the need for the laws of the soul and for the truth as to individual unfoldment to be made clear to those who, rejecting the old tradition, and refusing recognition to the mystic, yet seek to know themselves as liberated souls. With that knowledge will come the steady growth of the Building Mystics, for when a man has found his soul and recognizes its relationship to its mechanism of expression, the threefold lower man, he automatically passes into the consciousness of the subjective life, begins to work with cause and is no longer lost in the world of effects. Then he finds himself standing shoulder to shoulder with the mystics and knowers of all time. This is the trend of the religious impulse at this time and this is the glory of the coming age.

If it is true that there is being gathered together in the background of our present world-state a group of mystics who are distinguished by knowledge, vision, and a power to work on mental levels, unseen and unrecognized by men, it could also be noted that this band is not confined to the strictly religious types.

Men and women in every branch of human thought are found among this group including scientists and philosophers.

Like all else at this time, science itself is in process of transformation, and little as it is realized by many, their work with what they call matter, and their investigations of the atom are entering into a new field. In this field the older techniques and mechanisms will gradually be discarded and a new approach and a different fundamental concept as to the nature of matter will mark the new age. Within the next twenty-five years, emerging out of the two seemingly different ideas as to the nature of the atom, a recognition of certain energy impulses will be seen and this will be based on the discovery of those energies which (playing on the atom and on atomic forms) produce the tangible concrete shapes to which we give names in the various kingdoms of nature. The truth of certain basic premises of the Ageless Wisdom will be demonstrated, such as:

1. The soul is the form-building principle, producing attraction and cohesion.

2. This soul is an aspect or type of energy, distinguished from that of matter itself.

3. The atom has been recognized as an energy unit, but as yet the energy which sweeps atoms into aggregates which we call organisms and forms has not been isolated. This the mystics in the scientific world will sense and work to demonstrate during the next generation. It is this type of energy, the energy of the form building aspect of manifestation which is the source of all magical work; and it is this energy in the various kingdoms of nature that produces form, shape, species, kind, type and the differentiations which mark and distinguish the myriad forms through which life itself manifests. It is the quality of the energy which produces the quantity of forms; it is the light which causes the emergence into consciousness of the race of heterogeneous shapes which aggregates of atoms can assume.

4. This type of energy which produces the shapes and forms and coherent organisms in all the kingdoms of nature is not the life principle. The life principle will remain undiscovered and unrecognized until such time as the soul or qualifying principle, the builder of the forms is studied, recognized and in its turn investigated.

5. This is only possible as man steps forth into a fuller conscious possession of his divine heritage, and working as a soul and in control of his mechanism (physical, emotional, and mental) can work consciously en rapport with the soul in all forms.

This will be possible only as the race grasps the above hypothesis, and recognizes it as a possibility and seeks to demonstrate the fact of the soul-factor lying back of its structure or body of manifestation, or equally, seeks to disprove it. All great scientists and workers in the realm of objective nature have worked as souls, and all the most amazing of the developments in the realm of physics and chemistry, as in other departments of human knowledge, have been made when the worker in any particular field has launched forth with faith in some hypothesis he has formed, and has investigated and progressed his work forward stage by stage until he has contacted an aspect of the truth hitherto unformulated by man. Then, having through the use of his intuition entered into a new realm of thought, he takes the knowledge there discovered and formulates it in such way by theory, principle, experiment and mechanical contrivance that it becomes the possession of the group, and in due time is understood and utilized by the world. But in its genesis it has been mystical work and based on a mystical intuition.

It might be noted here that three great discoveries are imminent and during the next two generations will revolutionize modern thought and life.

One is already sensed and is the subject of experiment and investigation, the releasing of the energy of the atom. This will completely change the economic and political situation in the world, for the latter is largely dependent upon the former. Our mechanical civilization will be simplified, and an era ushered in which will be free from the incubus of money (its possession and its non-possession), and the human family will recognize universally its status as a bridging kingdom between the three lower kingdoms of nature and the fifth or spiritual kingdom. There will be time and freedom for a soul culture which will supersede our modern methods of education, and the significance of soul powers and the development of the superhuman consciousness will engross the attention of educators and students everywhere.

A second discovery will grow out of the present investigations as to light and color. The effect of color on people, animals and units in the vegetable kingdom will be studied and the result of those studies will be the development of etheric vision or the power to see the next grade of matter with the strictly physical eye. Increasingly will people think and talk in terms of light, and the effect of the coming developments in this department of human thought will be triple.

a. People will possess etheric vision.
b. The vital or etheric body, lying as the inner structure of the outer forms, will be seen and noted and studied in all kingdoms of nature.
c. This will break down all barriers of race and all distinctions of color; the essential brotherhood of man will be established. We shall see each other and all forms of divine manifestation as light units of varying degrees of brightness and shall talk and think increasingly in terms of electricity, of voltage, of intensity and of power. The age and status of men, in regard to the ladder of evolution, will be noted and become objectively apparent, the relative capacities of old souls, and young souls will be recognized, thereby re-establishing on earth the rule of the enlightened.

Note here, that these developments will be the work of the scientists of the next two generations and the result of their efforts. Their work with the atom of substance, and their investigations in the realm of electricity, of light and of power, must inevitably demonstrate the relation between forms, which is another term for brotherhood, and the fact of the soul, the inner light and radiance of all forms.

The third development, which will be the last probably to take place, will be more strictly in the realm of what the occultists call magic. It will grow out of the study of sound and the effect of sound and will put into man's hands a tremendous instrument in the world of creation. Through the use of sound the scientist of the future will bring about his results; through sound, a new field of discovery will open up; the sound which every form in all kingdoms of nature gives forth will be studied and known and changes will be brought about and new forms developed through its medium. One hint only may I give here and that is, that the release of energy in the atom is linked to this new coming science of sound.

The significance of what has happened in the world during the last century in the realm of sound is not appreciated yet nor understood. Terrific effects are however being produced by the unbelievably increased noise and sound emanating from the planet at this time. The roar of machines, the rumble of the transportation mechanisms in all parts of the world—trains, vessels and airplanes—the focussing of the sounds of men in such congested areas as the great cities, and, at this time, the universal use of the radio bringing musical sounds into every home and into street life are producing effects upon the bodies of men and upon all forms of life everywhere which will become apparent only as time elapses.

Some forms of life in the animal kingdom, but primarily in the vegetable kingdom, will disappear and the response of the human mechanism to this world of sound, uproar and music in which it will increasingly find itself will be most interesting.

These three developments will usher in the new age, will produce in this transition period the needed changes, and will inaugurate a new era wherein brotherhood will be the keynote, for it will be a demonstrated fact in nature. It will be an age wherein men will walk in the light, for it will be a world of recognized inner radiance, wherein the work of the world will be carried forward through the medium of sound, and eventually through the use of words of power and the work of the trained magician. These trained workers in substance, understanding the nature of matter, seeing always in terms of light and comprehending the purpose of sound will bring about those structural changes and those material transformations which will establish a civilization adequate for the work of the coming race. This work will be that of the conscious unification of the soul and its vehicle of manifestation. Those cultural methods also which will take the undeveloped of the race and carry them forward to a better manifestation, and a truer expression of themselves will be established and this it is the privilege of the coming generation of scientific investigators to bring about.

The outstanding characteristic, however, of the coming cycle will be an outgrowth of psychology. It will be the emergence of a new factor from the standpoint of the modern psychologist of the materialistic school and will involve the recognition of the soul.

The mechanistic school of psychologists has served and is serving an invaluable purpose, and the findings of the behaviorists are sound in fact, though erroneous in conclusion. They serve as a needed brake upon the more speculative and mystical school, which is dignified by the name of introspectionist. Like much else in the world at this time, from two great lines of thought, such as the mechanistic and the introspective or subjective mentioned above, a third will manifest which will embody the truth in both positions and duly adjust them to each other. On a larger scale this is working out in the fusing of occident and orient, of mysticism and occultism. We have no quarrel with either, but in the evolution of thought the main trends of ideas at this time are rapidly approaching each other and from them a synthesis will emerge which will prove an adequate platform upon which the coming cycle may make its stand.

It might be of value here if we noted the tendency of three lines of thought, roughly speaking in the field of psychology.

1. The mechanistic, laying the emphasis upon structure, ascribing the reactions of the human organism, mental, emotional, and physical—entirely to the material aspect, and regarding the structure as responsible for and giving rise to all the lines of conduct and characteristics which man displays, both abnormal and normal.

2. The introspective school, positing a self or a conscious something which is responsible for conditions and which, as has sometimes been said, is "aware of awareness". This school of psychologists recognizes the structure but goes further and regards certain aspects of conduct, and certain reactions and problems as insoluble under the pure mechanistic process. They approach more nearly the occult position, but do not go so far.

3. Then there are what I might call the vitalists, or that group of psychologists who, admitting the fact of the structure, yet regard it as subjected to the influences of energies and forces emanating from an

outer environment. These are the energies of a wider nature than those arising entirely within a man's own self, and number among them the great basic urges for which nature itself is responsible and which can be seen and felt in units of organic life, other than the human.

The truth which is safeguarded in all these schools is one truth and each aspect of it is correlated.

There is a mechanism through which the real man functions, and there is a structure which he has built up in conformity to the laws of nature and which he can learn to use and control. But, in accordance with the more subjective and speculative school he must learn to differentiate between himself, as the conscious centre of awareness, the "I" upon the throne of intelligence, and the apparatus through which he can contact the outer world. When the "I", the user of the mechanism, can do this he becomes aware of another fact and that is that not only is he a generator and user of energy, and the director of a quota of vitality which is his own, but that there are energies and forces in nature and the planet, and also extra-planetary or cosmic, to which he can also respond and which he can learn to use and adapt. The three present schools are therefore, in embryo, custodians of these three factors. Under the present system of quarrel and separation, these three schools are occupied largely with disproving each other's theories. But they are all three of them correct in their facts though wrong in their deductions. They all three need each other and from a blending of the three presentations there will emerge the fourth, which will be nearer the truth than any of the separated three.

When we come to the consideration of other basic trends in the world of current thought it becomes apparent that one of the most dominant is the increasing emphasis laid upon group consciousness, or environal awareness. This has been recognized by the man in the street as a sense of responsibility and indicates in the individual an egoic vibration. It is one of the first signs that the soul is beginning to use its mechanism. No longer does the man live in the interests of the separated self but he begins to realize the need for adjustment to and in the condition of his neighbor. He assumes the duty of being in a very real sense his brother's keeper, and realizes that in reality progress, contentment, peace of mind and prosperity do not exist for him apart from that of his brother. This realization is steadily expanding from the individual to the state and nation, from the family unit to the world, and hence the big organizations, fraternities, clubs, leagues and movements which have for their objective the uplift and welfare of men everywhere. The necessity of giving instead of getting is growing in the racial consciousness and the recognition of certain of the basic concepts connected with brotherhood is steadily growing. Brotherhood as a fact in nature is as yet largely a theory, but brotherhood as an ideal is now fashioned in the racial consciousness.

One of the great schools of thought or trend of ideas which is destined to pass away is that of the current philosophies as we now know them. Philosophy in its technical sense as the love of wisdom will increase as men understand increasingly the meaning of wisdom and become epochally wiser, but the present schools of philosophy have nearly served their purpose. This has been the formulation of ideas concerning God and His relation to man, concerning divinity, eschatology and spiritual relationships.

The last great gestures of the philosophical schools remain yet to be made. Their place will be taken in later centuries by those who will in deed and in truth be cosmologists, for once the Word of Mankind is understood and grasped and the significance of the individual appreciated, the Word of the Cosmos will receive due and more correct attention, and the laws and nature of that great Being in Whom we live and move and have our being will be studied. The cosmic Christ can never be known by any except the individual Christ.

Man, as we shall see as we proceed, is on the verge of establishing his divinity. Evolution has carried forward the perfecting of the mechanism to such an extent that it is now a coordinated integrated organism, a usable structure and ready for the divine user. In the course of the next few decades the fact of the soul will be established, and the work of the introspective thinkers, the mystics and occult students will be carried forward to the point where soul force will be established as a racial concept, and the laws of the soul will be recognized as superseding, though not abrogating (for the lesser is ever included in the greater) the laws of man. This in the sense that the law is ever kept by a manifesting soul, for, since there is no inclination to break it, there is no tendency on his part to infringe it.

This growing conviction as to the soul as the self is evidenced by the opposition to the theory called forth by the schools of thought which emphasize the dominance of matter and trace all phenomena, objective and subjective, to the activity of matter. Through the wrestling of those holding differing points of view truth emerges into the light, just as in a larger case, spirit "mounts on the shoulders of matter" back to its original position, plus the gain in quality which is the result of the experience. This being so, knowledge will take the place of theory, and direct evidence that of speculation. The theorising of men as to their divine nature must shortly give place to conviction and their philosophising to direct investigation of the soul. That which is recognized and admitted, even if not understood, is the object of attention and investigation and the day will dawn before so very long when an experimental science of the soul will have its place in the universities and public endowments and not the proving of the soul, but an analysis of its nature, purposes, and life will receive an attention equal to that now gives by modern scientists in their varying branches to the mechanism the soul seeks and eventually will use, for naught can arrest that great evolutionary development.

Certain words of warning I would like to give and also a summarisation of much earlier said:

First, hold not on to the form no matter what it be. All forms are but experiments, and reach the point where they are in balance—to be either discarded or vivified.

Secondly, remember that all personalities (your own included) have their periods of ebb and flow, under the law. The periods of ebb in the case of those holding prominent position cause at times consternation to all those who follow their personalities, and not the inner God within their own heart.

Thirdly, bear in mind, also, that just as in the individual life there come the periods wherein the vision is obscured, the valley is traversed, and the stars shut out by the fog, so in connection with groups will the same be seen. But bear equally in mind that after the valley is crossed (for all aspirants and for all truly spiritual groups) the Mount of Initiation is seen and ascended; after obscuration succeeds the vision, and after night comes the day. In the great cycles affecting cosmic groups this also can be seen; in the lesser cycles, controlling the races, the same eventuates and the same law persists in all the lesser groups down to the groups of tiny lives that hold sway in the vehicles of man. This needs emphasis.

Fourthly, do not permit yourselves to be discouraged. Discouragement is due to three causes. Paramountly it is due to the lowering of the vitality of the bodily organism. When such is the case, the astral body makes too strong a demand upon the physical, and in the endeavour to respond and in the sensed incapacity to do so adequately, lies one cause of the sense of discouragement. This often attacks those of you who are finely organised in the physical vehicle. The cure for this type of discouragement is obvious, is it not? Rest and relaxation build anew, and give time for nature to adjust the trouble. The sun too revitalises with prana and this should be considered. After all, sound common sense is the special requirement, and also the realisation that one's work is adjusted to one's capacity, and not to the overwhelming need. Meditate on this.

Another basis for discouragement is the over-development of the concrete mind, which in its turn makes too great a demand upon the emotional nature, and consequently again upon the physical. Too great a capacity to see all around a subject, too disproportionate a comprehension of the world's need, and too quick an apprehension of the many issues involved in connection with some particular matter produce a violent vibration in the astral body. This leads to a shattering of the physical vehicle, and the result sensed we term discouragement. It is here that a sense of proportion must be cultivated, that the faculty of wise balancing enters, and that mental equilibrium must be achieved. The cure lies in the realisation that time, eternity, evolution (call it what you will) brings all things to pass, and that everything does not depend upon individual effort. It is possible for wise souls to hasten the good work, but the end, nevertheless, is sure. If the wise souls are not forthcoming yet the force of evolution brings all things to pass, even if more slowly. Do not forget this, but when discouragement from mental sources settles down upon you, in quietness adjust yourself, and in contemplation sense the ultimate achievement of that great factor, Time.

A third cause lies in more occult realms, and is due to the balancing of the pairs of opposites. When the pendulum swings—as it must and does—towards that which we call dark, evil, and undesirable, it produces in those of you who are oriented towards the light a tension which results in discomfort in all the bodies, and is specially sensed as depression by the physical body. The more sensitive your body, the greater your responsiveness to this form of temptation. It is one of the things which specially hinders the aspirant. It renders him negative and receptive from the form side, and slows down his vibration. It prevents achievement and his service to the world suffers in consequence. The cure for discouragement does not lie in cultivating a violent counter vibration. It lies in the wise use of the mental body, and in a capacity to reason logically and to see the cause of the conditions, which lies either in your own personality or in your environment. Thus poise will he attained. It lies also in the appreciation of Time as a solvent as aforesaid. It lies also in the stilling of the concrete mind and a subsequent linking up with the soul and, via the soul, with the egoic group and consequently with the Master. It must never be forgotten that contact with the Master is made in this order, and that he who comes more and more under the guidance of the soul is he who more and more enters into the consciousness of his Master.

Then having with unselfish intent linked up with the Master, there comes next the deliberate and concentrated effort to work with pure dispassion, and with no desire to see the fruit of action. This process, long continued and pursued with patience, will result eventually in the attaining of an equilibrium which nothing can disturb.

I would like to state that there are five things which those who choose the path of occultism need to cultivate, and that the group should specially seek to attain. They are as follows:

1. Consecration of motive.
2. Utter fearlessness.
3. The cultivation of the imagination, balanced wisely by the reasoning faculty.
4. A capacity to weigh the evidence wisely, and to accept only that which is compatible with the highest instinct and intuition.
5. A willingness to experiment.

These five tendencies, coupled with purity of life and regulation of thought will lead to the sphere of achievement. Remember too that it is not purposed that you should find out all the knowable, but only just as much of it as may be employed wisely for the illumination of the race and of those whom you can each, in your own place, influence.

A real problem, as you all realise, lies in the achieving of utter fearlessness. All fear, doubt, and worry have to be eliminated. If this can be done the development of the inner point of contact and the knowledge of how to tap the sources of inspiration will increase in a wonderful manner. So many close the sources of information through an uncontrolled emotional nature. The astral body can be controlled. How?

1. By direct inhibition. This method can be used to advantage by beginners, but it is not the best method to follow. It reacts on the physical body, leads to congestion in the astral body, and to a similar condition in the etheric vehicle. It often produces headache, congestion of the liver and other disorders.

2. By a direct realisation of the issues at stake and the consciousness that, for a pupil of the Master, nothing comes to pass but what can lead to increased knowledge and development, and greater usefulness in service. Fear with many is not based on timidity (a paradoxical statement!) but is often based on a mental condition, such as pride. Those who are becoming polarised in the mental body, find their fears allied to the intellect. They are therefore harder to overcome than the fears of a person polarised in the astral body. The latter can bring the intellect to bear on the elimination of fear in the astral body. The mental types have to call directly on the Ego, for always the higher must be called in to deal with the lower. Hence the necessity for always keeping the channel clear. Do not crush out fear. Force it out by the dynamic power of substitution. This leads to my third suggestion that students in the group should cure the fear habit by—

3. A direct method of relaxation, concentration, stillness and flushing the entire personality with pure white light. Proceed in the following manner:

You are, we will say, in a state of panic; suggestions of great unpleasantness are crowding in; your imagination is running riot, and your mind enforces the riot. Forget not that the fears of an emotional person are not so potent as yours. Having a strong mental body, you clothe your fear reactions with mental matter, highly vitalised, which causes a powerful thoughtform to be created. This circulates between you and the feared event. Realising this you will proceed to seek quietness. You will relax your physical body, endeavour to quiet your astral body as far as may be, and to steady the mind. Then visualizing yourself (the personality), the soul and the Master—He, as the apex of the triangle,—you will with deliberation call down a stream of pure white light, and, pouring it through your lower vehicles, you will cleanse away all that hinders. Continue this process until you realise that the needed work is accomplished. At first you may have to do it many times. Later just once will suffice, and later still the whole process may be needless, for you will have achieved conquest.

This applies to the fears connected with the personality. You use the love aspect, flooding yourself with love and light. The legitimate fears which arise from things connected with the circumstances of the work to be done, and from the knowledge of materialised obstructions to the work must be treated somewhat differently. Here again a definite method must be followed:

Still the physical body.
Quiet by temporary inhibition the astral body.

Link up with the Ego, and definitely reason out the proper method of procedure in meeting the difficulty. Having exhausted all the higher rational methods and having clearly seen your course of action, you then—

Raise your vibration as high as may be and call down, from intuitional levels, added light on the difficulty. If your intuition and reasoning faculty produce harmony and thus show the way out, then proceed. As an occult fact past all controversy, you know that naught can now happen but what is for the best. You are sure of guidance, and he who sees thus the end from the beginning makes no error.

A third class of fears—which aspirants contact more and more as they grow in strength and usefulness in service—is based on the realisation of the forces that are working against the Plan and hindering the work to be done. Occult attacks and occult powers, warring militantly against the aspirant will occur; they may make their power felt in one or other of the vehicles and—in rare cases—where the aspirant is important enough, on all at once. Sometimes they will be attacks directed against the individual worker, sometimes against groups of workers. To counter them you employ the first method with the following additions and changes. You link yourself up either as an individual or forming one of a group with your own soul and *with the Lodge of Masters,* not simply with your own Master, but with the Brotherhood for which you are working. Then when stillness has been achieved, you visualise those Masters of whom you know, and raising your vibration higher still, you connect up, if possible, with the Chohans, with the Christ and the Manu, according to the line, religious or political, with which you may be working, and along which the attack will come. You then pour through the linking chain, and through all the vehicles, a stream of violet light. This method is only for use when the need is dire and the necessity great. The reason for caution lies in the etheric vehicle, which responds most violently to the colour violet.

With these precautions in mind the fear vibration can be faced and eventually eliminated. Fears fall into two categories for the worker:—Fear of what the future holds, and, secondly, doubt as to the outcome of any effort. With most people it is a combination of the two. Most aspirants have no basic doubt as to the ultimate issue, but they do doubt at times the working out of those issues in the present time, and they shrink back also from the path of endeavour, knowing—and rightly knowing—that it leads through trial and loneliness to the Feet of the Hierophant. They are likewise distressed by troubles and high vibrations which seem to emanate from high spiritual sources. Strong vibrations will come with ever increasing frequency, and as the race progresses in evolution the vibrations will wax stronger and their reactions must be dealt with in wisdom.

Two things manifest when the spiritual vibration is exceedingly potent. All good aspirations and synchronous high vibrations are stimulated and, secondly, all that we term "evil" is likewise stimulated. Aspirants should bear this carefully in mind. There may demonstrate such a factor as a crime wave, but there will also demonstrate an increasing number of groups that stand for spiritual endeavor and high aspiration. The effect of the heightening of the vibration on you, the aspirant, may manifest in various ways also. It may result in bodily fatigue and this must be dealt with—not so much by sleep and by rest, though a just proportion of them is necessary—but above all by a change of vibration, of recreation and of amusement. Secondly, it results frequently in a profound depression, in an utter sinking of the heart as the future is faced. Face that future, however, and remember that what the future holds is not revealed, but that "joy cometh in the morning". It results also in a sensitiveness of the astral body that is, perhaps, even more hard to bear. This must be dealt with by the individual as best he may, bearing in mind the suggestions that I have given him. It results also in a permanent stimulation of the atoms in the various vehicles and their coherent, stabilized vibration. It lifts a little nearer to the goal, though perhaps the aspirant may not realize it.

Everything depends upon the pupil's ability to grasp the inner meaning of all events. His entire progress upon the Path rests upon his attitude in making the teaching his own. It is only as we transmute the lessons on the inner planes into practical knowledge that they become part of our own experience and are no longer theoretical. Expansion of consciousness should be an ever increasing practical experience. Theories are of no value until we have changed them into fact. Hence the value of meditating on an ideal. In the meditation our thoughts vibrate temporarily to the measure of the conception, and in time that vibration becomes permanent.

Those who, with open eyes, enter on occult training need indeed to count the cost. The reward at the end is great, but the path is rough and the true occultist walks it alone. The capacity to stand alone, to assume responsibility, and then to carry all through single-handed, and to brave evil for the sake of the good achieved is the mark of a White Brother. Be prepared then for loneliness, for dangers of a dim and obscure character, and expect to see your life spent for no reward that touches the personality. It is only as the consciousness expands, and one finds one's true position in the cosmic whole that the reward becomes apparent; but cease from fear, and know that the personality is only temporary, and what matter if it suffer? Some good gained for the universal Brotherhood, some law explained and demonstrated in the life of every day, may make the Master say eventually (yes, eventually, after all is over) well done! Let your eyes therefore look straight on. Turn not to the right hand nor to the left. The path leads upward and on to greater rapidity of vibration and to greater sensitiveness. Seek the point of balance in your work and keep that balance, for the years hold much work, much pressure and much suffering.

Are you strong enough to see the world's woe, to see disaster and yet keep joyful? Can you be a partner in the work of furthering the evolution of the race and see the necessity for trouble and for discipline and yet not move to stem the tide of sorrow? Picked and tried souls are being trained all over the world at the present time. The Masters are overwhelmed with the work and Their time is over-occupied. They give what They can but on the individual aspirant depends the use made of that which is given.

Those of us who watch and guide on the inner side of life realize more than perhaps you who bear the burden and heat of physical plane existence know. We know your physical disabilities and some day may be able to help definitely in the building up of strong bodies for world service. Now such is the astral miasma—it is well nigh impossible for you, our struggling brethren, to have good health; the karma of the world prohibits it. The astral corruption and the foul cesspools of the lower levels of the mental plane infect all, and lucky is he who escapes. We watch with tenderness all of you, who, with weak and sensitive bodies, struggle, work, fight, fail, continue and serve. Not one hour of service, given in pain and tension, not one day's labor followed with racked nerves, with head tired and with heart sick, is allowed to pass unnoticed. We know and we care, yet, we may do naught that you, struggling in the field of the world, can do of that which is needed. The world's karma engulfs each of you at this epoch. If you could but realize it, the time is short, and rest, joy and peace are on their way.

The half-gained victory, the days lived through with a certain measure of success, yet with an unachieved ideal, the minutes of exhaustion of soul and body when the emptiness of everything, even of service itself, seems the only noticeable thing, the weeks and months of endeavor and of struggle against apparently insuperable odds, against the stupendous power of the forces of evolution, against the roaring tide of the world's ignorance,—all are known. Take comfort in the assurance that love rules all; take courage from the realization that the Hierarchy stands.

Those who are to teach the world more about the Masters and who are being trained to be focal points of contact are put through a very drastic disciplining. They are tested in every possible way and taught much through bitter experience. They are taught to attach no importance to recognition. They are trained not to judge from the appearance but from the inner vision. Capacity to recognize the Master's purpose and the ability to love are counted of paramount importance. Aspirants who seek to be chosen for work as disciples must lose all desire for the things of self and must be willing at any cost to pay the price of knowledge. If proof is to be given to the world of the subjective realm of reality it will be bought with the heart's blood, for only "in the blood of the heart" can power be safely gained and wisely wielded. As you go on and, as aspirants, study the hidden laws of nature, you will realize the need for the price paid. The spiritual unfoldment of the disciple's character must keep pace with his inner knowledge. This knowledge grows in three ways:

1. By definite expansions of consciousness, which open up to the disciple a realization of the points to be attained. This produces in his mind a formulation of what lies ahead to be grasped and is the first step towards acquirement. An aspirant is definitely taken on the inner planes and shown by a more advanced chela what is the work to be done, much in the same way as a pupil is shown by his master the lesson to be learned.

2. The next step is the mastering of the lesson and the working out in meditation and experiment of the truths sensed. This is a lengthy process, for all has to be assimilated and made part and parcel of the disciple's very self before he can go on. It resembles the working out of a sum—figure by figure, line by line, the working out being carried forward until the answer is achieved. This work is done both on the inner planes and on the physical. In the Hall of Learning the pupil is taught nightly for a short time before proceeding with any work of service. This teaching he brings over into his physical brain consciousness in the form of a deep interest in certain subjects, and in an increasing aptitude to think concretely and abstractly on the various occult matters that are occupying his attention. He attempts to experiment and tries various methods of studying the laws and in process of time arrives at results that are of value to him. Time passes and as he appropriates and knows more, his knowledge takes a synthetic form and he becomes ready to teach and to impart to others the residue of knowledge of which he is sure.

3. In teaching others comes further knowledge. The definition of truth in teaching crystallises the facts learnt, and, in the play of other minds, the aspirant's own vibration becomes keyed up to ever higher planes, and this fresh intuition and fresh reaches of truth pour in.

When one lesson has, in this way, been mastered, a further one is set, and when a pupil has learnt a particular series of lessons he graduates and passes an initiation. The whole group he teaches is benefited by his step forward, for every disciple carries those he instructs along with him in a curious indefinable sense. The benefit to the unit reacts upon the whole. A Master carries His disciples on and up with Him in a similar manner. The matter is abstruse and largely one of the secrets of the law of vibratory expansion. The initiation of the Logos has a universal effect.

You are right in your assumption that the probationary path corresponds to the later stages of the period of gestation. At the first initiation what is called in the New Testament "the babe in Christ" starts upon the pilgrimage of the path. The first initiation simply stands for commencement. A certain structure of right living, of thinking and of conduct has been attained; the form that the Christ is to occupy has been constructed and now that form is to be vivified and indwelt. The Christ life enters and the form becomes alive. Therein lies the difference between theory and making that theory a part of yourself. You can have a perfect picture or image but it lacks the life. You have a person who has modelled his life on the divine as far as he can. He has a good copy yet something is lacking. What is this something? The manifestation of the indwelling Christ. The germ has been there but it has lain dormant. Now it is fostered and brought to birth, and the first initiation is attained. Much then remains to be done. The analogy is complete. Many years were spent by the disciple Jesus between the birth and baptism. The remaining three initiations were taken in three years. You have the same situation on the path of the aspirant.

The second initiation marks the crisis of the control of the astral body. After baptism there remain the three temptations, demonstrating the complete control of the three lower vehicles. Then comes the Transfiguration, followed by knowledge of the future and complete self-abnegation. Therefore, you have the following:

1. The moment of conception—i.e. individualization.
2. Nine months gestation—i.e. the wheel of life.
3. First initiation—i.e. the birth hour.

The path is, therefore, a path on which steady expansion of consciousness is undergone with increasing sensitivity to the higher vibrations. This works out at first as sensitiveness to the inner voice and this is one of the most necessary faculties in a disciple. The Great Ones are looking for those who can rapidly obey the inner voice of their soul. The times are critical and all aspirants are urged also to render themselves sensitive to the voice of their Master as well. His time is fully occupied and disciples must train themselves to be sensitive to His impression. A slight hint, a pointed finger, a hurried suggestion, may be all that He has time to give, and each disciple must be upon the watch. The pressure upon Them is great now that They are moving closer to the physical plane. More souls are conscious of Them than when They worked on mental levels only and They also, working on denser planes, are finding conditions more difficult. The devas and disciples, aspirants and those upon the probationary path are being gathered around Them now and are being organized into groups with special work assigned. Some souls can work only in mass formation, banded together and unified by a common aspiration. Such are the majority of Christians, for instance, in the churches. These, knowing not the laws of occultism, and only sensing the inner truth, work on broad lines of preparation. They are aided by bands of lesser devas or angels who suggest, guide and control.

Others more advanced work in smaller groups. They idealize more and in them you see the thinkers and leaders of social reform, of humanitarian regeneration and of church leadership, either Christian or Oriental. The higher devas guide them, the blue and yellow devas, as the former group are guided by the blue and rose.

Back of them stand the still more advanced—the aspirants, probationers and disciples of the world. They work singly or in twos or threes and never in groups exceeding nine—the occult significance of these numbers being necessary to the success of their work. Great white and gold devas attend their labours.

Back again of these three groups stand the Masters and the devas of the formless levels—a Great Brotherhood, pledged to serve humanity.

Movements are being set on foot to transmute, if possible, the labours of destruction into constructive work. The time is critical, for a pause has come in the work of the destroyers. There is opportunity for the tide to turn and for the re-building of the body social.

It is for this reason that each one of you needs to make a fresh dedication of himself to the work of the redemption. Personalities must be submerged. Aspirants must live harmlessly in thought and word and deed. In this way each one of you will provide a pure channel, will become an outpost for the consciousness of the Master and provide a centre of energy through which the Brotherhood can work.

The prime problem of the aspirant is to dominate the emotional nature. Then he stands victor on the field of Kurukshetra; the clouds have rolled away, and henceforth he can walk in the light. Let it here be remembered that this very freedom to walk in the light carries with it its own problems. You ask how this can be? Let me give one simple, yet (I think you will find) convincing argument.

When a man literally walks in the light of his soul and the clear light of the sun pours through him—revealing the Path,—it reveals at the same time the Plan. Simultaneously however, he becomes aware of the fact that the Plan is very far as yet from consummation. The dark becomes more truly apparent; the chaos and misery and failure of the world groups stand revealed; the filth and dust of the warring forces are noted, and the whole sorrow of the world bears down upon the astounded, yet illuminated, aspirant. Can he stand this pressure? Can he become indeed acquainted with grief and yet rejoice forever in the divine consciousness? Has he the ability to face what the light reveals and still go his way with serenity, sure of the ultimate triumph of good? Will he be overwhelmed by the surface evil and forget the heart of Love which beats behind all outer seeming? This situation should ever be remembered by the disciple, or he will be shattered by that which he has discovered.

But with the advent of the light, he becomes aware of a new (for him) form of energy. He learns to work in a new field of opportunity. The realm of the mind opens up before him, and he discovers that he can differentiate between the emotional nature and the mental. He discovers also that the mind can be made to assume the position of the controller, and that the sentient forces respond with obedience to mental energies. "The light of reason" brings this about—light that is always present in man but which only becomes significant and potent when seen and known, either phenomenally or intuitionally.

Much false teaching is going about these days in connection with the mind and the soul. It might be summed up in the teaching of one school which shall be nameless, as follows:

Nature is cruel and selective. She works by the Law of the survival of the fittest; in the process of selection, millions of lives are sacrificed and much birthing of forms comes to naught. Hence the achieving of soul life is a rare event. Few people have souls and only a few therefore possess immortality and go hence to their own place of power to return no more. The rest are lost, submerged and swallowed up in the general process of nature, and the human kingdom as a whole is a dead loss except for a few emerging and significant figures, which the past and the present produce. They have achieved through the sacrifice of the many.

But the reaction of men themselves to this teaching is an adequate answer. The sense of immortality, the surety of an eternal future, the innate belief in God, the revelation of the light, the achieving of a wisdom which helps and aids is not the prerogative of the Senecas, of the St. Pauls, of the Akbars of the race. It is found (and sometimes in its purest form) in the humblest peasant. Words of wise counsel fall from the lips of the illiterate, and a knowledge of God and a belief in the soul's immortality are discovered to be latent in the hearts of the most unlikely and oft of the most sinful. But when the highly evolved and the most intelligent of the race discover in themselves the divine Flame, and awaken the power of the supreme Controller, seated at the heart of their being, they are very apt to place themselves in a higher category than other people, and to classify those who do not have their mental grasp of the differentiations of the evolutionary development as differing so widely from them as not to deserve the name of Sons of God. They regard all not working in mental energy as lacking souls and hence as lacking eternal persistence as individuals. This is only a glamour of the mind, is part of the great heresy of separateness, and indicates faintly the coming period wherein the mind will be as dominant and as misleading as is the sentient body at this time.

Let us therefore study the types of mental energy with which the individual has to work and see how this great heresy of separateness and the "fallacy of repudiation", as it is sometimes called, can be offset.

One of the first things we have to remember as we consider these types of energy is that their trend and work can be grasped more easily in a larger sense in relation to humanity than can their effects in an individual use of mental energy. Only a few human beings are as yet consciously using this type of force and only a few can therefore understand what it really entails. Increasingly men will come, as units, into possession of their intellectual heritage but, numerically speaking, scarce one in ten thousand is utilising this inherent power and knowingly functioning in his mental body.

When however we look at humanity as a whole and cast our eyes back over the past racial development, we can see how mental energy has had a most definite effect and has produced outstanding results. The use of two factors differentiates man from the animal, whether he uses them consciously or unconsciously. Both are latent in the animal but man is the only entity in the three worlds who can *consciously* reap benefit from them. One of these factors is *pain*, and the other is the faculty of *discrimination*. Through the means of pain and a subsequent process of analysis, of relation plus memory and visualisation, man has learnt what to avoid and what to cultivate. This works in the realm of physical plane happenings and of sensory experience. Through discrimination as to ideas and as to thought currents, man has learnt to decide upon what to base his activities in all departments of human affairs, even though he has but an imperfect grasp as to the true nature of ideas and his application of the truths sensed is quite imperfect. That he often chooses unwisely, that the ideas governing group conduct are not of the highest, that public opinion is proverbially moulded by personal and selfish interests may be only too sadly true. Nevertheless through pain and learning to utilise the power of choice in the realm of ideas—man is steadily forging ahead towards full liberty and full control of the earth, which it is his right to inherit. The *Old Commentary* says in relation to these two characteristics of man something that conveys much of beauty, couched in symbolic language. The phrases run as follows and it must be borne in mind whilst pondering upon them that water symbolises sentiency or astral reaction, and fire is the symbol of the mentality.

"The assuaging waters cool. They slowly bring relief, abstracting form from all that can be touched. The quivering fever heat of long repressed desire yields to the cooling draught. Water and pain negate each other. Long is the process of the cooling draught.
"The burning fire releases all that blocks the way of life. Bliss comes and follows after fire, as fire upon the waters. Water and fire together blend and cause the great Illusion. Fog they produce and mist and steam and noise, veiling the Light, hiding the Truth and shutting out the Sun.
"The fire burns fiercely. Pain and the waters disappear. Cold, heat, the light of day, the radiance of the rising sun and perfect knowledge of the Truth appear.
"This is the path for all who seek the light. First form, and all its longing. Then pain. Then the

assuaging waters and the appearance of a little fire. The fire grows, and heat is then active within the tiny sphere and does its fiery work. Moisture likewise is seen; dense fog, and to the pain is added sad bewilderment, for they who use the fire of mind during the early stage are lost within a light illusory.
"Fierce grows the heat; next comes the loss of power to suffer. When this stage has been outgrown, there comes the shining of the unobstructed sun and the clear bright light of truth. This is the path back to the hidden Centre.
"Use pain. Call for the fire, oh, pilgrim in a strange and foreign land. The waters wash away the mud and slime of nature's growth. The fires burn the hindering forms which seek to hold the pilgrim back and so they bring release. The living waters, as a river, sweep the pilgrim to the Father's Heart. The fires destroy the veil hiding the Father's Face."

Perhaps one of the first things that every student has to learn, as he seeks to grasp the nature and use of mind, is that public opinion has to give place to individual consciousness of right, and that then that individual consciousness has to be so employed and concentrated that it is seen in its right proportion as that living germ which can expand into the divine flower of the Son of Mind, the Manasaputra, and as the thread which leads back into the realm of the Universal Mind. This thread and this consciousness, when followed, will lead the individual into the Council Chamber wherein the plan and the purpose of the great Life will stand revealed, and wherein all human selfishness and self-seeking fade out in the clear light of the Will of God. Through right understanding and right use and control of the astral nature and a comprehension of the nature of the sentient consciousness, man can penetrate into the very heart of God Himself and know past all controversy that all is well, for all is Love. Through right use of the mind, and through correct understanding of the nature of the intellect, man can enter into the mind of God and know that all is well, for all is planned, and divine purpose is steadily working out its objectives.

The work of the Atlantean Adepts was to impress upon the world consciousness the fact that God is Love. This is a symbolic expression of the truth as is the use of the word God. The work of the Aryan Adepts is to impress upon the world consciousness that God is Will. To do this for the human family, They work with the intellect so as to bring it into control, to subordinate other forms to the mind and through the mind to reveal to man the vision of what is and what will be. Man is therefore brought into line with the esoteric head centre of the one Life. In the animal kingdom, through the development of sentiency and its allied unfoldment through pain, They are bringing those types of forms into line with the heart centre in Nature. This is a phrase conveying a truth which cannot be more clearly expressed until man has become more inclusive in his consciousness. Through colour in the vegetable Kingdom those forms of divine manifestation are also brought into vibratory contact with that centre of force in Nature which is analogous to the throat centre in man.

In using these words I refer primarily to the Life which is expressing itself through our planet, to our planetary Logos, but the idea can (needless to say) be progressed to include the great Life of which our planetary Logos is but a reflection and an expression. Man, the brain of nature; the animals, the expression of the heart; the vegetable world, the expression of the creative force or of the throat centre; these three kingdoms in nature forming, in a peculiar manner, correspondences to the three higher centres in man, as the three kingdoms on the involutionary arc correspond to the three lower centres, and the mineral kingdom—abstruse as the idea may seem to those of you who have not the consciousness of the life-aspect—corresponding to the solar plexus, the great clearing house between that which is above and that which is below.

These analogies change as time progresses. In Lemurian days, viewing it as a kingdom in nature, humanity expressed the solar plexus aspect, whilst the animal kingdom stood for the sacral centre, and the centre at the base of the spine was symbolised by the vegetable kingdom. In the middle of the Atlantean period, when certain great changes and experiments were wrought, a shift in the entire process took place; certain egos came in, as you know, as related in the *Secret Doctrine* and in a *Treatise on Cosmic Fire*, and a tremendous stepping forward became possible through their efforts. The chitta or mind-stuff became more vibrant and now we have the period of its intensest activity in the concrete sense.

We are told in the esoteric teaching that all three aspects of Divinity are themselves triple, and hence we can divide the energy of mind as far as humanity is concerned into three aspects also. We have therefore:

1. The lower concrete mind, called the chitta or mind-stuff in the *Yoga Sutras of Patanjali*.
2. The abstract mind, or that aspect of the mind which is related to the world of ideas.
3. The intuition or pure reason which is for man the highest aspect of the mentality.

These three find their overshadowing or enveloping field of expression in the third aspect of the Logos, which we call the Universal Mind, the active intelligent Deity. The lines of force from these three lower aspects lead back (if one may use so inadequate an expression) on to the third plane, as the astral lines of force lead back to the second or monadic plane, though as far as man's consciousness is concerned they only lead back to the buddhic or intuitional plane.

It is interesting to note that just as the Monad, impelled by desire, produces that form of life which we call the personality, so the mind aspect, as part of the purpose working out through the Universal Mind, in its form produces that manifestation which we call a Manasaputra, the great Son of Mind on the mental plane. Hence it is the mind principle in humanity which brings into manifestation the egoic body, the causal vehicle, the karana sarira, the twelve-petalled lotus. We are of course talking entirely in terms of the form aspect here. The reason for this lies back on the cosmic planes, whereon the planetary Logos has His life. From the cosmic astral plane comes the impulse which produces form existence and concrete expression—for all form-taking is the result of desire. From the cosmic mental plane comes the will-to-be in time and space, which produces the seven groups of egoic lives and the third outpouring.

It will be seen then inferentially, how the right use of energy by the initiate puts him en rapport not only with the higher planes of the solar system but also with those cosmic planes whereon our Logos has His Personality aspect, using these words in symbolic fashion. The right use of physical energy by the initiate gives him the freedom of the cosmic physical plane. The right use of astral energy gives him power on the cosmic astral, and the correct use of mental energy gives him entrance on to the cosmic mental. Inferentially then, the three higher centres in man when functioning perfectly play their part in this work of carrying energies from these exalted spheres into the field of activity of the initiate and of being doorways into realms hitherto closed to him.

Each centre or chakra is composed of three concentric interblending whorls or wheels which in the spiritual man upon the probationary path move slowly in one direction, but gradually quicken their activity as he nears the portal of the Path of Initiation. On initiation, the centre of the chakra (a point of latent fire) is touched, and the rotation becomes intensified, and the activity, fourth dimensional. It is difficult to express these ideas in words that can be comprehended by the uninitiated, but the effect could be described as a changing from a measured turn to one of a scintillating radiation, a 'wheel turning upon itself, as the ancient Scriptures express it. Hence, when by purification, conformity to rule, and an aspiration that brooks no hindrance and that ceases not for pain, the aspirant has caused his centres to pulsate and to rotate, then—and only then—can the Master lead him into the Presence of the Hierophant. The Initiator then, with full knowledge of the disciple's ray and of his sub-ray, both egoic and personal, and recognising any karma that still may cling, touches the centre or centres which are in line for vivification, and the hidden fire will then rush up and become focalised. Remember always that in the vivification of a centre there is always a corresponding vitalisation of the analogous head centre, till eventually the seven centres in the body and the seven centres in the head rotate in unison. Remember also that just as the four minor rays pass into the three major rays, so the four minor centres carry on the correspondence and pass into pralaya, finding their focal point in the throat centre. Thus you will have the three centres—head, heart and throat—carrying the inner fire, with the three major head centres vibrating in unison also.

I realise that this is all intricate and technical. It has its place and value however, and much that here is communicated will find its usefulness when you are all passed over to the other side and a fresh band of aspirants will follow in your footsteps. The training of the mental body has a value, and many evade such technicalities, hiding behind an emphasis upon the life side of truth, all due to an inherent mental laziness. This that you now receive is but the A. B. C. of esotericism. Waste not time however in too detailed deduction. All that is now possible is a broad general outline, patient reserve, a willingness to recognise physical brain limitations and the accepting of an hypothesis. Believe these hypotheses possible unless your intuition revolts or they are contradicted by past teaching given by other of the Lodge's Messengers. I do not dogmatise to you. I only in these instructions give you certain information,—the correctness of which I leave the future to demonstrate. I simply ask that you make record and in the coming years much that may now seem peculiar or mayhap even contradictory will be elucidated, slowly unravelled, and more easily comprehended. A little knowledge leads to much confusion unless laid aside for future use when the years of instruction have increased the store.

To return to our theme:—The heart centre in man opens the door into what is called "the heart of the Sun." The throat centre opens the way into full understanding of the path of the physical Sun and all true astrologers must eventually have that centre functioning. The head centre opens the way to the central spiritual Sun, each passing, via the planetary correspondence, to one of the cosmic planes.

Thus we have a summation of technicalities, and of facts, which are (under the Law of Analogy) of purely academic interest and no more. Even those of us who are initiate know practically nothing of the cosmic planes beyond the cosmic physical. Our consciousness is only beginning to be solar, and we are labouring in our small measure to overcome those planetary limitations which hold us back from solar knowledge and life. For aspirants who have not even a knowledge of what planetary consciousness signifies, the above information has only one value and that is, that it emphasises the synthetic nature of the great plan and the fact that the smallest unit is an integral part of the whole. It enforces the idea that energy is a life fluid circulating throughout the entire body of the Logos, and vivifying therefore even the tiniest atom in that whole. It is valuable to endeavour to grasp the picture and to vision the wonder of what is transpiring. It is waste of time, nevertheless, to ponder upon the cosmic astral plane, for instance, when even the plane of the ego (the fifth subplane of the cosmic physical plane, counting from above downwards) is as yet inaccessible to the average man and is the goal for all his aspiration and meditation.

For man, therefore, the Universal Mind can best be grasped as it expresses itself through what we call the concrete mind, the abstract mind, and the intuition or pure reason.

The concrete mind is the form building faculty. Thoughts are things. The abstract mind is the pattern building faculty, or the mind which works with the blue prints upon which the forms are modelled. The intuition or pure reason is the faculty which enables man to enter into contact with the Universal Mind and grasp the plan synthetically, to seize upon divine Ideas or isolate some fundamental and pure truth.

The goal of all the work of an aspirant is to understand those aspects of the mind with which he has to learn to work. His work therefore might be summed up as follows:

1. He has to learn to think; to discover that he has an apparatus which is called the mind and to uncover its faculties and powers. These have been well analysed for us in the first two books of the *Yoga Sutras of Patanjali*.

2. He has to learn next to get back of his thought processes and form building propensities and discover the ideas which underlie the divine thought-form, the world process, and so learn to work in collaboration with the plan and subordinate his own thought-form building to these ideas. He has to learn to penetrate into the world of these divine ideas and to study the "pattern of things in the Heavens" as it is called in the Bible. He must begin to work with the blue prints upon which all that is, is modelled and moulded. He becomes then a student-symbolist, and from being an idolater he becomes a divine idealist. I use these words in their true sense and connotation.

3. From that developed idealism, he must progress even deeper still, until he enters the realm of pure intuition. He can then tap truth at its source. He enters into the mind of God Himself. He intuits as well as idealises and is sensitive to divine thoughts. They fertilise his mind. He calls these intuitions later, as he works them out, ideas or ideals, and bases all his work and conduct of affairs upon them.

4. Then follows the work of conscious thought-form building, based upon these divine ideas, emanating as intuitions from the Universal Mind. This goes forward through meditation.

Every true student knows that this involves *concentration* in order to focus or orient the lower mind to the higher. Temporarily the normal thought-form building tendencies are inhibited. Through *meditation* which is the mind's power to hold itself in the light, and in that light become aware of the plan, he learns to "bring through" the needed ideas. Through *contemplation* he finds himself able to enter into that silence which will enable him to tap the divine mind, wrest God's thought out of the divine consciousness and to *know*. This is the work before each aspirant and hence the necessity of his understanding the nature of his mental problem, the tools with which he must perforce work, and the use he must make of what he learns and gains through right use of the mental apparatus.

How is this to be done? How bring through and how build afterwards?

No matter how small or unimportant an individual thinker may be, yet in cooperation with his brethren, he wields a mighty force. Only through the steady strong right thinking of the people and the understanding of the correct use of mental energy can progressive evolution go forward along the desired lines. Right thinking depends upon many things, and it might be useful to state some of them very simply:

1. An ability to sense the vision. That involves a capacity in a faint measure to realise the archetype on

which the Lodge is endeavouring to fashion the race. It involves cooperation in the work of the Manu, and the development of abstract as well as synthetic thought, the flashing forth of the intuition. The intuition wrests from the high places a touch of the ideal plan as it lies latent in the mind of the Logos. As men develop this capacity, they will touch sources of power that are not on mental levels at all but which constitute those from which the mental plane itself draws sustenance.

2. Then, having sensed the vision and glimpsed a fraction of the beauty (how little men see is astounding!) in your hands lies the opportunity to bring down to the mental plane as much of the plan as you possibly can. Nebulous and faint at first is your grasp after it, yet it will begin to materialise. Seldom at first will you find that you can contact it, for the vision comes through the medium of the causal body and few can hold that high consciousness for a long time. But the struggle to apprehend will lead to results, and little by little the idea will seep through to the concrete levels of the mental plane. Then it becomes a concrete thought, something that can be definitely visualised and appropriated as a basis for thought.

3. This accomplished, what comes next? A period of gestation, a period wherein you build your thought-form of as much of the vision as foul can bring through into your consciousness. Slowly must this be done, for a stable vibration and a well built form is desired. Hurried work leads nowhere. As you build there will gradually be sensed a longing, a desire to see this vision brought to earth, and see it becoming known to others among the sons of men. Then you vitalise the thoughtform with the power of your will, you seek to make it *be*; the rhythm becomes heavier and slower, the material built into your form is necessarily coarser, and you find that your thought-form of the vision is clothed in matter of the mental and astral planes.

4. Happy the disciple who can bring the vision nearer still to humanity, and work it into existence on the physical plane. Remember this, that the materialisation of any aspect of the vision on the physical plane is never the work of one man. Only when it has been sensed by the many, only when they have worked at its material form can their united efforts draw it into outer manifestation. Thus you see the value of educating public opinion; it brings the many helpers to the aid of the few visionaries. Always the Law holds good;—in descent, differentiation. The two or three sense the plan intuitively; then the rhythm they set up with their thought sweeps the mental plane matter into activity; thinkers seize hold of the idea. This is a hard thing to learn and difficult to do but the reward is great.

To those who wrestle, strive, and hold on, the joy is doubled when the materialisation comes. The joy of contrast will be yours, for knowing the past of darkness you will revel in the light of fruition; the joy of tried and tested companionship will be yours, for years will have proved to you who are your chosen associates, and in community of suffering will come the strengthened link; the joy of peace after victory will be yours, for to the tired warrior the fruits of achievement and rest are doubly sweet; the joy of participation in the Masters' [Plan 369] plan will be yours, and all is well that associates you closely with Them; the joy of having helped to solace a needy world, of having brought light to darkened souls, of having healed in some measure the open sore of the world's distress, will be yours, and in the consciousness of days well spent, and in the gratitude of salvaged souls, comes the deepest joy of all,—the joy a Master knows when He is instrumental in lifting a brother up a little higher on the ladder. This is the joy that is set before you all—and not so very far ahead it lies. So work, not *for* joy but *towards* it; not for reward, but from the inner need to help; not for gratitude, but from the urge that comes from having seen the vision and realisation of the part you have to play in bringing that vision down to earth.

It is helpful to differentiate between happiness, joy and bliss:

First, *happiness*, which has its seat in the emotions, and is a personality reaction.

Second, *joy*, which is a quality of the soul and is realised in the mind, when alignment takes place.

Third, *bliss*, which is the nature of the Spirit and about which speculation is fruitless until the soul realises its oneness with the Father. This realisation follows upon an earlier stage wherein the personal self is at-oned with the soul. Therefore speculation and analysis as to the nature of bliss is profitless to the average man whose metaphors and terminologies must perforce be personal and related to the world of the senses. Does the aspirant refer to his happiness or joy? If he refers to the latter it must come as the effect of group consciousness, of group solidarity, of oneness with all beings, and may not be interpreted in terms of happiness after all. Happiness comes when the personality is meeting with those conditions which satisfy it in one part or other of its lower nature; it comes when there is a sense of physical well being, of contentment with one's environment or surrounding personalities, or of satisfaction with one's mental opportunities and contacts. Happiness is the goal of the separated self.

When however we seek to live as souls, the contentment of the lower man is discounted and we find joy in our group relationships and in bringing about those conditions which lead to the better expression of the souls of those we contact. This bringing of joy to others in order to produce conditions in which they may better express themselves may have a physical effect as we seek to better their material conditions, or an emotional effect as our presence brings to them peace and uplift, or an intellectual result as we stimulate them to clarity of thought and understanding. But the effect upon ourselves is joy, for our action has been selfless and nonacquisitive, and not dependent upon the aspirant's circumstance or worldly state. Much happiness is necessarily foregone when ill-health makes its pressure felt, as the environment is difficult and the "accumulated karma of many births" presses down, or as the troubles of the family, nation or race weigh upon the sensitive personality. The happiness of youth or the self-centred contentment of the selfish insulated person (hiding himself behind the shield of his protective desires) must not be confounded with joy.

It is a platitude as well as an occult paradox to say that in the midst of profound personality distress and unhappiness, the joy of the soul may be known and felt. Such however is the case, and it is for this the student must aim. Some people are happy because they shut their eyes to truth, or are self-hypnotised, hiding themselves within a shell of illusion. But the aspirant has frequently reached the stage wherein his eyes are wide open; he has learnt to speak truth to himself, and has built up no separating wall between himself and others. He is awake and alive; he is sensitive and frequently suffering. He wonders why apparently what the world calls happiness and peace have left him, and asks what is to be the outcome.

We who watch and guide on the inner side, watch with loving care all of you who struggle in the thick of the fray. We are like the General Headquarters staff who follow the course of the battle from a secure eminence. In our security lies your ultimate success, for we hold in our hands the solution of many problems, and apply that solution when the battle goes contrary. One thing always would I have you remember. It is of vital importance. It is this statement, that in the destruction of the form lies hid the secret of all evolution. Think not this is truism. You will see it in constant application and need to be prepared for its demonstration. The Masters utilize the form to the uttermost; They seek to work through it, imprisoning the life in confining walls for just as long as the purpose is served and the race instructed through that form. Then the time comes that the form no longer serves the purpose intended, when the structure atrophies, crystallises and becomes easily destructible. Its destruction then becomes the matter of greatest concern and usefulness, and it goes, whilst a new form takes its place. Watch and see if this be not so. Always the building of the form, always its utilisation for as long as possible, always the destruction of the form when it hinders and cramps the expanding light, always then the rapid reconstruction of a new form. Such has been the method since the commencement of the aeon.

In the infancy of the race the forms endured for a long time. Evolution moved more slowly, but now on the upward trend of all things, the form has but short duration. It lives vitally for a brief period; it moves with rapidity and then is succeeded by another form. This rapidity will increase not decrease as the consciousness or inner expansion of the life of the race vibrates ever to a faster and lighter rate of rhythm.

It is necessary likewise that you arrive at the realization that one of the principal objects of endeavor at the present time on the part of those whom you call the Elder Brothers of the race, is to stimulate, purify and coordinate the etheric body. This etheric body is not only the transmitter of prana but is the medium for all the energies which we are considering. Its importance also lies in other directions:

a. Being of physical plane matter, literally, etheric consciousness is the next step ahead for the race. This will demonstrate at first as the ability to see etherically and to cognize etheric matter.
b. It is the field of exploration immediately ahead of the modern scientist. In ten years time, many medical practitioners will be recognizing it as a fact of nature.
c. Most of the diseases that the physical body suffers from at present have their roots in the etheric body. There are few, if any, purely physical diseases. Disease has its source in astral and etheric conditions.
d. The secret of safe and sane clairvoyance and clairaudience depends upon the purification of the etheric vehicle.
e. The etheric emanations of people can be great contaminators. In the purification, therefore, of this body lies the secret of a sweeter and saner humanity.

Hence, the importance of the etheric. There are many other reasons which will later be emphasized. In beginning to form your ideas on the subject, however, it is the part of wisdom to adhere to wide generalities until the whole matter has taken clear shape in your mind.

Work on the etheric body, however, from the standpoint of the Hierarchy is not confined only to the bodies of men. It is a planetary process. The etheric body of the earth itself is being subjected to a definite stimulation. The spirit of the earth, that mysterious entity—not the planetary Logos—is being vivified in a new sense and in his vivification many interesting developments eventuate. In three ways this is being attempted:

1. By an increased rate of vibration of the etheric atoms, caused by the coming in of the ceremonial ray. This must not be pictured as a sudden and violent change. From the standpoint of the human student the rate of increase is apparently so slow and gradual as to be inappreciable. Nevertheless, the stimulation exists, and in the course of centuries will be recognized.
2. By the play of certain astral forces on the etheric body that leads to slow but definite changes in the internal structure of the atom, the coming into consciousness of another of the spirillae and a general tightening up of the whole cosmos of the atom.
3. By the use on the inner planes by the Mahachohan of one of the powerful talismans of the seventh ray.

The spirit of the earth, it might be noted, is of slow and gradual arousing. He is on the involutionary arc and passes on to the evolutionary in some dim and distant future. Therefore, he will not carry us with him. He but serves our purpose now, offering us a home within his body, yet remaining dissociated from us. The devas of the ethers from this very stimulation are consequently hastening forward in evolution and approximating also nearer to their ideal.

In all I have said anent the etheric body of men, anent the planet, anent the spirit of the earth, the crux of the whole situation lies in the fact that the five rays at this time have the seventh ray as their predominating ray. The seventh ray is the ray that controls the etheric and the devas of the ethers. It controls the seventh sub-plane of all planes but it dominates at this time the seventh sub-plane of the physical plane. Being in the fourth round also, when a ray comes into definite incarnation, it not only controls on planes of the same number but has a special influence on the fourth sub-plane. Note how this works at this time in the three worlds:

1. The fourth ether, the lowest of the ethers, is to be the next physical plane of consciousness. Etheric matter is even now becoming visible to some, and will be entirely visible at the end of this century to many.
2. The fourth sub-plane of the astral holds the majority of men when they pass over and consequently much work on the greatest number can therefore be accomplished.
3. The fourth mental sub-plane is the plane of devachan.

THE FOUNDING OF THE HIERARCHY

The various energies which play upon the human being and produce his unfoldment constitute his field of experience. Those two words—unfoldment and experience—should ever be linked, for each produces the other. As one is subjected to experience in the form world, a paralleling unfoldment of consciousness is carried forward. As that unfoldment produces constant changes in realisation and a consequent constant reorientation to a new state of awareness, it necessarily leads to new experience—experience of fresh phenomena, of new states of being, and of dimensional conditions hitherto unknown. Hence the frequent reaction of the disciple to the fact that for him, as yet, there is no point of peace. Peace was the objective of the Atlantean aspirant. Realisation is that of the Aryan disciple. He can never be static; he can never rest; he is constantly adjusting himself to new conditions; constantly learning to function therein, and then subsequently finding them pass away to give place, in their turn, to new. This goes on until the consciousness is stabilised in the Self, in the One. Then the initiate knows himself to be the onlooking Unity watching the phenomenal phantasmagoria of life in form.

He passes from one sense of unity to a sense of duality, and from thence again into a higher unity. First, the self identifies itself With the form aspect to such an extent that all duality disappears in the illusion that the self is the form. We have then the form constituting apparently all that there is. This is followed by the stage wherein the indwelling self begins to be aware of Itself as well as of the form, and we talk then in terms of the higher and the lower self; we speak of the self and its sheaths, and of the self and the not-self. This dualistic stage is that of the aspirant and of the disciple, up to the time of his training for the third initiation. He begins with a knowledge that he is a spiritual entity confined in a form. His consciousness for a long period of time remains predominantly that of the form. Gradually this changes,—so gradually that the aspirant learns the lesson of endurance (even to the point of enduring the not-self!) until there comes a life of balance, wherein neither preponderates. This produces in the man a state of apparent negativity and inertia which may last for one life or two, and he

175

seems to accomplish little in either direction. This is, for workers, a valuable hint in their dealings with people. Then the point of balance changes, and the soul appears to dominate from the standpoint of influence, and the entire consciousness aspect begins to shift into the higher of the two aspects. Duality however, still persists, for the man is sometimes identified with his soul and sometimes with his form nature; this is the stage wherein so many most earnest disciples are at this time to be found. Little by little however he becomes "absorbed" in the soul, and thus comes en rapport with all aspects of the soul in all forms until the day dawns when he realises that there is nothing but soul and then the higher state of unity supervenes.

These points need consideration and are valuable, for there are schools of thought (such as the Vedanta and other mystical groups of thinkers) which emphasise the life aspect and appear to negate duality. Other schools (such as the Theosophical, in spite of denial) teach the fact of the self and the not-self, and hence can be interpreted in terms of duality. Both are right and both need each other. It should be remembered that in the process of manifestation we work from a relative unity, through duality, to another unity, in the following way:

1. The unity of form, wherein the self is identified apparently with the form, and is absorbed in form life.
2. Duality, with a fluctuating shift backward and forward between the self and the form, the focus of consciousness being sometimes in one and sometimes in the other.
3. The unity of the soul, wherein naught but soul is seen to exist, and only *being* is registered in consciousness.

Thus it will be found that both schools are right, and that the dualistic concept is a step upon the way to essential union with the One Life.

It should be remembered that just as the battle ground (the kurukshetra) for the *aspirant* or probationer is the astral plane, so the battle ground for the *disciple* is the mental plane. There is *his* kurukshetra. The aspirant has to learn to control his emotional psychic nature through right control of the mind, and this Krishna seeks to emphasise as he trains Arjuna to take the next step towards right vision. The disciple has to carry forward this mental attention, and, through right use of the mind, achieve a higher realisation, and bring into active use a still higher factor,—that of the intuition.

In himself, the aspirant repeats the racial unfoldment, and re-enacts the racial drama; and to comprehend this certain facts about that drama and the work of the Hierarchy should be grasped and I here enumerate them:

1. The movement for the spreading of the Secret Doctrine is eighteen million years old.

2. Only four of the original Instigators still remain with us. The work (impulsive and controlling) lies now in the hands of three groups of lives, if it may be so expressed:

a. In the hands of those of our Earth Humanity who have equipped themselves so as to serve.
b. In the hands of certain Existences who have come into our earth scheme of evolution from other planetary schemes.
c. In the hands of a large number of devas of superhuman evolution.

These in their aggregate, form the occult Hierarchy of the planet, working in three main divisions, and in seven groups as outlined in many Theosophical books and summarized in *Initiation, Human and Solar*.

3. In the very early stages, this Hierarchy was called by various names; among others it was called the Temple of Ibez.

4. Let us consider the founding of the Temple of Ibez. To do this it will be necessary to consider the period of the coming of the White Brotherhood to earth and the immediate problem before Them; this will involve the recognition of certain facts that have never been adequately considered. It is an acknowledged fact in occultism that for our earth humanity the advent of the occult Hierarchy was epochal; it brought about two things:

The definite crystallization of that group soul which is now called the fourth or human kingdom.

The arousing of manas or mind in animal man in a triple way.

a. By the direct incarnation of certain members of the White Brotherhood, in which way They brought in the new and necessary factors by transmission to their children.
b. By the definite implantation of what is called in the occult Scriptures "the spark of mind" in animal man. This is simply a pictorial way of picturing the creation, by a direct act, of the necessary mental unit or mental apparatus of thought, within the causal or spiritual body.
c. By the gradual stimulation of the mental faculty in animal man, and the steady vitalisation of the latent germ of mind until it flowered forth as manifested mind.

This covered a vast period of time, and though the Brotherhood made its headquarters at Shamballa and directed its activities from there, it was found necessary during the first sub-race of the Atlantean Root Race to make certain efforts, if the evolution of the race was to proceed according to plan. Students of these mysteries need to remember that though Shamballa is spoken of as existing in physical matter and as occupying a definite location in space, the physical matter referred to is etheric, the Lord of the World and His assistants of the higher degrees occupying bodies formed of etheric matter.

5. It was decided about seventeen million years ago (the coming of the Hierarchy and the founding of Shamballa being about eighteen and a half million years ago) to have on the dense physical plane an organization and a headquarters for the mysteries, and to have a band of Adepts, and Chohans who would function in dense physical bodies and thus meet the need of the rapidly awakening humanity.

6. The first outpost for the Shamballa Fraternity was the original temple of Ibez and it was located in the centre of South America, and one of its branches at a much later period was to be found in the ancient Maya institutions, and the basic worship of the sun as the source of life in the hearts of all men. A second branch was later established in Asia, and of this branch the Himalayan and southern Indian adepts are the representatives, though the work is materially changed. At a later date than the present, discoveries will be made, revealing the reality of the old form of hierarchical work; ancient records and monuments will be revealed, some above ground and many in subterranean fastnesses. As the mysteries of central Asia in the land stretching from Chaldea and Babylon through Turkestan to Manchuria, including the Gobi desert, are opened up, it is planned that much of the early history of the Ibezhan workers will be revealed.

We might here note the fact that the word Ibez is literally in the nature of an acrostic veiling the true name of the planetary Logos of the earth, one of Whose principles is working in Sanat Kumara, making Him thus a direct incarnation of the planetary Logos and an expression of His divine consciousness. These four letters are the first letters of the real names of the four Avatars on the four globes of our earth chain who have embodied four of the divine principles. The letters I B E Z are ·not the true Sensar letters, if such an inaccurate expression can be used of an ideographic language, but are simply a Europeanized distortion. The true meaning is only conveyed at the fourth initiation when the nature of the planetary Logos is revealed and His four Avatars are definitely contacted through the direct mediatory work of Sanat Kumara.

7. A word now as regards the work of the Ibezhan adepts and Their mysteries; it is necessary here to point out that the whole trend of Their work was in a way different and necessarily so, to that of the adepts at this time. Their objective was to stimulate mysticism and the stimulating of the kingdom of God within the human atom. The nature of Their work is most difficult for the average man of this time to comprehend, owing to the different state of his consciousness. The Ibezhan adepts had to deal with a humanity which was in its infancy, whose polarization was most unstable, and whose coordination was very imperfect. There was very little mentality to be found and men were practically altogether astral; they functioned even more consciously on the astral plane than on the physical, and it was part of the work of these early adepts, working under instruction from Shamballa to develop the energy centres of the human unit, stimulate the brain and make him fully self-conscious on the physical plane. Their objective was to bring about a realization of the kingdom of God within, and little attention was paid (in Their training of Their disciples) to the bringing about of the realization of God in nature or in other units. It was necessary in those days to employ methods more definitely physical than are permissible now, and these methods of physical stimulation were employed and the laws of energy as they work through the various centres were taught until the time came when another big change was made in the hierarchical methods, and the door from the animal kingdom into the human was closed and the door of initiation was opened. It was felt at that time that man was then self-centered enough and individualized enough to permit of a drastic change in method and practice. All this took a vast period of time and it is the remnants of the earlier Temple practices which have come down to us in degraded phallic teaching, in Tantrik magic and the practices of Hatha Yogis. The infant humanity of Lemurian and early Atlantean days had to be taught what they were by means of symbols and methods which to us would be crude, impossible and of a nature which the race should have transcended for many millions of years.

8. At the time the door of initiation was opened, many millions of years ago the Lodge came to two decisions:

That individualisation must cease until man had not only coordinated the physical and astral bodies and could think self-consciously but until he had also transcended the physical and the astral. When he is becoming group-conscious, then the door into the kingdom of self-consciousness will again be opened.

That the path of mysticism must lead eventually to the occult path, and that plans must be made to impart teaching, and mysteries must be organized which would reveal the nature of God in all that is seen, and not only in man. Man must be taught that though an individual, he is but part of a greater whole and that his interests must be made subservient to those of the group. Gradually the teaching was re-organized, and the curriculum increased; little by little the mysteries were developed as the people became ready for them until we have the marvelous schools of the Mysteries of Chaldea, Egypt, Greece and many others.

9. Three things might be mentioned:

a. The relatively low point of evolution of many men and their naturally physical polarization.
b. The work of the black adepts and the followers of the left hand path. When the Ibezhan adepts (again under instructions from the Masters at Shamballa) began to withdraw into the Temples, to make the mysteries more difficult of attainment and to work against abuses and distortions, a number of Their erstwhile followers, many of great power and knowledge, fought Them and thus we have one of the causes of the appearing of black and white magic, and one of the reasons of the purifying waters of the flood being deemed necessary.
c. The powerful thought-forms built up in the early Ibezhan mysteries and which (particularly in America) are as yet undestroyed. This gigantic "Dweller on the Threshold" of all the true Mysteries has to be slaughtered before the aspirant can pass on.

10. The work of the Ibezhan adepts and the mysteries of the Temple of Ibez are still persisting and are being carried on by the masters and adepts in physical incarnation throughout the world. They teach the meaning of the psyche, the ego or the soul and of the human unit, so that the man may indeed be what he is, a God walking on earth, his lower nature (physical, astral and mental) completely controlled by the soul or the love aspect, and this not in theory but in deed and truth. When this is the case, the physical body will have no lure for the real man, the emotional nature and desire body will no longer lead astray nor will the mind shut out that which is true and spiritual, but the God will use the three bodies as vehicles of service to the race. Then will the human kingdom be transcended and man pass into the spiritual kingdom, there to have further lessons just as infant humanity when passing out of the animal kingdom was trained and taught its functions and work by the Ibezhan teachers.

In Atlantean days, the goal that the Hierarchy of Teachers set before Themselves was the awakening in man of the love nature, as a step towards the awakening of the heart centre. To do this, the Teachers at that time were Themselves focussed (deliberately and of intent) in the heart centre, and chose to work entirely through that centre, subordinating Their mental equipment and the mental energy They could use to the need of the time, They kept Their mental force in abeyance when training the initiates until the time the third initiation was reached. In our race, the condition is reversed. The Hierarchy is working now entirely on mental levels, though basing all endeavour upon past achievements in connection with the heart centre. Up to the third initiation therefore, disciples have to endeavour to work entirely with mental energy in an effort to control, master and use it. Their attempt is concentrated then upon transmitting (from egoic levels) the will aspect of the soul. That will has to be imposed upon the personality until it has become the automaton of the soul. Then the intuition takes control, and energies from the intuitional or Buddhic plane begin to make their impact upon the form nature, the personality. Prior to this period of intuitional control, there are many lives wherein the intuition may begin to play its part, and the student learns the meaning of illumination. Until after the third initiation, however, it is the illumined mind which is the dominant factor, and not the pure intuitive perception, or pure reason. After this great initiation, which marks a definite transition out of the form consciousness, the initiate can function at will on the plane of the intuition, and the mind is steadily relegated into the background till it becomes a part of the instinctual apparatus—as much a part of the subconscious instinctual nature as is the instinctual nature which the materialistic psychologist so much stresses. Intuitive perception, pure vision, direct knowledge, and an ability to utilise the *undifferentiated* energies of the Universal Mind are the main characteristics of the Aryan adepts. I use the word 'undifferentiated' in the sense of freedom from multiplicity; certain main distinctions will still be found to exist. The will of the soul, regarding that soul as having its place on one of the seven Rays, is superseded by the will of the Whole.

These are words meaning but little, or having at best only a theoretical significance to students in this group. When I say to you that the will which is transmitted through the medium of the controlled mind is embodied in seven types of energy, and to these seven types, there are corresponding types of humanity, you say doubtless that that is clear and not so difficult to grasp. Yet do you indeed understand? Seven types of energy, and seven types of responsive mentalities, dependent upon the seven ray types! In this statement, we note the differentiations of the soul aspect as grasped by the mind. These are the seven differentiations which take the place of the multiplicity of differences into which the form aspect falls. They are, nevertheless, distinctions and differentiations, and persist in their hold over man until the third initiation. By them he is swept into certain major activities and life tendencies, according to his particular ray. These are mental distinctions. All souls on the mental plane take the forms of the solar Angels, of the divine Sons of mind. Hence we have these groupings, and hence the focussing of the energies through which the Plan of the Ages works out through seven main departments.

At a later stage, when certain great transitions in consciousness have taken place and the form has lost its hold, even these divisions disappear, and the plan is seen as a whole, the Life is known in its essential oneness, and the term, monad, begins to have some real significance.

Students must always remember that all distinctions and categories are mental productions, and are due to the modifications of the thinking principle, and to the control of form by mental energy. As the central Thinker of the Universe works through the power of thought, the problem of surmounting these distinctions and differences is well nigh insuperable until such time as the aspirant comes under complete control of the second aspect of divinity, and passes out of the domination of the third or matter aspect. But up to the third initiation even the second aspect (the aspect of love) implies duality, for it is inherent in love itself. Ever there is the Lover and the loved, the Desirer and the desired, the seeker and the sought. It is only as the first aspect, that of energising unifying Life (which sweeps all forms and all dualities into one great synthesis) is sensed at the third initiation, that the words I have here dictated convey any practical meaning or realisation.

Let us simplify matters, if we can, by three clear statements; in them we will sum up the work the disciple accomplishes, as he struggles with and masters the energies of the mental world.

1. Work on the mental plane produces realisation of duality. The disciple seeks to blend and merge the soul with its vehicle and to do this consciously. He seeks to fuse them into a unity. He aims at the realisation that, here and now, they are ONE. The unification of the self and of the not-self is his objective. The first step in this direction is taken when he begins to cease identifying himself with the form, and recognises (during this transitional period) that he is a duality.

2. The mind, rightly used, becomes therefore a recorder of two types of energy or of two aspects of the manifestation of the One Life. It records and interprets the world of phenomena. It records and interprets the world of souls. It is sensitive to the three worlds of human evolution. It becomes equally sensitive to the kingdom of the soul. It is the great mediating principle, in this interim of dual recognition.

3. Later, the soul and its instrument become so unified and at-one that duality disappears, and the soul knows itself to be all that is, all that has been and all that will be.

There is a curious and ancient Atlantean chant which is no longer used but in those far off times was chanted by the initiate who took the third initiation—the consummating initiation of that period. It goes as follows. The translation of the symbols in which it was written necessitates the loss of rhythm and potency.

"I stand between the Heavens and Earth! I vision God; I see the forms God took. I hate them both. Naught do they mean to me, for one I cannot reach, and for the lower of the two I have no longer any love.

"Torn I am. Space and its Life I cannot know, and so I want it not. Time and its myriad forms I know too well. Pendant I hang betwixt the two, desiring neither.

"God from high Heaven speaks. There is a change. I hear with ear attentive, and, listening, turn my head. That which is visioned, yet visioning could not reach, is nearer to my heart. Old longings come again, yet die. Old chains with clamour snap. Forward I rush.

"Myriads of voices speak and halt me in my tracks. The thunder of the sounds of earth shuts out the voice of God. I turn me on my forward path, and vision once again the long held joys of earth, and flesh and kin. I lose the vision of eternal things. The voice of God dies out.

"Torn again am I, but only for a little time. Backward and forward shifts my little self, e'en as a bird soars into heaven and settles back again upon the tree. Yet God, in His high place, outlasts the little bird. Thus do I know that God will victor be and later hold my mind and me in thrall.
*
"Hark to the joyous paean that I chant; the work is done. My ear is deaf to all the calls of earth, except to that small voice of all the hidden souls within the outer forms, for they are as myself; with them I am at-one.

"God's voice rings clear and in its tones and overtones the little voices of the little forms dim and fade out. I dwell within a world of unity. I know all souls are one.

"Swept am I by the universal Life and as I sweep upon my onward way—the way of God—I see all lesser energies die out. I am the One; I, God. I am the form in which all forms are merged. I am the soul in which all souls are fused. I am the Life, and in that Life, all little lives remain."

These words, chanted in the ancient formulas on peculiar and selected notes, were most potent and brought definite results in certain ancient ceremonies that have long since died out.

To the three concise statements above made we might add a fourth as follows:

4. When the chitta, or mind stuff, is swept into activity by abstract ideas (the embodied thoughts of the divine mind, carrying the energy of their creator and consequently the cause of phenomenal effects in the three worlds) and when to this is added divine understanding and synthetic apprehension of the will and purpose of God, then the three aspects of mind are unified. These we touched upon earlier, and called them:

1. Mind stuff, or chitta.
2. Abstract mind.
3. Intuition or pure reason.

These have to be unified in the consciousness of the aspirant. When this has happened, the disciple has built the bridge (the antaskarana) which links:

1. The spiritual triad.

2. The causal body.
3. The personality.

When this is done the egoic body has served its purpose, the solar Angel has done its work, and the form side of existence is no longer needed, as we understand and utilise it, as a medium of experience. The man enters into the consciousness of the Monad, the ONE. The causal body disintegrates; the personality fades out, and illusion is ended. This is the consummation of the Great Work, and another Son of God has entered into the Father's home. That he may go out from there into the world of phenomena in order to work with the Plan is probable, but he will not need to undergo the processes of manifestation as humanity does. He can then construct, for the work, his body of expression. He can work through and with energy as the Plan dictates. Note these last words, for they hold the key to manifestation.

Our study of the energies which have been brought to our attention as we studied Rule X has brought us to a consideration of:

Personality Energy: emanating from:

a. Coordinated man.
b. Dominant human beings.
c. Groups: such as

1. The Hierarchy of Adepts.
2. The integrating Group of Mystics of the New Age.

This will be an important consideration, for this group of mystics is gaining each year in potency.

Planetary Energies: emanating from:

a. The seven planets.
b. The Earth.
c. The Moon.

Only a few things can be noted about this section of energies and about the next, for this is a series of Instructions for the aspirant and not a treatise on energy.

Solar Energies: emanating from:

a. The physical sun.
b. Cosmic sources.

In all thoughts concerning these energies it should be remembered that they are passed to us through, or rather constitute the bodies of, certain lives whom we call the devas, in their greater and lesser groups, and that therefore we are all the time working in the bodies of lives and hence influencing them. Some of you therefore who have made a study of *A Treatise on Cosmic Fire* may find it of value to note the following items of information:

1. The lowest types of devas or builders on the evolutionary Path are violet devas; next come the green,

and, last of all, the white devas. These are all dominated by a fourth and special group. These control the exoteric processes of physical plane existence.

2. It must not be forgotten, however, that, on a lower scale of the evolutionary ladder, are other groups of lives, wrongly entitled devas, which work in obedience to the law, and are controlled by the higher entities. There are, for instance, the denser forms of gaseous life, termed often salamanders, the elementals of the fire. These are directly under the control of the Lord Agni, Lord of the mental plane, and, in this mental age, we have the element of fire entering into the mechanics of living as never before. Eliminate the products which are controlled by heat and you will bring our civilisation to a stop; you will bring all means of transportation to an end and all modes of lighting; you would throw all manufactories into the discard. Basically again, these fiery lives, are found in all that burns, and in the warmth that holds all life formation on earth and causes the flourishing of all living things.

3. Under the Law of Correspondences the mental plane has an analogy in the third subplane of the physical plane, the plane into which science is now entering. Mind has, for its main expression in the material world what we call our scientific civilisation.

4. Agni rules on the mental plane, and has domination likewise on the third subplane of the etheric planes. He is the Lord of the fifth or mental plane, counting from above downwards, if one must employ these terms for the sake of symbolism. For this world cycle, Agni is the dominating influence, though Indra, Lord of the buddhic or intuitional level has a subtle control which is steadily waxing stronger. All humanity is striving towards the fourth plane of union between the three higher and the three lower, but, at this present moment, the plane of mind or of fire is the most important.

5. We need to remember that just as in particular incarnations, men are focussed or polarised in various bodies—sometimes the astral and sometimes the mental—so at this time one might infer that our planetary Logos Himself is focussed in His mental body. He, it has been said, is striving towards the fourth cosmic initiation, which makes possible *our* attainment of the fourth Initiation, for He carries us forward with Him, and, on our particular level, we achieve as cells in His Body.

6. As time progresses, Indra will swing into control and the age of air will be ushered in. More and more as the buddhic principle manifests and at-one-ment is achieved shall we see this age of air coming into being. A corroboration of this can be seen in the gradual control by men of the air. In an esoteric sense, all in the future will become *lighter*, more rarefied and more etherealized. I am choosing my words with care.

7. "Our God is a consuming Fire" refers primarily to Agni, the controlling factor in this age. The devas of the fire will play an increasingly important part in all earth processes. To them is given the work of inaugurating the New Age, the new world and civilisation and the new continent. The last great transition was governed by Varuna.

8. Agni controls not only the fires of the earth and rules the mental plane but he is definitely associated with the work of arousing the sacred fire, the kundalini. Note how the correspondence works out. A great part of the fifth root-race, three-fifths perhaps, stand close to the Probationary Path, and with the coming in of the new age and the advent of the Christ in due time and in His own place (note the care with which I express this; dogmatic assertions in terms of men's concrete minds are inadvisable) many will find it possible to make the adequate extra effort, entailed in the taking of the first major Initiation. They will begin to pass from the fifth to the fourth plane. The Lord of Fire will achieve his peculiar

work for this cycle by arousing the fire of kundalini in the large numbers of those who are ready. This will be begun in this century, and carried forward actively for the next one thousand years.

In your work you may later be shown—all depends upon your aptitude—methods of approach to these dominating forces, but this will come subjectively and not through magical work and formulas. The attainment of a right vibration will work automatically in the production of right conditions and right rapports.

I would again point out that we shall not waste time in planetary intricacies and the interplay of solar energies, but will concern ourselves with the laws of practical spiritual living. I seek but to give a few thoughts which have relation to the coming age, and which will enable man to go forward to that glorious heritage which is his and into which he must inevitably enter under the good Law and through the experience of rebirth. Through rebirth he learns to dominate and utilise form correctly.

All forms, in themselves, are not expressions of a personality. To warrant the term, three types of energy must be present, three types, fused, blended and coordinated into one functioning organism. A personality is therefore a blend of mental energy, of emotional energy and of vital force, and these three are masked, hidden or revealed (note this terminology) by an outer shell or form of dense physical matter. This outer crust is in itself a form of negative energy. The result of this union of three energies in an objective form is self-consciousness. Their fusion produces that sense of individuality, which justifies the use of the word 'I', and which relates all occurrences to a self. Where this central conscious entity exists, utilising the mind, reacting sensuously through the emotional body and energising the dense physical (via the vital body) then one has a personality. It is self-conscious existence in form. It is awareness of identity in relation to other identities, and this is equally true of God or man. It is a sense of identity, however, which persists only during the creative process, and for as long as the matter aspect and the consciousness aspect present the eternal duality of nature. In our evolutionary development it is not realised in the sub-human forms; it is realised in the human kingdom, and is realised but merged into and negated by the greater forms and consciousness which we call the superhuman.

Personality is that state of awareness which has its conditioning factor in the mind stuff, but this can be transcended when that mind stuff no longer controls. As the individual mind stuff is an integral part of the Universal Mind, and as the principle of mind is inherent in all forms, the sense of individuality and of self-awareness is always eternally possible. In the higher states of consciousness, it is however, eventually relegated to a subordinate position. God, for instance, can always and eternally be aware of that reality which constitutes the self, and which governs the integrity of the solar system, and of the solar interplay with other systems, but the consciousness of divinity and the awareness of the solar Deity is not primarily occupied with selfhood. That—as a result of past world periods and experience—is below the threshold of the divine consciousness, and has become as much a part of the cosmic instinctual nature as are any of the human instinctual attributes. The focus of the Eternal Attention (if I may use so unusual a phrase where words are necessarily almost worthless!) lies in realms of awareness beyond our comprehension. They lie as far beyond our ken as the awareness of a Master of the Wisdom lies beyond the ken of an ant or a mouse. It is therefore fruitless for us to dwell upon it. For us, there is the achieving of personality, or of a full registration or awareness of the indwelling self; there lies then the utilisation of that personality, and its sacrifice eventually to group good, with a consequent merging of the self in the one self and the fusion of the individual soul (consciously and willingly) in the Oversoul.

184

'I am'—the cry of every human being; 'I am That',—the cry of every personality, who realises his selfhood and uses his personality in order to express the will of the indwelling entity, the true person. 'I am that I am'—the cry of the individual soul as it is lost in the whole and realises its oneness with the soul or self of all.

The characteristics of the individual who is beginning to function as a personality might be briefly enumerated as follows. They are simple and clear and preeminently selfish. Let it not be forgotten that the primitive step on the way to selfhood of necessity is selfishness. Let it be equally well remembered that the prime hindrance to the advanced and highly evolved personality is selfhood, or the prolongation of the selfish attitude. The characteristics therefore are in their sequential development as follows:

1. The ability to say I am, I wish, I desire, I will.
2. The consciousness of being in the centre of one's tiny universe. "Around me the Heavens move and the stars in their courses revolve" is the motto of this stage.
3. The sense of drama and the capacity to visualise oneself as the centre of one's environment.
4. The sense of responsibility and the aptitude to regard the surrounding members of the human family as dependent upon one.
5. The sense of importance—the outgrowth of the above. This demonstrates in power and influence where there is a real and steadily awakening entity behind the persona, and in braggadocio and bombast where a small selfish creature functions.
6. The power to use the entire equipment so that the mind and brain function synchronously and the emotional nature is thereby subordinated, inhibited or controlled. This involves the steady growth of the power to use thought.
7. Capacity to live a coordinated life so that the entire man functions and is guided by purpose (expressing the energy of will), by desire (expressing the energy of the emotional or psychic nature), and by vitality which swings the physical vehicle into line with purpose and desire.
8. Power to influence, sway, guide and hold others within the range of individual purpose and desire.

When this stage has been reached the three energies which constitute a personality have been successfully fused and merged and the mechanism or instrument of the indwelling self is a usable and valuable asset. The man is a potent personality and becomes the centre of a group; he finds himself to be a focal point for other lives, and is an influential magnetic individual, swaying others, coordinating human units into groups, and organisms. He becomes the head of organizations and of parties, of religious and political bodies and of nations in some cases. Thus do the dominant personalities come into being and find themselves; they discover thus the distinction between the centre of power, the self, and the equipment; they finally become conscious of vocation in the true sense of the term.

It should be noted that this sequential development is paralleled by an inner growth of soul awareness, though the mode of expression of that inner growth is largely dependent upon the ray upon which the spiritual Entity is found.

One point should be here noted and upon this point aspirants should exercise care. The usual connotation of the words spiritual growth is largely that of religious growth in understanding. A man is deemed spiritual if he is interested in the world Scriptures, if he is a Church member and if he lives a saintly life. But this is no true definition for it is not sufficiently comprehensive. It has grown out of the impress set upon human thought and terminologies by the Piscean Age, and through the influence of the sixth ray, and the work of the Christian Church—all most necessary and all inherent in the great plan, but which (divorced from their eternal context) lead to the over-emphasis of certain divine expressions, and the overlooking of other as vital manifestations of the divine consciousness. is far wider and more inclusive than their manifestation through the medium of religious and mystical literature and organisations for the imparting of metaphysical truth. Power, purpose and will are divine qualities and expressions, and show themselves with equal clarity through a Mussolini or through a Pope. In both cases the mechanism of expression modifies and steps down the qualities and serves as a handicap. A potent personality may function in any field of human expression and his work will warrant the word spiritual just in so far as it is based on high idealism, the greatest good of the largest number, and self-sacrificing endeavour. these three—idealism, group service and sacrifice—are characteristics of those personalities who are becoming increasingly sensitive to the soul aspect, the qualities of that soul being knowledge, love and sacrifice.

This is why the emphasis in all schools of true esotericism is laid on *motive*. People who are strongly individual and are developing a group consciousness inevitably, in some life, find their way into esoteric schools and have to be guided in such a manner that the soul nature enfolds, overpowers and uses the personality.

The outstanding characteristics of those personalities who are not as yet soul-centered or controlled, are dominance, ambition, pride and a lack of love to the whole, though they frequently possess love for those who are necessary to them or to their comfort.

You have therefore in the sequential development of humanity the following stages:

1. That of the animal consciousness.

2. The emotionally polarised individual, selfish and governed by desire.

3. The two above stages, plus a growing intellectual grasp of environing conditions.

4. The stage of responsibility to family or friends.

5. The stage of ambition and of longing for influence and power in some field of human expression. This leads to fresh endeavor.

6. The coordinating of the personality equipment under the above stimulus.

7. The stage of influence, selfishly used and frequently destructive, because the higher issues are not registered as yet.

8. The stage of a steadily growing group awareness. This is viewed:

a. As a field of opportunity
b. As a sphere of service.
c. As a place wherein sacrifice for the good of all becomes gloriously possible.

This latter stage puts a man upon the path of discipleship, which includes, needless to say, that of the earlier phase, probation or testing.

The problem consists in ascertaining upon which step of the ladder and in which phase one finds oneself at any particular time. Behind each human being stretches a long series of lives and some are now headed towards the stage of dominant selfish personality expression and are making themselves individuals in full conscious awareness. This is, for them, as much a step forward as is discipleship for all of you. Others are already personalities and are beginning to experiment with the energy flowing through them and to gather around themselves those people who vibrate to their note and for whom they definitely have a message. Hence the myriads of small groups all over the world, working in every known field of human expression. Others have passed beyond that stage and are becoming decentralised from the personality expression in the three worlds of human life and are motivated by an energy which is the higher aspect of the personality energy. No longer do they work and plan and struggle to express their personalities and to make their individual impact upon the world or to gather magnetically around themselves a group of people who look up to them and thus feed the springs of their pride and ambition and who make them both influential and important. They are beginning to see things in a newer and truer perspective. In the light of the Whole, the light of the little self fades out, just as the light that is inherent in every atom of the body is gathered together and obliterated in the light of the soul when that blazes forth in all its glory.

When this stage of selflessness, of service, of subordination to the One Self, and of sacrifice to the group becomes the objective, a man has reached the point where he can be received into that group of world mystics and knowers and group workers which is the physical plane reflection of the planetary Hierarchy.

THE NEW GROUP OF WORLD SERVERS

We have spoken often of the integrating group of knowers who are beginning to function upon the earth, gathered together in loose formation and held by the inner spiritual tie and not by any outer organisation. The planetary Hierarchy has always existed and from time immemorial and right down the ages those sons of men who have fitted themselves for work and who have measured up to the requirements, have found their way into the ranks of those who stand behind the world evolution and guide the destinies of the little ones.

Their grades and works are theoretically known, and names of some have been given out to the masses,—at what cost and personal sacrifice those masses will never know. With the Hierarchy of adepts I do not propose to deal. The books upon the subject are easily available and should be read with the needed reservations as to symbolical interpretations and the limiting effects of words.

An event is however transpiring upon earth which is, in its way, as momentous and as important as that crisis in Atlantean times when the physical, vital and astral bodies were coordinated and formed a functioning unit. Then the `yoga of devotion' or bhakti yoga was initiated for the training of the aspirants at that time. A physical plane replica (as far as such a replica was then possible) was organised of those who could work devotedly and who could learn, through the use of ceremonial and pictures, some mode of activity which would carry on the hierarchical work on earth and thus constitute a training school for those who later would be admitted into the ranks of the Hierarchy. The remnants of this Atlantean group remain with us in the modern Masonic movements, and the work of the Hierarchy was thus perpetuated in sign and symbol. There has thus been preserved in the consciousness of the race a pictorial presentation of a momentous planetary condition which worked out in the human family in this threefold coordination. But it was primarily objective. Form and symbol, tool and furniture, temple and tone, office and externalities were the prominent factors; they veiled the truth and therefore preserved the 'outer and visible form of an inner and spiritual' reality. Only those were, in those days, allowed to participate in these mysteries and work who felt within themselves the longing and desire for the mystical vision, and who loved deeply and were devoted to the spiritual ideal. They were not required to possess active mentalities, and their intellectual powers were practically nil. They liked and needed authority: they learnt through ceremonial; they were devoted to the Great Ones Whose names and forms stood behind the office holders in the esoteric lodges. Mind entered not in. This must be remembered. There were no personalities.

Today, in the world, another great moment of crisis has arrived. I refer not to the present world condition, but to the state of the human consciousness. Mind has arrived at a functioning power, personalities are coordinated. The three aspects of man are being blended; another formation or precipitation from the Hierarchy of adepts has become possible. On the physical plane, without any exoteric organisation, ceremonials, or outer form, there is integrating—silently, steadily and powerfully—a group of men and women who will supersede eventually the previous hierarchical effort. They will supersede all churches, all groups, and all organisations and will eventually constitute that oligarchy of elect souls who will govern and guide the world.

They are being gathered out of every nation, but are gathered and chosen, not by the watching Hierarchy or by any Master, but by the power of their response to the spiritual opportunity, tide and note. They are emerging out of every group and church and party, and will therefore be truly representative. This they do, not from the pull of their own ambition and prideful schemes, but through the very selflessness of their service. They are finding their way to the top in every department of human knowledge, not because of the clamour they make about their own ideas, discoveries and theories, but because they are so inclusive in their outlook and so wide in their interpretation of truth that they see the hand of God in all happenings, His imprint upon all forms and His note sounding forth through every channel of communication between the subjective reality and the objective outer form. They are of all races; they speak all languages; they embrace all religions, all sciences and all philosophies. Their characteristics are synthesis, inclusiveness, intellectuality and fine mental development. They own to no creed, save the creed of Brotherhood, based on the one Life. They recognise no authority, save that of their own souls, and no Master save the group they seek to serve, and humanity whom they deeply love. They have no barriers set up around themselves, but are governed by a wide tolerance, and a sane mentality and sense of proportion. They look with open eyes upon the world of men and recognise those whom they can lift and to whom they can stand as the Great Ones stand,—lifting, teaching and helping. They recognize their peers and equals, and know each other when they meet and stand shoulder to shoulder with their fellow workers in the work of salvaging humanity. It does not matter if their terminologies differ, their interpretations of symbols and scriptures vary, or their words are few or many. They see their group members in all fields—political, scientific, religious, and economic—and give to them the sign of recognition and the hand of a brother. They recognise likewise Those who have passed ahead of them upon the ladder of evolution and hail Them Teacher, and seek to learn from Them that which They are so eager to impart.

This group is a product of the past and upon that past I will touch; I will also indicate the present situation and forecast somewhat the general lines along which their association and future work will run. That such a group is forming is true and holds a good augury for the coming decades. In quiet and subtle ways they are already making their presence felt but theirs is as yet primarily a subjective influence.

Let us begin with the past. About the year 1400, the Hierarchy of Masters was faced with a difficult situation. As far as the work of the second ray was concerned (which had to do with the impartation of spiritual truth) there had come to be what I might call a complete exteriorisation of that truth. The activity of the first ray had also brought about an intense differentiation and crystallisation among the nations and governments of the world. These two conditions of concrete orthodoxy and political differences persisted for many generations and are still manifesting. Today we have a similar condition both in the world of religion and in that of politics. This is true whether one is considering India or America, China or Germany, or whether one is studying the history of Buddhism with its many sects, Protestantism with its myriads of warring groups, or the many schools of philosophy in the orient or the occident. The condition is widespread, and the public consciousness tremendously diversified, but this state of affairs marks the summation of the period of separativeness and the end, before so many centuries, of this intense distinctiveness of thought.

After noting and watching this trend of affairs for another one hundred years, the Elder Brothers of the race called a conclave of all departments about the year 1500 A.D. Their object was to determine how the urge to *integration*, which is essentially the keynote of our universal order, could be hastened, and what steps could be taken to produce that synthesis and unification in the world of thought which would make possible the manifestation of the purpose of the divine life which had brought all into being. When the world of thought is unified, then the outer world will fall into a synthetic order. It should be remembered here that the Masters think in large terms and work in the wider cycles of evolutionary endeavour. The tiny and temporary cycles, the small ebb and flow of the cosmic processes do not engage Their attention in the first instance.

At this conclave They had three things to do:

1. To view the divine plan on as large a scale as possible, and refresh Their minds with the vision.

2. To note what influences or energies were available for use in the large endeavour to which They were pledged.

3. To train the men and women who were then probationers, chelas and initiates so that in due time They could have a satisfactory band of assistants on whom They could in future centuries rely.

They had, in connection with these aspirants, two problems:

1. They had to deal with the failure on the part of even the most advanced disciples to preserve continuity of consciousness, a failure even now manifested by even initiates.

2. The Masters found the minds and brains of chelas curiously insensitive to the higher contacts, and this again is a condition which still prevails. The chelas, then as now, possessed aspiration, a desire to serve humanity, devotion and occasionally a fair mental equipment, but that telepathic sensitivity, that instinctive response to hierarchical vibration, and that freedom from the lower psychism which are the needed prerequisites to intensive intelligent work were singularly lacking. For that matter, they are still distressingly so. Telepathic sensitivity is decidedly on the increase as a result of world conditions and the evolutionary trend, and this is (for the workers on the inner plane) a most encouraging sign, but love of psychic phenomena and failure to differentiate between the vibrations of the various grades of hierarchical workers still greatly hinder the work.

You might here ask and rightly so: What is this plan? When I speak of the plan I do not mean such a general one as the plan of evolution or the plan for humanity which we call by the somewhat unmeaning term of soul unfoldment. These two aspects of the scheme for our planet are taken for granted, and are but modes, processes and means to a specific end. The plan as at present sensed, and for which the Masters are steadily working, might be defined as follows:—It is the production of a subjective synthesis in humanity and of a telepathic interplay which will eventually annihilate time. It will make available to every man all past achievements and knowledges, it will reveal to man the true significance of his mind and brain and make him the master of that equipment and will make him therefore omnipresent and eventually open the door to omniscience. This next development of the plan will produce in man an understanding —intelligent and cooperative—of the divine purpose for which the One in Whom we live and move and have our being has deemed it wise to submit to incarnation. Think not that I can tell of the plan as it truly is. It is not possible for any man, below the grade of initiate of the third degree, to glimpse it and far less understand it. The development of the mechanism whereby a disciple may be en rapport with Those responsible for the working out of the plans, and the capacity to know (and not just dimly sense) that tiny aspect of the whole which is the immediate step ahead and with which cooperation is possible, that can be achieved by all disciples and should be held as the goal before all aspirants. With the exception of probationary disciples who are not as yet sufficiently stable in their endeavour, all can therefore strive towards achieving continuity of consciousness and at awakening that inner light which, when seen and intelligently used, will serve to reveal other aspects of the Plan and specially that one to which the illumined knower can respond and usefully serve.

To bring this about has been the objective of all training given during the past 400 years, and from this fact you can vision the utter patience of the Knowers of the race. They work slowly and with deliberation, free from any sense of speed, towards Their objective, but—and herein lies the immediate interest of what I have to communicate—They do have a time limit. This is based upon the Law of Cycles. It concerns the operation of certain periods of opportunity which necessarily have their term. During these times of opportunity, forces, influences, and energies are temporarily at work, and of these the Masters seek to make use.

Looking ahead, during the conclave to which I have made reference, the assembled servers of the race noted the future coming in of the Aquarian age, with its distinctive energies and its amazing opportunities. These They noted and They sought to prepare man for that period which would approximate 2500 years, and which could if duly utilised, bring about the unification, consciously and intelligently, of mankind, and so produce the manifestation of what I prefer to call "scientific brotherhood" in contradistinction to the sentimental connotation of the term now so prevalent.

It appeared to Them at that time that it would be necessary to do two things before the coming potencies of the Aquarian age could profitably be employed. First of all, humanity must have its consciousness elevated to the mental plane; it must be expanded so that it included not only the world of emotion and of feeling but also that of the intellect. The minds of men must be made widely and generally active, and the entire level of human intelligence must be raised. It was necessary, secondly, that something should be done to break down the barriers of separateness, of isolation and of prejudice which were keeping men apart from each other and which They foresaw would increasingly do so. Cycle by cycle, men were becoming more and more wrapped up in their own selves—satisfaction and exclusiveness, and racial pride. The result of this would lead inevitably to wide cleavages and the erection of world barriers between nation and nation, and between race and race.

This determination of the members of the Hierarchy to train the minds of men more rapidly and to build towards a more synthetic unity brought them to a decision which involved the formation of group units, and brought about the emergence of those groups of workers and thinkers who, through their activities, have so largely governed and moulded our world for the past three or four centuries. We have therefore, dating from this conclave, the inauguration of definite and specific group work along clearly defined lines, with each group standing for some peculiar presentation of truth and for some aspect of the knowledge of reality.

These groups fall generally into four major divisions; cultural, political, religious, and scientific. In more modern times three other groups have definitely emerged; they are the philosophical, the psychological, and the financial groups. Philosophers have, of course, always been with us, but they have been for the most part isolated units who have founded schools characterised by partisanship and separativeness. Now there are no outstanding figures as in the past, but groups who represent certain ideas. It is of profound importance that the work of these seven groups of thinkers be recognised as part of the hierarchical programme, designed to produce a certain situation, to bring about certain preparatory conditions, and as playing a definite part in the work of world evolution as far as humanity is concerned.

Under the influence of the different rays as they cycled in and out of activity, little groups of men emerged, played their part *in group formation*, and disappeared, often unaware of their inherent synthesis and of their co-workers. As can be seen in any intelligent historical retrospect, the work that they did for the race and their contribution to the pageant of the progress of mankind stands out with clarity. I have not the time to take this procession of groups, each custodian of a special contribution, and trace for you the work they did or the subjective impulses under which they worked. I can but indicate the trend of their endeavour, and leave to some illumined student of history the delineation of the golden thread of their spiritual work as they raised the mental standard of the race and put man en rapport with the world in which he lived, opening his eyes not only to the nature of matter and of form but also to the hidden depths of his own being. Through their activities we now have a humanity in close relation, though not at-one, and a humanity characterised by three things:

1. An amazing interrelation and intercommunication, of which the radio, the press, modern transportation, and the telephone and telegraph are the servants.

2. A wide-spread philanthropic enterprise, and the growth of the sense of responsibility for one's brother, which was totally unknown in the year 1500. Movements such as the Red Cross, educational foundations, hospitals, and the present economic relief measures to be found in every country are its exoteric manifestations.

3. A division of the entire human family, consciously or unconsciously, into two basic groups: first, those who stand for the old order of things, who are reactionary, and separative. They represent separative nationalism, boundaries, servitude, and servile obedience; they exemplify religious sectarianism and dependence upon authority. They are against all modern innovations and progress. Secondly, those who vision a unified world wherein love of God means love of one's neighbour, and where the motives underlying all religious, political and educational activities are characterised by a world consciousness and the welfare of the entire body and not of the part.

The unification to which the forward looking people aspire does not involve the neglect of any part, but it does involve the care and nurture of each part in order that it may contribute to the well being of the entire organism. It involves, for instance, the right government and proper development of every national unit so that it can adequately perform its international duties, and thus form part of a world brotherhood of nations. This concept does not even involve the formation of a world state, but it does involve the development of a universal public consciousness which realises the unity of the whole, and thus produces the determination that each must be for all and all for each as it has been said. Only in this way can there be brought about an international synthesis which will be characterised by political and national unselfishness. This universal state of mind will not again inevitably involve the founding of a world or universal religion. It requires simply the recognition that all formulations of truth and of relief are only partial in time and space, and are temporarily suited to the temperaments and conditions of the age and race. Those who favour some particular approach to the truth will nevertheless achieve the realisation that other approaches and other modes of expression and terminologies, and other ways of defining deity can be equally correct and in themselves constitute aspects of a truth which is greater and vaster than man's present equipment can grasp and express. Even the Great Ones Themselves but dimly sense reality and though They are aware of deeper underlying purposes than are Their chelas, yet even They see not the ultimate goal. They too are forced to use such unmeaning terms in Their teaching as Absolute Reality, and Ultimate Realisation.

Hence, during the past three centuries, group after group has appeared and played its part, and we today reap the benefit of their accomplishment. Under the cultural group for instance we find emerging the poets of the Elizabethan age, and the musicians of Germany and of the Victorian era. Groups of artists are likewise to be found, giving us the famous schools which are the glory of Europe. Two famous groups, one cultural and the other political, also played their parts, the one producing the Renaissance and the other bringing about the French Revolution. The effects of their work are still to be felt, for the modern humanistic movement with its emphasis upon the past which is completed in the present, and its search for the roots of man's equipment in the earlier trends, harks back to the Renaissance. Revolution and the determination to fight for the divine rights of man find their prime inaugurating influence and impetus in the revolution in France. Revolt, the formation of political parties, the class warfare which is so rampant today and the splitting of every country into warring political groups, though sporadic always, have become universal during the past two hundred years, and are all the results of the group activity started by the Masters. Men have grown thereby and have learnt how to think, and even though they may think wrongly and may initiate disastrous experiments, the ultimate good is inevitable and unavoidable. Temporary discomforts, passing depressions, war and bloodshed, penury and vice may lead the unthinking into the depths of pessimism. But those who know and who sense the inner guiding hand of the Hierarchy are aware that the heart of humanity is sound and that out of the present chaos and perhaps largely because of it, there will emerge those competent to deal with the situation and adequate to the task of unification and synthesis. This period has been occultly called the "age of restoration of what has been broken by the fall". The time has come when the separate parts can be reunited and the whole stand together again in its earlier perfection.

The religious groups have likewise been many,—so many that their enumeration is hopeless. We have the groups of Catholic mystics who are the glory of the occident, there are also the protesting Lutherans, Calvinists and Methodists, the Pilgrim Fathers—those sour and earnest men—the Huguenot and Moravian martyrs, and the thousands of modern sects in every group. These have all served their purpose and have led man to the point of revolt and away from acquiescence in authority. They have driven man to the stage of thinking for himself by the force of their unique example. They stood for freedom and the personal right to know.

These latter groups have acted largely under the influence of the sixth and second rays. The cultural emerged under that of the fourth ray, whilst the first ray has impelled the political activities which have

A Treatise on White Magic

brought such changes in the nations. Under the fifth and third ray impulses, groups of scientific investigators have arisen, working with the forces and energies that constitute the divine Life, dealing with the outer garment of God, searching from without towards the within, and demonstrating to man his essential unity with all creation and his relationship, intrinsic and vital, with all forms of life. The names of the individuals in any group are legion and of relatively no importance. It is the group and its interrelated work that counts. It is interesting to note that in the scientific group the underlying unity is particularly noticeable, for its members are singularly free from sectarianism and selfish competition. This cannot be said of the religious and political groups.

In relation to the many nations and the myriads of men on earth, these moulding groups under the various divisions are few in number. Their personnel, their contribution to the growth of human expression, and their place in the plan can quite easily be traced. The point to be emphasised is that these have all been motivated from the inner subjective side of life; they have come forth under a divine urge and with a specific work to accomplish; they have all been composed in the primary stage of disciples and initiates of the lesser degrees; they have all been subjectively guided step by step by their own souls, which have, in their turn, been cooperating consciously with the Hierarchy of Knowers. This has been the case even when the individual man has been totally unaware himself or his place in the group and that group's divine mission. Let it be remembered also that *there has not been a single failure*, though again and again the individual has not been cognisant of success. The mark of these workers is that they build for posterity. That those who have followed them have failed, and that those who have responded to this work have not been true to the ideal is disastrously true, but the initial group has uniformly achieved. This surely negates pessimism and demonstrates the exceeding potency of the subjective activity.

The three groups to which I earlier referred require a word of comment. Their work is curiously different to that of the other groups and their ranks are recruited from all the ray groups, though the members of the third group (that of the financiers) are found primarily upon the seventh ray, that of ceremonial organisation. In the order of their emergence, they are the groups of philosophers, psychologists and business men.

The group of philosophers of more modern date are already powerfully moulding thought, whilst the ancient schools of Asiatic philosophers are just beginning to influence western ideas. Through analysis, correlation and synthesis, the thought power of man is developed and the abstract mind can be unified with the concrete. Through their work therefore that interesting sensitivity of man, with its three outstanding characteristics of instinct, intellect and intuition is brought to a condition of intelligent coordination. Instinct relates man to the animal world, intellect unites him to his fellow men, whilst the intuition reveals to him the life of divinity. All these three are the subject matter of philosophical investigation, for the theme of the philosophers is the nature of reality and the means of knowledge.

The two most modern groups are the psychologists who work under the Delphic injunction "Man, know thyself", and the financiers who are the custodians of the means whereby man can live upon the physical plane. These two groups necessarily, and in spite of apparent divergences and differences are more synthetic in their foundational aspects, than any of the others. One group concerns itself with mankind, with the varying types of humanity the mechanism employed, and man's urges, characteristics, and with the purpose—apparent or hidden—of his being. The other group controls and orders the means whereby he exists, controlling all that can be converted into energy and constituting a dictatorship over all modes of intercourse, commerce and exchange. They control the multiplicity of form—objects which modern man regards as essential to his mode of life. Money, as I have before said, is only crystallised energy or vitality,—what the oriental student calls pranic energy. It is a concretisation of etheric force. It is therefore vital energy externalised, and this form of energy is under the direction of the financial group. They are the latest group in point of date, and their work (it should be borne in mind) is most definitely planned by the Hierarchy. They are bringing about effects upon the earth which are most far reaching.

Now that centuries have elapsed since the conclave in the sixteenth century, these external groups have played their part and performed most notable service. The results achieved have reached a stage where they are internationally effective, and their influence is not confined to one nation or race. The Hierarchy is now faced with another situation which requires careful handling. They must gather up and weld together the various threads of influencing energy and the differing trends of thought power which the work of the groups since the year 1500 has produced. They have also now to offset some of the effects which are tending towards a further differentiation. This must inevitably be so when force is brought into contact with the material world. Initial impulses have in them potency both for good and for evil. As long as the form remains of secondary importance and relatively negligible, we call it good. Then the idea and not its expression controls. As time elapses and the energy of the thought makes its impact upon matter and lesser minds seize upon the particular type of energy or are vitalised by it, then evil begins to make its presence felt. This finally demonstrates as selfishness, separateness, pride and those characteristics which have produced so much harm in the world.

About seventeen years ago the Masters met and came to a momentous decision. Just as it had been decided at the earlier conclave to gather out of the inchoate masses of men, groups of workers along various lines, and set them the task of elevating humanity and expanding the human consciousness, so now it was felt wise to gather out of the many groups, a group which should contain (as does the Hierarchy itself) men of all races, of all types and tendencies. This group has a specific mission, and some of the facts about it might be stated as follows:

It is first of all an attempt at an externalisation of the Hierarchy upon the physical plane, or a small working replica of this essentially subjective body. Its members are all in physical bodies but must work entirely subjectively, thus utilising the inner subjective apparatus and the intuition. It is to be composed of men and women of all nations and ages, but each one must be spiritually oriented, all must be conscious servers, all must be mentally polarised and alert, and all must be inclusive.

One of the essential conditions imposed upon the personnel of the group is that they must be willing to work without recognition, on the subjective levels. They must work behind the scenes as do the Great Ones. Its members therefore must be free from all taint of ambition, and from all pride of race and of accomplishment. They must be also sensitively aware of their fellowmen and of their thoughts and conditioning environment.

It is a group that has no esoteric organisation of any kind, no headquarters, no publicity, no group name. It is a band of obedient workers and servers of the WORD—obedient to their own souls and to group need. All true servers everywhere therefore belong to this group, whether their line of service is cultural, political, scientific, religious, philosophical, psychological or financial. They constitute part of the inner group of workers for humanity, and of the world mystics, whether they know it or not. They will be thus recognised by their fellow group members when contacted in the casual ways of world intercourse.

This group gives to the word "spiritual" a wide significance; they believe it to mean an inclusive endeavour towards human betterment, uplift and understanding; they give it the connotation of tolerance, international synthetic communion, religious inclusiveness, and all trends of thought which concern the esoteric development of the human being.

It is a group therefore without a terminology or Bible of any kind; it has no creed nor any dogmatic formulations of truth. The motivating impulse of each and all is love of God as it works out in love for one's fellow man. They know the true meaning of brotherhood, without distinction of race. Their lives are lives of willing service, rendered with utter selflessness and without any reservations.

The personnel of the group is known only to the Elder Brothers of the race, and no register of names is kept, and there are only three main requirements:

1. A certain amount of at-one-ment between the soul and its mechanism is essential, and that inner triplicity, usually dormant in the majority, of soul-mind-brain must be in alignment and active.

2. The brain has to be telepathically sensitive in two directions and at will. It must be aware of the world of souls and also of the world of men.

3. There must also exist a capacity for abstract or synthetic thought. This will enable a man to leap over racial and religious barriers. When this is present also there is an assured belief in the continuity of life and its correlation to the life after death.

To sum up the situation, it must be noted that the groups in the past have stood for certain aspects of truth and have demonstrated certain ray characteristics. The new group will express all the aspects and have in it members on all the rays. The majority of the workers in the many groups have carried forward certain details of the plan, and added their quota of energy to the forward urge of humanity, but they have for the most part done this without any true understanding of what they were accomplishing, and without any real comprehension of that body-soul relationship which leads to really intelligent work, unless we except a few prominent mystics such as Meister Eckhart. They have been primarily groups of personalities, with that added touch of genius which indicates a certain contact with the soul. The group that is now in process of formation is composed of those who are aware of the fact of the soul, and have established a soul intercourse that is real and lasting; they look upon the mind, emotions and body nature as simply an equipment whereby human contacts can be established, and their work, as they see it, is to be carried forward through the medium of this equipment, acting under the direction of the soul. They are therefore living souls, working through personalities, and not personalities actuated by occasional soul impulses. The members of the many groups were all somewhat one-sided and their talents ran along some specific line. They demonstrated a capacity to write as Shakespeare, to paint like a da Vinci, to produce musical masterpieces like a Beethoven, or to bring about world changes like a Napoleon. But the new type of group worker is a rounded out individual, with a capacity to do almost anything to which he sets his hand, but with a basic impulse to network on thought levels more than on the physical plane. He is therefore of use to the Hierarchy as he can be used in a variety of ways, for his flexibility and experience, and his stability of contact can be all subordinated to the group requirements.

The true exponent of this new group type will of course not appear for many decades. He will be a true Aquarian with a universal touch, an intense sensitivity, a highly organised mental apparatus, an astral equipment which is primarily responsive to the higher spiritual vibrations, a powerful and controlled energy body, and a sound physical body, though not robust in the ordinary use of the term.

What then is the present situation in connection with the integrating group of mystics? Let me be somewhat explicit.

In every European country, in the United States of America, and in parts of Asia and South Africa are to be found certain disciples, usually unrecognised in the world at large, who are *thinking truth*. Let me call your attention to that phrase. The most important workers in this new group and those who are closest to the Great Ones are those whose daily thought life is oriented by the new ideal. That this thought life of theirs may work out in definite esoteric activities may be true, but they are first of all and always those who live in and work from the "high and secret place". Their influence is wielded silently and quietly and they lay no emphasis upon their personalities, upon their own views and ideas, or upon their methods of carrying forward the work. These possess a full realisation of their own limitations, but are not handicapped thereby, but proceed to think through into objective manifestation that aspect of the vision which it is their mission to vivify into form. They are necessarily cultured and widely read, for in these difficult transitional times they have to cultivate a world grasp of conditions and possess a general idea of what is going on in the different countries. They possess in truth no nationality in the sense that they regard their country and their political affiliations as of paramount importance. They are equipped to organise, slowly and steadily, that public opinion which will eventually divorce man from religious sectarianism, national exclusiveness, and racial biases.

One by one, here and there they are being gathered out and are gathering to them those who are free from the limitations of past political, religious and cultural theories. They, the members of the one group, are organising these forward looking souls into groups which are destined to bring in the new era of peace and of good will. These latter who are being influenced by the group members are as yet only a few thousands among the millions of men, and out of the four hundred accepted disciples working in the world at this time, only about 156 are equipped by their thought activity to form part of this slowly forming group. These constitute the nucleus of what will be some day a dominant force. During the next twenty-five years their influence will become potent enough to attract political attention, provided those of you who have seen the vision of *a powerful subjective body of thinking Souls* can speak the needed words, and outline those concepts which will hasten the work of integration, and put the units in this group in touch with one another. Do your utmost to see that this is done and make this the message and keynote of the work you all do wherever you are.

What should therefore be the work of the immediate present? Let me outline the programme as far as I can.

The first thing to be done is to strengthen the ties and establish firmly the link between yourselves and all those whom you recognise as possible working disciples in the new group. To do this, acquaint yourselves with the work of the leaders of groups in the various countries of the world—such as Switzerland, the United States, Holland, Germany and Great Britain. From their reaction to the vision of this new age type of work you can then make a temporary decision. Watch them at their work. Note the emphasis laid by them upon personalities. If personal ambition seems to govern their activities, if their position is one of a determination to work in the group of mystics because of its novelty or because it gives them a certain standing or because it intrigues their imagination or gives them scope for gathering people around them, then proceed no further, but—preserving silence—leave time and the law to correct their attitude.

Secondly, be receptive towards those who seek you out and seem to vibrate to the same note. When I say you, I mean the group to which you all subjectively belong. They will come if you work with decision and sound out the note of unity so clearly that they are in no doubt as to your motives and your disinterested activity. Some of the 156 who form the present nucleus will be known to you and will work in unison with you, though maybe not in your peculiar field of action.

The picture to be held before your eyes is that of a vast network of groups, working along the many possible lines, but having at their heart or behind them—working silently and persistently influencing through soul contact—one or more members of the new slowly emerging group. These focal points through which the Hierarchy is now seeking to work stand together telepathically and exoterically they must work in the completest understanding, preserving always an attitude of non-interference, and leaving each worker free to teach his own group as he sees fit. The terms used, the methods employed, the types reached, the truths taught, the discipline of life demonstrated concern no one but the working disciple.

The members of this group of new age workers will, however, possess certain general characteristics. They will impose no enforced dogmas of any kind, and will lay no emphasis upon any doctrine or authorities. They are not interested in having any personal authority nor do they rest back upon traditional authority, whether religious, scientific, cultural or any other form of imposed truth. Modes of approach to reality will be recognised and each will be free to choose his own. No discipline will be imposed by these workers upon those who seek to cooperate with them. The ideas of any one person or leader as to how the units in his particular sphere of activity should live and work, should meditate and eat, will be regarded as of no special value. The members of this new group work esoterically with souls, and deal not with the details of the personality lives of the aspirants they seek to inspire.

This is a basic rule and will serve to eliminate many worthy aspirants from this group of world servers now in process of forming. The tendency to impose one's own point of view indicates a lack of understanding and it will rule many out.

Again, the young and promising aspirants must be sought out and carefully inculcated with the trend of the new ideals. They must be taught to look for the divine and the good in all—both people and circumstances. Breadth of vision must be developed and that wide horizon pointed out which will enable the aspirant to live through this transitional period which is now with us, so that when they reach middle life they will stand as pillars of strength in the new world. Do not narrow them down to the ancient disciplines and teach them not to lay emphasis upon diet, celibacy, times and seasons, and so distract their attention away from the newer and sacred art of being and the wonder of living as a soul.

Forget not that when a man is living as a soul and his entire personality is therefore subordinated to that soul, unselfish purpose, purity of life, conformity to law and the setting of a true example of spiritual living will normally and automatically follow. Food, for instance, is frequently a matter of climatic expediency and of taste, and that food is desirable which keeps the physical body in condition to serve the race. Again, a divine son of God can surely function as freely and as effectively when in the married state as in the celibate; he will however brook no prostitution of the powers of the body to the grosser satisfactions, nor will he offend against established custom, nor lower the standards which the world has set for its highest and best. The issues have been confused and the emphasis has been too often laid upon the physical acts and not upon the life of the actor when the attention is fixed upon the soul, the physical plane life will be rightly handled. It will be realised that there is greater hindrance to

197

the growth of the man in spiritual being through a critical attitude or a state of self satisfaction than by the eating of meat.

Two rules of life activity must be taught the young aspirant:

He must be taught to focus on constructive activity and to refrain from pulling down the old order of living. He must be set to building for the future, and to thinking along the new lines. He must be warned not to waste time in attacking that which is undesirable, but must instead bend all his energies to creating the new temple of the Lord through which the glory may be manifested. In this way public attention will gradually be focussed upon the new and beautiful, and the old established creations will fall into decay for lack of attention and so disappear.

He must be taught also that partisanship is in no way a sign of spiritual development. He will not therefore use the words *anti* this or *pro* that. Such terms automatically breed hatred and attack, and effort to resist change. They put the user on the defensive. Every class of human beings is a group of brothers. Catholics, Jews, Gentiles, occidentals and orientals are all the sons of God.

As regards the future of this world group of which we have been speaking much depends upon two things.

First, it is necessary for all those isolated disciples working in every country in the world, to become aware of one another and then to enter into telepathic rapport. This may seem to you to be a wonderful but impractical vision. I assure you that this is not so. The work of establishing this rapport may indeed be slow, but it is an inevitable effect of the growing sensitivity of all the souls who are working in the field of the world. The first indication of it is that instinctive recognition of those who constitute part of this group when they meet and contact each other in the ways of world intercourse. There comes to them an immediate flashing forth of the light, an instantaneous electrical interplay, a sudden sensing of a similarity of vision and of objective, or a vital opportunity to aid in and to cooperate with each other in the work in which it is realized that all are interested.

Working disciples everywhere when they meet each other will know at once that their work is identical, and will advise with each other as to where cooperation and supplementary endeavour may be possible. In about thirty years the interrelation between the units in this group (scattered as they may be all over the world) will be so close that daily they will meet each other at a set time and in the secret place. This only becomes possible when the triplicity of soul-mind-brain are all aligned in the individual and when each aspect of it can be simultaneously in touch with members of the group. At present all the souls of the group of mystics do work in unison; a number have succeeded in bringing the soul and the mind also into a close and established relation, but as yet the lowest aspect of this aligned and linking triangle, the physical brain, remains totally unresponsive to the waves of force emanating from the higher aspects of the disciples engaged thus in laying the foundations of the new age civilisation.

It is therefore largely a matter of perfecting the mechanism of the brain so that it can rightly register and correctly transmit the soul impressions and the group purposes and recognitions. This involves:

1. The awakening into conscious activity of the centre between the eyebrows, called by the oriental student, the ajna centre.

2. The subordinating then of the activity of this centre to that of the head centre, so that the two vibrate in unison. This produces the establishment of three things:

a. Direct conscious alignment between soul-mind-brain.
b. The appearance of a magnetic field which embraces both the head centres and so definitely affects the pineal gland and the pituitary body.
c. The recognition of this field of dual activity in two ways: as of a light in the head, an interior radiant sun, or as a dynamic centre of energy through which the will or purpose aspect of the soul can make itself felt.

3. The development of a facility which will enable a man to:

a. Use the mind in any direction he chooses, turning it externally towards the world of phenomena, or internally towards the world of spiritual being.
b. Produce consciously and at will a corresponding responsiveness in the physical brain, so that it can register accurately any information coming from the physical world, and the emotional or astral world.
c. Discriminate intelligently between all these spheres of sentient activity.

This will all be eventually covered by a new psychological approach which will emerge out of the old and be a blend of the mechanical schools, the introspective and the more purely oriental position, plus the conclusions of two new schools which will shortly arise but which are as yet too small to warrant a name. They are in the embryo stage. One school will deal with the energy aspects of the individual and his responsiveness to the energy of the universe in which he is immersed; the other will consider man as a unit of electricity. Both will be quite one-sided but the contributions of the various schools will some day be unified into one synthetic presentation.

The second requirement which will establish relation between the working disciples in this group is the capacity to preserve a constant and sequential recollection of both the inner and the outer life. We call it continuity of consciousness, and by this we mean the power to be fully aware of all happenings in all spheres and departments of man's being during the entire twenty-four hours of the day. As yet this is far from being the case. There is no real awareness of existence during the hours of sleep. The dream life as related is as full of illusion as any of the more definitely lower psychic experiences. The slowly growing interest in dreams from the standpoint of psychology and the investigation of their probable source are the first weak attempts towards establishing the awareness on a really scientific basis. There is as yet no conscious registering of mental activity during such times, for instance, as when the emotional body holds the centre of the stage. With what is the mind occupied during a long period of emotional upset? It has, we know, its own life and its laws. Again, what are the activities of the soul when the development of consciousness will have reached the stage where there will be a sentient reaction in all the departments of man's nature and all of it recorded by the brain? Already men are aware both of physical plane activity and emotional aliveness simultaneously. That is for the majority a common and ordinary condition. Where two activities can be registered at once, why not three or even four? Such is the future ahead for the race, and the disciples, actively employed, will be the first to express and demonstrate this extended consciousness.

Thus telepathic interplay and extended sentiency must be developed and are closely interlinked with each other.

I have therefore pointed out the immediate future development of the individual disciple. What lies ahead in the immediate future for the group?

First of all, a preliminary period of emergence into the public consciousness, and thus of making its presence felt. This will be done through the steady communication of the new ideals and the constant emphasis laid upon the essential oneness of all humanity. It will be the result of the uniformity and inclusiveness of the note sounded by one here and another there. During this stage there must be no hurried work and no precipitate action of any kind. The growth of the group and of its ideas will be slow and sure. The group exists already. It has not to be formed and organised, and there is therefore for none of you the assuming of any sense of responsibility nor the organising of any activity desired to lure these disciples, who have chosen thus to work subjectively, into publicity. Such are not the methods approved by the Elder Brothers of the race, nor is it the way that They Themselves work.

Know each of you for yourselves whether you stand for the new position, the new attitude towards work, and for the subjective method. Decide once and for all whether you prefer to work in the old exoteric ambitious manner, building and vitalising an organisation, and so producing all the mechanism which goes with such a method of work. Remember that such groups are still greatly needed and are useful. It is not yet the new age and the little ones must not be left exposed to the new forces, nor turned out bereft of the nursery to which they naturally belong.

Should the new mode of work appeal to you, see to it that the personality is subordinated, that the life of meditation is kept paramount in importance, that sensitivity to the subjective realm is cultivated, and any necessary outer activities are handled from within outwards. Avoid a purely mystical introspection or its opposite extreme, an over-emphasised organising spirit, remembering that a life of truly occult meditation must inevitably produce outer happenings, but that these objective results are produced by an inner growth and not by an outer activity. An ancient Scripture teaches this truth in the following terms:

"When the sun progresses into the mansion of the serving man, the way of life takes the place of the way of work. Then the tree of life grows until its branches shelter all the sons of men. The building of the Temple and the carrying of the stones cease. The growing trees are seen; the buildings disappear. Let the sun pass into its appointed place, and in this day and generation attend ye to the roots of growth."

Little groups will spring up here and there whose members respond to the new note and whose growth into the world group will be watched over by one or more working disciples. But these latter do not organise the groups; they grow as a man in this place and another in that place awakens to the new vision or comes into incarnation in order to take his place in the work and bring in the new era. These groups will demonstrate no sense of separateness; they will be unaware of personal or of group ambition; they will recognise their unity with all that exists, and will stand before the world as examples of pure living, constructive building, creative activity subordinated to the general purpose, beauty and inclusiveness. Perhaps in the early stages of integration, the words friendliness and cooperativeness best describe them. They are not interested in dogmas or doctrines and have no shibboleths. Their outstanding characteristic will lie in individual and group freedom from a critical spirit. This non-criticism will not grow out of an inability to see error, or failure to measure up to an idea; falsity, impurity and weakness will be recognised for what they are, but when noted will only serve to evoke a loving helpfulness.

Little by little these groups will come to know each other and to meet with one another at set times and places. They will come to these mutual conferences with no desire to impress one another and with no thought of relative numerical strength; they will demonstrate no ambition to increase their ranks. How should they when they know themselves all to be members of the one world Group? They have no teaching to give of a doctrinal nature and will not seek to demonstrate learning. They will meet solely to discuss modes of world helpfulness, the formation of a platform so universal and composed of such basic truths that it can be presented under all the varying methods and utilise the many terminologies. They will endeavour to employ each other's terms, and to familiarise themselves with each other's approach to reality and symbology.

Little by little also the special contribution and note of each group will be recognised and where a need exists for just that special approach and the particular note or method of interpretation in any part of the world, there will be an immediate and united impulse to facilitate the work that that special group could do in that place.

These groups, with the one subjective group of conscious living souls behind them, will be too busy with world service and interests to waste time on trifling nonessentials. They will not have the time to play around with group names and insignia and badges and the technicalities of fraternities when they meet together. World needs, world opportunities, and the rapid development of the consciousness of mankind and the initiation of humanity into the spiritual realities will so engross their attention that they will have no interest in purely physical plane arrangements, nor in laying the emphasis upon their own personal growth. They will be well aware that response to world need in service and the life of focussed meditation will promote their growth. Their eyes are not upon themselves, upon their own good characters, or upon their individual accomplishments.

Later as a result of their telepathic relationship and their united conferences, there may emerge certain esoteric groups and schools for development in order more rapidly to equip them for world service. In these schools modes of meditation, the intensification of vibration and the laws of the universe will be taught, and the right use of colour and of sound. But all will be subordinated to the idea of service and the uplift of humanity. Also the schools referred to in *Letters on Occult Meditation* will gradually come into being.

But what use is it for me to forecast the future in more explicit terms and hold out a picture of an intriguing quality when at the present time the integration of the group of world mystics and its close welding is not an accomplished fact?

World unity, brotherhood in its true sense, the growth of telepathic interplay, the elimination of the non-essentials which serve to separate the thoughts of men and bring about separateness on the physical plane, and the laying of a true emphasis upon the fundamentals of the Ageless Wisdom, the manifestation of a true understanding, the bringing about of at-one-ment with the soul, the recognition of those who belong to the group of world Saviours—this is the immediate work to be done and this must engross your attention.

This and this alone warrants the expenditure of all that any of you have to give—love and life, time and money.

This and this alone justifies your existence and calls forth from all of you who respond to the vision that utter self-sacrifice which is so rare and so far-reaching in its effects. The casting of all that one has at the feet of the Lord of Life in order that the work of world salvage may go forward, the elimination

201

out of one's life of all that can possibly hinder, the giving of all that one has until it hurts to give, the ruling of one's life on the basis of surrender, asking oneself all the time: What can I relinquish in order that I may help more adequately? That and more than that lies ahead of all of you who hear the call and respond to the need and opportunity.

Let me tell you this—this group now in process of becoming, will in time develop its own "yoga" and school of training which will gradually supersede that of the raja yoga and bhakti yoga schools. The method of training will only be given to those who have trained the mind and learnt to control the emotions. Hence the key to what is now going on. The mode of training will be no easy short cut to the goal. Only the intelligent can attain it and only coordinated personalities will be eligible to the teaching. The keynote of the new yoga will be synthesis; its objective will be conscious development of the intuitive faculty. This development will fall into two categories: first, the development of the intuition and of true spiritual perception, and secondly, the trained utilisation of the mind as an interpreting agent.

In the book *Agni Yoga*, some of the teaching to be given has filtered through but only from the angle of the will aspect. No book has as yet made its appearance which gives in any form whatsoever the "yoga of synthesis". We have had "bhakti yoga" or union through devotion. Raja Yoga is now receiving emphasis, which is union through the mind. It sounds like a redundancy to speak of union through synthesis, but it is not so. It is union through identification with the whole—not union through realisation or through vision. Mark well this distinction, for it holds the secret of the next step for the personalities of the race. *The Bhagavad Gita* gives us primarily the key to the yoga of devotion. Patanjali teaches us the yoga of the mind. In the Gospel story we have the portrayal of realisation, but the key or the secret of identification is still withheld. It lies in the custody of a few in this integrating group of mystics and knowers and will be brought out into manifestation in the furnace of their individual experience and thus given to the world. But the time is not yet. The group must grow in strength and knowledge and in intuitive perception.

You ask me: What keeps a man from becoming a member of such a group? I tell you with emphasis that four things only keep a man from affiliation.

First: an uncoordinated personality. This involves necessarily an untrained mind and a feeble intellect.
Second: a sense of separateness, of distinction, and of being set apart or different from one's fellow men.
Third: the possession of a creed. No matter how good a formula of beliefs it may be, it inevitably produces exclusiveness. It bars some out.
Fourth: pride and ambition.

You ask again: How shall one qualify? The rules are simple, and are three in number. First, learn to practice harmlessness; then desire nothing for the separated self, and thirdly look for the sign of divinity in all. Three simple rules, but very hard to accomplish.

Behind this group of mystics, which includes thinkers in every department of human thought (let me reiterate the word *thinkers* and of human knowledge stands the Hierarchy of Masters and in between these two groups stand also a band of teachers, of whom I am one. These act as intermediaries and as transmitters of energy. May I repeat and beg you to attend, that this group which is slowly forming is gathered out of every imaginable group of thinking and intelligent men. As yet, and this may surprise a few, there are not very many occultists (so-called) among them. This is due to the fact that the occultists are numerically few in relation to the masses of humanity, and also to their tendency to be sectarian, exclusive and self-righteous. Selfless humanitarian workers are there; political leaders and economists and scientific workers in the world's laboratories are also there; churchmen and religious adherents from all the world religions are there and the practical mystics and a few occultists. The true occultist is rare.

The group is and will be kept entirely subjective. Its members are linked telepathically, or they recognise each other through the quality of the work they are doing in the outer world and the inclusiveness of the note they sound. It is inspired from above by the souls of its members and the Great Ones, and is energised into activity by the need of humanity itself. It is composed of living conscious souls, working through coordinated personalities. Its symbol is a golden triangle enclosing an even-armed cross with one diamond at the apex of the triangle. This symbol is never reproduced in form at all. It shines above the heads of all who are in the group and cannot be seen by anyone (not even a clairvoyant) except a group member, and then only if—for purposes of work—his recognition needs stimulation. The motto of the group is *The Glory Of The One.*

More I may not tell you now, but this will give you some idea of the reality of the work that is going on. It may serve as an incentive to fresh effort on the part of all working to equip themselves for selfless service.

We are to take up now a very brief consideration of two types of energy of a major kind, which are, in themselves, composed and blended of coordinating energies. The subject matter is therefore of so advanced a nature that it is useless for the aspirant to give much time to its study. Volumes would be necessitated likewise if all that could be said were written, and it will only be possible in this book to outline some broad generalisations, and to indicate certain facts of interest. The main reason that it profits us not to study these energies too closely is because the planetary Spirit or Logos and the planetary Entity are the two forms in active manifestation which respond most forcibly to the impact of these energies. The human being responds, and that only subconsciously, because (in his form nature) he constitutes a part of the planetary expression.

The planetary Spirit is a Being Who, ages ago, passed through the state of consciousness which we call the human state and has left it far behind. He (using the personal pronoun simple for the sake of terminological clarity) has an origin which lies outside the solar system altogether; his life is focussed in the planet; his consciousness lies in realms beyond the concept of the highest adept in our planetary Hierarchy. The planetary Entity is the sum total of the forms which constitute the form through which the planetary spirit is manifesting, and therefore is the synthesis of the planetary physical, astral and mental elementals. For the purposes of our consideration, this Entity is the sum total of all physical, mental, astral and mental forms, which, blended and fused, constitute our planet. Each is the embodiment of energy, and these two major streams which produce the form and the consciousness aspects of our planetary existence make their impact on the human being. The life of the planetary spirit makes its impact via the soul; and the life of the planetary Entity is registered through the medium of the personality mechanism.

The duality of these energies is primarily astral-buddhic, and the bias of the life forces and the general trend of the impulses influencing humanity in this great cycle are the attractive energy of the intuitional nature of the planetary Logos, and the potent force of the astral (desire) body. In other words, the astral elemental, which embodies the desire nature of the planetary Logos is exceedingly potent, particularly in this present cycle, but the strength of the spiritual and intuitional nature of the One in Whom we live and move and have our being is steadily increasing. On the one hand, you have the devastating expression of the wild hunt for pleasure, of sex and of the crime incident to the satisfying of desire. This characterises our present civilisation and is now at its height; it may be said that it is even on the decline, little as you may sense it. At the same time, there is found the open door of initiation. Both these opportunities (if I might so term them) are found simultaneously present, but the strength of the one is weakening, and the trend towards the other is growing. Thus the way out can be seen.

In the above paragraph, the dominant planetary urges present in evolution are summed up and man's reaction to them noted.

Solar energies have also a dual effect. First, there is what we might call the *pranic* effect, which is the result of the impact of solar force, emanating from the physical sun. This produces definite results upon the objective forms, and these are termed physical or vital. These enter the human body—via the spleen and also via a centre found between the shoulder blades; this centre is between the throat centre and the heart centre in the spinal column, but nearer the heart than the throat. Secondly, there are energies which emanate from what is esoterically called "the heart of the sun"; these sweep through one or other of the planets in seven great streams and power into the soul of man and produce that sensitivity which we call awareness. These seven types of energy produce the seven types of souls or rays, and in this thought you find the secret of soul unity. During manifestation, owing to the seven types of energy impacts, playing upon the matter of space, one finds the seven types of soul, the seven fields of expression, and the seven grades of consciousness and of ray characteristics. These differentiations as you well know are like the colouring that the prism takes when subjected to the rays of the sun, or to the tracery of pattern found in reflection upon a limpid pool.

ASTROLOGY AND THE ENERGIES

To these two energies, a third group of energies must be added, and these are the basis of much of our astrological research. They emanate from the twelve constellations which form our solar zodiac. Their effect is infinite and the permutations of these three groups of energies lead to the infinite complication which we find in nature. The claims of the astrologers as to the reality of the energies playing upon the human organism can be seen to be true; their claims as to their capacity to interpret are for the most part unfounded. So little is really known by the highest intelligence on the planet; for, forget not, that the adepts utilise primarily the intuition. These energies leave their mark upon every form in every kingdom in nature, acting as a retrograding or a stimulating force. They carry one type of energy on to a fuller expression of the quality of any form, or hold another back from a developed manifestation.

It is not opportune here to outline the nature of true astrology. That astrology is a science, and a coming science, is true. That astrology in its highest aspect and its true interpretation will enable man eventually to focus his understanding and to function rightly is equally true. That in the revelations that astrology will make in time to come will be found the secret of the true coordination between soul and form is also correct. But *that* astrology is not yet to be found. Too much is overlooked and too little known to make astrology the exact science that many claim it is. The claim will be fulfilled at some future date, but the time is not yet.

Certain factors which astrologers should bear in mind, and certain conditions they are only too apt to forget, may however be briefly noted. For the sake of clear understanding we will simply tabulate a number of statements which should be studied with care by the average investigator in this field. I cannot here write a treatise on the energies with which astrology should deal, sorely as such a treatise is needed.

Astrologers concern themselves primarily with three types of energy:

a. The energy of the constellation in which the Sun is posited at the time of birth.
b. The rising sign to which the man should respond.
c. The moon which governs his form aspect, and particularly the physical form.

The energy of the particular constellation or sign in which a man is born is more deeply significant than has ever yet been suggested. It embodies or indicates his present problem, sets the pace or tempo of his life, and is related to the quality of his personality. It governs, if I may so express it, the rajasic or activity aspect of his life during incarnation.

The ascendant or rising sign indicates the line along which his energy as a whole can flow if he is to fulfill the purpose of any incarnation. This, of course, if rightly handled. It holds the secret of his future, and in its symbolism and understanding he can find the clue to his life problem and an indication of what he can be and achieve. It presents to him the type of force which will enable him to succeed. This, when duly consummated, might be regarded as producing the sattvic, or harmony aspect of his life, for when it plays its part and is utilised, it produces harmony with the will of the soul during any particular incarnation.

In the moon influence, we have indicated the native's past. It summarises the limitations and handicaps under which he must work, and therefore might be regarded as embodying the tamasic aspect of matter, or that which "holds back" and which—if permitted to influence unduly—will produce inertia. In the body with which man is equipped lies hid the secret of past experience, and every lunar form through which we have to arrive at due expression is in itself the product or synthesis of all the past. Let me see if I can put the present truth about astrology in such simple guise that they who know naught of this intricate science may understand.

The birth month indicates the day of opportunity. The door stands open. The particular month in which a soul comes into incarnation is indicated to that soul by the month in which it passed out of incarnation in a previous life cycle. If it, for instance, died in the month governed by the sign Leo, it will return into incarnation in the same sign, picking up the thread of experience where it left it, and starting with the same type of energy and the peculiar equipment with which it passed away from earth life, plus the gain of thought and conscious onlooking. The quality of the energy and the nature of the forces to be manipulated during life are indicated to the soul in this way.

The rising sign, embodying another type of energy, should wax in strength during the incarnation, for it indicates the nature of the soul force that the incarnated son of God is seeking to wield through the medium of a particular personality, possessing certain characteristics.

The influence of the moon is primarily physical. The prison of the soul is thus indicated. The handicaps to be met are thus secured; the type of body or of bodies through which the force of the native's sign and the quality of the energy which will bring him to his goal are thus defined. Through the medium of the lunar lords and what they have given him as the result of past experience down the ages must he express himself upon the physical plane.

Owing to the precession of the equinoxes, a situation is brought about in which a fourth type of force makes itself felt. The sun is, in reality, many degrees away in the great round of the heavens from where it is stated to be, as far as the greater zodiac is concerned. This is, of course, from the standpoint of time. As the sweep of the sun through a constellation covers a period of approximately two thousand two hundred years, the shift in the course of the centuries is very slight, so slight that little difference would be noted in the casting of the planetary horoscope. In the casting of the horoscope of a solar system it would be of vital importance, but this is so far beyond the capacity of the wisest astrologer on our planet that discussion is immaterial.

In casting the horoscope of a human being who is born in a particular month, however, it should be borne in mind (which it seldom is) that now the month and the sign do not coincide at all. The sun is really not in Leo, for instance, during the month of August. The correct interpretation therefore of a chart is largely psychometrical and dependent upon the thought-form of the constellation which has been built up for ages by the astrologers. Energy follows thought. For thousands of years certain types of energy and their consequent qualifying effects on substance and form have been considered to be thus and so. Therefore, thus they are, except in the case of the highly evolved, of the true aspirant who has oriented himself, and is thus escaping from the wheel of existence and beginning to govern his stars, and so is no longer under their rule and domination.

Astrology now deals primarily with the personality for whom the horoscope may be cast and with the events of the personality life. When, through meditation and service, plus the discipline of the lunar bodies, a man comes consciously and definitely under his soul ray, then he comes as definitely under the influence of one or other of the seven solar systems, as they focus their energy through one or other of the constellations and subsequently one or other of the seven sacred planets. Eventually, there will be twelve sacred planets, corresponding to the twelve constellations, but the time is not yet. Our solar system, as you know, is one of seven. When a man has arrived at this point in evolution, birth months, mundane astrology, and the influences which play upon the form aspect become of less and less importance. This circle of solar systems affects paramountly the soul and it becomes the focal point of spiritual energies. This is the problem of the soul on its own plane,—responsiveness to these types of energy, and, of them, the personality is totally unaware.

The signs which fall therefore into the four categories of earth, water, fire and air, concern primarily the man who lives below the diaphragm, and who utilises the lower four centres:—the centre at the base of the spine, the sacral centre, the solar plexus and the spleen. The inner group of seven major or systemic energies produce their effect upon the man who is living above the diaphragm, and work through the seven representative centres in the head. Four of them focus through the throat centre, the heart centre, the ajna and head centres. Three are held latent in the region of the head centres (the thousand petalled lotus) and only enter into functioning activity after the third initiation. It will be evident therefore how complicated from the standpoint of the horoscope (as well as of the individual problem) is this meeting of the energies of two types of constellations in the case of the man who is neither purely human nor purely spiritual. The ordinary horoscope is negated. The horoscope is not possible as yet of delineation. The only horoscope, which is basically and almost infallibly correct is that of the entirely low grade human being who lives entirely below the diaphragm and is governed by his animal nature alone.

Astrologers must remember also that there are several undiscovered planets which are producing pulls and shifts and focussing streams of energy upon our earth which tend to complicate the problem still further. Pluto is one of them, and having now emerged into manifestation (or rather into recognition) to it will be assigned all the unexplained conditions. Pluto will be made the scapegoat for faulty astrology for a long time to come. This chart failed to work and be true because Pluto must be influential in it and we know little about Pluto. So the story will run. Yet Pluto has always been revolving around our sun and producing its effects. It governs however the death or cessation of old ideas and emotions, and its influence is therefore largely cerebral and in that you have the clue to its late discovery. Mankind is only on the verge of becoming mental. Its effects are felt first in the mental body. The names of the planets are not the result of arbitrary choice but the planets name themselves.

Astrologers will eventually find it necessary to cast three horoscopes or three charts:—one purely physical dealing with the body of nature; one primarily emotional, and dealing with the quality of the personality and with its sensitivity, or state of awareness; the third will be the chart of the mental impulses and conditions. It will be found that these three charts will take certain geometrical lines, the lines of energies will form patterns. These three charts, superimposed one upon the other, will give the personality diagram, the individual life pattern. Amazing symbolic charts and lineal forms will be found to emerge when this his done, and the "geometry of the individual" will grow out of this, for it will be found that each line will function in relation to another line, and the trends of the life energies will become apparent. Eventually, even in this department of knowledge, "the star will shine forth" This will constitute a new branch of psychology and its true exponent for our age will duly be found. I but indicate the lines of the future astrology in order to safeguard the present.

One thing astrologers need at this time to do and that is to make due allowance for this transition period out of Pisces into Aquarius. This is seldom done, but it is evident that the tremendous turmoil incident to these transitions affects the individual chart, and frequently offsets individual destiny or karma. People are submerged in planetary and racial destinies, and their own tiny affairs are offset almost entirely and sometimes completely negated. It is not possible to cast the horoscope of the planet, and those who propose to do so are deceiving themselves and others. The horoscope of the fourth kingdom in nature, of humanity, will eventually be cast, but it will be done by initiates, and there are no initiate astrologers working on the physical plane at this time. One hint here I give.

The Sun was in Sagittarius when the first human tendencies struggled to the fore. The stage of animal man was completed and when Sagittarius was dominant (from our planetary standpoint—I am using words with care) the great event of individualisation took place. But the brain of the then human being failed to register what had happened. In the words of the *Old Commentary*:

"The sons of God shot forth like arrows from the bow. The forms received the impulse and lo! a God was born. The tiny babe knew not the great event."

This took place twenty-one million years ago. Cycles passed and when at a later date the sun was in Leo (approximately eighteen million years ago) the first instances of coordination between brain and mind took place and the human being was definitely self-conscious. He registered his individuality. The figures for the first date (though exactness is not possible in a system of mutation such as ours) are 21,688,345 years ago. These figures are useless at this time for they can neither be proved correct nor incorrect. Later investigation will prove their usefulness, when the nature of time is better understood. Sagittarius governs human evolution, for it symbolises progress towards a conscious goal. Leo governs the human consciousness in the human kingdom for the energy pouring through it enables man to say "I am".

It might be of value if I here attempted a translation necessarily inadequate, of the key word of each sign. These fall into two categories as far as humanity is concerned. There is the key word for the form aspect and the keyword for the soul aspect. In the first case, the word is expressed; in the second it is consciously spoken by the soul. Translated into modern terms much is lost, but the underlying thought which directs the work of the emanating energies is of value. For our world period they are as follows:

For the aspirant who progresses from Aries to Pisces and has therefore re-oriented himself we have:

Aries------------I come forth, and from the plane of mind I rule.
Taurus---------I see, and when the eye is opened, all is illumined.
Gemini --------I recognise my other self and in the waning of that self I grow and glow.
Cancer---------I build a lighted house and therein dwell.
Leo--------------I am That and That am I.
Virgo ----------I am the Mother and the Child, I God, I matter am.
Libra------------I choose the Way that leads between the two great lines of force.
Scorpio --------Warrior I am, and from the battle I emerge triumphant.
Sagittarius-----I see the goal. I reach the goal and see another.
Capricorn -----Lost am I in light supernal and on that light I turn my back.
Aquarius ------Water of life am I, poured forth for thirsty men.
Pisces----------I leave the Father's home and turning back, I save.

From the standpoint of the form, the life proceeds in a reverse direction, and the work of nature is seen under the following words:

Pisces ----------------And the Word said: Go forth into matter.
Aquarius-------------And the Word said: Let desire in form be ruler.
Capricorn------------And the Word said: Let ambition rule and the door stand wide.
Sagittarius-----------And the Word said: Let food be sought.
Scorpio --------------And the Word said: Let Maya flourish and deception rule.
Libra -----------------And the Word said: Let choice be made.
Virgo ----------------And the Word said: Let matter reign.
Leo--------------------And the Word said: Let other forms exist, I rule.
Cancer --------------And the Word said: Let isolation be the rule and yet the crowd exists.
Gemini---------------And the Word said: Let instability do its work.
Taurus ---------------And the Word said: Let struggle be undismayed.
Aries -----------------And the Word said: Let form again be sought.

It will be noted that all these ideas concern the work of energy in some form or another and in the last grouping with the work of the so-called unregenerate selfish individual, full of desire for satisfaction. The group of mantric words used by the aspirant in the power of his own soul, are positive.

It seems needless to deal further with the various types of force and we shall now turn our attention to Rule XI.

RULE ELEVEN

Three things the worker with the law must now accomplish. First, ascertain the formula which will confine the lives within the ensphering wall; next, pronounce the words which will tell them what to do and where to carry that which has been made; and finally, utter forth the mystic phrase which will save him from their work.

Analysis of the Three Sentences.
Salvation from our Thought-Forms.
Salvation from Death.

ANALYSIS OF THE THREE SENTENCES

This rule is, as you know, the last of those governing work on the astral plane and the magical task of motivating those thought-forms which are to be the expression of some type of energy. We have considered the various energies with which men work and the power a man can wield through building thought-forms. We have seen also how a man can manipulate the various grades of matter until the embodied idea has clothed itself with mental matter and with astral matter. It is therefore a vital entity, on the verge of materialising upon the physical plane. Nothing, it should be noted, can now stop its emergence into objectivity except the expressed act of the will of its creator, for the form, being vitalised by that creator, is subject always to his will, until he has severed his connection with it by the utterance of the "mystic phrase". We will assume that emergence into effective existence is the decision and that the creative work is carried forward.

It will here be noted that this work is either conscious or unconscious. In the unconscious building of thought-forms such as is the case with the average human being, many never produce the desired physical plane effects, and fail in their intended purpose. As long however, as man is animated by selfishness and by hatred, this is a beneficent thing. Fortunately for the human race, few people as yet work in mental matter. Most of them work with astral or desire matter and these forms are fluidic and changeable, and are powerful only through the faculty of persistence. There is an occult basis for the statement that if one desires a thing for a sufficiently long period of time one will possess it. Such is the law governing the return to incarnation of the average human being. Lacking the one-pointedness of the mental plane matter as it is influenced by a concentrated mind, these desire forms fail to do the damage they otherwise might. Their effect is felt largely by the creator of these kama-manasic forms and not by his environing associates. The moment that the mind factor enters in and becomes dominant, that moment a man becomes dangerous or useful as the case may be—dangerous not only to himself but to those around him, or useful in the working out of the plan of evolution. He can then create thought-forms, capable of producing outward manifesting results and tangible effects. Given aspiration, however, and spiritual impulse, a man can become a true occultist, and produce organised results, and functioning organisms upon the physical plane. I use the word "organism" deliberately, for it will serve to convey the idea that any thought-form is regarded by us as a subjective and existing entity, clothed in subtle matter, and capable of manifestation. This is called popularly sometimes "the working out of an idea", or the "carrying through of a project"; it is termed at other times a "discovery", or an " invention", or something of that nature. All the time, quite unrealising it, man is talking in occult terms and evidencing an inner appreciation of the methods whereby all that has been thought (by God or man) comes into existence.

The embodied idea or thought (the former being potentially far more potent than the latter) has worked its way through to the verge of physical manifestation. Its creator who, in the case of a "white magician" is not an emotionally centred person, is consciously bringing it to the stage when its inner purpose and plan can be demonstrated. He holds the thought-form in his consciousness and gives it shape and energy through the power of his own one-pointed mental focus.

We are told in the rule under consideration that the aspirant has three things to do:

1. Ascertain the formula which will crystallise the form he has built, much in the same way that we find architects and bridge builders reducing the desired form to a mathematical formula.

2. Pronounce certain words which will give the form vitality and so carry it forth on to the physical plane.

3. Utter the phrase which will detach the thought-form from his aura and so save the drain upon his energies.

It will be noted that the *formula* has relation to the thought-form, the *words of power* to the objective for which the form has been constructed, and the *mystic phase* concerns the severing of the magnetic link which binds together the creator and his creation. One therefore concerns the form, another the soul embodied in the form (whose lowest characteristic is desire, the reflection of love) and the last the life aspect with which the creator has endowed the creation. We are consequently face to face again with the eternal triplicities of spirit, soul and body. It should be remembered that the Rules for Magic, as understood by the true esotericist, are as true of a created universe, solar system or planet as they are true of the tiny thought creations of a chela or aspirant.

The first reaction of the average student on reading the above is to think immediately of the body nature as it expresses some type of energy. Thus duality is the thing noted and that which employs the thing is present in his mind. Yet one of the main necessities before occult aspirants at this time is to endeavour to think in terms of the one Reality which is Energy itself and nothing else. Therefore it is of value to emphasize in our discussions of this abstruse subject the fact that spirit and energy are synonymous terms and are interchangeable. Only in the realisation of this can we arrive at the reconciliation of science and religion and at a true understanding of the world of active phenomena by which we are surrounded and in which we move.

The terms organic and inorganic are largely responsible for much of the confusion, and the sharp differentiation existing in the minds of many people between body and spirit, between life and form, have led to a refusal to admit the essential identity in nature of these two. The world in which we live is regarded by the majority as really solid and tangible, yet possessing some mysterious power lying concealed within it which produces movement, activity and change. This is of course putting it crudely but it suffices to sum up the unintelligent attitude.

The orthodox scientist is largely occupied with structures, relationships, with the composition of form and with the activity produced by the component form parts and their interrelations and dependencies. The chemicals and elements and the functions and parts they play, and their mutual interactions as they compose all forms in all the kingdoms of nature are the subject of their investigation. The nature of the atom, of the molecule and the cell, their functions, the qualities of their force manifestations and the varying types of activity, the solving of the problem as to the character and nature of the energies—focalised or localised in the differing forms of the natural or material world—demand the consideration of the ablest minds in the world of thought. Yet the questions—What is Life? What is Energy? or What is the process of Becoming and the nature of Being? remain unanswered. The problem as to the why and the wherefore is regarded as fruitless and speculative, almost insoluble.

Nevertheless, to the pure reason and through the correct functioning of the intuition, these problems can be solved and these questions answered. Their solution is one of the ordinary revelations and attainments of initiation. The only true biologists are the initiates of the mysteries, for they have an understanding of life and its purpose and are so identified with the life principle that they think and speak in terms of energy and its effects, the planetary Hierarchy, are based on a few fundamental formulas which concern life as it makes itself felt through its three differentiations or aspects:—energy, force, matter.

It should be noted here that only as a man understands himself can he arrive at an understanding of that which is the sum total that we call God. This is a truism and an occult platitude, but when acted upon leads to a revelation which makes the present "Unknown God" a recognised Reality. Let me illustrate:

Man knows himself to be a living being and calls death that mysterious process wherein that something, which he commonly designates as the breath of life, is withdrawn. On its withdrawal, the form disintegrates. The cohesive vitalising force is gone, and this produces that falling apart into its essential elements of that which has hitherto been regarded as the body.

This life principle, this basic essential of being and this mysterious elusive factor is the correspondence in man of that which we call spirit or life in the macrocosm. Just as the life in man holds together, animates, vitalises and drives into activity the form and so makes of him a living being, so the life of God—as the Christian calls it—performs the same purpose in the universe and produces that coherent, living, vital ensemble which we call a solar system.

This life principle in man manifests in a triple manner:

1. As the directional will, purpose, basic incentive. This is the dynamic energy which sets the being functioning, brings him into existence, sets the term of his life, carries him through the years, long or short, and abstracts itself at the close of his life cycle. This is the spirit in man, manifesting as the will to live, to be, to act, to pursue, to evolve. In its lowest aspect this works through the mental body or nature, and in connection with the dense physical makes itself felt through the brain.

2. As the coherent force. It is that significant essential quality which makes each man different, which produces that complex manifestation of moods, desires, qualities, complexes, inhibitions, feelings and characteristics which produce a man's peculiar psychology. This is the result of the interplay between the spirit or energy aspect, and the matter or body nature. This is the distinctive subjective man, his colouring, or individual note; this it is which sets the rate of vibratory activity of his body, produces his particular type of form, is responsible for the condition and nature of his organs, his glands, and his outer aspect. This is the soul and—in its lowest aspect—it works through the emotional or astral nature and in connection with the dense physical, through the heart.

3. As the activity of the atoms and cells of which the physical body is composed. It is the sum total of those little lives of which the human organs, comprising the entire man are composed. These have a life of their own and a consciousness which is strictly individual and identified. This aspect of the life principle works through the etheric or vital body and in connection with the solid mechanism of the

tangible form through the spleen.

It is not, of course, possible to give the mantric words and phrases which are mentioned in Rule XI. They would be profoundly incomprehensible to all but the initiate, and therefore need not engross our attention. It should be noted that much in these Instructions is in advance of modern thought and both these Instructions and the *Treatise on Cosmic Fire* will only be fully understood towards the end of this century.

Let us consider this rule sentence by sentence, and arrive at that one of the interpretations which is the easiest for the average aspirant. All these rules can be read from the standpoint of intelligent man, and will mean but little; they can be read from the standpoint of the aspirant, and will then convey certain practical ideas which are susceptible of daily application and can be wrought out in the crucible of life experience. They will achieve meaning as the aspirant learns to handle energies, to work in mental matter and to cooperate creatively with the Purpose underlying the evolutionary plan. From the angle of vision of the disciple, these Rules carry certain potent instructions and will lead him to an understanding of the process of the creative work in nature, which is necessarily sealed to the mind of the aspirant. As to the comprehension of the initiate, these words convey definite commands which only his illumined intuition can rightly interpret. With the higher grades of intelligences we need not concern ourselves. We will consider this Rule therefore solely from the angle of vision of the average aspirant, leaving other interpretations to those individuals who have the internal equipment which will enable them to understand.

I. *Ascertain the formula which will confine the lives within the ensphering wall.*

All forms in nature, as we well know, are made up of myriads of tiny lives, holding a certain measure of awareness, of rhythm, and of coherency according to the force of the Law of Attraction, utilized by the builder of the form. This is true both of the Macrocosm and of the infinite world of microcosmic lives, which are contained within the greater whole. Embryo solar systems, coming into being under the impulse of divine thought, are at first fluidic and nebulous, are shifting in outline and are held together loosely by the central nucleus of energy—another way of expressing the embodied idea. As time progresses, they pass on to other conditions, they take more definite form, they enter into peculiar relations with allied and neighboring forms, and adjust themselves to varying relations of an internal nature with those forms, which in the earlier stage was not possible. Eventually we find a solar system such as ours and myriads of others—a solar system functioning as a sun with its revolving and rotating planets, preserving their differing orbits, holding their stated and relative positions, active as independent and inter-dependent organisms, and yet presenting, to the eye of the astronomer, a coherence, a unity and a structure that is unique in each case and yet which functions under cosmic law. It measures up to some vast purpose, conceived and held steadily in the Universal Mind, which is in its turn an aspect of that group-conscious and self-conscious entity who is the author of its being and the creator of its form.

This one intelligent Life may be posited as creating in his meditation (or its, if you prefer, for what do words matter when all is futile to express reality as it is!) and consequently in his reflective mind, that which we call a thought-form. This thought-form has four main characteristics:

1. It is brought into being through the conscious use of the Law of Attraction.

2. It is formed of an infinite number of living entities who are attracted by the mind of the divine

Creator and thus enter into relation with each other.

3. The form is the externalization of something that its Creator has:

a. Visualized.
b. Built intelligently and "coloured" or "qualified", so as to meet the purpose for which it was intended.
c. Vitalized by the potency of his desire and the strength of his living thought.
d. Held in shape as long as it is needed in order to perform its specific work.
e. Connected to himself by a magnetic thread—the thread of his living purpose and the strength of his dominant will.

4. This interior purpose, which has clothed itself in mental, astral and vital substance, is potent on the physical plane just as long as:

a. It remains consciously in its Creator's thought.
b. It "keeps its distance" occultly from its Creator. Many thought-forms remain futile as they are "too close" to their Creator.
c. It can be directed in any desired direction, and under the law of least resistance, can find its own place, thus performing its desired function and carrying out the purpose for which it was created.

The "formula" therefore might be regarded as the idea emanating from the divine Thinker; it might be defined as the dynamic purpose, the thing, as the Thinker sees it and externalizes it in his mind, and visualizes it as the carrier of his intent. The mathematics which underlie the construction of a bridge, such as any of the great spans which signalize human achievement, convey naught to the uninitiated, but to those who know and understand, they are the bridge itself, reduced to its essential terms. They are the bridge in latency, and in these mathematical formulas lie hid the purpose, the quality and the form of the completed structure and its eventual usefulness. So it is with the concepts and the ideas which give birth to a thought-form. These occult formulas exist on the archetypal plane which (for the aspirant) is the plane of the intuition, though in reality it is a state of consciousness far higher still. These formulas underlie a world of forms and must be contacted by those who are duly equipped to work under the Great Architect of the Universe. There are, symbolically speaking, three great books of formulas. Note the words "symbolically speaking", and forget them not. There is first the Book of Life, read and eventually mastered by initiates of all degrees. There is the Book of Divine Wisdom, read by aspirants of all degrees, sometimes called the Book of Knowing Experience, and there is the Book of Forms which is compulsory reading for all in whom the intelligence is awakening to functioning activity. It is with the Book of Forms that we are now concerned.

Patanjali speaks in one place of the "rain-cloud of knowable things" of which the soul is consciously aware. The aspirant, weary of the eternal round of his own futile and unimportant thoughts, seeks to tap the resources of this "rain cloud" and so precipitate upon the earth some of the thoughts of God. He seeks to work so that he can further the manifestation of the ideas of the Creator. To do this he has to fulfill certain initial requirements, which might be briefly stated as follows:

1. Know the true meaning of meditation.

2. Align with facility the soul, the mind and the brain.

3. Contemplate, or function as the soul on its own plane. It then becomes possible for the soul to act as

the intermediary between the plane of divine ideas and the mental plane. You see how this matter of participation in the divine creative process works out as the objective of all true meditation work?

4. Register the idea, received by the soul intuitively, and recognize the form which it should take. These last seven words are of vital importance.

5. Reduce the vague and misty idea to its essentials, discarding all vain imaginings and the formulations of the lower mind, so equipping oneself to leap readily into activity, and, through steadfastness in contemplation, receive accurately the vision of the inner structure, or of the subjective skeleton, if I may so term it, of the form which is to be.

6. This, as recorded consciously by the soul upon the mind, is as consciously registered by the mind, held steady in the light, and might be regarded as the reduction of the formula to the blue print. It is not the formula itself, but the secondary process. According to the strength, the simplicity and the clarity of the embodiment of the formula in a simple outlined structure, so will be the finally furnished building and the consequent form, which will confine within the periphery of the outer form itself the lives used in its construction.

This, in reality, resembles the stage of conception. Latent within the germ (the result of male—female interrelation) lie all the potencies and capacities of the finished product. Latent within the idea which has been materially conceived, but which has been inspired by the Spirit aspect, lie hid the potencies of the finished thoughtforms. The matter aspect, represented by the mind, has been fecundated by the Spirit aspect, and the triplicity will eventually be completed by the created form. But in the early stages there is as yet only the "formula"—the conceived idea, the latent yet dynamic concept. It is potent enough to draw to itself the essentials for growth and form, yet who shall say whether it will prove an abortion, a mediocre and feeble product, or a creation of real beauty and value?

Every externalized idea is, therefore, possessed of form, animated by desire, and created by the power of the mind. The desire plane is the one upon which the mind imposes its conceptions in order to produce the "idea incarnate", to clothe the idea in form. It is therefore the gestation ground. The mind previously has been the recipient of the archetypal idea, as grasped and visualized by the soul. In its turn the soul is the recipient of the formula as presented to it in the world of ideas. You have thus the "presented-idea", the " perceived-idea" and the "formulated-idea", and the idea working out into manifestation.

It is well to bear in mind that the following factors govern the emergence of the idea out of the Universal Mind into the world of tangible forms. These are:

1. The energies emanating from the archetypal plane. This plane is the focus of the attention of the highest group of Intelligences on our planet. Their consciousness can respond and be inclusive to this sphere of activity whereon the Mind of God expresses itself, free from the limitations of what we understand as form. They are the custodians of the formula; they are the mathematicians who prepare the blue prints of the great Plan; they calculate the effects of the forces with which the work is carried forward, and the energies which must be manipulated; they allow for the strains and stresses to which the forms must be subjected under the impact of the life force, they deal with the cyclic impulses to which the evolutionary process must respond; they concern themselves with the relation between the form aspect and the life urge.

2. The intuitional state of awareness. On this level of consciousness, we find the Masters of the Wisdom carrying on Their work, and it is in this sphere of influence that They work with the greatest ease and facility, as much so as does normally intelligent man work on the physical plane. Their minds are constantly in touch with the archetypal minds, who are the custodians of the formulas, and They— taking the blue prints (I speak again in symbolic fashion), deal with the specifications, look for those suitable for the control of the work, and assemble the needed personnel. Among Their disciples, They search until They find the one most suited to be the focal point of information on the physical plane, or the group most eligible to carry into manifestation the desired part of the Plan. They work with those so chosen, impressing upon their minds that eternal triplicity of idea-quality-form until the details begin to emerge, and the work of what is literally a "precipitation" can go forward.

3. The activity of the mental state of consciousness. It is on the mental plane that much of this work is necessarily done, and here is reason sufficient for the development, on the part of the aspirant, of a trained intellect. The "rain cloud of knowable things" precipitates first of all on the mental plane, and a further precipitation goes forward when disciples and aspirants are the recipients. These latter, in their turn, seek to impress and guide the lesser workers and aspirants, who, karmically or by choice, lie within their radius of influence. Thus the "idea" presented is seized upon by many minds and the formula aspect of the great work has played its part.

It will be seen how this work is consequently and essentially *group work*, and is therefore only truly possible for those who have somewhat mastered the meditation process, and can "hold the mind steady in the light". This light in reality streams forth from the Universal Mind and is of varying kinds and was (esoterically speaking) generated in a previous solar system and must be used and developed in this one.

In the words "the light of the intuition" we have conveyed to our minds that type of energy which embodies the purpose, the will of God, the Plan, as we regard it. In the words "the light of the soul", we have an expression which sums up the purpose, the plan, the will of those entities, who, incarnated in human form, and at times functioning out of the body, have the responsibility of materializing the divine concepts in the four kingdoms in nature. The human kingdom is, par excellence, the medium of expression for the Universal Mind, and when the sons of God in human form are perfected, the problems of the natural world will be solved in a large measure. The fully conscious sons of God, aware of themselves whilst in the human form (and they are few as yet), constitute literally the brain of the planetary life.

There is a truly occult significance to the words "to throw the light" upon a problem, a condition, or a situation. In its essential meaning it connotes the revelation of the presented idea, of the principle which underlies the outer manifestation. It is the recognition of the inner and spiritual reality which produces the outer and visible form. This is the keynote of all work in symbolism. The work of ascertaining the formulas, of drawing up the subjective charts or plans of intuitive impression and of intense activity on the mental plane is the sole work of the organized planetary hierarchy. The second phase of the work is carried on by those workers, who, co-operating consciously with the hierarchy, demonstrate the reality of that work in the three worlds of human evolution. They bring the germ of the idea, and the embryonic concept into outer and completed existence, through the process of right thought, the awakening of desire, and the nurturing of right public opinion. They thus bring about the needed physical activity.

Aspirants, group leaders and thinkers in all parts of the globe can be available for this work, provided their minds are open and focussed. According to the simplicity of their approach to truth, according to the clarity of their thought, according to their group influence and state of inclusive awareness, and according also to their power for long sustained effort will be the approximation of the outer form to the inner idea and the spiritual subjective reality.

The point I seek to make is that the average reader of these Instructions has nothing to do with the formulas. They are grasped and understood by the great Knowers Who stand back of the evolutionary process and are responsible for its functional activity. The hierarchy of Masters, of the senior initiates, and disciples is proceeding steadily with that work but is dependent, under the Law, upon those on the physical plane who are to produce the outer forms. If they fail to respond, there will be delay or incorrect building; if they make mistakes, there will be lost time and energy, and again delay; if they lose interest and cease to work, or are primarily interested in their own affairs and personalities, the Plan will have to wait, and energy which would otherwise be made available for the solving of human problems and the guidance of humanity will have to find its outlet in other directions. There is never anything static in the creative process; energy which is flowing forth in the pulsation of the one Life, and its rhythmic and cyclic activity—never ending and never resting—must be somewhere utilized, and must find its way in some direction, often (when man fails in his duty) with catastrophic results. The problem of cataclysms, the cause, for instance, of the steadily increasing insect peril, will be found to be related to the inflow of unused and unrecognized energy which is capable of right direction and right purpose and for the furthering of the Plan, if the aspirants and disciples of the world will shoulder their group responsibilities, submerge their personalities, and achieve true realization. Humanity must be more diligent and more intelligent in the working out of its true destiny and karmic obligations. When men are universally en rapport with the custodians of the plan and their minds and brains are illumined by the light of the intuition, of the soul and of the universal mind, when they can train themselves to respond intelligently to the timely impulses which cyclically emanate from the inner side of life, then there will be a steady adjustment between life and form and a rapid amelioration of world conditions. It is an interesting point to hear in mind that the first effect of the response of the more advanced of the sons of men to the formulas as translated and transmitted by the Knowers will be the establishing of right relations between the four kingdoms in nature, and right relations between units and groups in the human family. A step in this direction is being made. Relations between the four spheres of activity which we call human, animal, vegetable and mineral are now badly adjusted because the energy of matter is primarily the governing factor. In the human kingdom, the working of this energy demonstrates in what we call selfishness. In the animal kingdom, it demonstrates in what we call cruelty, though, where the sense of responsibility is nonexistent and only instinctual and temporary parental responsibility is found, there is no criticism to be given. In the vegetable kingdom this maladjustment expresses itself during this planetary period of misuse as disease.

This surprises you? Disease has its roots primarily in maladjustments and misdirected force in the vegetable kingdom; this affects The animal and mineral kingdoms and subsequently the human. It is too far ahead for this to be demonstrated, but when this condition is understood, it will be in that kingdom in nature that the attention of the investigators must be focussed, and the eradication of disease will eventually find its solution.

II. *Pronounce the words which will tell them what to do and where to carry that which has been made.*

Let us remember in connection with this Rule that it is only potent in so far as the "worker with the Law" is en rapport with the inner reality within himself, with the soul. It is essential that through him, in full waking consciousness, the soul should be functioning. It is the soul who pronounces the words.

It is the soul who utters forth the mystic phrase, but it is the soul as controller or ruler of the mechanism, of the form-apparatus. This control is only possible where there is alignment of the brain and mind and soul. Again, it is necessary to remember that this Rule, being an expression of the creative work, applies to all creative process, whether macrocosmic or microcosmic, whether we are dealing with God as the creator of the solar system, with the soul as the creator of the human mechanism, or with the man as he attempts to master the technique of the magical work and so become a creator of forms in his own little sphere. All have to work out the true significance of the Rule, for God works under the law of His Being, and this Law demonstrates to us as the laws of nature.

The ideas of ordered activity and of a conscious and purposeful goal are bound up in the phrase we are considering. The builder of any form is first of all a controller of lives and the arbiter of the destinies of certain entities. In this thought we have light thrown upon the subject of free will and upon the Law of Cause and Effect. It must not be forgotten however that the mystery of causes lies hid in past universes—all, in their day, the "forms indwelt by God". For us there can be no such thing as pure cause, but only the working out of major effects. Just as for us such a reality as pure reason is totally incomprehensible and unattainable, so with pure cause. These factors antedate our solar system and therefore speculation about them remains unrewarded, except in so far as it tends to develop the mental apparatus. This solar system is a system of effects, which in their turn generate causes. Only in the human family and only among those human beings who are consciously using mind power are any causes of any kind being generated. All causes, being initiated by a mind of some kind, functioning consciously and thinking clearly, posit a Thinker, and this is profoundly the position of the occult sciences. Our solar system is a thought-form but one having real existence just as long as thought persists. All that is forms part of the current of ideas emanating from the divine Thinker. All thoughts are part of a divine stream. The mass of people think not, and so do not generate causes that must in due time produce their effect.

You ask, where then the truth of the statement made in many occult modern books that the trend of life or cycle of lives indicates necessarily the future, and that the causes initiated in one life work out as effects in another? Where lives are predominantly emotional and are physically oriented, it is not a particular life that sets the pace but the group of lives, simultaneously interacting with each other, predisposes the future along certain lines. This is eternally true of all human beings at a certain level of conscious development where they are swayed by mass ideas, moulded unthinkingly by tradition and public opinion, are frankly immersed in selfish interests, and are not "taking hold" of conditions themselves but are being carried forward on the tide of evolution. It is a form of group activity (groups governed by the vibration of physical and astral forms) which produces the characteristics and tendencies which cause the situation and environing circumstances. In this realization lies hid the secret of racial and national karma and conditions. In these groups, the ordinary feeling, active man is immersed, and out of this immersion he must find his way by discovering and using his mind. Instinct must give place to intellect. For cycles of lives, groups of souls incarnate through the pull of the material forms towards which they are attracted. These attractive energies have earlier been utilized by the soul—finally being discarded and disintegrated. It is the potency of form which in the first case draws the soul into incarnation, for in the first half of the evolutionary process matter—highly organized in a previous solar system—is the dominant factor. Later, we know, spirit mounts on the shoulder of matter. The mass interplay of spirit and matter is now so potent that one of the major experiences that a soul undergoes is the achieving of the stage wherein the pull of matter begins to wane and the soul learns to detach itself. This is the experience through which humanity is now passing—again a group activity on a higher turn of the spiral.

Large generalizations are indeed safer than the detailed and oft erroneous information anent the rules governing the taking and relinquishing of form, found in much of our puerile literature, but e'en these generalizations should be regarded with much distrust. All that can be posited is that, under the Law of Cause and Effect, spirit and matter coalesced and the worlds were made. Governed by the same law, forms were created and became material expressions of the life urge. They were swept in and out of manifestation according to a rhythmic cyclic beat, initiated in still earlier solar systems, than the one immediately preceding ours. Groups of forms appeared and disappeared, and were governed almost entirely by their group coherence and vibration. So the life progressed through the elemental or involutionary kingdoms, through the three lower kingdoms in nature and on into the human kingdom.

In the lower human stages and in the stage of animal man, the same group activity reigns, only (as in the involutionary kingdoms) becoming smaller and smaller groups as the individual units achieve—one by one—the status of truly self-conscious individuals, and begin to work as souls. Then they not only become creators, with the power of standing alone, with the faculty of clear thinking and accurate visualization, but demonstrate also that they are the possessors of the creative art or faculty of creative imagination. They pass through life after life of self-sufficiency in which the personality is developed and used; then they begin to find their subjective group which will eventually take the place of the outer material groups in their consciousness. Thus they regain again group existence, only this time in full awareness and control.

In the group with which they find themselves subjectively affiliated, will be found those who have worked with them in the earlier mass state, so that they work in close association with those who have been nearest to them and who have been linked with them in the great life cycle.

There are certain names given to these stages in the occult archives which are suggestive and illuminating; they are of course symbolic. It might be of interest if I gave some of these ancient cryptic utterances which convey three items of information, namely, the name of the stage, its esoteric colour, and its symbol. I would like to point out, however, that these intriguing pieces of information which I at times convey and which some of the students seem to regard as of vital importance are of far less importance than the injunction to live kindly, speak words of gentleness and of wisdom, and practice self-forgetfulness. The occult data is read and noted, the familiar instructions are skipped and overlooked. We, who work with aspirants, smile oft at the foolishness and lack of judgment evinced by those we teach. Say to a student: Practice with steadfastness the law of loving-kindness, and he will say that indeed he will attempt to do, but within himself the very familiarity of the injunction palls and is deemed, at best, a needed platitude. Say to the student: I will give you some occult phrases or some items of information anent the Great Ones, and with keenness, with excitement, and with smug self-satisfaction and with a pleased curiosity, he prepares for the important revelation. Yet the earlier injunction is the conveyer of occult information and indicates a law which—if rightly followed—leads to release and liberation. The latter concerns phenomena and the knowledge of it leads not the weary pilgrim to the gates of heaven. Some of you need this reminder.

Those stages which precede the human are omitted as none who will read these words possess the equipment to comprehend their inner sense. We will begin therefore with the stages in the human kingdom.

Stage I

The life has climbed the stairway long through daily use of form. Through the lesser three, with

218

progress slow, the long path has been travelled. Another door stands open now. The words sound forth: "Enter upon the way of real desire."

The life, that only knows itself as form, enshrouds itself in vivid red, the red of known desire, and through the red all longed-for forms approach, are grasped and held, used and discarded, until the red changes to rose and rose to palest pink, and pink to white. Forth flowers then the pure white rose of life.

The tiny rose of living life is seen in bud; not yet the full blown flower.

Stage II

The picture changes form. Another voice, coming from close at hand utters another phrase. The life continues on its way. "Enter the field where children play and join their game." Awakened to the game of life, the soul passes the gate.

The field is green and on its broad expanse the many forms of the one moving Life disport themselves; they weave the dance of life, the many patterned forms God takes. The soul enters "the playground of the Lord" and plays thereon until he sees the star with five bright points, and says: "My Star."

The star is but a point of light, not yet a radiant sun.

Stage III

The way of red desire fails. It loses its allure. The playground of the sons of God no longer holds appeal. The voice which has twice sounded from out the world of form sounds now within the heart. The challenge comes: "Prove thine own worth. Take to thyself the orange ball of thy one-pointed purpose." Responsive to the sounded word, the living soul, immersed in form, emerges from the many forms and hews its onward way. The way of the destroyer comes, the builder and again the tearer down of forms. The broken forms hold not the power to satisfy. The soul's own form is now the great desire, and thus there comes the entering of the playground of the mind.

But in these dreams and fantasies, at times a vision comes—a vision of a folded lotus flower, close petalled, tightly sealed, lacking aroma yet, but bathed in cold blue light.

Orange and blue in some more distant time will blended be, but far off yet the date. Their blending bathes the bud in light and causes future opening. Let the light shine.

Stage IV

Into the dark the life proceeds. A different voice seems to sound forth. "Enter the cave and find your own; walk in the dark and on your head carry a lighted lamp. The cave is dark and lonely; cold is it and a place of many sounds and voices. The voice of the many sons of God, left playing on the playground of the Lord, make their appeal for light. The cave is long and narrow. The air is full of fog. The sound of running water meets the rushing sound of wind, and frequent roll of thunder.

Far off, dim and most vaguely seen, appears an oval opening, its color blue. Stretched athwart this space of blue, a rosy cross is seen, and at the centre of the cross, where four arms meet, a rose. Upon the upper limb, a vibrant diamond shines, within a star five-pointed.

The living soul drives forward towards the cross which bars his way to life, revealed and known.

Not yet the cross is mounted and therefore left behind. But onward goes the living soul, eyes fixed upon the cross, ears open to the wailing cries of all his brother souls.

Stage V

Out into radiant life and light! The cave is left behind; the cross is overturned; the way stands clear. The word sounds clear within the head and not within the heart. "Enter again the playground of the Lord and this time lead the games." The way upon the second tier of stairs stands barred, this by the soul's own act. No longer red desire governs all the life, but now the clear blue flame burns strong. Upon the bottom step of the barred Way he turns back and passes down the stairs on to the playground, meeting dead shells built in an earlier stage, stepping upon forms discarded and destroyed, and holding forth the hands of helpfulness. Upon his shoulder sits the bird of peace; upon his feet the sandals of the messenger.

Not yet the utter glory of the radiant life! Not yet the entering into everlasting peace! But still the work, and still the lifting of the little ones.

Here in symbolic form we have pictures of human life and progress, of life in form and growing through the building process which marks the creative work. It is only a bald translation of some mantric phrases, and of some basic symbols, and must in no way be considered to be anything except indicative of a process, veiled and couched so that only those who know can understand. Esotericists will understand that these five stages cover the life period of every form, no matter whether the creator is cosmic, planetary or human.

Every form is built by an impulsive spark of life, emanated by a creator, and growing stage by stage under the law of accretion—an aspect of the law of attraction, which is the law of life. This law cooperates with the Law of Cause and Effect, which, as we know, is the law governing matter. Cause, attraction or desire, accretion and effect—these four words govern the construction of any thought-form. When the latter is a completed entity, it is an effect built by accretion under the power of an organized cause.

The race has evolved now to a point where we think of effects primarily in terms of quality rather than in terms of matter. A thought-form exists for us in order to produce an effect. The raison d'être of all forms we have come to feel is to express some subjective quality which will give us the key to its creator's purpose. Ponder on these words. Hence, we find in this Rule XI that the purpose of the word pronounced is to tell the lives which constitute the form "what to do and where to carry that which has been made." Thus we find the idea of purpose, activity and goal.

There is no need for me to add to the vast amount of literature which has been put forth or to emphasize the significance of purpose in connection with such a thoughtform as a solar system, a planet, a kingdom in nature or a human being. In some respects this subjective triplicity of purpose, activity and goal is well known and in others it is of too high and too inscrutable a nature for us to deal with in these Instructions and wander into the realms of speculation. With the goal, religion has long sought to deal; with the activity aspect, the scientist is now attempting to deal; and with the Will of God the most advanced thinkers and philosophers are constantly speculating. Only when man submits himself to the discipline of his own spiritual will and controls the activity of the lives within his form nature and so orients himself to the goal as it progressively makes its appeal to his vision, will he arrive at a true understanding of the plan, which constitutes the will of God as far as human beings can grasp it.

But with the thought-forms which he is beginning to create as he daily learns to think, we can concern ourselves for it is the first lesson soon to be learnt in the magical work. The creator in mental matter has:

a. To learn to build intelligently.
b. To give the impulse, through right speech which will animate that which he has built, and so enable the thought-form to convey the intended idea.
c. To send out his thought-form correctly oriented to his goal, and so truly directed that it will reach the objective and accomplish its sender's purpose.

The necessity for clear thinking and the elimination of idle, destructive and negative thoughts becomes increasingly apparent as the aspirant progresses upon his way. As the power of the mind increases and as the human being differentiates his thought increasingly from mass thought, he inevitably builds thought substance into form. It is at first automatic and unconscious. He cannot help so doing, and fortunately, for the race, the forms constructed are so feeble that they are largely innocuous, or so in line with mass thought that they are negligible in their effect. But as man evolves his power and his capacity to harm or to help increases, and unless he learns to build rightly and correctly to motivate that which he has built he will become a destructive agency and a centre of harmful force—destroying and harming not only himself, as we shall see shortly, but equally hurting and harming those who vibrate to his note.

Granted all this you might appositely inquire: Are there some simple rules which the earnest and sincere beginner could apply to this science of building and which are so clear and concise that they will produce the needed effect? There are, and I will state them simply so that the beginner will, if he follows them, escape the dangers of black magic, and learn to build in line with the plan. He will, if he follows the rules I give, avoid the intricate problem which he has himself blindly constructed and which will indeed shut out the light of day, darken his world, and imprison him in a wall of forms which will embody for him his own peculiar great illusion.

These rules may sound too simple for the learned aspirant but for those who are willing to become as little children they will be found to be a safe guide into truth and will eventually make them able to pass the tests for adeptship. Some are couched in terms symbolic, others are necessarily blinds, still others express the truth just as it is.

1. View the world of thought, and separate the false out of the true.

2. Learn the meaning of illusion, and in its midst locate the golden thread of truth.

3. Control the body of emotion for the waves that rise upon the stormy seas of life engulf the swimmer, shut out the sun and render all plans futile.

4. Discover that thou hast a mind and learn its dual use.

5. Concentrate the thinking principle, and be the master of thy mental world.

6. Learn that the thinker and his thought and that which is the means of thought are diverse in their nature, yet one in ultimate reality.

7. Act as the thinker, and learn it is not right to prostitute thy thought to the base use of separative desire.

8. The energy of thought is for the good of all and for the furtherance of the Plan of God. Use it not therefore for thy selfish ends.

9. Before a thought-form is by thee constructed, vision its purpose, ascertain its goal, and verify the motive.

10. For thee, the aspirant on the way of life, the way of conscious building is not yet the goal. The work of cleaning out the atmosphere of thought, of barring fast the doors of thought to hate and pain, to fear, and jealousy and low desire, must first precede the conscious work of building. See to thy aura, oh traveler on the way.

11. Watch close the gates of thought. Sentinel desire. Cast out all fear, all hate, all greed. Look out and up.

12. Because the life is mostly centered on the plane of concrete life, thy words and speech will indicate thy thought. To these pay close attention.

13. Speech is of triple kind. The *idle words* will each produce effect. If good and kind, naught need be done. If otherwise, the paying of the price cannot be long delayed.

The *selfish words*, sent forth with strong intent, build up a wall of separation. Long time it takes to break that wall and so release the stored-up, selfish purpose. See to thy motive, and seek to use those words which blend the little life with the large purpose of the will of God.

The *word of hate*, the cruel speech which ruins those who feel its spell, the poisonous gossip, passed along because it gives a thrill—these words kill the flickering impulses of the soul, cut at the roots of life, and so bring death.

If spoken in the light of day, just retribution will they bring; when spoken and then registered as lies, they strengthen that illusory world in which the speaker lives and holds him back from liberation.

If uttered with intent to hurt, to bruise and kill, they wander back to him who sent them forth and him they bruise and kill.

14. The idle thought, time selfish thought, the cruel hateful thought if rendered into word produce a prison, poison all the springs of life, lead to disease, and cause disaster and delay. Therefore, be sweet and kind and good as far as in thee lies. Keep silence and the light will enter in.

15. Speak not of self. Pity not thy fate. The thoughts of self and of thy lower destiny prevent the inner voice of thine own soul from striking upon thine ear. Speak of the soul; enlarge upon the plan; forget

thyself in building for the world. Thus is the law of form offset. Thus can the rule of love enter upon that world.

These simple rules will lay right foundations for the carrying forward of the magical work, and will render the mental body so clear and so powerful that right motive will control and true work in building will be possible.

Much of the significance of this rule must remain theoretical, and be considered as holding a challenge until such time as the real magical work of thought-form building becomes universally possible. The *formula*, as we have seen, will remain unknown to all save the members of the Hierarchy of Adepts for long ages to come. The *directional words* are capable of ascertainment, but only to those who are working consciously under the guidance of their own souls, and who, through mind control merging into deep meditation, can manipulate the matter of thought and become "knowing creators." These can, and do, speak the impulsive words which bring into being those new forms and organisms, those expressions of ideas and those organisations which live their life cycle and serve their purpose, and so come, duly, to their timely and appointed end. These creators are the leaders and organisers, the teachers and the guides in all phases of human living. Their sound does go forth into all lands and their note is internationally recognised. Hundreds of such names are easily remembered and spring unhidden to the mind. They live in the memory of the multitude and that which lives is the sound of their accomplishment, be that good or bad.

But in the sentence which we must consider we find portrayed a universal function, even though it is as yet carried forward for the most part unconsciously. The words to be dealt with are as follows:

III. *Finally, to utter forth the mystic phrase which will save him from their work.*

Therefore it appears that at the close of the magical work of creation, a phrase must be enunciated which effects a salvation and produces a liberation of a dual kind,—a liberation of the creating agent from the form which he has created, and the emancipation of that form from the control of the one who has brought it into being.

It is obvious that already the nature of speech in relation to embodied ideas is being somewhat understood. Study the method of talk which is now the main factor employed to "launch an idea." Note how all inventions (which are neither more nor less than embodied concepts) come into exoteric being on the physical plane through the power of the spoken word, and consider also with care the occult significance underlying all conferences, all meetings, all consultations, and all discussions which concern themselves with the launching of some idea or set of ideas upon the sea of public necessity. May it not be possible that under the modes of activity employed by the advertising agencies and the constant training given to salesmen in the use of the spoken word as a means of approach to the public in order to sell an idea, we shall find the first distorted indications of the emanations of those mystic phrases which will bring into being the creation of the soul in all fields of creative enterprise?

The training of public opinion, the utilisation of catch words and slogans, the tendency to embody the concepts of campaigners in trite and apposite phrases are part of the growing realisation as to the magical work. All these means are employed blindly and without true realisation; they constitute a part of the emerging activities of a humanity which is on the verge of real creative work, the principles of which are not yet understood nor scientifically applied. But they do point the way, and under the simplification which marks the return to synthesis, we shall have the cessation of speech and the utilisation of simpler forms. Under the evolutionary urge, we have had the creative Sound, the Word, Speech. The latter, in its turn, has been differentiated into words, phrases, sentences, paragraphs, books, until we now have the era wherein this differentiation is at its height, and we have speeches at all hours of the day and night; we have the utilisation of the public platform to reach the public ear, and of the radio to reach all classes and races of humanity in an effort to mould public opinion and bring certain ideas and concepts into the public consciousness. We have the publication of books literally in their millions, and all playing their part in the same great work, and we have as yet both methods of communication being prostituted to the selfish ends and ambitious purposes of those who speak and write. Yet there are a few true creators who are endeavouring to make their sound heard, to speak those mystical words which will enable humanity to see the vision. Thus will be dispersed eventually the clouds of thought-forms which at this time shut out the clear light of Cod.

The subject is too large for me to elaborate in this *Treatise*. I but seek to make suggestions which will carry to the intelligent reader some idea of the enormous progress which has been made in the magical work. In this way he will be enabled to go forward with optimism knowing that hitherto all has been good inasmuch as man has progressed in knowledge. Out of the present welter of speech and of words, of lectures and of books, a few clear concepts will surely emerge which will find an echo in the hearts of men. Thus also will men be led on into the new age, wherein "talk will die out and books come to naught" for the lines of subjective communication will lie open. Men will recognise that noise acts as a deterrent to telepathic intercourse. The written word will not be needed either, for men will use symbols of light and colour to supplement through the eye what the subjective hearing has recorded. But that day is not yet, even though the radio and television are the first steps in the right direction.

Putting the truth as simply as possible we might state that through the complexity of much speech-making and book-writing, ideas are now enabled to take form and so run through their cycle of activity. But this method is as unsatisfactory in the field of knowledge as is the ancient tallow dip in the field of illumination. Electric light has superseded it, and some day the true telepathic communication and vision will take the place of speech and of writings.

Carrying the same concepts into the field of real esoteric work we have the worker in thought-matter building his thought-form and "confining the lives" which express and respond to his idea within a "ring-pass-not". This latter persists for as long as his mind attention and hence his ensouling energy is directed upon it. We have him pronouncing the words which will enable his thought-form to do its work, fulfill the mission for which it has been constructed, and carry out the purpose for which it was created. All that has been given out hitherto in connection with the words used in the creative work is the sevenfold sacred Word, AUM. This, when rightly used *by the soul on the mental plane* vitalises and expedites all thought-forms, and so produces successful enterprise. It is interesting to note that in Atlantean days, the word used was TAU, enunciated explosively and so forcefully, that the thought-forms thus energised and expedited acted inevitably like a boomerang, and returned to the one who sent them forth. This word TAU is likewise, in its symbolic form, the symbol of reincarnation. It is desire for form which produces the use of form and causes cyclic and constant rebirth in form. It was the constant use of the TAU likewise, which brought about the final overwhelming with water, which swept away the ancient Atlantean civilisation; the few who used the AUM in those days were not potent enough to offset the force of desire. The mind bodies of the race could not respond to that newer creative sound. Humanity was still swept entirely by longing and desire to such an extent that the united desire for possessions and for the enjoyment of form drove men esoterically "into the waters". Desire for form still forces upon humanity the constant process of rebirth until such time as the TAU influence is exhausted and the AUM sound can dominate. The former influence is however weakening, and the AUM is increasing in potency until it will be the dominating factor. To this latter sound, the word of the soul must eventually succeed, until AUM in its turn is entirely superseded.

The sound of many waters (which is the symbolic way of expressing the TAU influence) will cease, and the time will come, as we are assured in the Christian Bible, when there "will be no more sea". Then the sound of the AUM which is symbolically spoken of as the "roaring" of a blazing fire", and which is the sound of the mental plane will take its place. The word of the soul cannot be given except in the secret place of initiation. It has its own peculiar vibration and note, but this cannot be conveyed until such time as the AUM is used with correctness. Just as the TAU, carrying the note of desire and of the urge to have and to be, was misused and carried its civilisations to disaster, so AUM can also be misused and can carry its civilisations into the fire. This is the truth which really underlies the misunderstood Christian teaching anent hell-fire and the lake of fire. They portray symbolically the end of the age when the mental plane civilisations will come to a cataclysmic end, as far as the form aspect is concerned just as the earlier civilisations came to a watery consummation.

One hint here I will give, and one that is oft overlooked. On the mental plane, time is not; therefore the time equation enters not into the idea of a final ending by fire. There is no setting of a time for a disaster or a catastrophe. The full effect will take place in the realm of the mind, and may it not be said that even now the fire of anxiety, of foreboding, of worry, and of fear is burning up our thoughts and engrossing our mental attention? Its work is to purify and cleanse, so, let the AUM do its work and let all of you who can, employ it with frequency and with right thought so that the world purification may proceed apace. Much must be burned and consumed which bars the way for the emergence of the new ideas, the new archetypal forms. These will eventually dominate the new age and make it possible for the word of the soul to sound forth and be heard exoterically.

I realize that that which I have imparted here is difficult of comprehension, but the paragraphs above dictated hold warning for the careless and much instruction for the earnest seeker after light.

There are two aspects of this phrase which we are considering with which I seek briefly to deal. There are many which I might take up, but two will suffice to carry practical suggestion, and to indicate ideas which aspirants everywhere would do well to grasp. The thought of salvation from the effect of form-embodied ideas must be considered, and I would like also to cover the idea of "a saving-from" under two headings. The aspirant has to be saved from the thought-forms built daily during his mental life, and a soul in incarnation has also to be saved from the form attachments which during the ages have grown and strengthened, and from which he has to be released through the process we call death. We will therefore divide our subject as follows:

I. Salvation from the power exerted by the thoughtforms we have ourselves created.

II. Salvation from the power of the threefold body which the soul has built, through the magical release called death.

It is with the latter that I wish primarily to deal, but certain things must be said concerning the power of thought-forms, and concerning their danger, and the mode whereby they can be rendered innocuous.

SALVATION FROM OUR THOUGHT-FORMS

I speak now for aspirants, who, through concentration and meditation, are gaining power in thought. I speak for the thinkers of the world, who, through their one-pointed application and devotion to business, to science, to religion or to the varying modes of human activity have oriented the mind (not the emotions but the mentality) to some line of constant action which is necessarily a part of the divine activity in the large sense.

It is right here, in the use of thought, that the difference between black and white magic can be seen. Selfishness, ruthlessness, hatred, and cruelty characterise the worker in mental substance whose motives are, for many lives, centred around his own aggrandisement, focussed on his personal acquisition of possessions, and directed entirely to the attainment of his own pleasure and satisfaction, no matter what the cost to others. Such men are happily few, but the way to such a point of view is easy to achieve, and many need to guard themselves lest they tread unthinkingly the way towards materiality.

A gradual and steady growth in group consciousness and responsibility, a submergence of the wishes of the personal self and the manifestation of a loving spirit characterise those who are oriented towards the life side of the divine whole. It might be said that human beings fall into three main groups:

1. The vast majority, who are neither good nor bad, but simply unthinking and entirely submerged in the evolutionary tide, and in the work of developing a true self consciousness, and the needed equipment.

2. A small, a very small number, who are definitely and consciously working on the side of materiality—or (if you prefer so to express it) on the side of evil. Potent are they on the physical plane, but their power is temporal and not eternal. The law of the universe, which is the law of love, is eternally against them, and out of the seeming evil good will come.

3. A goodly number who are the pioneers into the kingdom of the soul, who are the exponents of the new age ideas, and the custodians of that aspect of the Ageless Wisdom which is next to be revealed to mankind. This group is constituted of the unselfish and intelligent men and women in every field of human endeavour, of the aspirants and disciples, of the initiates who sound the note for the various groups and types, and of the Occult Hierarchy itself. The influence of this band of mystics and knowers is exceedingly great and the opportunity to work in cooperation with it at this time is easier of attainment than at any other time in racial history.

The first group is unthinking; the two other groups are beginning to think and to employ the laws of thought. It is with the use of thought by the aspirant that I seek to deal. Much about thought will be found in *A Treatise on Cosmic Fire*, but I intend to give some practical ideas and suggestions which will help the average aspirant to work as he should.

Let us remember first of all that no aspirant, no matter how sincere and devoted, is free from faults. Were he free, he would be an adept. All aspirants are still selfish, still prone to temper and to irritability, still subject to depression and even at times to hatred. Oft that temper and hatred may be aroused by what we call just causes. Injustice on the part of others, cruelty to human beings and to animals, and the hatreds and viciousness of their fellow men do arouse in them corresponding reactions, and cause them much suffering and delay. One thing must ever be remembrance. If an aspirant evokes hatred in an associate, if he arouses him to temper, and if he meets with dislike and antagonism, it is because he himself is not entirely harmless; there are still in him the seeds of trouble, for it is a law in nature that we get what we give, and produce reactions in line with our activity be it physical, emotional or mental.

There are certain types of men who do not come under this category. When a man has reached a stage of high initiation, the case is different. The seed ideas he seeks to convey, the work he is empowered to do, the pioneering enterprise he is endeavouring to carry forward, may—and often do—call forth from those who sense not the beauty of his cause and the rightness of the truth he enunciates, a hatred and a fury which causes him much trouble and for which he is not personally responsible. This antagonism comes from the reactionaries and the devotees of the race and it should be remembered that it is largely impersonal even though focussed on him as the representative of an idea. But with these high souls I deal not, but with students of the Ageless Wisdom who are learning not only that they seldom think, but that when they do they are oft thinking wrongly, for they are forced into a thought activity by reactions which have their seat in their lower nature, and are based on selfishness and lack of love.

There are three lessons which every aspirant needs to learn:

First, that every thought-form which he builds is built under the impulse of some emotion or of some desire; in rarer cases it may be built in the light of illumination and embody, therefore, some intuition. But with the majority, the motivating impulse which sweeps the mindstuff into activity is an emotional one, or a potent desire, either good or bad, either selfish or unselfish.

Second, it should be borne in mind that the thoughtform so constructed will either remain in his own aura, or will find its way to a sensed objective. In the first case, it will form part of a dense wall of such thoughtforms which entirely surround him or constitute his mental aura, and will grow in strength as he pays it attention until it is so large that it will shut out reality from him, or it will be so dynamic and potent that he will become the victim of that which he built. The thought-form will be more powerful than its creator, so that he becomes obsessed by his own ideas, and driven by his own creation. In the second case, his thought-form will find its way into the mental aura of another human being, or into some group. You have here the seeds of evil magical work and the imposition of a powerful mind upon a weaker. If it finds its way into some group, analogous impulsive forms (found within the group aura) will coalesce with it, having the same vibratory rate or measure. Then the same thing will take place in the group aura as has taken place within the individual ring-pass-not,—the group will have around it an inhibiting wall of thought-forms, or it will be obsessed by some idea. Here we have the clue to all sectarianism, to all fanaticism, and to some forms of insanity, both group and individual.

Thirdly, the creator of the thought-form (in this case an aspirant) remains responsible. The form remains linked to him by his living purpose and therefore the karma of the results, and the ultimate work of destroying that which he has built must be his. This is true of every embodied idea, the good as well as the bad. The creator of all of them is responsible for the work of his creation. The Master Jesus, for instance, has still to deal with the thought-forms which we call the Christian Church, and has much to do. The Christ and the Buddha have still some consummating work to carry through, though not so much with the forms which embody Their enunciated principles, as with the souls who have evolved through the application of those principles.

With the aspirant, however, who is still learning to think, the problem is different. He is still prone to use thought matter to embody his mistaken apprehension of the real ideas; he is still apt to express his likes and dislikes through the power of thought; he is still inclined to use the mind stuff to make possible his personality desires. To this every sincere aspirant will bear witness.

Much concern is being felt among many of you as to the guarding of thoughts and the protection of formulated ideas. Some thoughts are ideas, clothed in mental matter and keep their habitat on the plane of thought matter. Such are the abstract conceptions and the scarcely sensed facts of the inner occult or mystic life that pass through the mind of the thinker. They are not so difficult to guard, for their vibrations are so high and light that few people have the power to clothe them adequately in mental matter, and those few are so very scarce that the risk of such statements being unwisely promulgated is not very great.

Then there are the communications involved in occult teaching. The circle of those who apprehend them is widening somewhat and these thought-forms frequently take to themselves astral matter from the desire in the heart of the student to verify, corroborate, and share with the group whose knowledge is as vital as his. Sometimes this is possible, and sometimes not. If prohibited what is the method of protection then? Largely a refusing to allow the matter of the astral plane to adhere to the mental thought-form. Fight the matter out on the desire level, and inhibit that type of matter from formulating. Where no desire to speak exists, and where the striving is to prevent the gathering of the material around the nucleus, another thought-form is built up, one that intervenes and protects.

Still another type of thought-form comes forth,—the most prevalent and the one that causes the most trouble. These are the facts of information, the detailed material, the news (if so you like to call it), the basis of what may degenerate into gossip, that concerns either your work, administrative or otherwise, and that which concerns other people. How shall you prevent your mind from transmitting to another facts such as these? These are facts that have their origination in physical plane occurrence, and therein lies the difficulty. The inner facts of the occult life, and those that originate on the mental plane are not so difficult to hide. They do not come your way till your vibrations are keyed high enough for them, and as a rule, when that is so, character of sufficient stability and wisdom goes alongside. But it is not thus with a physical plane fact. What must be done? The other thoughts descend from above; these latter work upwards from the physical plane and are increased in vitality by the knowledge of the many, often of the many unwise. One kind starts nebulously on the mental plane, and only the higher type of mind can formulate it, and clothe it with matter in geometrical precision, and such a mind usually has the wisdom that refuses to clothe it in astral plane matter. Not so with the physical plane fact. It is a vital entity, robed in material of the astral plane and the mental plane when first you meet and contact it. Will you vitalise it, or will you arrest it? Arrest it by a rush and wave of love for the party implicated, that envelops the thought-form and sends it back to the originator, borne on the wings of a surge of astral plane matter, strong enough to sweep through and around, mayhap disintegrating, but most certainly returning it harmlessly to the sender. Perhaps it is an evil piece of information, a lie or item of gossip. Devitalise it by love, break it in pieces by the power of a counter thought-form of peace and harmony.

Or again, it may be true, some sad or evil occurrence or deed of some mistaken brother. What then is there to do? Truth cannot be devitalised or disintegrated. The Law of Absorption will aid you here. Into your heart you absorb the thought-form you encounter and there transmute it by the alchemy of love. Let me be practical and illustrate, for the matter is of importance.

Some brother comes to you and tells to you a fact about another brother—a fact involving what the world would call wrongdoing on that brother's part. You who know so much more than the average man of the street, will realise that that so called wrongdoing may be but the working out of karma, or have its basis in a good motive wrongly construed. You add not to the talk, you do not hand on the information, as far as you are concerned the thought-form, built around the fact, has wandered into what you call a cul-de-sac.

What do you then? You build a counter stream of thoughts which (on a wave of love) you send your apparently erring brother: thoughts of kindly assistance, of courage and aspiration, and of a wise application of the lessons to be learnt from the deed he has accomplished. Use not force, for strong thinkers must not unduly influence other minds, but a gentle stream of wise transmuting love. We have here three methods, none strictly occult, for those later shall be imparted, but methods available for the many.

1. The thought form kept to the mental levels, i.e. the inhibiting of astral plane matter.

2. The thought-form broken up and disintegrated by a stream of love-force well-directed.

3. The absorbing of the thought-form, and the formulation of a counter-thought of loving wisdom.

Inhibition—Disintegration—Absorption

There are three main penalties which attach to the wrong use of thought substance, and from these the aspirant must learn to save himself, and to avoid those activities; eventually this will make the process of salvation unnecessary.

1. A potent thought-form can act like a boomerang. It can return, charged with increased velocity, to the one who sent it on its mission. A strong hatred, clothed in mental matter, can return to its creator charged with the energy of the hated person, and can hence work havoc in the life of the aspirant. Hate not, for hatred returns ever from whence it came. There is a depth of truth in the ancient aphorism: "Curses, like chickens, come home to roost."

A potent desire for material acquisition will eventually return bringing inevitably that which has been desired, only to find in the majority of cases that the aspirant no longer aches for possession, but regards it as an incubus, or, in the meantime, already possesses more than he needs and is satiated and knows not what to do with all that he has gained.

A potent thought-form embodying an aspiration for spiritual illumination or for recognition by the Master may bring such a flood of light as to blind the aspirant, and make him consequently the possessor of a wealth of spiritual energy for which he is unready, and which he cannot use. Again, it may attract to the aspirant a thought-form of one of the Great Ones, and thus swing him deeper into the world of illusion and of astralism. Hence the need for humility, for a longing to serve and a resulting self-forgetfulness if one is to build truly and correctly. Such is the law.

2. A thought-form can also act as a poisoning agent, and poison all the springs of life. It may not be potent enough to swing out of its creator's aura (very few thought-forms are), and find its goal in another aura there to gather strength and so return from whence it came, but it may have a vitality of its own which can devastate the life of the aspirant. A violent dislike, a gnawing worry, a jealousy, a constant anxiety and a longing for something or someone may act so potently as an irritant or poison

that the entire life is spoilt, and service is rendered futile. The entire life is embittered and devitalised by the embodied worry, hatred or desire. All relationships with other people are rendered equally futile or even definitely harmful, for the worried or suspicious aspirant spoils the home circle or his group of friends by his inner poisonous attitude, governed by an idea. His relation to his own soul and the strength of the contact with the world of spiritual ideas is at a standstill, for he cannot progress onward and is held back by the poison in his mental system. His vision becomes distorted, his nature corroded, and all his relationships impeded by the wearing, nagging thoughts which he has himself embodied in form and which have a life so powerful that they can poison him. He cannot rid himself of them no matter how hard he tries or how clearly he sees (theoretically) the cause of his trouble. This is one of the commonest forms of difficulty, for it has its seat in the selfish personal life, and is ofttimes so fluidic that it seems to defy direct action.

3. The third danger against which the aspirant must guard himself is becoming obsessed by his own embodied ideas, be they temporarily right or basically strong. Forget not that all right ideas are temporary in nature and must eventually take their place as partial rights and give place to the greater truth. The fact of the day is seen later as part of a greater fact. A man can have grasped some of the lesser principles of the Ageless Wisdom so clearly and be so convinced of their correctness that the bigger whole is forgotten and he builds a thought-form about the partial truth which he has seen which can prove a limitation and keep him a prisoner and hold him back from progress. He is so sure of his possession of truth that he can see the truth of no one else. He can be so convinced of the reality of His own embodied concept of what the truth may be that he forgets his own brain limitations and that the truth has come to him via his own soul and is consequently coloured by his ray, being subsequently built into form by his personal separative mind. He lives but for that little truth; he can see no other; he forces his thought-form on other people; he becomes the obsessed fanatic and so mentally unbalanced, even if the world regards him as sane.

How shall a man guard himself from these dangers? How shall he rightly build? How shall he preserve that balance which will enable him to see truth, judge rightly, and so preserve his mental contact with his soul and with the souls of his fellow men?

First and foremost, by the constant practice of Harmlessness. This involves harmlessness in speech and also in thought and consequently in action. It is a positive harmlessness, involving constant activity and watchfulness; it is not a negative and fluidic tolerance.

Secondly, by a daily guarding of the doors of thought, and a supervision of the thought life. Certain lines of thought will not be permitted; certain old thought habits will be offset by the institution of constructive creative thinking; certain preconceived ideas (note the esoteric value of that phrase), will be relegated to the background so that the new horizons will be visioned and the new ideas can enter. This will entail a daily, hourly watchfulness, but only until ancient habits have been overcome and the new rhythm established. Then the aspirant will discover that the mind is so focussed on the new spiritual ideas that the old thought-forms will fail to arrest the attention; they will die of inanition. There is encouragement in this thought. The first three years' work will be the hardest. After that the mind will be engrossed by the ideas and not by the thought-form.

Thirdly, by refusing to live in one's own thought world and by entering the world of ideas and the stream of human thought currents. The world of ideas is the world of the soul, and of the higher mind. The stream of human thoughts and of opinions is that of the public consciousness and of the lower mind. The aspirant *must* function free in both worlds. Note this with care. The thought is not that he must function freely, which involves more the idea of facility but that he must function as a free agent in both worlds. Through constant daily meditation he does the first. Through wide reading and sympathetic interest and understanding he accomplishes the second.

Fourthly, he must learn to detach himself from his own thought creations, and leave them free to accomplish the purpose for which he intelligently sent them forth. This fourth process falls into two parts:

1. By the use of a mystic phrase he severs the link which holds an embodied idea in his thought-aura.

2. By detaching his mind from the idea, once he has sent it on its mission, he learns the lesson of the *Bhagavad Gita* and "works without attachment".

These two points will vary according to the growth and status of the aspirant. Each has, for himself, to formulate his own "severing phrase", and each has for himself, alone and unaided, to learn to look away from the three worlds wherein he works in his effort to push his idea of the work to be done. He has to teach himself to withdraw his attention from the thought-form he has built, wherein that idea is embodied, knowing that as he lives as a soul, and as spiritual energy pours through him so his thought-form will express the spiritual idea and accomplish its work. It is held together by the life of the soul, and not by personality desire. The tangible results are ever dependent upon the strength of the spiritual impulse animating his idea, which is embodied in his thought-form. His work lies in the world of ideas and not in physical effects. Automatically the physical aspects will respond to the spiritual impulse.

SALVATION FROM DEATH

We come now to the second phase of our study of the final words of Rule XI. We have dealt with salvation from the dangers incident to the creation of thoughtforms by a human being who has learnt, or is learning, to create on the mental plane. Much could have been said from the standpoint of the inability of the majority of students to think with clarity. Clear thinking involves capacity to dissociate oneself, temporarily at least, from all reactions and activities of an emotional nature. As long as the astral body is in a state of restless movement, and its moods and feelings, its desires and emotions are powerful enough to attract attention, positive pure thought processes are not possible. Until the time comes when there is a more general appreciation of the value of concentration and of meditation, and until the nature of the mind and its modifications are more universally understood, any further teaching on the subject would be futile.

In these Instructions I have sought to give an indication of the first steps in esoteric psychology, and have dealt primarily with the nature and mode of training of the astral body. Later on in this century, the psychology of the mind, its nature and modifications may be handled in more detail. But the time is not yet.

Our subject now is salvation from the body nature through the process of death.

Two things must be borne in mind as we seek to study the means of this salvation:

First, by the body nature I mean the integrated personality, or the human equipment of physical body, vital or etheric vehicle, the matter (or mode of being) of the desire nature, and the mind stuff. These constitute the sheaths or outer forms of the incarnated soul. The consciousness aspect is sometimes

231

focussed in one and sometimes in another, or is identified with the form or with the soul. The average man works with facility and self-consciousness in the physical and astral bodies. The intelligent and highly evolved man has added to these two the conscious control of his mental apparatus, though only in certain of its aspects, such as the memorising or analysing faculties. He has also, in some cases, succeeded in unifying these three into a consciously functioning personality. The aspirant is beginning to understand something of the principle of life which is animating the personality, whilst the disciple is utilising all three, because he has coordinated or aligned the soul, the mind, and the brain and is therefore beginning to work with his subjective apparatus or energy aspects.

Secondly, this salvation is brought about through a right understanding of the mystical experience we call *death*. This is to be our theme, and the subject is so immense that I can only indicate certain lines along which the aspirant may think, and posit certain premises which he can later elaborate. We shall confine ourselves also primarily to the death of the physical body.

Let us first of all define this mysterious process to which all forms are subject and which is frequently only the dreaded end—dreaded because it is not understood. The mind of man is so little developed that fear of the unknown, terror of the unfamiliar, and attachment to form have brought about a situation where one of the most beneficent occurrences in the life cycle of an incarnating Son of God is looked upon as something to be avoided and postponed for as long a time as possible.

Death, if we could but realise it, is one of our most practised activities. We have died many times and shall die again and again. Death is essentially a matter of consciousness. We are conscious one moment on the physical plane, and a moment later we have withdrawn onto another plane and are actively conscious there. Just as long as our consciousness is identified with the form aspect, death will hold for us its ancient terror. Just as soon as we know ourselves to be souls, and find that we are capable of focussing our consciousness or sense of awareness in any form or on any plane at will, or in any direction within the form of God, we shall no longer know death.

Death for the average man is the cataclysmic end, involving the termination of all human relations, the cessation of all physical activity, the severing of all signs of love and of affection, and the passage (unwilling and protesting) into the unknown and the dreaded. It is analogous to leaving a lighted and a warmed room, friendly and familiar, where our loved ones are assembled, and going out into the cold and dark night, alone and terror stricken, hoping for the best and sure of nothing.

But people are apt to forget that every night, in the hours of sleep, we die to the physical plane and are alive and functioning elsewhere. They forget that they have already achieved facility in leaving the physical body; because they cannot as yet bring back into the physical brain consciousness the recollection of that passing out, and of the subsequent interval of active living, they fail to relate death and sleep. Death, after all, is only a longer interval in the life of physical plane functioning; one has only "gone abroad" for a longer period. But the process of daily sleep and the process of occasional dying are identical, with the one difference that in sleep the magnetic thread or current of energy along which the life force streams is preserved intact, and constitutes the path of return to the body. In death, this life thread is broken or snapped. When this has happened, the conscious entity cannot return to the dense physical body and that body lacking the principle of coherence, then disintegrates.

It should be remembered that the purpose and will of the soul, the spiritual determination to be and to do, utilises the thread soul, the sutratma, the life current, as its means of expression in form. This life current differentiates into two currents or two threads when it reaches the body, and is "anchored", if I might so express it, in two locations in that body. This is symbolic of the differentiations of Atma, or Spirit, into its two reflections, soul and body. The soul, or consciousness aspect, that which makes a human being a rational, thinking entity, is "anchored" by one aspect of this thread soul to a "seat" in the brain, found in the region of the pineal gland. The other aspect of the life which animates every atom of the body and which constitutes the principle of coherence or of integration, finds its way to the heart and is focussed or "anchored" there. From these two points, the spiritual man seeks to control the mechanism. Thus functioning on the physical plane becomes possible, and objective existence becomes a temporary mode of expression. The soul, seated in the brain, makes man an intelligent rational entity, self-conscious and self-directing; he is aware in varying degree of the world in which he lives, according to the point in evolution and the consequent development of the mechanism. That mechanism is triple in expression. There are first of all the nadis and the seven centres of force; then the nervous system in its three divisions: cerebro-spinal, sympathetic, and peripheral; and then there is the endocrine system, which might be regarded as the densest aspect or externalisation of the other two.

The soul, seated in the heart, is the life principle, the principle of self-determination, the central nucleus of positive energy by means of which all the atoms of the body are held in their right place and subordinated to the "will-to-be" of the soul. This principle of life utilises the blood stream as its mode of expression and as its controlling agency, and through the close relation of the endocrine system to the blood stream, we have the two aspects of soul activity brought together in order to make man a living, conscious, functioning entity, governed by the soul, and expressing the purpose of the soul in all the activities of daily living.

Death, therefore, is literally the withdrawal from the heart and from the head of these two streams of energy, producing consequently, complete loss of consciousness and disintegration of the body. Death differs from sleep in that *both* streams of energy are withdrawn. In sleep only the thread of energy, which is anchored in the brain is withdrawn, and when this happens the man becomes unconscious. By this we mean that his consciousness or sense of awareness is focussed elsewhere. His attention is no longer directed towards things tangible and physical but is turned upon another world of being and becomes centred in another apparatus or mechanism. In death, both the threads are withdrawn or unified in the life thread. Vitality ceases to penetrate through the medium of the blood stream and the heart fails to function just as the brain fails to record, and thus silence settles down. The house is empty. Activity ceases except that amazing and immediate activity which is the prerogative of matter itself and which expresses itself in the process of decomposition. From certain aspects, therefore, that process indicates man's unity with everything that is material; it demonstrates that he is part of nature itself and by nature we mean the body of the one life in whom "we live and move and have our being". In those three words—living, moving and being—we have the entire story. *Being* is awareness, self consciousness and self-expression and of this man's head and brain are the exoteric symbols. *Living* is energy, desire in form, coherence and adhesion to an idea and of this the heart and the blood are the exoteric symbols. *Moving* indicates the integration and response of the existing, aware, living entity into the universal activity, and of this the stomach, pancreas and liver are the symbols.

It is interesting, though incidental to our subject, to bear in mind that in cases of imbecility and idiocy and in that stage of old age which we call senile decay, the thread which is anchored in the brain is withdrawn, whilst that which conveys the life impulse or urge remains still anchored in the heart. There is life but no intelligent awareness; there is movement but no intelligent direction; in the case of senile decay, when there has been a high grade apparatus utilized in life, there may be the appearance of intelligent functioning but that is an illusion due to old habit and to old established rhythm but not to coordinated coherent purpose.

It must be noted also that death is, therefore, undertaken at the direction of the ego, no matter how unaware a human being may be of that direction. The process works automatically with the majority, for when the soul withdraws its attention the inevitable reaction on the physical plane is death, either by the abstraction of the dual threads of life and reason energy, or by the abstraction of the thread of energy which is qualified by mentality, leaving the life stream still functioning through the heart but no intelligent awareness. The soul is engaged elsewhere and occupied on its own plane with its own affairs.

In the case of highly developed human beings we often find a sense of pre-vision as to the death period; this is incident upon egoic contact and awareness of the wishes of the ego. It involves sometimes a knowledge of the very day of death, coupled to a preservation of self-determination up to the final moment of withdrawal. In the case of initiates there is much more than this. There is an intelligent understanding of the laws of abstraction and this enables the one who is making the transition to withdraw consciously and in full waking awareness out of the physical body and so to function on the astral plane. This involves the preservation of continuity of consciousness so that no hiatus occurs between the sense of awareness on the physical plane and that of the after death state. The man knows himself to be as he was before, though without an apparatus whereby he can contact the physical plane. He remains aware of the states of feeling and of the thoughts of those he loves, though he cannot perceive or contact the dense physical vehicle. He can communicate with them on the astral plane or telepathically through the mind if they and he are en rapport, but communication that involves the use of the five physical senses of perception lies necessarily out of his reach. It is useful to remember, however, that astrally and mentally the interplay can be closer and more sensitive than ever before for he is freed of the handicap of the physical body. Two things, however, militate against this interplay: one is the grief and violent emotional upset of those left behind and, in the case of the average human being, the other is the man's own ignorance and bewilderment as he stands faced by what are to him new conditions, though they are really old conditions, if he could but realize it. Once men have lost the fear of death and have established an understanding of the after-death world which is not based on hallucination and hysteria or on the conclusions (oft unintelligent) of the average medium, who speaks under the control of his own thought-form (built by himself and the circle of sitters), we shall have the process of death properly controlled. The condition of those left behind will be carefully handled so that there is no loss of relationship and no false expenditure of energy.

There is a big difference now between the scientific method of bringing people into incarnation and the perfectly blind and oft frightened and surely ignorant way in which we usher them out of incarnation. I seek today to open the door in the occident to a newer and more scientific method of handling the process of dying, and let me make myself perfectly clear. What I have to say in no way abrogates modern medical science with its palliatives and skill. All I plead for is a sane approach to death; all I seek to make is a suggestion that when pain has worn itself out and weakness has supervened, the dying person be permitted to prepare himself, even if apparently unconscious, for the great transition. Forget not that it takes strength and a strong hold on the nervous apparatus to produce pain. Is it impossible to conceive of a time when the act of dying will be a triumphant finale of life? Is it impossible to vision the time when the hours spent on the death bed may be but a glorious prelude to a conscious exit? When the fact that the man is to discard the handicap of the physical sheath may be for him and those around him the long waited for and joyous consummation? Can you not visualize the time when instead of tears and fear and the refusal to recognize the inevitable, the dying person and his friends would mutually agree on the hour and that nothing but happiness would characterize the passing? That in the minds of those left behind the thought of sorrow will not enter and death beds will be regarded as happier occasions than births and marriages? I tell you, that before so very long this will be deeply so for the intelligent of the race, and little by little for all.

You say there are as yet only beliefs as to immortality and no sure evidences. In the accumulation of testimony, in the inner assurances of the human heart, in the fact of belief in eternal persistence as an idea in the minds of men lies sure indication. But indication will give place to conviction and knowledge before another hundred years has elapsed, for an event will take place and a revelation be given to the race which will turn hope into certainty and belief into knowledge. In the meantime, let a new attitude to death be cultivated and a new science of death be inaugurated. Let it cease to be the one thing we cannot control and which inevitably defeats us and let us begin to control our passing over to the other side, and to understand somewhat the technique of transition.

Before I take up this subject in greater detail I would like to make reference to the "web in the brain", which is intact for the majority but is non-existent for the illumined seer.

In the human body, as you know, we have an underlying, interpenetrating vital body which is the counterpart of the physical, which is larger than the physical and which we call the etheric body or double. It is an energy body and is composed of force centres and nadis or force threads. These underlie or are the counterparts of the nervous apparatus—the nerves and the nerve ganglia. In two places in the human vital body there are *orifices of exit* for the life force. One opening is in the solar plexus and the other is in the brain at the top of the head. Protecting both is a closely woven web of etheric matter, composed of interlacing strands of life energy.

During the process of death, the pressure of the life energy beating against the web produces eventually a puncturing or opening. Out of this the life force pours as the potency of the abstracting influence of the soul increases. In the case of animals, of infants and of men and women who are polarized entirely in the physical and astral bodies, the door of exit is the solar plexus and it is that web which is punctured, thus permitting the passing out. In the case of mental types, of the more highly evolved human units, it is the web at the top of the head in the region of the fontanelle which is ruptured, thus again permitting the exit of the thinking rational being.

In psychics and in the case of mediums and lower seers (clairvoyant and clairaudient people) the solar plexus web is permanently ruptured early in life and easily therefore they pass in or out of the body, going into trance, as it is called, and functioning on the astral plane. But for these types there is no continuity of consciousness and there seems no relation between their physical plane existence and the happenings which they relate whilst in trance and of which they usually remain totally unaware in the waking consciousness. The whole performance is below the diaphragm and is related primarily to animal sentient life. In the case of conscious clairvoyance and in the work of the higher psychics and seers there is no trance, obsession or mediumship. It is the web in the brain which is punctured and the opening in that region permits the inflow of light, information and inspiration; it confers also the power to pass into the state of Samadhi which is the spiritual correspondence to the trance condition of the animal nature.

In the process of death these are, therefore, the two main exits: the solar plexus for the astrally polarized, physically biased human being and therefore of the vast majority, and the head centre for the mentally polarized and spiritually oriented human being. This is the first and most important fact to remember and it will easily be seen how the trend of a life tendency and the focus of the life attention determine the mode of exit at death. It can be seen also that an effort to control the astral life and the emotional nature and to orient one's self to the mental world and to spiritual things has a momentous effect upon the phenomenal aspects of the death process.

If the student is thinking clearly, it will be apparent to him that one exit concerns the spiritual and highly evolved man, whilst the other concerns the low grade human being who has scarcely advanced beyond the animal stage. What then of the average man? A third exit is now in temporary use; just below the apex of the heart another etheric web is found covering an orifice of exit. We have, therefore, the following situation:

1. The exit in the head, used by the intellectual type, by the disciples and initiates of the world.

2. The exit in the heart, used by the kindly, well-meaning man or woman who is a good citizen, an intelligent friend and a philanthropic worker.

3. The exit in the region of the solar plexus, used by the emotional, unintelligent, unthinking man and by those whose animal nature is strong.

This is the first point in the new information which will slowly become common knowledge in the West during the next century. Much of it is already known by thinkers in the East and is in the nature of a first step towards a rational understanding of the death process.

The second point to be grasped is that there can be a technique of dying and a training given during life which will lead up to the utilization of that technique.

As regards the training to which a man can submit himself I will give a few hints which will be found to convey a new meaning to much work now being done by all aspirants. The Elder Brothers of the race who have guided humanity through long centuries, are now busy preparing people for the next great step to be taken. This step will bring in a continuity of consciousness which will do away with all fear of death and link the physical and astral planes in such a close relation that they will in reality constitute one plane. Just as an at-one-ment has to be brought about between the various aspects of man, so a similar unification has to take place in connection with the various aspects of the planetary life. The planes have to be at-one-ed as well as soul and body. This has already been largely accomplished between the etheric plane and the dense physical plane. Now it is being rapidly carried forward between the physical and the astral.

In the work being done by seekers in all departments of human thought and life, this unification is proceeding and in the training now suggested to earnest and sincere aspirants, there are other objectives than just the one of producing soul and body at-one-ment. No emphasis, however, is laid upon them, owing to the ability of man unduly to emphasize the wrong objectives. It might well be asked if it is possible to give a simple set of rules that would be followed now by all who seek to establish such a rhythm that life itself is not only organized and constructive, but when the moment for vacating the outer sheath arrives, there will be no problem nor difficulty. I will, therefore, give you four simple rules that link up with much that all students are now doing:

1. Learn to keep focussed in the head through visualization and meditation and through the steady practice of concentration; develop the capacity to live increasingly as the king seated on the throne between the eyebrows. This is a rule that can be applied to the every day affairs of life.

2. Learn to render heart service and not an emotional insistence on activity directed towards handling the affairs of others. This involves, prior to all such activity, the answering of two questions:—Am I rendering this service to an individual as an individual, or am I rendering it as a member of a group to a group? Is my motive an egoic impulse, or am I prompted by emotion, ambition to shine and love of being loved or admired? These two activities will result in the focussing of the life energies above the diaphragm and so negate the attractive power of the solar plexus. Hence, that centre will become increasingly inactive and there will not be so much danger of puncturing the web in that locality.

3. Learn, as you go to sleep, to withdraw the consciousness to the head. This should be practiced as a definite exercise as one falls to sleep. One should not permit oneself to drift off to sleep, but should endeavor to preserve the consciousness intact until there is a conscious passing out onto the astral plane. Relaxation, close attention, and a steady drawing upwards to the center in the head should be attempted, for until the aspirant has learned to be steadily aware of all processes in going to sleep and to preserve at the same time his positivity, there is danger in this work. The first steps must be taken with intelligence and followed for many years until facility in the work of abstraction is achieved.

4. Record and watch all phenomena connected with the withdrawing process, whether followed in the meditation work or in going to sleep. It will be found, for instance, that many people wake with an almost painful start just as they have dropped asleep. This is due to the slipping out of the consciousness through a web which is not adequately clear and through an orifice which is partially closed. Others may hear an intensely loud snap in the region of the head. This is caused by the vital airs in the head of which we are not usually aware and is produced by an inner aural sensitivity which causes awareness of sounds always present but not usually registered. Others will see as they fall asleep, or clouds of color, or banners and streamers of violet, all of which are etheric phenomena. These phenomena which are of no real moment, are all related to the vital body, to pranic emanations, and to the web of light.

The carrying on of this practice and the following of these four rules over a period of years will do much to facilitate the technique of the death bed, for the man who has learned to handle his body as he falls asleep, has an advantage over the man who never pays any attention to the process.

In relation to the technique of dying it is only possible for me at this time to make one or two suggestions. I deal not here with the attitude of the attendant watchers, I deal only with those points which will make for an easier passing over of the transient soul.

First, let there be silence in the chamber. This is, of course, frequently the case. It must be remembered that the dying person may usually be unconscious. This unconsciousness is apparent but not real. In nine hundred cases out of a thousand the brain awareness is there, with a full consciousness of happenings, but there is a complete paralysis of the will to express and complete inability to generate the energy which will indicate aliveness. When silence and understanding rule the sick room, the departing soul can hold possession of its instrument with clarity until the last minute and can make due preparation.

Later, when more anent color is known, only orange lights will be permitted in the sick room of a dying person, and these will only be installed with due ceremony when there is assuredly no possibility of recovery. Orange aids the focussing in the head, just as red stimulates the solar plexus and green has a definite effect upon the heart and life streams.

Certain types of music will be used when more in connection with sound is understood, but there is no music as yet which will facilitate the work of the soul in abstracting itself from the body, though certain notes on the organ will be found effective. At the exact moment of death, if a person's own note is sounded, it will coordinate the two streams of energy and eventually rupture the life thread, but the knowledge of this is too dangerous to transmit yet and can only later be given. I would indicate the future and the lines along which future occult study will run.

It will be found also that pressure on certain nerve centers and on certain arteries will facilitate the work. (This science of dying is held in custody, as many students know, in Tibet.) Pressure on the jugular vein and on certain big nerves in the region of the head and on a particular spot in the medulla oblongata will be found helpful and effective. A definite science of death will inevitably later be elaborated, but only when the fact of the soul is recognized and its relation to the body has been scientifically demonstrated.

Mantric phrases will also be employed and definitely built into the consciousness of the dying person by those around him, or employed deliberately and mentally by himself. The Christ demonstrated their use when he cried aloud, "Father, into Thy hands I commend my spirit." And we have another instance in the words, "Lord, now lettest Thou Thy servant depart in peace." The steady use of the Sacred Word chanted in an undertone or on a particular key (to which the dying man will be found to respond) may later constitute also a part of the ritual of transition accompanied by the anointing with oil, as preserved in the Catholic Church. Extreme unction has an occult, scientific basis. The top of the head of the dying man should also symbolically point towards the East and the feet and the hands should be crossed. Sandalwood only should be burned in the room and no incense of any other kind permitted, for sandalwood is the incense of the first or destroyer ray and the soul is in process of destroying its habitation.

This is all I can at this time communicate on the subject of death for the consideration of the general public. But I conjure all of you to push the study of death and its technique as far as possible and to carry forward occult investigation of this matter.

RULE TWELVE

The web pulsates. It contracts and expands. Let the magician seize the midway point and thus release those "prisoners of the planet" whose note is right and justly tuned to that which must be made.

Interludes and Cycles.
The Prisoners of the Planet.

INTERLUDES AND CYCLES

We now come to the four rules which concern the physical plane. In many ways their understanding is far more difficult than was the case in the other rules, in just the same way that practical application is far harder than theorising. We can frequently think with clarity and desire rightly but the working out into physical plane manifestation of the subjective ideas, under law and constructively, is never an easy thing to do. It is however just at this point that a white magician begins to do his real work, and it is just here that he encounters failure and finds that his inner grasp of reality does not necessarily result in correct creative activity. In *A Treatise on Cosmic Fire*, there will be found certain points of interest for us to consider, and I would like to quote a few words from them:

"It might be useful here to remember that in the work of creation the white magician avails himself of the current ray influences. When the fifth, third and seventh rays are in power, either coming in, at full meridian, or passing out, the work is much easier than when the second, sixth or fourth are dominant. At the present time, the seventh ray, as we know is rapidly dominating, and it is one of the easiest of the forces with which man has to work. Under this ray it will be possible to build a new structure for the rapidly decaying civilisation, and to erect the new temple desired for the religious impulse. Under its influence the work of the numerous unconscious magicians will be much facilitated." Pages 1021-1022.

It is apparent therefore that the day of opportunity is with us, and that the coming generation can, if it so wishes, perform the magical work with many of the factors present which will tend to produce satisfactory results. The fifth ray is passing out, but its influence can still be felt; the third ray is at full meridian, and the seventh ray is rapidly coming into right activity. Much will consequently occur to make man successful, provided he can preserve constantly a right orientation, purity of motive and of life, a stabilised and receptive emotional body and that inner alignment which will make his personality a true vehicle for his soul or self.

A very interesting analogy works out as we study the words: "The web pulsates. It contracts and expands". The underlying thought is that of pulsation, of diastole and systole, of ebb and flow, of cyclic activity, of the day of opportunity and the night of inactivity, of inflow and output, and of those many appearances and disappearances which mark the sweep of all lives in all kingdoms and dimensions. This day and night cycle which is the inevitable mark of manifested existence has to be recognised. One of the things which every disciple has to learn (putting the truth in the simplest terms) is to achieve that wisdom which is based on a knowledge of when to work and when to refrain, and on an understanding of those periods or interludes which are characterised by speech and by silence. It is here that mistakes are made and here that many workers fail to make good.

This entire rule might be given in the following paraphrase which will merit careful thought and which I will elucidate somewhat.

God breathes and His pulsating life emanates from the divine heart and manifests as the vital energy of all forms. It flows, pulsating in its cycles, throughout all nature. This constitutes the divine inhalation and exhalation. Between this breathing out and the breathing in comes a period of silence and the moment for effective work. If disciples can learn to utilise these interludes, they can then release the "prisoners of the planet," which is the objective of all magical work, performed during this world period.

With the manner in which this One Life of the solar system works in these vast interludes of meditative silence, called technically a pralaya, we need not concern ourselves. The activity of the Universal Mind and its comprehensive purpose can only be perceived when each son of God enters consciously into his divine heritage. The mode of working by means of which our planetary Life utilises the cycles of silence concerns Him alone, and it must be remembered that each planetary Logos has a different pulsation, a varying periodic interlude, and His Own unique method of procedure.

What does concern the student of these Instructions however is how he can himself attain a definite constructive activity in *his* interludes. These interludes, for the purpose of our discussion, fall into three categories:

1. Life interludes, or those periods wherein the spiritual man is out of incarnation and has withdrawn into the egoic consciousness. These, for the little evolved, are practically nonexistent; they cycle in and out of incarnation with amazing rapidity. The physical plane analogy of this rapidity of activity is to be found in the intense rushing to and fro of the ordinary man as he meets the exigencies of existence and also in the difficulty he evidences in patience and in waiting and in achieving the meditative poise. As growth takes place, the periods of withdrawal from incarnation steadily lengthen, until the point is reached when the periods out of physical manifestation greatly exceed those spent in outer expression. Then the interlude dominates. The periods of outgoing (exhalation) and of inbreathing (inhalation) are relatively brief and—the point to be emphasised—these two periods are coloured and controlled by the purposes of the soul, formulated and recorded on the mind during the interlude between the two more active stages of experience. The inner life, slowly developed during the cyclic interludes, becomes the dominating factor. The man gradually becomes subjective in his attitude and the physical plane expression is primarily then the result of the inner thought life and not so much the result of reaction to physical plane occurrences and the restlessness of the desire nature.

2. The ebb and flow of daily life during a particular incarnation will also demonstrate its interludes, and these the aspirant has to learn to recognise and to utilise. He has to register the distinction between intense outgoing activity, periods of withdrawal, and interludes wherein the outer life seems static and free from active interest. This he must do if he is to avail himself fully of the opportunity which life experience is intended to furnish. The whole of life is not concentrated in one furious continuous stretch of rushing forth to work, nor is it comprehended in one eternal siesta. It has normally its own rhythmic beat and vibration and its own peculiar pulsation. Some lives change their rhythm and mode of activity every seven years; others alter every nine or eleven years. Still others work under shorter cycles and have months of strenuous endeavour followed by months of apparent non-effort. Some people again are so sensitively organised that, in the midst of work, events and circumstances are so staged that they are forced into a temporary retirement wherein they assimilate the lessons learnt during the preceding period of work.

Two groups of human beings work with apparently no physical plane ebb and flow, but manifest steadily an urge to work. These are people who are so little evolved and so low down (if one might thus express it) on the ladder of evolution and so predominantly animal that there is no mental reaction to circumstances but simply a response to the call of physical needs, and the use of time for the satisfaction of desire. This never lets up and therefore there is little that can be called cyclic in their expression. They include the unthinking toiler and the uncivilised man. Then there are those men and women who are on the opposite scale, and have climbed relatively high on the ladder of progress. These are so emancipated from the purely physical and are so aware of the nature of desire that they have learnt to preserve a continuous activity—based on discipline and service. They work consciously with cycles and understand somewhat their nature. They know the divine art of abstracting their consciousness into that of the soul in contemplation and can control and wisely guide their work in the world of men. This is the lesson which all disciples are learning and this is the high achievement of the initiates and trained workers of the race.

3. The third type of interlude, and the one with which we are here primarily concerned as we consider the magical work on the physical plane, is the interlude achieved and utilised during the meditation process. With this the student must familiarise himself, for otherwise he will be unable to work with power. This interlude or period of intense silence differentiates itself into two parts:

There is first of all the interlude which we call contemplation. I would remind you of the definition given in a book by Evelyn Underhill which describes contemplation as "an interlude between two activities". This period of silence succeeds upon the activity (found so difficult by the beginner) of making the alignment between soul-mind-brain, of quieting the emotional body, and of achieving that concentration and meditation which will serve to focus and reorient the mind upon a new world, and place it within the sphere of influence of the soul. It is analogous to the period of inhalation. In this cycle, the outgoing consciousness is gathered in and lifted up. When success crowns this effort, the consciousness then slips out of what we call the personality, the mechanism aspect, and becomes a changed consciousness. The soul on its own plane becomes active and of this activity the mind and brain are aware. From the standpoint of personality activity, an interlude takes place. There is a point of inspired waiting. The mechanism is entirely quiescent. The mind is held steady in the light and the soul in the meantime thinks, as is its habit, in unison with all souls, taps the resources of the Universal Mind, and formulates its purposes in line with the universal plan. This cycle of recorded soul activity is followed by what might be called the process of exhalation. The interlude comes to an end; the waiting mind again becomes active and in so far as it has been rightly oriented and held in a purely receptive attitude, it becomes the interpreter and instrument of the soul, which has now turned the "light of its countenance upon the attentive personality". Through that medium it can now work out the plans formulated in the interlude of contemplation. The emotional nature is swept by desire to make objective the plans with which the reoriented mind seeks to colour its experience, and subsequently the brain receives the transmitted impression and the physical plane life is then adjusted so that those plans can properly materialise. This of course delineates a mechanism, trained and adjusted and rightly responsive—a rare thing indeed to find. The second part of the interlude only becomes possible when the first or contemplative interlude has been achieved.

The disciple who is seeking to cooperate with the Hierarchy of Masters and to manifest this cooperation by active participation in Their work on the physical plane has to learn to work not only through the contemplative realisation but through a scientific utilisation of the interludes, developed in breathing, between points of inhalation and exhalation in the purely physical sense of the term. This is the true science and objective of pranayama. The brain consciousness is necessarily involved. The interlude between breaths is only capable of right use where a man has achieved the power to follow the interlude of contemplation affecting the soul and the mind and the brain. Just as the mind has been held in the light, and has been receptive to the soul impression so the brain has to be held receptive to impression from the mind.

One interlude therefore (from the standpoint of the united soul and personality) takes place *after* the period of soul inhalation, when the outgoing consciousness has been gathered inward, and the other takes place at the close of that interlude when the soul again becomes outgoing consciously to the objective world; exhalation takes the place of inhalation and also has its interlude. The disciple has to learn facility in utilising these two soul interludes—one of which produces effects upon the mind, and the other upon the brain.

There is, as always, a physical plane analogy of this process of divine inhalation and exhalation with its two interludes of silence and of thought. Let me again re-iterate the consequences of these interludes.

In the higher interlude, abstract or divine thought impresses the soul and is transmitted to the waiting mind; in the other, the mind, through concrete thought and an attempt to embody divine thought in form, impresses the brain and produces action through the medium of the physical body.

Students of occultism who have demonstrated their devotion and their mental poise, and who (to use the ancient formula of the schools of meditation) have kept the five commandments and the five rules, and have achieved right poise, can begin to use the interludes between the two aspects of physical breathing for intense activity and the use of the power of will to produce magical effects. The consciousness, focussed in the brain and having participated in the work of contemplation can now proceed to the work of materialising the plan upon the physical plane by the focussed energy of will, used in the silence by the conscious man. As can be seen, these breathing interludes are also two in number, after inhalation and after exhalation and the more experienced the disciple, the longer will be the interlude and the greater the opportunity therefore for focussed magical work and for the utterance of those words of power which will make divine purpose to *be*.

It would not be right nor proper for me to enlarge here upon the work of utilising these "midway points", as they are called in Rule XII, which the magician seizes and which he employs in constructive work. In them he consciously uses energy, directing it as he sees it; in them, he consciously comes in contact with those forces and lives which he can employ and command to bring to him what he requires for the furtherance of spiritual purposes and for the work of constructing those forms and organisms which may be needed; in them, he goes forward with the work of releasing the "prisoners of the planet"; and in them he becomes conscious of his fellow workers, of the group of world mystics, and of the hierarchy of souls.

In Instructions such as these, which are to be read by the general public it would be most unwise to give more explicit directions. Enough has been left unsaid to make it impossible for any but a deeply learned student to arrive at the necessary correlations which will enable him to carry forward the "work of the interludes", in which alone magical work can be done. You might ask: Why is this so? Why are the secrets of the breath so carefully guarded? Because the efficacy of black magic is found right here. There is a point where both black and white magic employ necessarily one similar stage in the work. Certain men, with potent wills and clear and trained minds, but animated by purely selfish purpose, have learnt to use the lower of the two soul interludes—that which concerns the relation of mind and brain. Through an intense application and a knowledge of the science of the centres they have been enabled to work out their selfish plans and to impose their will and mental authority upon the "prisoners of the planet". Thus they have wrought much harm. They have no desire to participate in the higher interlude wherein the soul is active, and the mind responsive. The intellectual activity and the responsiveness of the brain to mind impression is all that concerns them. Both white and black magicians, as you see, employ the lower interlude, and both know the significance of the physical breathing interludes. But the white magician works from the soul level out into the manifested world and seeks to carry out the divine plan, whilst the black magician works from the level of the intellect as he seeks to achieve his own separative ends. The difference is not only that of motive, but also of alignment and the radius of the consciousness and its field of expansion. Hence you will see why such extreme caution is evidenced by all true teachers, as they endeavor to teach the nature of the magical work. Only the tested and the true, only the unselfish and the pure can be given the full instructions. All can be given the information concerning the major interludes of soul-mind and mind-brain. Only a few can as yet be trusted with the significant information concerning the minor interludes, carried on in the physical body between breaths and in the brain consciousness.

One other point might be of interest before I proceed to speak of the "prisoners of the planet" and the work to be done with them.

Humanity at this time is passing through a cycle of excessive activity. For the first time in human history this activity embraces mankind on a large scale in the entire three aspects of the personality consciousness. The physical bodies, the emotional and mental states of consciousness are all in a condition of potent upheaval. This unified triple activity is increased by a cycle of equally intense planetary activity, due to the coming in of a new age, the passing of the sun into a new sign in the Zodiac and the preparation consequently going on to fit man to work easily with the new forces and energies playing upon him. At the centre of human life, the integrating group of new World servers must meet therefore a very real need. Their work must primarily be to keep such a close link with the soul of humanity—made up of all souls on their own level of being—through their own organised soul activity that there will always be those who can "work in the interludes" and so keep the plan progressing and the vision before the eyes of those who cannot as yet themselves enter into the high and secret place. They have, as I oft times have said, to learn to work subjectively, and this they must do in order to preserve—in this cycle of activity and exoteric expression—the power, latent in all, to withdraw into the centre. They constitute the door, speaking symbolically. Capacities and powers can die out for lack of use; the power of divine abstraction and the faculty to find what has been called "the golden path which leads to the clear pool and from thence to the Temple of Retreat" must not be lost. This is the first work of the Group of World Mystics, and they must keep the path open and the way clear of obstructions. Otherwise white magic might temporarily die out and the selfish purposes of the form nature assume undue control. This dire event happened in Atlantean days and the then group of workers had to withdraw from all external activity and "abstract the divine mysteries, hiding them away from the curious and the unworthy."

Now a new attempt is being made to free the "prisoners of the planet". The Hierarchy, through the Group of World Servers now in process of formation is seeking to externalise itself, and to restore the mysteries to humanity to whom they truly belong. If the attempt is to succeed it is basically necessary that all of you who have sensed the vision or seen a part of the intended plan should re-dedicate yourselves to the service of humanity, should pledge yourselves to the work of aiding to the utmost of your ability (ponder those words and search out their significance) all world servers, and should sacrifice your time and give of your money to further the endeavor of the Great Ones. Rest not, above all, from your meditation work; keep the inner link; think truth at all times. The need and the opportunity are great and all possible helpers are being called to the forefront of the battle. All can be used in some way, if the true nature of sacrifice is grasped, if skill in action is developed and if work without attachment is the effort of each and all of you.

THE PRISONERS OF THE PLANET

Having dealt with the work of the magician in his own interior consciousness and with the need for him to learn the importance of seizing the "midway point" in his work of using the interludes, both major and minor, we come now to the consideration of the objective of all his work, that is if he is a true white magician. It is stated clearly that this is to release the "prisoners of the planet". It would profit us therefore to study who these prisoners are and what is the mode of their release to be employed by the working disciple.

These prisoners of the planet fall into two major groups, which embody necessarily certain subdivisions. Inclusively they constitute all forms of life that we usually call subhuman, but these words must be given a wider connotation than is normally the case. They must be extended to include all lives which are embodied in forms.

The two divisions are as follows:

First, the substance of all forms, or the multiplicity of tiny atomic lives which, through the power of thought, are drawn into the form aspect through which all existences or all souls, mineral, vegetable, animal and the animal body of man, express themselves. This opens up a wide horizon and covers practically the work of creation on the physical plane so that we cannot even touch upon it. Under the Law of Magnetic Attraction and owing to the impulsive activity of the Universal Mind as it works out the purposes of the solar Logos or of the planetary Logos these constituents of the matter of space, these atoms of substance, are drawn together, manipulated in a rhythmic manner and held together in form. Through this mode of creation, existences come into manifestation, participate in the experience of their particular cycle, whether it is ephemeral, like the life of a butterfly or relatively permanent like the ensouling life of the planetary deity, and vanish. The two aspects concerned, spirit and matter, are brought thus into a close rapport, and necessarily exert an effect upon each other. Matter, so-called, is energised or "lifted up" in the occult sense of the term by its contact with spirit so-called. Spirit, in its turn, is enabled to enhance its vibration through the medium of its experience in matter. The bringing together of these two divine aspects results in the emergence of a third, which we call the soul, and through the medium of the soul, spirit develops a sentiency and a conscious awareness and capacity to respond which remains its permanent possession when the divorce between the two comes around eventually and cyclically.

Much anent this will be found in *A Treatise on Cosmic Fire* and there is no need for me to repeat myself here. This second treatise is intended to be more practical and generally useful. It deals primarily with the training of the aspirant so that he can, in his turn, act as a conscious creator, and as he works serve the higher ends of the Life which enfolds him. Thus he aids in the materialising of the plans of God. The training of the aspirant, the indicating to him of possible trends and lines of evolution, and the definition of the underlying purpose is all that it is wise to impart at the present stage in which the average aspirant finds himself. This has been attempted in these Instructions and there has been given also some new teaching anent the emotional vehicle. In the next century, when man's equipment is better developed and when a truer meaning of group activity is available, it will be possible to convey more information, but the time is not yet. All that is possible for me is to grope for those feeble words which will somewhat clothe the thought. As they clothe it they limit it and I am guilty of creating new prisoners who must ultimately be released. All books are prison houses of ideas, and only when speech and writing are superseded by telepathic communication and by intuitive interplay will the plan and the technique of its expression be grasped in a clearer fashion. I talk now in symbols; I manipulate words in order to create a certain impression; I construct a thought-form which, when dynamic enough, can impress the brain of a transmitting agent, such as yourself. But, as I do so, I know well how much must be left unrelated and how seldom it is possible to do more than point out a cosmology, macrocosmic or microcosmic, which will suffice to convey a temporary picture of divine reality.

I talk to you of laws, and I seek to formulate them intelligently but I am dealing really with those divine impulses which emanate from a cosmic Creator and become laws as they produce effects in the matter of space, meeting therein practically no resistance. Other divine impulses which also cyclically stream forth have not as yet carried such a strong vibration, and have not therefore been as powerful as the vibration of the combined substance affected. These latter are those impulses to which we give the name spiritual, and which we look forward to seeing established as the laws of the new era, and which will then supersede or coalesce with the present laws of the universe. Together they will bring in the new synthetic world.

But how can the whole be comprehended by the part? How can the entire plan be noted by a soul which sees as yet but a tiny fraction of the structure? Bear this steadily in mind as you study and ponder these Instructions and remember that, in the light of the future knowledge of humanity, all that is here conveyed is like a fifth reader in grammar school to the test books utilised by a college professor. It will serve however to graduate the aspirant out of the Hall of Learning into the Hall of Wisdom, if he uses the information given.

Learn to be telepathic and intuitive. Then these forms of words and these ideas, clothed in form, will not be needed. You can then stand face to face with naked truth, and live and work in the terrain of *ideas* and not in the world of *forms*.

So we leave the vast expanse of lives, covered by the unmeaning phrase "atomic substance," and pass on secondly to a consideration of those prisoners of the planet which can be more easily contacted, whose general plight can be more specifically understood, and who stand in a closer relation to man. Men are not yet equipped to comprehend the nature of those units of electrical energy which embody what we call the soul of all things and which has been termed the "anima mundi"—the life and soul of the One in whom all embodied existences live and move and have their being.

To do this, it will be necessary to understand somewhat the part that the fourth kingdom in nature plays in relation to the whole, and the purpose for which that aggregate of forms which we call the human family exists. We must study this from the standpoint of the relation of the fourth kingdom to the whole, and not from the standpoint of man's own individual progressive development and the part he plays as a human unit within the ring-pass-not of the human family. We will use the word humanity, and speak of its mission and function in the big scheme and the working out of the plan. We will infer a humanity which is composed of all the sons of men. It includes on the one hand the hierarchy of adepts who have deliberately incarnated on the physical plane in order to work within the limits of the human kingdom, and on the other we find the undeveloped types which are more animal than human. Between these two extremes we find the many and varied types, the developed and the undeveloped, the intelligent and the unintelligent—all who are covered by the word man.

Humanity constitutes a centre of energy within the cosmos, capable of three activities.

I. First of all, humanity is responsive to the inflow of spiritual energy. This pours into it from the cosmos, and speaking symbolically these energies are basically three in number:

1. Spiritual energy, as we inadequately term it. This emanates from God the Father and reaches humanity from the level of what is technically called the monadic plane, from the archetypal sphere, the highest source of which a man can become conscious. To this type of energy there are few so equipped that they can respond. It is for the majority practically nonexistent. I use the words "God the Father" in the sense of the One Self-Existent Life, or Absolute Being.

2. Sentient energy—the energy which makes man a soul. It is the principle of awareness, the faculty of consciousness, that something, inherent in matter (when brought into relation with spirit), which awakens responsiveness to an outer and far-reaching field of contacts. It is that which eventually

develops in man a recognition of the whole, of the self, and which leads him to self-determination and self-realisation. When these are developed, as they are not in the subhuman kingdoms, a man can become aware of the first type of energy, mentioned above. This energy of sentient consciousness comes from the second aspect of deity, from the heart of the sun, just as the first, technically but symbolically speaking, emanates from the central spiritual sun. The parallel to these two types of force in a human being is the nervous energy working through the nervous system with headquarters in the brain, and the life energy which is seated in the heart.

3. Pranic energy, or vitality. This is that vital force, inherent in matter itself and in which all forms are immersed, as they constitute functioning parts of the greater form. To this all forms respond. This type of energy comes from the physical sun and works actively upon the vital bodies of every form in the natural world, including the physical form of humanity itself.

In the terminology of the Ageless Wisdom, these three are called electric fire, solar fire, and fire by friction, and their purpose in relation to each other is summed up for us in the words of *The Secret Doctrine* as follows:

"Matter is the Vehicle for the manifestation of Soul on this plane of existence, and Soul is the Vehicle on a higher plane for the manifestation of Spirit and these three are a Trinity, synthesized by Life which pervades them all." S. D. I. 80.

Humanity, being the meeting-place for all the three types of energy, constitutes therefore a "midway point," in the consciousness of the Creator. This "midway point" has to be seized by the active creating agent in some such manner as the aspirant has to learn to seize his midway points in the tiny bit of magical and creative work which he is seeking to carry forward. Humanity is intended to be the medium wherein certain activities can be instituted. It is in reality the brain of the planetary Deity, its many units being analogous to the brain cells in the human apparatus. Just as the human brain, made up of an infinite number of sentient responsive cells, can be suitably impressed when quiescence has been achieved, and can become the medium of expression for the plans and purposes of the soul, transmitting its ideas via the mind, so the planetary Deity, working under the inspiration of the Universal Mind, can impress humanity with the purposes of God and produce consequent effects in the world of phenomena.

The members of the hierarchy represent those who have achieved peace and quiescence, and can be impressed; aspirants and disciples represent those brain cells which are beginning to fall into the larger divine rhythm. They are learning the nature of responsiveness. The mass of men are like the millions of unused brain cells which the psychologists and scientists tell us we possess but do not employ. This analogy you can think out in greater detail for yourself, but even superficially it will be apparent to you that when this point is grasped, the purpose for which humanity exists, the objective before the group of world mystics and workers, and the ideal set before the individual aspirant, are the same as in the individual meditation; the achieving of that focussed attention and mental quiet wherein reality can be contacted, the true and the beautiful can be registered, divine purpose can be recorded, and it becomes possible to transmit to the phenomenal form, upon the physical plane, the needed energy whereby the subjective realisation can be materialised. The aspirant does this in connection with his own soul purpose if he is successful in his endeavour; the disciple is learning to do this in relation to group purpose, and the initiate cooperates with the planetary purpose. These constitute the inner group of vitally alive brain cells in the planetary brain, the entire human group, and it is evident that the more powerful their united vibration and the clearer the light which they reflect and transmit, the more rapidly will the present inert mass of human cells be brought into activity. The occult hierarchy is to the planetary Life what the light in the head is to the average awakened disciple, only on so much vaster a scale, and with such an adequate inner alignment that students such as those who read these Instructions cannot understand the true significance of the words. The point to be grasped is that through humanity on the physical plane, the nature of reality will be revealed; the true and the beautiful will be manifested; the divine plan will eventually work out, and that energy be transmitted to all forms in nature which will enable the inner spiritual reality to emerge.

II. The second type of activity of which man is capable is an intense progressive and spiral development within the human ring-pass-not. This sentence covers the mode of development and the entire procedure of unfoldment of all the evolving units that we call men. With this I seek not here to deal. The history of the human structural growth, the entire field of the unfolding human consciousness and the history of all races and peoples that have lived or are living upon our planet can be dealt with under this heading. It concerns the use humanity has made of all the energies available within the natural world of which it is a part, inherent in the fourth kingdom itself and coming to it also from the world of spiritual realities.

III. The third type of activity which should occupy the attention of humanity, and one as yet little understood, is that it should act as a transmitting centre of spiritual forces—soul force and spiritual energy united and combined—to the prisoners of the planet and to the lives, held in embodied existence in the other kingdoms of nature. Human beings are apt to be primarily concerned with their higher group relations, with their return to the Father's home, and with the trend which we call "upwards" and away from the phenomenal world. They are principally occupied with the finding of the centre within the form aspect, that which we call the soul and, having found it, with the work then of acquainting themselves with that soul and thus finding peace. This is right and in line with divine intention but it is *not* all of the plan for man, and when this remains the prime objective, a man is dangerously near falling into the snare of spiritual selfishness and separateness.

When the centre is found by any human being and he becomes at-one with, and enters into relation with his soul, then he automatically shifts his position in the human family and—again speaking in symbols—finds himself part of the centre of light and understanding which we call, esoterically, the occult hierarchy, the cloud of witnesses, the disciples of the Christ, and other names according to the trend of the disciple's convictions. This hierarchy is also attempting to externalise itself in the form of the group of World Workers, and when a man has found his soul and the principle of unity is sufficiently revealed to him he shifts also into this more exoteric group. All who find the centre do not as yet link up with both the interior and exterior groups. Then he is pledged to the magical work, to the salvaging of souls, to the releasing of the prisoners of the planet. This is the goal for humanity as a whole, and when all the sons of men have attained the objective, these prisoners will be released. The reason for this will be that the magical work will be carried forward intelligently and perfectly and human beings in group formation will act as transmitters of pure spiritual energy, which will vivify every form in every kingdom in nature.

In considering the problem of the prisoners of the planet and their eventual release, it must be remembered that one of the forces which lie back of the entire evolutionary scheme is that of the Principle of Limitation. This is the primary impulse which brings about the act of creation, and is intimately linked with that of will and its lower reflection, desire. Will is desire, formulated so clearly and carried so powerfully to an intelligent climax that the mode of its materialisation is grasped with such accuracy and energised with such intent that the result is inescapable. But pure will is only possible to a coordinated thinker, to truly self-conscious entities. Desire is instinctual or rather inherent in all forms, for all forms and organisms constitute part of some primary thinker and are influenced by the powerful intent of that primary force.

The Principle of Limitation therefore is the outcome of the purposeful will and formulated desire of some thinking Being, and governs consequently the form-taking process of all incarnated lives. This Principle of Limitation controls the scope of an incarnation, sets its measure and rhythm, determines the radius of its influence, and brings about that illusory appearance of reality which we call manifestation.

The "prisoners of the planet" fall into two categories:

1. Those lives which act under the influence of a conscious purpose, and who "limit the life that is in them" for a time. They consciously take form, knowing the end from the beginning. These Beings in their turn fall into three main groups.

a. The Being Who is the life of our planet, the One in Whom we live and move and have our being. This being, or sum total of organised lives is sometimes called the planetary Logos, sometimes the Ancient of Days, sometimes God, and sometimes the One Life.
b. Those lives who constitute the Principle of Limitation in a kingdom of nature. The Life that is, for instance, expressing itself through the medium of the animal kingdom is a self-conscious intelligent entity, working in full awareness of intent and objective, and limiting his sphere of activity in order to provide due opportunity and expression for the myriad lives that find their life and being and sustenance in him. See you how the law of sacrifice runs throughout creation.
c. The sons of mind, human souls, solar Angels, the divine sons of God who in full self-consciousness work out certain well seen ends through the medium of the human family.

2. Those lives who are limited in form because they are not self-conscious but are unconscious constituent parts of a greater form. They have not yet evolved to the point where they are self-conscious entities.

It might be said that this second category includes all existences, but the line of demarcation between self-produced limitation and unrealised form-taking lies entirely in the realm of consciousness. Some lives are prisoners and know it. Others are prisoners and know it not. The clue to suffering lies right here in the realm of mind. Pain and agony, rebellion and the conscious urge towards betterment and the changing of conditions are only found where what we call individuality is present, where the "I" complex is controlling, and where a self-conscious entity is functioning. There is of course the equivalent to pain in kingdoms below the human, but it enters into another differentiation. It is not self-related. Sub-human forms of life suffer and undergo discomfort and are subject to the throes of death but they lack memory and prevision, and possess not that mental apprehension which will enable them to relate past and present and anticipate the future. They are exempt from the agony of foreboding. Their entire reaction to what are called evil conditions is so different to that of humanity that it is difficult for us to grasp it. The *Old Commentary* describes these two groups in the following terms:

"The Sons of God, who know and see and hear (and knowing, know they know) suffer the pain of conscious limitation. Deep in the inmost depths of conscious being, their lost estate of liberty eats like a canker. Pain, sickness, poverty and loss are seen as such, and from them every son of God revolts.

He knows that in himself, as once he was before he entered prisoner into form, he knew not pain. Sickness and death, corruption and disease, they touched him not. The riches of the universe were his, and naught he knew of loss.

"The lives that enter into form alone with lives self-conscious, the deva lives which build the forms indwelt by all the Sons of God, they know not pain or loss or poverty. The form decays, the other forms retire, and that which is required to nourish and keep strong the outer, lacks. But lacking also will and planned intent, they feel no aggravation and know no clear revolt."

A word about pain might be in place here, though I have naught of an abstruse nature to communicate anent the evolution of the human hierarchy through the medium of pain. The devas do not suffer pain as does mankind. Their rate of rhythm is steadier although in line with the Law. They learn through application to the work of building and through incorporation into the form of that which is built. They grow through appreciation of and joy in the forms built and the work accomplished. The devas build and humanity breaks and through the shattering of the forms man learns through discontent. Thus is acquiescence in the work of the greater Builders achieved. Pain is that upward struggle through matter which lands a man at the Feet of the Logos; pain is the following of the line of the greatest resistance and thereby reaching the summit of the mountain; pain is the smashing of the form and the reaching of the inner fire; pain is the cold of isolation which leads to the warmth of the central sun; pain is the burning in the furnace in order finally to know the coolness of the water of life; pain is the journeying into the far country, resulting in the welcome to the Father's Home; pain is the illusion of the Father's disowning, which drives the prodigal straight to the Father's heart; pain is the cross of utter loss, that renders back the riches of the eternal bounty; pain is the whip that drives the struggling builder to carry to utter perfection the building of the Temple.

The uses of pain are many, and they lead the human soul out of darkness into light, out of bondage into liberation, out of agony into peace. That peace, that light and that liberation, with the ordered harmony of the cosmos are for all the sons of men.

With the problem of limitation is closely linked that of liberation. Into the prison house of form enter all that live; some enter consciously and some unconsciously, and this we call birth, appearance, incarnation, manifestation. Immediately there sweeps into activity another law or the working out of an active principle which we call the Law of Cycles. This is the principle of periodic appearance—a beneficent operation of the lower wisdom of innate divinity, for it produces that sequence of the states of consciousness which we term Time. This produces therefore in the world field of awareness a gradual and slow growth towards self-expression, self-appreciation, and self-realisation. To these principles of Limitation and of Cycles is added another principle, that of Expansion. This brings about the development of consciousness so that the latent germ of sentiency or of sensitive response to environment may be fostered in the living unit.

We have therefore three Principles:

1. The Principle of Limitation.
2. The Principle of Periodic Manifestation.
3. The Principle of Expansion.

These three Principles together constitute the factors underlying the Law of Evolution as men call it. They bring about the imprisonment of the Life in its various appearances or aspects; they produce the environing forms, and they lead the imprisoned lives on into ever more educational prison houses.

Finally the time arrives when the Principle of Liberation becomes active and a transition is effected out of a prison house which cramps and distorts into one which provides adequate conditions for the next development of consciousness.

It is interesting here to note that death is governed by the Principle of Liberation, and not by that of Limitation. Death is only recognised as a factor to be dealt with by self-conscious lives and is only misunderstood by human beings, who are the most glamoured and deluded of all incarnated lives.

The next point to be noted is that each kingdom in nature acts in two ways:

1. As the liberator of the kingdom of forms which has not reached its particular stage of conscious awareness.
2. As the prison house of lives that have transmitted into it from the level of consciousness next beneath it.

Let it be remembered always that each field of awareness in its boundaries constitutes a prison, and that the objective of all work of liberation is to release the consciousness and expand its field of contacts. Where there are boundaries of any kind, where a field of influence is circumscribed, and where the radius of contact is limited there you have a prison. Ponder on this statement for it holds much of truth. Where there is an apprehension of a vision and of a wide unconquered territory of contacts then there will inevitably be a sense of imprisonment and of cramping. Where there is realisation of worlds to conquer, of truths to be learnt, of conquests to be made, of desires to be achieved, of knowledges to be mastered, there you will have a festering sense of limitation, goading on the aspirant to renewed effort and driving the living entity on along the path of evolution. Instinct, governing the vegetable and animal kingdoms, develops into intellect in the human family. Later intellect merges into intuition and intuition into illumination. When the superhuman consciousness is evoked these two—intuition and illumination—take the place of instinct and of intelligence.

Illumination—what does that lead to? Straight to the summit of achievement, to the fulfillment of cyclic destiny, to the emergence of the radiant glory, to wisdom, power, God consciousness. These words however mean but little or nothing in comparison with a Reality which can only be sensed by any human being when his intuition is awakened and his mind illumined.

Grasping these facts anent imprisonment how, to be practical, can a man become a releasing agent for the "prisoners of the planet"? What can humanity as a whole achieve along this line? What can the individual do?

The task of humanity fails primarily into three divisions of labour. Three groups of prisoners can be released and will eventually find their way out of their prison house through the instrumentality of man. Already human beings are working in all three fields.

1. Prisoners within the human form. This involves working with one's fellow men.
2. Prisoners within the animal kingdom, and already much is being done in this field.
3. Prisoners within the forms of the vegetable world. A beginning has been made here.

Much work is being accomplished by man for men, and through the agency of scientific, religious and educational endeavour, the human consciousness is steadily expanding until one by one the Sons of God are breaking through their limitations into the world of souls. In the retrospect of history, the picture of the emerging prisoner, Man, can be seen in clear delineation. Little by little he has mastered the planetary boundaries; little by little, he has grown from the stage of cave man to that of a Shakespeare, a Newton, a Leonardo da Vinci, an Einstein, a St. Francis of Assisi, to a Christ and a Buddha. The capacity of man to achieve in any field of human expression seems practically unlimited, and if the past few thousand years have seen such a stupendous growth, what shall we see in the next five thousand years! If prehistoric man, little more than an animal, has grown into the genius, what unfoldment is not possible as more and more of innate divinity makes its presence felt? The superman is with us. What will the world manifest when all mankind is tending towards a concrete manifestation of superhuman powers?

Man's consciousness is being released in varying directions and dimensions. It is expanding into the world of spiritual realities and beginning to embrace the fifth or spiritual kingdom, the kingdom of souls. It is interpenetrating, through scientific research, the world of super-human endeavour, and investigating the many aspects of the Form of God, and of the forms that constitute the Form.

In touching upon the work of humanity in releasing the units of which it is constructed, and in releasing the prisoners in the vegetable and animal kingdoms, I want to point out two things, both of profound importance:

First, in order to release the "prisoners of the planet" that come under the title of *subhuman*, man has to work under the influence of the *intuition*; when working to release his fellow men he has to know the meaning of *Illumination*.

When the true nature of Service is comprehended, it will be found that it is an aspect of that divine energy which works always under the destroyer aspect, for it destroys the forms in order to release. Service is a manifestation of the Principle of Liberation, and of this principle, death and service, constitute two aspects. Service saves, liberates and releases, on various levels, the imprisoned consciousness. The same statements can be made of death. But unless service can he rendered from an intuitive understanding of all the facts in the case, interpreted intelligently, and applied in a spirit of love upon the physical plane, it fails to fulfil its mission adequately.

When the factor of spiritual illumination enters into that service, you have those transcendent Lights which have illumined the way of humanity and have acted like search-lights, thrown out into the great ocean of consciousness, revealing to man the Path he can and must go.

I would like to point out another thing. I have given no specific rules for releasing the prisoners of the planet. I have made no classification of the prisons and their prisoners, nor of methods of work nor of techniques of release.

I urge only upon each and all who read these Instructions the necessity for renewed effort to fit themselves for service by a conscious and deliberate effort to develop the intuition and to achieve illumination. Every human being who reaches the goal of light and wisdom automatically has a field of influence which extends both up and down, and which reaches both inwards to the source of light and outwards into the "fields of darkness". When he has thus attained he will become a conscious centre of life giving force, and will be so without effort. He will stimulate, energise and vivify to fresh efforts all lives that he contacts, be they his fellow aspirants, or an animal, or a flower. He will act as a transmitter of light in the darkness. He will dispel the glamour around him and let in the radiance of reality.

When large numbers of the sons of men can so act, then the human family will enter upon its destined work of planetary service. Its mission is to act as a bridge between the world of spirit and the world of material forms. All grades of matter meet in man, and all the states of consciousness are possible to him. Mankind can work in all directions and lift the subhuman kingdoms into heaven and bring heaven down to earth.

RULE THIRTEEN

The magician must recognize the four; note in his work the shade of violet they evidence, and thus constructed the shadow. When this is so, the shadow clothes itself, and the four become the seven.

The Quaternaries to be Recognised.
The Precipitation of Thought-forms.

THE QUATERNARIES TO BE RECOGNISED

This rule is for me one of the most difficult to explain, the reason for this being threefold:

One: The number of people in physical incarnation at this time who can work in a truly creative manner and profit by the information given in this Rule is exceedingly few. Only to the white magician, and he experienced in his work, can the real interpretation be given. There is much danger in imparting the significance of these rules to those who are not qualified in themselves to work correctly. We will, therefore, consider the qualifications required of those who are entitled to this knowledge so that the student can begin to develop in himself that which may be lacking.

Two: The danger of minute and detailed instructions consists in the fact that were they now to be given to the world, we should be flooded with thought-forms and these thought-forms would be created in order to express purely selfish desire and mental matter would be swept into activity in line with the fancies and the whims of the undeveloped along spiritual lines. It must be remembered that every human thought, whether the potent mass thoughts or individual dynamic ideas, must eventually emerge objectively on the physical plane. This is an inevitable and unalterable rule and due consideration of this law which governs mental substance will show the danger of wrong thought and the power of right. The potency of human thought at this time is primarily of mass description, for few there are who can think creatively. Public opinion, mass ideas, the tendencies of human desire and thought, are not at this time of the highest order, and the physical precipitation of these vague and inchoate thoughts distinguished by a vast similarity, and colored by selfish intent and personal behest, and based upon likes and dislikes, prejudices and longings, can be seen in the most interesting precipitation. The vast assembly of insects which now haunt our planet and cause increasing concern to the scientist, agriculturist, and all those dealing with the welfare of the human animal, are the direct result of thought precipitation.

I have not time to enlarge upon this fact, but I can assure you that as men learn to think with more unselfishness and with greater purity, and as malice and hatred and competition give place to brotherhood, kindness and cooperation, the insect pest, as it is now called, will most surely die out.

Three: Another difficulty which I experience in elucidating these rules lies in the fact that it is today more easy to prove the fact that there is a realm of mind than it is to prove that there is a realm of the ether, even though scientists use the word widely. This rule concerns the four grades of etheric substance which constitute the etheric envelope of all forms in nature, from a mountain to an ant, and from a plant to an atom. Certain scientists recognize the fact of an etheric body, vast numbers do not, and from the standpoint of the masses of humanity, it remains unrecognized. That which lies closest to us and in our immediate foreground is often overlooked, and it has interested those of us who teach and guide to note how much emphasis is laid upon psychic and astral phenomena, and how little attention is paid to the more obvious and more easily discerned etheric forms and forces! Given a slight change in the present mode of visual focussing it will be found that the human eye is capable of including an entirely new field of perception and of awareness. Blindly men introvert their consciousness and become aware of astral objects and that illusive world of ever changing forms in which we live and move and have our being, and yet, they fail to see that which lies immediately before them.

These three difficulties of:

1. Lack of qualification,
2. Dangers inherent in unconscious form-building.
3. Etheric blindness,

make it well nigh impossible for me to do full justice to this rule and to elucidate the work on etheric levels, and hence the relative brevity of the elucidation.

In dealing with the subject of qualification and answering the question: What constitutes the equipment needed by a white magician? I would say one thing:—all students realize that certain requirements must be met if a man is to be entrusted with any measure of understanding of the technique of the Great Work. I take it for granted, however, that the *character* qualifications are not those to which our question refers. All aspirants know, and down the ages have been taught, that a clean mind and a pure heart, love of truth, and a life of service and unselfishness, are prime prerequisites, and where they are lacking, naught avails and none of the great secrets can be imparted. You might well say here: We have also been taught that there exist those who work in the four ethers and who undoubtedly perform magical deeds, yet who do not possess this essential purity and loving-kindness to which reference has been made. This is undoubtedly true; they belong to a group of workers in matter whom we call Black Magicians; they are highly developed intellectually and can motivate mental substance or mind stuff in such a manner that it can achieve objectivity on the physical plane and bring about their deep intent. About this group there is much misunderstanding and profound ignorance. It is perhaps as well, for their destiny is tied up with the future race, the sixth, and their end and the cessation of their activities will come about in that far distant aeon which is technically called the Sixth Round. The final break or division between the so-called black and white forces, for this particular world cycle, will take place during the period of the sixth root race in the present round. Towards the close of the sixth root race, before the emergence of the seventh, we shall have the true Armageddon about which so much has been taught. A small cycle, corresponding to this final battle and cleavage, will appear during the sixth subrace which is now in process of formation. The world war which has just taken place and our present cycle of separativeness and upheaval, do not constitute the real Armageddon. The war which is told to us in the Mahabharata and the present war had the roots of their trouble and the seeds of the disasters which they brought about, one in the lower and one in the higher astral world. Selfishness and desire of a low order were the impulses back of them both. The coming great division will have its roots in the mental world and will consummate in the sixth subrace. In the sixth root race it will have the seeds of portentous disaster in the coordinated triplicity of mind, astralism, and physical nature, which will bring about a climaxing moment for the planetary duality.

Beyond that we need not go, for the humanity of the sixth round will be so different in nature to ours and those who will differentiate into the black and the white forces will be so unlike what we now understand by the words, that we need not concern ourselves with that far distant problem.

Let it be remembered that the true black magician (I refer not here to a person with a tendency to black magic) is a soulless entity. He is a being in whom the Ego is—as we understand the term today—non-existent. It is oft overlooked and seldom grasped or told that they, therefore, do not exist in physical bodies. Their world is ever the world of illusion. They work, from the lower mental plane, on desire matter and on the sentient desire bodies of those on the physical plane who are swept by delusion and held in the bonds of extreme selfishness and self-centeredness. What the ignorant call a black magician on the physical plane is only some man or woman sensitive to or en rapport with a true black magician on the astral plane. This relationship is only possible when there have been many lives of selfishness, low desire, perverted intellectual aspiration, and love of the lower psychism, and this only when the man has been held willingly in thrall by them. Such men and women are few and far between, for unadulterated selfishness is rare indeed. Where it exists, it is exceedingly potent, as are all one-pointed tendencies.

The clue to the requirements of a more esoteric kind is given to us in Rule XIII. "The magician must recognize the four." He has presumably built up a fine character. He has educated himself for service. His aspiration is true and steady. He is living purely and unselfishly. He has mastered somewhat the meaning of meditation. He now has to begin to train himself in what is called "occult recognition."

This rule is a most interesting example of the many connotations and numerous correspondences which can be conveyed in a few simple words. We are told that he must "recognize the four". The *Treatise on Cosmic Fire* tells us:

"This means literally that the magician must be in a position to discriminate between the different ethers and to note the special hue of the different levels, thereby insuring a balanced building of the `shadow.' He `recognizes' them, in the occult sense; that is, he knows their note and key and is aware of the particular type of energy they embody. Enough emphasis has not been laid upon the fact that the three higher levels of the etheric plane are in vibratory communication with the three higher planes of the cosmic physical plane, and they (with their ensphering fourth level) have been called in the occult books `the inverted Tetraktys.' It is this knowledge which puts the magician in possession of the three types of planetary force and their combination, or the fourth type, and thus releases for him that vital energy which will drive this idea into objectivity. As the different types of forces meet and coalesce, a dim shadowy form clothes itself upon the vibrating astral and mental sheath, and the idea of the solar Angel is attaining definite concretion."

The obvious and most apparent meaning is, therefore, recognition of the four ethers, but this is in its turn dependent upon other meanings and based upon the recognition of other quaternaries. I would like to give a short *resume* of some of the qualifications needed by the white magician and of some of the recognitions which will gradually emerge in his consciousness.

First, he must recognize "the four that constitute the One." In other words, the first quaternary that he must know and know well is that which he is essentially himself:

1. Physical body, sensitive emotional nature, mind and soul;
2. Soul, mind, brain and the outer world of forces;
3. Spirit, soul and body within the great Whole.

This presupposes real spiritual attainment and the capacity, therefore, to function as a soul. Until this has been achieved, one can be an aspirant to the practice of white magic, but one is not yet a white magician.

Second, he must recognize "the city that stands foursquare." He must understand the meaning, of "man, the cube", and this in three ways:

1. Himself as a human being;
2. His fellow man in relation to himself and the Whole;
3. The fourth kingdom in nature, the human kingdom, viewing that entire kingdom as an entity, an organized life functioning on the physical plane, indwelt by soul, animated by spirit.

This means, therefore, that as a man he is responsive to his kind and is aware also of the purpose of the kingdom to which he belongs. This can best be expressed in some wonderful words from an ancient writing in the Masters' Archives. It is said to date back to early Atlantean times. The material on which the writing is found is so old and so frail that all that the Masters themselves can touch and see is a precipitation made from it, the original being kept at Shamballa. It runs thus, with certain deletions, which it is wiser not to insert:

"At the four corners of the square, the four angelic...are seen. Orange they are, but veiled in rosy light. Within each form the yellow flame is seen and round each form the blue...
"Four words they utter forth, one for each human race, but not the sacred sound which bringeth forth the seventh. Two words have died away, four sound today. One sounds in realms so high that man can enter not as man. Thus are the seven words of man ringing around the square, passing from mouth to mouth.
"Each day of man the words take form and different seem. In...the words will be as follows:
"From out the North a word is chanted forth which means...be pure.
"From out the South the word peals out: I dedicate and...
"From out the East, bringing a light divine, the word comes swinging round the square: Love all.
"From out the West, answer is thrown back: I serve."

This is a faint effort to express in English these ancient Atlantean phrases, older than Sanskrit or Senzar, and known only to a mere handful of the members of the present hierarchy. But in the thoughts of purity, dedication, love and service, are summed up the nature and the destiny of man, and it should be remembered that they do not stand for so-called spiritual qualities, but for potent occult forces, dynamic in their incentive and creative in their result. This should be pondered on carefully by all aspirants. We have, consequently, with these four, added to the first one, spiritual attainment, five of the qualifications of the white magician.

Third, the white magician must recognize the cross which stands in the Heavens upon which the cosmic Christ is crucified and on which the white magician, being a cell in the body of the cosmic Christ, is also crucified. Technically and astrologically speaking, in this present aeon he must understand the inner significance of Taurus, of Leo, of Scorpio and of Aquarius, for they are potent in our world cycle. He must, if I may express it symbolically, and yet at the same time accurately, be able to utter forth the achievement which is the goal of his endeavor in each of these four signs and under each of these four powers. In Taurus he must be able to say: "I seek illumination and am myself the light." In Leo he will say: "I know myself to be the one. I rule by Law." The word he will utter forth in Scorpio will be: "Illusion cannot hold me. I am the bird that flies with utter freedom." In Aquarius the words spoken will be: "I am the server, and I the dispenser am of living water."

These occult qualifications upon which I have thus lightly touched, must be closely studied by the aspirant and as he studies them and lives by these rules, various qualifications will emerge and will distinguish him. It must be remembered that all that I have here said has a different meaning on each plane and in relation to the seven stages of consciousness as these express themselves in these seven fields of awareness.

Finally, as far as the aspirant who reads these instructions is concerned, he must have transcended the four noble truths, learned the meaning of the four gospels, understood the significance and purpose of the four elements—earth, water, fire and air, and, esoterically speaking, passed as a Saviour through the four kingdoms. This latter phrase will only be really understood at the fourth initiation. When he has done this, he can say: "Desire holds me not, with freedom now I stand. I desire all and nothing. I live and die, am offered up and rise again: I come and go at will. Earth lies beneath my feet and water laves my form. The fire destroys that which impedes my way, and master of the air am I. Through all the world of forms my feet have passed. All now exists for me and I, the servant of the whole, persist." Study these words and note how the concept of the ideal requirements which constitute the equipment of the white magician has steadily grown.

I could enlarge on many other quaternaries, but the few just quoted suffice to show some of the recognitions towards which the aspirant strives. The only other one which I will note is that referred to as the violet four, or the four types of energy which constitute the vital or etheric body of all forms in the natural world. Here again we have a higher three and a lower one, which ever indicates the three aspects or principles of divinity and the form through which these three must manifest. Spirit, soul and body express the same idea from another angle, added to that which is produced through their interaction. It must ever be remembered that from the point of view of Reality what we call the dense physical body, tangible and objective, is but an illusion. We are told again and again in the ancient writings that it is not a principle. Why is this so? Because it is only an *appearance* brought about by the merging of the higher three and the fourth, and this appearance is a fiction or a figment of the human mind. I speak not in parable; I utter only facts in nature and one that is slowly coming into mature consideration among the philosophers of both hemispheres. Both in the solar system, the macrocosm of the microcosm, and likewise in the microcosm, there are ever the three highest planes which embody the principles and produce the dynamic purpose, and which constitute the four levels of the etheric body of both God and man, viewing them from what we call the energy or physical angle. These four are reflected in the four levels of the etheric division of the physical plane as regards the physical body of all forms. These four etheric levels, or these four grades of vital substance constitute what is called the "true form" of all material objects or phenomena, and they are responsive to the four higher types of spiritual energy which we usually call divine. This relation between the prototypal trinity and its plane of merging and the etheric reflection is found in all forms according to the type of energy which predominates. In each of the four kingdoms in nature all four types are found, but the fourth etheric is found in fuller degree in the mineral kingdom than in the human, whilst the highest of the four ethers is found in greater proportion in the human than in the other three kingdoms. This which I tell you is apt to be found confusing by the neophyte for the words energy, dynamic purpose, vitality and etheric substance mean little to the beginner, but they serve to indicate some of the knowledge which the worker in white magic has to grasp. This I might illustrate, for instance, by stating that working in the mineral kingdom, the fourth kingdom in nature from the standpoint of God, and the first from the standpoint of time and space, he will work with the fourth cosmic ether (buddhic energy) utilizing ether of the fourth grade in his own body as the transmitting agent, and so on, in connection with the other three kingdoms in nature. One of the secrets not yet revealed, fortunately, is concerned with the question as to whether light violet is the color of the highest or the lowest of the four and this will not be revealed for some time to come.

The consideration of these various quaternaries which it is necessary that the white magician understand, and the qualifications which he must possess before he is permitted to carry forward the magical work, leads to the following question: Is there some basic formula or proposition which must govern the magical activity?

This question is, of course, too general and vague, but until the inclusiveness of the human mind is greater than is now the case, such questions will inevitably be asked. I can, however, give a short reply which holds in it the clue to the entire process. When correctly understood, it will govern the method of work and the thought life of the worker in white magic. My answer is this: Potencies produce precipitation. In those three words lies the entire story. They sum up the history of the Creator and the life story and environing conditions of every human being. They account for all that is, and lie back of the law of rebirth. These potencies are driven into activity by the power of thought and hence, in training them to be creators and in teaching them to govern and control their own destinies, the Teachers of the race begin with the mind aspect of aspirants. They emphasize that which will govern the potencies; they deal with that which produces the objective form, which is qualified by them, is energized by them and which fulfills the purpose of the Thinker.

A thinker, then, is the essential factor, and it will become apparent to you, therefore, as you study these words, just what is going on in the world of today. The trend of our modern civilization, in spite of all its mistakes and errors, is to produce thinkers. Education, books, travel, in its many and varied forms, enunciations of science and of philosophy, and the driving inner urge which we call religious, but which is, in fact, the drive towards truth and its mental verification—all these factors have one objective, and this is to produce thinkers. Given a real thinker, you have an incipient creator and (unconsciously at first, but consciously later on) one who will wield power in order to "precipitate" or cause to emerge objective forms. These forms will either be in line with Divine purpose and plan and, consequently, will further the cause of evolution, or they will be animated by personal intent, characterized by separated, selfish purpose, and constitute, therefore, part of the work of the retro-active forces and the material element. They will be of the nature of black magic.

Again the four appear:

1. The thinker.
2. The potency.
3. The quality of that potency.
4. The precipitation.

THE PRECIPITATION OF THOUGHT FORMS

What is a precipitation? Many definitions could be given and most of them—being clothed in words—would lose much of their true significance, but some idea may be conveyed in the following terms:

"A precipitation is an aggregation of energies arranged in a certain form, in order to express the idea of some creative Thinker, and qualified or characterized by the nature of his thought and held in that peculiar form as long as his thought remains dynamic."

These words are an attempt to express a symbol found in the same ancient book, or rather compilation, referred to earlier, in our consideration of Rule XIII. Certainly these symbols emerging from the remote past constitute the working tools, if I might so express it, of the Thinkers Who guide our racial and planetary evolution. This particular symbol might be described as follows:

A blazing sun forms the background and at the very center of that sun appears an eye; projecting downwards toward the right from this eye pours forth a stream of energy in the form of a beam of light. It rays outward, widening towards the end, into a second circle and in that circle is a cross resembling what is called a Maltese cross. At the center of the cross is another eye and within the eye the Sacred Word. Between the arms of the cross forming, therefore, another cross, is the Swastika, the arms emerging from behind the Maltese cross. At the bottom of the page whereon this symbol is found are four geometrical forms. Some of these are referred to by H. P. B. and were taken by her from this ancient picture. They are well known but seldom applied by esotericists to the creative work. They are the cube, the five pointed star, the six pointed star and the eight sided diamond, superimposed one upon the other. They constitute, therefore, the base of the symbol. H. P. B. refers also to the point, the line and the circle, but these, with the triangle, have been exoterically applied to Deity and the manifested universe. Later these other forms will also be applied to God and to man, in the exoteric sense. But this will only be when the truths of the Ageless Wisdom are universally recognized.

The laws of thought are the laws of creation, and the entire creative work is carried forward on the etheric level. This constitutes practically a second formula. The Creator of the solar system confines his attention to the work performed on what we call the four higher planes of our system. The lower three, constituting the cosmic dense physical plane, are in the nature of precipitation. They are objective, because the matter of space responds to, or is attracted by the potency of the four higher etheric vibrations. These, in their turn, are motivated or swept into activity by the dynamic impact of the divine thought. There is a similar procedure where man is concerned. Just as soon as man becomes a thinker and can formulate his thought, desire its manifestation and can energize "by recognition" the four ethers, a dense physical manifestation is inevitable. He will attract by his pranic energy, colored by desire high or low, and animated by the potency of his thought, just as much of the responsive matter in space as is needed to give body to his form.

Much of this is dealt with in *A Treatise on Cosmic Fire* and as these Instructions are intended to deal with the inner development of the aspirant, I shall not carry these ideas further beyond prophesying that within fifty years the true significance of precipitations will be engrossing the attention of the scientists. Occult students would do well to give the subject careful thought. It can be approached in two ways. There is, first of all, the study of the objective world in which the individual aspirant finds himself. He will need to consider the fact that his body of manifestation is a precipitation, that it is a result of his potent thought and desire and of his "recognition" of the four ethers. He will need to understand that this form which he has created will persist just as long as the dynamic power of his thought holds it together, and that it will dissipate when he (occultly speaking) "takes his eye away". He will need to consider also that his environment is the result of the work of an aggregate of group thinkers—group to which he belongs. This concept can be traced back all the way from a family group to the group of egos who, closely interlinked, form a group on the higher level of the mental plane, and on again to the seven major thinkers of the universe, the Lords of the seven rays. These seven, in their turn, are swept into activity by the three supreme magical workers, the manifested Trinity. These Three, in due course, will be recognized as responsive to the thought of the One Creator, the Unmanifested Logos.

The word "recognition" is one of the most important in the language of occultism and holds the clue to the mystery of Being. It is related to karmic activity and on it the Lords of Time and Space depend. It is hard to illustrate this in simple terms, but it might be said that the problem of God Himself consists in this, that He must manifest a threefold recognition:

1. Recognition of the past, which necessarily involves a recognition of that matter in space which is, through past association, already colored by thought and purpose.
2. Recognition of the four grades of lives which, again through past association, are capable of response to His new thought for the present and can, therefore, carry out His plans and work in collaboration with Him. They subject their individual purposes to the one divine plan.
3. Recognition of the objective which exists in His Mind. This, in its turn, necessitates a one pointed focussing upon the goal and the holding of the purpose intact throughout the vicissitudes of the creative work, and in spite of the potency of the many divine Thinkers who have been attracted to Him by similarity of idea.

It is hopeless to attempt to avoid the use of personal pronouns when talking pictorially and symbolically. If the student will bear in mind that such an attempt to reduce cosmic principles and concepts to words is in itself ridiculous and that the only possible thing to do is to present a picture, then no harm can eventuate. But the pictures change, as evolution proceeds upon its way, and the picture of today will at a later date be deemed no better than a child's rough scrawl. A new picture will then be presented, simpler and more harmonious, and more beautiful, until it, in its turn, is deemed inadequate.

The same recognitions, on a lesser scale, govern the activities of the solar Angel as he proceeds with the work of incarnation and of manifestation upon the physical plane. He has in his turn to recognize the matter of the three planes of human expression which are already, through past association, colored by his vibration; he has to recognize the groups of lives with which he has had relation and with which he again must work. Finally, he has, throughout the tiny cycle of an incarnation, to hold his purpose steady and to see that each life carries that purpose forward into fuller manifestation and completion.

The work of the human being also, as he endeavors to become a creative thinker, lies along analogous lines. His creative work will be successful if he can recognize the tendency of his mind as that tendency emerges through the medium of his present interests, for these have their roots in the past. It will be successful if he can recognize the vibration of the group of lives in line with whose thought his creative work must proceed, for unlike the Deity in the solar system, he cannot work sole and alone. And who shall say whether in those greater spheres of existence in which our Deity plays His part, He is any more free from cosmic group influences than the human individual is free from impression by his environing impulses? He has to recognize the purpose for which he has deemed it wise to build a thought-form and he must hold that purpose steady and unimpaired throughout the whole period of objectivity. This we call one pointed attention, and this creative work is one of the, as yet unrecognized, goals of the meditation process. Hitherto the emphasis has been laid on the achieving of a focussed attention and on the necessity, when that has been attained, of coming in touch with the soul, the spiritual thinker. But later decades will see the emerging of a technique of creation. When soul, mind and brain are unified and facility in unification has been achieved, further instructions will be given in the creative art. Meditation is the first basic lesson given when men have achieved the capacity to function on the mental plane.

Down the great cycle upon the wheel of rebirth "the idea of the solar Angel is attaining definite concretion". *A Treatise on Cosmic Fire*, p. 1024. Each life sees the initial purpose clarified and time is literally the length of a thought. This same basic truth underlies the creation of all forms on the physical plane, whether it is a thought-form embodying the urgent desire of a man for selfish acquisition or that thought-form which we call a group or an organization and which is animated by the unselfish purpose and embodies some disciple's mode of helping humanity. It underlies group work, regarding a group as an entity. If a group could appreciate the power of this fact, and "recognize" its opportunity, it could, by its one-pointed fixity of purpose and its focussed attention to the spiritual objective, perform miracles in salvaging the world. I here appeal to all who read these words to reconsecrate themselves and to recognize the opportunity they have of an united effort towards world usefulness.

It might be of use here if I expressed quite simply the requirements needed to bring about the manifestation of individual spiritual purpose or of group spiritual purpose. These can be summed up in three words:

1. Power.
2. Detachment.
3. Non-criticism.

So often simple words are used because of their every day connotation their true significance and esoteric value are lost.

Let me give you a few thoughts anent each of these, with application only to the creative work of white magic.

Power is dependent for expression upon two factors:

a. Singleness of purpose.
b. Lack of impediments.

Students would be amazed if they could see their motives as we see them who guide on the subjective side of experience. Mixed motive is universal. Pure motive is rare and where it exists there is ever success and achievement. Such pure motive can be entirely selfish and personal, or unselfish and spiritual, and in between, where aspirants are concerned, mixed in varying degree. According, however, to the purity of intent and the singleness of purpose, so will be the potency.

The Master of all the Masters has said, "If thine eye be single, thy whole body shall be full of light". These words which He enunciated give us a principle underlying all the creative work and we can link up the idea which He clothed in words with the symbol I have earlier described in this *Treatise*. Power, light, vitality, and manifestation! Such is the true procedure.

It will be obvious, therefore, why the manifested unit, man, is urged to be vital in his search and to cultivate his aspiration. When that aspiration is strong enough, he is then urged to achieve the capacity to "hold his mind steady in the light". When he can do this, he will achieve power and possess that single eye which will redound to the glory of the indwelling divinity. Before, however, he has mastered this process of development, he may not be trusted with power. The procedure is as follows: The individual aspirant begins to manifest somewhat soul purpose in his life on the physical plane. He is transmuting desire into aspiration and that aspiration is vital and real. He is learning the meaning of light. When he has mastered the technique of meditation (and with this certain schools in existence at present are concerned) he can proceed to handle power, because he will have learned to function as a divine Thinker. He is now cooperative and is in touch with the divine Purpose.

As all true students know, however, the number of impediments is legion. Hindrances and obstacles abound. Singleness of purpose may occasionally be realized in high moments, but it does not abide with us always. There are the hindrances of physical nature, of heredity and environment, of character, of time and conditions, of world karma, as well as individual karma. What shall then be done? I have only one word to say and that is, *persist*. Failure never prevents success. Difficulties develop the strength of the soul. The secret of success is ever to stand steady and to be impersonal.

The second requirement is *detachment*. The worker in white magic must hold himself free as much as he can from identifying himself with that which he has created or has attempted to create. The secret for all aspirants is to cultivate the attitude of the onlooker and of the silent watcher, and, may I emphasize the word *silent*. Much true magical work comes to naught because of the failure of the worker and builder in matter to keep silent. By premature speech and too much talk, he slays that which he has attempted to create, the child of his thought is still-born. All workers in the field of the world should recognize the need for silent detachment and the work before every student who reads these Instructions must consist in cultivating a detached attitude. It is a mental detachment which enables the thinker to dwell ever in the high and secret place and from that center of peace calmly and powerfully to carry out the work he has set before himself. He works in the world of men; he loves and comforts and serves; he pays no attention to his personality likes and dislikes, or to his prejudices and attachments; he stands as a rock of strength and as a strong hand in the dark to all whom he contacts. The cultivation of a detached attitude personally, with the attached attitude spiritually, will cut at the very roots of a man's life; but it will render back a thousandfold for all that it cuts away.

Much has been written anent attachment and the need to develop detachment. May I beg all students in the urgency of the present situation to leave off reading and thinking about it aspirationally and to begin to practise it and to demonstrate it.

Non-criticism is the third requirement. What shall I say about that? Why is it regarded as so essential a requirement? Because criticism (analysis and, consequently, separativeness) is the outstanding characteristic of mental types and also of all coordinated personalities. Because criticism is a potent factor in swinging mental and emotional substance into activity and so making strong impress upon the brain cells and working out into words. Because in a sudden burst of critical thought, the entire personality can be galvanized into a potent coordination, but of a wrong kind and with disastrous results. Because criticism being a faculty of the lower mind can hurt and wound and no man can proceed upon the Way as long as wounds are made and pain is knowingly given. Because the work of white magic and the carrying out of hierarchical purpose meets with basic hindrances in the relations existing between its workers and disciples. In the pressure of the present opportunity there is no time for criticism to exist between workers. They hinder each other and they hinder the work.

I have upon me at this time a sense of urgency. I urge upon all those who read these Instructions to forget their likes and their dislikes and to overlook the personality hindrances which inevitably exist in themselves and in all who work upon the physical plane, handicapped by the personality. I urge upon all workers the remembrance that the day of opportunity is with us and that it has its term. This present type of opportunity will not last forever. The pettiness of the human frictions, the failures to understand each other, the little faults which have their roots in personality and which are, after all, ephemeral, the ambitions and illusions must all go. If the workers would practise detachment, knowing that the Law works and that God's purposes must come to an ultimate conclusion and if they would learn never to criticize in thought or word, the salvaging of the world would proceed apace and the new age of love and illumination would be ushered in.

RULE FOURTEEN

The sound swells out. The hour of danger to the soul courageous draweth near. The waters have not hurt the white creator and naught could drown nor drench him. Danger from fire and flame menaces now, and dimly yet the rising smoke is seen. Let him again, after the cycle of peace, call on the Solar Angel.

The Centres and Prana.
The Use of the Hands.
The Treading of the Way.
The Awakening of the Centres.

THE CENTRES AND PRANA

The nearer we approach in our thought to the physical plane, the more difficulty is experienced by the magician, whether he be the solar Angel occupied with the magical work of manifestation, or an expert worker under the plan. This is due to two causes:

1. The automatic response of dense physical matter to substance, remembering always that substance is force.

2. The dangers incident to working with the fires or with the pranas of the Universe. This latter danger is that with which Rule XIV concerns itself.

There are many ways in which this Rule can be interpreted. We can study the work of the solar Angel as he approaches the dense physical plane to take incarnation and thus arrives at that critical point in his creative work wherein the threefold sheath is at the stage where it must, inevitably and unavoidably, make a contact with the matter aspect. It is the stage during which, expressing this truth in occult terms, it is literally called upon to "clothe itself and disappear into the light of day." The spiritual man is now veiled by a mental or by a fire sheath. He is clothed "in a watery mist", which is an ancient way of referring to the great illusion. This term conveys not only the concept of the possession of an astral or watery body, but also presents to the mind the effect which that body must have upon the hidden solar Angel. The latter looks out through the fire and through the mist and sees distortion and reflection. He sees that which must mislead.

Besides the sheath of fire and the sheath of mist he has clothed upon himself an outer web of closely interlocking streams of force. These constitute his etheric or vital body, which is in the nature of a web or mesh of energy nadis, which, in their tens of thousands, are woven together and form in certain localities in this energy body various focal points of force, of which the most important are the seven centers. There are, however, many such focal points.

When this clothing has been assumed by the solar Angel, a final stage is reached, and solar fire and fire by friction must be brought into contact with three "most ancient fires". These are the fires of the dense physical objective matter or of those material energy units which we normally cover by the words "gaseous, liquid and dense", a meaningless phrase and only of use to us, through its teaching of differentiation. These three ancient fires are an aspect of fire by friction.

At this point is the hour of danger for the soul courageous. It is the hour wherein the soul must bring into at-one-ment the etheric body and the gaseous envelope which is the highest aspect of the dense physical sheath, the instrument of tangible organic manifestation.

We can also study this Rule from the point of view of the initiate who is occupied with the wielding of forces and who, through the power of his thought, may have created a thought-form. This thought-form he has clothed with an astral or desire sheath, deliberately vitalized with his energy, and now seeks to give it objective existence and send it forth to accomplish his purpose and his intent. The crucial moment in all creative work is ever to be found at this stage. It is the stage wherein the vibrant subjective form has to attract to itself that material which will give it organization upon the physical plane. This fact has to be remembered, no matter what the magician is seeking to render objective. It refers equally to an organization, to a group or to a society; it may refer to the materialization of money or to the clothing or exteriorization of an idea. The moment of danger to the magician comes at this final stage. A point of fine discrimination is reached and the magician has to proceed now with caution. Many good plans fail to materialize and the reason lies right here. A plan is, after all, an idea let loose in time and space to seek a form and do its work. Many come to naught because their creator, or the creative mind from which they emanate, understands not this critical period. A right adjustment of forces has here to be arranged, so that neither too much energy is used in the work, nor too little. When too much energy is released through the medium of the vital body, then a fire blazes forth when the gaseous energy of the dense physical plane is brought in contact with vital etheric energy. Thus the embryo form is destroyed. Where there is not sufficient energy, or adequate persistent attention, and when the thought of the magician wavers, then the idea comes to naught, then the infant is still-born, and nothing comes into objective manifestation. This has a literal correspondence on the physical plane. Many infants are still-born for this very reason that the solar Angel wavers in his intent and is not sufficiently interested. Many fine ideas equally fail to materialize or have no persistent living existence "in the light of day," because there was not sufficient energy to generate that spark of living flame which must ever burn at the center of all forms. The danger, therefore, is twofold:

1. That of destruction by fire, owing to the expenditure of too much energy and the expression of too violent a purpose.

2. That of death, through lack of vitality and because the "directed attention" of the magician is not of adequate strength and duration to bring the form into being. The occult law holds good that energy follows thought.

We could study this Rule from the standpoint of the aspirant, as he learns to work with energy and with the forces of nature, as he learns the significance and the purpose of the vital body, and gains power in the control of the vital fires or the pranas of his own little system. It seems to me that for our particular purpose, this line of approach would be of the most use. These Instructions are intended for those who are definitely interested in the way of *liberation from form,* and who are seeking to prepare themselves to work in cooperation with the Great White Lodge. They are learning the first steps in the magical work and for them, therefore, an understanding of the fires and of the energies with which they must work, is of prime importance. We will, therefore, confine our attention to this phase of the great work and consider neither the work of the soul as it takes incarnation and manifests objectively through a form, nor with the work of the initiates, as they act as creative magicians under group impulse and through an intelligent understanding of the evolutionary plan. These Instructions are intended to be practical and to convey the teaching needed to those students who can read between the lines and who are developing the capacity to see the esoteric meaning behind the outer blinds and exoteric forms.

We are now going to consider the pranas, and I would here quote some paragraphs from *The Light of the Soul* which give a description of these pranas. We find in Book II, Sutra 39 that there are five aspects of prana, functioning through and, therefore, constituting the total etheric or vital body.

"Prana is fivefold in its manifestations, thus corresponding to the five states of mind, the fifth principle, and to the five modifications of the thinking principle. Prana in the solar system works out as the five great states of energy which we call planes, the medium of consciousness....The five differentiations of prana in the human body are:

"1. *Prana,* extending from the nose to the heart and having special relation to the mouth and speech, the heart and lungs.

"2. *Samana* extends from the heart to the solar plexus; it concerns food and the nourishing of the body through the medium of food and drink and has special relation to the stomach.

"3. *Apana* controls from the solar plexus to the soles of the feet; it concerns the organs of elimination, of rejection and of birth, thus having special relation to the organs of generation and of elimination.

"4. *Upana* is found between the nose and the top of the head; it has a special relation to the brain, the nose and the eyes, and when properly controlled produces the coordination of the vital airs and their correct handling.

"5. *Vyana* is the term applied to the sum total of pranic energy as it is distributed evenly throughout the entire body. Its instruments are the thousands of nadis or nerves found in the body, and it has a peculiar definite connection with the blood channels, the veins and arteries." (Pp. 329-330.)

"The etheric body is the force or vital body and it permeates every part of the dense vehicle. It is the background, the true substance of the physical body. According to the nature of the force animating the etheric body, according to the activity of that force in the etheric body, according to the aliveness or the sluggishness of the most important parts of the etheric body (the centers up the spine) so will be the corresponding activity of the physical body. Similarly and symbolically, according to the wholeness of the breathing apparatus, and according to the ability of that apparatus to oxygenate and render pure the blood, so will be the health or wholeness of the dense physical body." (Pp. 218-219.)

We find it also stated that the forces which make up the vital body or the various pranas of which it is constructed emanate:

"a. From the planetary aura. In this case it is planetary prana, and so concerns primarily the spleen and the health of the physical body.
"b. From the astral world via the astral body. This will be purely kamic or desire force and will affect primarily the centers below the diaphragm.
"c. From the universal mind or manasic force. This will largely be thought force and will go to the throat center.
"d. From the ego itself, stimulating primarily the head and heart centers." (P. 220.)

We read also that "most people receive force only from the physical and astral planes, but disciples receive force also from the mental and egoic levels." Finally we read:

"It may help the student if he realizes that the right control of prana involves the recognition that energy is the sum total of existence and of manifestation, and that the three lower bodies are energy bodies, each forming a vehicle for the higher type of energy and being themselves transmitters of energy. The energies of the lower man are energies of the third aspect, the Holy Ghost or Brahma aspect. The energy of the spiritual man is that of the second aspect, the Christ force, or buddhi. The object of evolution in the human family is to bring this Christ force, the principle of buddhi, into full manifestation upon the physical plane and this through the utilization of the lower triple sheath." (P. 227.)

This gives a general picture of the subject of our consideration and gives us the elementary facts upon which all our thoughts must be based. It becomes apparent, therefore, as we study the above that the aspirant has three things to do:

First, he has to learn the nature of the energies or pranas which have brought his magical creation, the physical body, into manifestation and which keep it in such a condition that he can or cannot rapidly achieve the spiritual objective of his soul. This lesson involves:

a. Arriving at a knowledge of those forces which are peculiarly potent in his life and which seem to direct his activities. This will bring to him the knowledge as to which centers of his etheric body are awakened and which are dormant. This all aspirants have to grasp before they really can apply themselves to the real training for discipleship.
b. Grasping the relation between these forces of nature which he has appropriated for his own use and which constitute the sum total of his personal, mental, sentient and vital energies, and those same forces as they are found in the natural world and govern the manifestation of the Macrocosm.
c. Learning to work with these energies in an intelligent manner in order to bring about three happenings:
An harmonious cooperation with his own solar Angel, so that solar force may impose its rhythm upon the lunar forces.
An intelligent response to and affiliation with the group of World Servers who at any given time have undertaken the work of directing, by the power of their thought, the forces of nature and so leading the whole creative body forward along the line of divine intent.
The production on the physical plane of a personality adequate for its creative task and capable of those forms of activity, emanating from the mind, which will enable him to further the work of the directing agencies.

Second, learn to live as a soul and, therefore, free from identification with the body nature. This brings out three things:

a. An ability to withdraw into the head consciousness and from that high place to direct the life of the personal self.
b. The power to pass through the various centers in the body those universal forces and energies which are needed for world work. This has to be done consciously and in full awareness of the source from which they come, of the mode of their activity and of the purpose for which they must be used. This involves also the understanding of which force is related to a center. This consequently involves the necessity to develop the centers, to bring them into a state of potency and to harmonize them into a unified rhythm.
c. The capacity, therefore, to work at will through the medium of any particular center. This is only possible when the soul can dwell as the Ruler on the "throne between the eyebrows" and when the Kundalini fire has been what is occultly called raised. This fire has to pass up through the spinal column and burn its way through the web which separates center from center on the "Golden Rod of Power."

Third, learn to study the reactions upon others of whatever energy he, through his personality, may be expressing, or which, if he be an initiate and, therefore, a conscious worker with the Plan, it may be his privilege to utilize or transmit. Through a close study of his personal "effect" upon his fellowmen, as he lives amongst them, and as he thinks, speaks and acts, he learns the nature of that type of force which may flow through him. He can arrive, therefore, at an understanding of its type, its quality, its strength, and its speed. These four words warrant consideration and elucidation.

A. The *type* of force as used by an aspirant will indicate to him its emanating source, and a study of it will begin to signify to him the Entity from which it has emanated. A knowledge of the type answers the question: Along what line of energy and upon what ray is this force to be found? A close watch upon this aspect of work will soon indicate to the aspirant:

1. upon what plane he himself may be working,
2. the nature of his ray, egoic ray and personality ray. Only the initiate of the third degree can ascertain his monadic ray,
3. the particular tattva which may be involved,
4. the center through which he may be transmitting the force.

It will be apparent, therefore, that a study of the types of energy is of practical usefulness and will tend to leave no part of the aspirant's nature untouched. Think for a minute of the lessons which can be learned by the man who submits the energy used in verbal expression, for instance, to the scrutiny of the Inner Ruler and who—after talking or after joining in the give and take of daily life—asks himself the questions: What was the type of energy used by me in my speech today? What was the force that I expended in my contacts with my fellowmen? You ask me if I can illustrate this for you? Now let me attempt to do so and so make simple what is deemed so oft to be abstruse and difficult. Let the student inquire of himself whether the position he held mentally and whether the words which he spoke on any particular occasion were prompted by a desire to impose his will upon his hearers. This imposition of his will could be either right or wrong. When right, it would mean that he was speaking under the impulse of his spiritual will, that his words would be in line with soul purpose and intent and would be governed by love and, therefore, would be constructive, helpful and healing. His attitude would be one of detachment and he would have no desire to take prisoner the mind of his brother. But if his words were prompted by self-will and by the desire to impose *his* ideas upon other people and so to shine in their presence, or to force them to agree with his conclusions, his method would then be destructive, dominating, aggressive, argumentative, forceful, rude or irritable, according to his personality trends and inclinations. This would indicate the right or the wrong use of first ray force.

Should the type of force he wields be that of the second ray, he can submit it to a similar analysis. He will then find it to be based on group love, service and compassion, or upon a selfish longing to be liked, on sentiment and on attachment. His words will indicate this to him if he will closely study them. Similarly, if he is using third ray force, in a *personal* manner, he will be devious in his propositions, subtle and elusive in his arguments, using manipulation in his relations with his fellowmen, or be an interfering busybody, actively engaged in running the world, in managing other people's lives for them, or in grasping so firmly the reins of government in his own self-interest that he will sacrifice everything and everybody in the work of furthering his own busy ends. If he is, however, a true disciple and aspirant, he will work with the Plan and will wield third ray force to bring about the loving purposes of the spiritual Reality. He will be busy and active and his word will carry truth, and will lead to the helping of others, for they will be detached and true.

THE USE OF THE HANDS

It is of value here when we are dealing with the wielding of force to give a little information anent the use of the hands in such work. One of the Masters has said, "It is but with armed hand and ready either to conquer or perish that the modern mystic can hope to achieve his object." I intend to speak a few words about the hands, for there is more occult teaching hidden in these words than is apparent on the surface.

In one of the old books, available for the instruction of disciples these words are found:

"The armed hand is an empty hand and this protects its possessor from the accusations of his enemies. It is a hand freed from the taint of the four symbolic evils—gold, lust, the dagger, and the finger of enticement."

These words are most significant, and it might be well to study briefly the type of hands and their quality which are distinctive of disciples. In all forms of esoteric teaching the hands play a great part and this for four reasons:

1. They are the symbol of acquisitiveness.
2. They are centres of force
3. They are wielders of the sword.
4. They are, when employed unselfishly

a. Instruments of healing.
b. Agencies whereby certain keys are turned.

Viewing them as *symbols of acquisitiveness* it must be remembered that in the average man they are employed to "grasp and to hold" and to acquire that which the man wants for himself and for the satisfaction of his selfish desire. In spiritual man, the hands are still symbols of acquisitiveness but he only grasps that which is needed for the helping of the group and releases at once towards that end that which he has thus acquired. The initiate holds nothing for himself; the saviour of the race may utilise all that is laid up in the divine storehouse but not for himself, only for those he seeks to help.

As *centres of force* the hands play a most potent part, and one that is little understood. It is an occult fact that the hands of a disciple (once he has acquired that acquisitiveness which is based on unselfish group work) become transmitters of spiritual energy. The "laying on of hands" is no idle phrase nor confined solely to the operations of the episcopate of any faith. The occult laying on of hands can be studied in four aspects:

1. *In healing.* In this case the force which flows through the hands comes from a dual source and via two etheric centres, the spleen and the heart.

2. *In the stimulation of any specific centre.* The energy employed in this case comes from the base of the spine, and the throat, and must be accompanied by appropriate words.

3. *In the work of linking a man up with his ego.* The force used here must be received from three etheric centres, the solar plexus, the heart, and the centre between the eyebrows.

4. *In group work.* Here energy is utilised emanating from the ego, via the head centre, the throat centre and the base of the spine.

It will be apparent therefore that the Science of the Hands is a very real one and the disciple has to learn the nature of the forces in the different centres, how to transmit and unify them and then by an act of the will how to pass them outward through the chakras in the hands. The hands do their work either directly, or through the projection of a steady flow once the blended currents have been tapped, or indirectly, or by manipulation. Through a knowledge of the law a disciple can not only utilise the current flowing through the centres of his own body, but can also combine them with the planetary or cosmic currents to be found in his environment. This is done unconsciously frequently by speakers who magnetically use the hands to any extent and the effects as seen by a clairvoyant are often amazing. When this work is done consciously a most potent factor is added to the equipment of any chela.

In this connection it must be borne in mind that the matter is a very abstruse one and that certain ray forces pass along the line of least resistance from left to right and others from right to left. Certain centres transmit their energies via the right hand and others via the left. Much knowledge is therefore required in order to work scientifically.

I have no time to take up in detail the meaning of the hands as they *wield the sword,* save to point out that the sword as a symbol stands for many things:

1. The sharp, two-edged sword is the discriminative faculty which reaches to the roots of the chela's being and separates the real and true from the false and impermanent. It is wielded by the ego from the mental plane and is spoken of as the "Sword of cold blue steel."

2. The sword of renunciation, or that double-bladed axe which the chela willingly applies to anything he considers as likely to hold him back from his goal. It is applied primarily to the things of the physical plane.

3. The sword of the Spirit is that weapon which in the hands of the disciple cuts down before the eyes of the group he is serving the obstacles which stand in the way of group progress. It is only wielded safely by those who have trained their arms to wield the other swords and in the hands of an initiate is a most potent factor.

The *Old Commentary* to which reference has been oft times made says:

"The steel is needed for the transmission of the fire. When the force of the inner man is coupled with the energy transmitted through the chakras of the palms, it passeth down the shining blade and blendeth with the force of the One Who is the ALL. Thus is the Plan consummated."

And thus it might be added is the energy of the unit augmented by the force of the greater Whole.

It is said in the occult books and likewise in *The Secret Doctrine* that all initiates must be *healers*; therefore, that all initiates use the palms of the hands in the work of healing. Only those therefore, who have wielded the sword dare lay the sword down and stand with empty hands, uplifted in blessing. Only the "armed hand" can safely be used in the work of salvation; only those who have "taken the kingdom of Heaven by force" and who are occultly known as the "Violent Ones" can take the heavenly supply and use it in the work of healing. This should be carefully borne in mind. The true healing force can only flow through those who in some degree either directly (by right of initiation or of advanced discipleship) or indirectly as being used on the inner side by some adept or advanced healer, are linked with the hierarchy. A man should know his status before he can rightly heal. This does not apply to those healers who are unconscious workers, being powerful transmitters of prana or solar vitality. Their name is legion and they do much good even though at times the energy they transmit serves to stimulate wrongly.

As regards *the use of the hands in turning keys* I will simply give a hint. Only those hands can turn the key in the door of initiation who have learnt the art of the centres", the significance of the hands in service, the wielding of the swords, and the four positions in which the hands are held in group service.

Study, therefore, the type of force which you usually wield; know along what line of ray energy it comes and so arrive at a truer knowledge of yourself and of your own inner capacities, and ascertain likewise what types of energy you may lack and how your equipment can be duly rounded out.

B. The *quality* of the force used is necessarily dependent upon the ray from which it may emanate. You ask me to differentiate between the words *type* and *quality*. I would say that the type of force indicates the life aspect, whilst the quality indicates the consciousness aspect, and that both of them are aspects of the entity or the being who is the embodiment of a ray. The type will manifest primarily through what we might call dynamic direction and through its power to produce an effect. This has, of course, to be coupled to right quality and skill in action. The quality will be indicated more by its power of attractive approach. It has in it more of the magnetic aspect than the type has. Students can arrive at the quality of the force they may be using by noticing what they attract to themselves, both in circumstances, in people, and in the reactions which people show to what the student may say or do. In the type there is a preponderance of the will aspect, in the quality the desire aspect is primarily to be found. It is profoundly true that according to a man's desires so will be the forms of life which he will, like a magnet, attract to himself.

C. The *strength* of a particular force brings us back to the Rule we are studying, for it involves in itself the factor of true persistence, and we have earlier seen that the emergence into functioning life and activity of any form is dependent upon the persistent attention of its creator. Energy can be used dynamically or steadily and the effects of these two modes of the application of energy differ. One is primarily used in destructive work, and this is the dynamic method. There are, for instance, certain dynamic words of power which, when employed by the Creative Destroyers, bring about the destruction of forms. With these, however, aspirants have naught to do. Their important work is to learn the meaning of persistence and of strength. It is literally a time-persistence, and *strength* is beyond all other things the power to endure, to hold out, to stand steady, and to go forward undeterred. Study, therefore, most carefully the types dynamic, the quality magnetic, and the strength persistent of the forces which constitute your equipment. When you can wield, either destructively or constructively, either selfishly or selflessly, or in line with the Plan Universal, or the plan selfish and personal then you will work consciously and will knowingly tread the right or the left hand path.

D. The *speed* of the force used is dependent upon these three previous factors. Speed in this sense has no essential relation to time, though it is hard to find another word to use in the place of speed. It relates to the world of effects as they emanate from the world of causes. It has, perhaps, essentially a relation to truth, for the truer an impulse is and the clearer the understanding of the subjective purpose, so will the right direction and the impact of the force, follow automatically. Perhaps speed would be more correctly translated by the words "correct direction", for where there is correct direction, true orientation, exact understanding of purpose and recognition of the type of force required, then there is an instantaneous effect. When the soul has registered the desired quality and possesses the strength of the Timeless One and the persistence of the One Who is from the beginning, the process of force expression and the relation between cause and effect is spontaneous and simultaneous, and not sequential. This can scarcely be understood by those who have not yet the consciousness of the eternal Now. But this spontaneous and simultaneous effect is the clue to the entire magical work and in these four words—type, quality, strength and speed—the story of the work of a White Magician is told. But more I dare not give and it is not permitted to me to speak more clearly. Few are yet fitted to be magicians and few (perhaps fortunately) have as yet all the seven centres awakened so that they can work freely on the seven planes and with the seven types of the seven ray energies.

I would point out that these four aspects of energy can be studied by the aspirant in his own nature. On the physical plane he is apparently the initiating cause and as he works with these energies they will call forth a response and a reaction from those who feel the impact of them and who demonstrate their effect. It is true, therefore, is it not, that we work and live in a world of forces? We need no distant field or special domain in which to live and learn and work, for we dwell in a world of force and energy; we are ourselves constituted of force or energy units; and we wield force, knowingly or unknowingly, throughout the twenty-four hours of the day. The field of our occult training is the field of the world and the world of our peculiar circumstances and environment.

THE TREADING OF THE WAY

We have seen, as we have considered Rule XIV that, in the magical work, the critical point of objectivity has now been reached by the aspirant. He is endeavouring to become a magical creator and to accomplish two things:

1. Re-create his instrument or mechanism of contact, so that the solar Angel has a vehicle, adequate for the expression of Reality. This involves, we noted, right type, quality, strength and speed.

2. Build those subsidiary forms of expression in the outer world through which the embodied Energy, flowing through the re-created sheaths, can serve the world.

In the first case, the aspirant is dealing with himself, working within his own circumference, and thus learning to know himself, to change himself and to rebuild his form aspect. In the other case, he is learning to be a server of the race, and to construct those forms of expression which will embody the new ideas, the emerging principles, and the new concepts which must govern and round out our racial progress.

Remember that no man is a disciple, in the Master's sense of the word, who is not a *pioneer*. A registered response to spiritual truth, a realised pleasure in forward-looking ideals, and a pleased acquiescence in the truths of the New Age do not constitute discipleship. If it were so, the ranks of disciples would be rapidly filled and this is sadly not the case. It is the ability to arrive at an understanding of the next realisations which lie ahead of the human mind which marks the aspirant, who stands at the threshold of accepted discipleship; it is the power, wrought out in the crucible of strenuous inner experience, to see the immediate vision and to grasp those concepts in which the mind must necessarily clothe it, which give a man the right to be a recognised worker with the plan (recognised by the Great Ones, if not recognised by the world); it is the achievement of that spiritual orientation, held steadily—no matter what the outer disturbance in the physical plane life may be—that signifies to Those Who watch and seek for workers, that a man can be trusted to deal with some small aspect of Their undertaken work; it is the capacity to submerge and to lose sight of the personal lower self in the task of world guidance, under soul impulse, which lifts a man out of the ranks of the aspiring mystics into those of the practical, though mystically minded, occultists.

This is an intensely practical work, on which we are engaged; it is likewise of such proportions that it will occupy all of a man's attention and time, even his entire thought life, and will lead him to efficient expression in his personality task (imposed by karmic limitation and inherited tendency) and to a steadfast application of the creative and magical work. Discipleship is a synthesis of hard work, intellectual unfoldment, steady aspiration and spiritual orientation, plus the unusual qualities of positive harmlessness and the opened eye which sees at will into the world of reality.

Certain considerations should be brought to the notice of the disciple which—for the sake of clarity—we will tabulate. To become an adept it will be necessary for the disciple to:

1. Enquire the Way.
2. Obey the inward impulses of the soul.
3. Pay no attention to any worldly consideration.
4. Live a life which is an example to others.

These four requirements may sound at the first superficial reading as easy of accomplishment, but if carefully studied it will become apparent why an adept is a "rare efflorescence of a generation of enquirers." Let us take up each of these four points:

1. *Enquire the Way.* We are told by one of the Masters that a whole generation of enquirers may only produce one adept. Why should this be so? For two reasons:

First, the true enquirer is one who avails himself of the wisdom of his generation, who is the best product of his own period and yet who remains unsatisfied and with the inner longing for wisdom unappeased. To him there appears to be something of more importance than knowledge and something of greater moment than the accumulated experience of his own period and time. He recognises a step further on and seeks to take it in order to gain something to add to the quota already gained by his compeers. Nothing satisfies him until he finds the Way, and nothing appeases the desire at the centre of his being except that which is found in the house of his Father. He is what he is because he has tried all lesser ways and found them wanting, and has submitted to many guides only to find them "blind leaders of the blind". Nothing is left to him but to become his own guide and find his own way home *alone*. In the loneliness which is the lot of every true disciple are born that self-knowledge and self-reliance which will fit him in his turn to be a Master. This loneliness is not due to any separative spirit but to the conditions of the Way itself. Aspirants must carefully bear this distinction in mind.

Secondly, the true enquirer is one whose courage is of that rare kind which enables its possessor to stand upright and to sound his own clear note in the very midst of the turmoil of the world. He is one who has the eye trained to see beyond the fogs and miasmas of the earth to that centre of peace which presides over all earth's happenings, and that trained attentive ear which (having caught a whisper of the Voice of the Silence) is kept tuned to that high vibration and is thus deaf to all lesser alluring voices. This again brings loneliness and produces that aloofness which all less evolved souls feel when in the presence of those who are forging ahead.

A paradoxical situation is brought about from the fact that the disciple is told to enquire the Way and yet there is none to tell him. Those who know the Way may not speak, knowing that the Path is constructed by the aspirant as the spinner spins its web out of the centre of his own being. Thus only those souls flower forth into adepts in any specific generation who have "trodden the winepress of the wrath of God alone" or who (in other words) have worked out their karma alone and who have intelligently taken up the task of treading the Path.

2. *Obey the inward impulses of the soul.* Well do the teachers of the race instruct the budding initiate to practise discrimination and train him in the arduous task of distinguishing between:

a. Instinct and intuition.
b. Higher and lower mind.
c. Desire and spiritual impulse.
d. Selfish aspiration and divine incentive.
e. The urge emanating from the lunar lords, and the unfoldment of the solar Lord.

It is no easy or flattering task to find oneself out and to discover that perhaps even the service we have rendered and our longing to study and work has had a basically selfish origin, and resting on a desire for liberation or a distaste for the humdrum duties of everyday. He who seeks to obey the impulses of the soul has to cultivate an accuracy of summation and a truthfulness with himself which is rare indeed these days. Let him say to himself "I must to my own Self be true" and in the private moments of his life and in the secrecy of his own meditation let him not gloss over one fault, nor excuse himself along a single line. Let him learn to diagnose his own words, deeds, and motives, and to call things by their true names. Only thus will he train himself in spiritual discrimination and learn to recognise truth in all things. Only thus will the reality be arrived at and the true self known.

3. *Pay no consideration to the prudential considerations of worldly science and sagacity.* If the aspirant has need to cultivate a capacity to walk alone, if he has to develop the ability to be truthful in all things, he has likewise need to cultivate courage. It will be needful for him to run counter

consistently to the world's opinion, and to the very best expression of that opinion, and this with frequency. He has to learn to do the right thing as he sees and knows it, irrespective of the opinion of earth's greatest and most quoted. He must depend upon himself and upon the conclusions he himself has come to in his moments of spiritual communion and illumination. It is here that so many aspirants fail. They do *not* do the very best they know; they fail to act in detail as their inner voice tells them; they leave undone certain things which they are prompted to do in their moments of meditation, and fail to speak the word which their spiritual mentor, the Self, urges them to speak. *It is in the aggregate of these unaccomplished details that the big failures are seen.*

There are no trifles in the life of the disciple and an unspoken word or unfulfilled action may prove the factor which is holding a man from initiation.

4. *Live a life which is an example to others.* Is it necessary for me to enlarge upon this? It seems as if it should not be and yet here again is where men fail. What after all is group service? Simply the life of example. He is the best exponent of the Ageless Wisdom who lives each day in the place where is the life of the disciple; he does not live it in the place where he thinks he should be. Perhaps after all the quality which produces the greatest number of failures among aspirants to adeptship is cowardice. Men fail to make good where they are because they find some reason which makes them think they should be elsewhere. Men run away, almost unrealising it, from difficulty, from inharmonious conditions, from places which involve problems, and from circumstances which call for action of a high sort and which are staged to draw out the best that is in a man, provided he stays in them. They flee from themselves and from other people, instead of simply *living the life.*

The adept speaks no word which can hurt, harm or wound. Therefore he has had to learn the meaning of speech in the midst of life's turmoil. He wastes no time in self pity or self justification for he knows the law has placed him where he is, and where he best can serve, and has learnt that difficulties are ever of a man's own making and the result of his own mental attitude. If the incentive to justify himself occurs he recognises it as a temptation to be avoided. He realises that each word spoken, each deed undertaken and every look and thought has its effect for good or for evil upon the group.

Is it not apparent therefore why so few achieve and so many fail?

THE AWAKENING OF THE CENTRES

Speaking more technically and therefore warranting the use of the word *Instructions* in connection with this treatise for aspirants and disciples, it must be carefully borne in mind that the main task of the aspirant is the handling of energies, both in himself and in the world of physical phenomena and externalisation. This consequently involves an understanding of the centres and of their awakening. But understanding must come first, and the awakening at a much later date in the sequence of time. This awakening will fall into two stages:

First, there is the stage wherein, by the practice of a disciplined life and by the purification of the thought life, the seven centres are automatically brought into a right condition of rhythm, vitality and vibratory activity. This stage involves no danger and there is no directed thought—in connection with the centres—permitted to the aspirant. By that I mean he is not allowed to concentrate his mind upon any one centre, nor may he seek to awaken or energize them. He must remain engrossed with the problem of purifying the bodies in which the centres are found, which are primarily the astral, etheric and physical bodies, remembering ever that the endocrine system and the seven major glands, in particular, are the effectual externalisations of the seven major centres. In this stage, the aspirant is working all around the centres and is dealing with their environing matter and with the living substance which completely surrounds them. This is all that can be safely undertaken by the majority, and it is with this stage that the bulk of the aspirants in the world today are engaged and with which they must remain engaged for a long the to come.

Secondly, there is the stage wherein the centres, through the effective work of the earlier stage, become what is esoterically called "released within the prison house"; they can now become the subject (under proper direction by a teacher) of definite methods of awakening and of charging,—the methods differing according to the ray, personality and egoic, of the aspirant. Hence the difficulty of the subject and the impossibility of giving general and blanket rules.

It is interesting here to note, even though it has no bearing on the matter of personal training, that this method, first of a long period of purification and later of energising scientifically, is the one employed by the guiding hierarchy which stands behind world affairs. Steadily They have been working at the task of clarifying world matter, and bringing about world purification on a large scale. This is the first stage of the work and only became generally possible when man became a more truly thinking entity, during the past few centuries, on a wide level. This purification is going on now in all departments of human existence, for humanity now stands, or rather three-fifths of it stands, on the path of probation. Through welfare and uplift movements and the wide spread of sanitation, the work goes forward on the physical plane; through political upheavals which reveal abuses; through economic discontent which is after all a striving to change that which is undesirable so as to give the human unit conditions of living which will lead to thought and from thought to soul control; through religious propaganda and the efforts of the many organisations and groups throughout the world which hold before the minds of men what I might symbolically call "the hope of Heaven" (using the word "Heaven" as a symbol of perfection and of purity), the work of this stage is going steadily forward. So successful has it been that now the filth and impurities which surround the world soul and which keep humanity from its true expression are known and recognised and there is consequently a steady drive towards betterment. All has been brought to the surface, and the result seems appalling and uncontrollable to those who only see the surface. But underneath, the deep river of purity and truth is flowing strong.

One evidence of the success of the world movement towards pure living and the destruction of that which hinders is that the work of the second stage is now in process of initiation. The hierarchy, for the first time in world history, can now work directly with the centres in the body of humanity. Thus we have now the formation of the new Group of World Workers, who, in their totality throughout the world, constitute the heart centre and the "centre between the eyebrows" of the etheric body of the human family. Through the one, spiritual life can begin to flow in and vitalise all the centres, and through the other, the vision can be seen and the inner worlds sensed and known.

I would here like to point out two other matters, and so clarify the entire situation. There is much confusion on the subject of the centres and much erroneous teaching leading many astray and causing a great deal of misapprehension.

First, I would state that no work such as an effort to awaken the centres should ever be undertaken whilst the aspirant is aware of definite impurities in his life, or when the physical body is in poor condition or is diseased. Neither should it be undertaken when the pressure of external circumstances is such that there is no place or opportunity for quiet and uninterrupted work. It is essential that for the immediate and focussed work on the centres there should be the possibility of hours of seclusion and of freedom from interruption. This I cannot too strongly emphasise, and I do so in order to demonstrate to the eager student that at this period of our history there are few whose lives permit of this seclusion. This is however a most beneficent circumstance and not one to be deplored. Only one in a thousand aspirants is at the stage where he should begin to work with the energy in his centres and perhaps even this estimate is too optimistic. Better far that the aspirant serves and loves and works and disciplines himself, leaving his centres to develop and unfold more slowly and therefore more safely. Unfold they inevitably will and the slower and safer method is (in the vast majority of cases) the more rapid. Premature unfoldment involves much loss of time, and carries with it often the seeds of prolonged trouble.

Over-stimulation of the brain cells is necessarily one of the results of the merging, by an act of will, of the fires which circulate in the human body. Such stimulation can produce insanity and the breaking down of the cellular structure of the brain, and through the over-activity of the cell life can also induce that internal friction between them which will eventuate in brain tumors and abscesses. This cannot be too strongly reiterated.

The underlying objective in all laya yoga work (or work with the centres) is based upon the fact that the energy of the cells which compose the body or the matter aspect (called in *The Secret Doctrine*, and in *A Treatise on Cosmic Fire*, "fire by friction") must be blended with the fire of consciousness. This latter is the energy, present in matter yet different from the fire of matter itself, which underlies the entire nervous system and because it so underlies it produces sensitivity and awareness. It is the cause of response to contact and confers the ability to register and record impression, as you well know. This fire is technically called "solar fire", and when it blends with the fire of matter and with the "electric fire" of the highest divine aspect, then man's being comes into its fullest manifestation and the great work is completed. But it is a most dangerous undertaking, when induced before the mechanism is ready to deal with it.

This triple blending can only be safely undertaken by the highly organised and rounded-out person, and by one who has achieved the capacity to focus his attention in the head and from that high point direct the entire process of fusion. It involves the ability to withdraw the consciousness literally into the etheric body and yet at the same time to preserve—in full awareness—a point of contact in the head, and from that point direct the automaton, the physical body. It presupposes, if successful, certain etheric conditions in the body. One of these is the process of burning through or destruction (partial or complete) of any obstructions found along the spinal cord which could prevent the free rising of the fire at the base of the spine, commonly called the kundalini fire, which lies quiescent, latent and potential in the lowest centre. This is "the sleeping serpent which must arise and uncoil".

Each centre in the spine is separated from the one above it and the one below it by an interlaced protective web which is composed of a curious blend of etheric and gaseous substance. This has to be burnt away and dissipated before there can be the free play of the fires of the body. A complete network of nadis and centres underlies and is the subtle counterpart of the nervous and endocrine systems. A little clear thinking therefore will demonstrate the need for excessive care, for there will obviously lie a direct effect upon the external apparatus and this in its turn will definitely affect what the psychologists call "behaviour". There are four of these interlaced circular "webs" lying between the five centres found on the rod of the spinal column, such as follows: 0/0/0/0/0, and three are to be found in the head. These three bisect the head, and form a series of crosses, as follows:

275

This is much like the cross upon the Union Jack, which has always had an esoteric significance for the student, and indicates a point in racial evolution. This cross in the head separates the ajna centre (the centre between the eyebrows) from the head centre, for it lies behind that centre in the forehead, and at the same time forms a protective shield between the ajna and throat centres.

These etheric webs are in reality disks, rotating or revolving at specific rates, which differ for the different centres, and according to the point in evolution of the system of centres concerned. Only when these webs are burnt away by the ascending and descending fires can the true centres really be seen. Many clairvoyants confuse the centres and their protective counterparts, for the latter have a radiance and light of their own.

As the life achieves an increasingly high vibration through purification and discipline, the fire of the soul, which is literally the *fire of mind*, causes the centres also to increase their vibration, and this increased activity sets up a contact with the protective "webs", or disks of pranic energy found on either side of them. Thus, through the interplay, they are gradually worn away, so that in the course of time they become perforated, if I might use such an inadequate term. Many aspirants feel convinced that they have raised the kundalini fire at the base of the spine and are consequently making rapid progress, whereas all that they have accomplished is to burn or "rub through" the web at some point or other up the spine. A sensation of burning or of pain in any part of the spine, when not due to physiological causes, is, in the majority of cases, due to the piercing of one or other of the webs, through the activity of the centres allied to them. This happens very frequently in the case of women in connection with the solar plexus centre, and with men in connection with the sacral centre. Both these centres—as a result of evolutionary development—are exceedingly active and highly organised, for they are the expression of the physical creative nature and of the emotional body. A sense therefore of burning and of pain in the back indicates usually undue activity in a centre, which produces destructive results upon the protective apparatus, and is no true indication of spiritual unfoldment and superiority. It may indicate the latter, but it should be remembered that, where there is true spiritual growth, pain and danger are in this connection practically eliminated.

There has been much loose talk about the raising of the kundalini fire and much misapprehension in the matter. Let me assure you that it is most difficult to raise, and can only be done by a definite act of the will and through the intense mental focussing and concentrated attention of the man, seated on the throne of consciousness in the head. The Masonic tradition has the teaching clearly held in its beautiful ritual of the raising of the great Master-Mason. Only when there is united effort of a fivefold kind, and only after repeated failure, does the vivifying life course through the entire body and bring to life the true man.

The second point I would touch upon is that all this deeply esoteric work must only proceed under the direction of the skilled teacher. Platitudinously, the aspirant is told that "when the pupil is ready, the Master will appear". He then settles comfortably back and waits, or focuses his attention upon an attempt to attract the attention of some Master, having apparently settled in his mind that he is ready or good enough. He naturally gives himself a spiritual prod at intervals, and attends spasmodically to the work of discipline and of purification. But steady and prolonged undeviating effort on the part of aspirants is rare indeed.

It is indeed true that at the right moment the Master will appear, but the right moment is contingent upon certain *self-induced* conditions. When the process of purification has become a life-long habit, when the aspirant can at will concentrate his consciousness in the head, when the light in the head shines forth and the centres are active, then the Master will take the man in hand. In the meantime he may have a vision of the Master, or he may see a thought-form of the Master, and may get much real good and inspiration from contact with the reflected reality, but it is not the Master and does *not* indicate the stage of accepted discipleship. Through the medium of the light of the soul, the soul can be known. Therefore seek the light of your own soul, and know that soul as your director. When soul contact is established, your own soul will, if I may so express it, introduce you to your Master. With all due reverence again may I add, that the Master waits not with eagerness to make your acquaintance. In the world of souls, your soul and His soul are allied, and know essential unity. But in the world of human affairs and in the process of the great work it should be remembered that when a Master takes an aspirant into His group of disciples, that aspirant is, for a long time, a liability and oft a hindrance. Students over-estimate themselves quite often, even when repudiating such an idea; subjectively they have a real liking for themselves and are frequently puzzled as to why the Great Ones give them no sign, nor indicate Their watching care. They will not and They need not until such time as the aspirant has used to the full the knowledge which he has gained from lesser teachers, and from books and printed scriptures of the world. Students must attend to the immediate duty and prepare their mechanisms for service in the world, and should desist from wasting time and looking for a Master; they should achieve mastery where now they are defeated and in the life of service and of struggle they may then reach the point of such complete self-forgetfulness that the Master may find no hindrance in His approach to them.

It will be apparent therefore from the above that I cannot give specific instructions as to the awakening of the centres and the burning of the etheric web which will result in the release of energy. Such information is too dangerous and too intriguing to be put in the hands of the general public, who are driven by desire for some new thing, and lack right poise and the needed mental development. The time has come however when the fact that there is an energy body underlying the nervous system must be recognized by the world at large, and when the nature of the seven centres, their structure and location should be grasped technically, and when the laws of their unfoldment should be widely known. But more than this cannot yet be safely given. The intricate nature of this science of the centres is too great for general usefulness. The teaching to be given in any particular case and the methods to be applied are dependent upon too many factors for a general rule and instruction to be given. The ray and type, the sex and point in evolution must be considered and also the *balance* of the centres. By this I mean the consideration as to their over-development in one case and under development in another and as to whether there is a preponderance of the force below or above the diaphragm, or whether the main energy is concentrated in that central clearing house, the solar plexus. The quality and the brilliance of the light in the head has to be studied, for it indicates the measure of soul control and the relative purity of the vehicles, and the various etheric "webs" have to be carefully dealt with, and also the rate of vibration of the web and the centre. A synchronisation has to be set up and this is most difficult to bring about. These are only a few of the points that the teacher has to note, and it is apparent therefore that only a teacher who has achieved synthetic vision and can see a man "whole," or as he really is, can give those instructions which will reverse the ancient rhythm of the centres, destroy without pain and danger the protective sheaths, and raise the kundalini fire from the base of the spine to the exit in the head.

Such teachers are found by the pupil when he has carried forward his life work under the direction of his soul, when he has grasped the theory of the science of the centres, and has mastered and controlled the astral nature and its corresponding centre, the solar plexus. The emphasis laid upon the dominance of the Christ principle by Christianity has laid a sure foundation for the work to be done. This truth is curiously substantiated in a study of the number "eight" in connection with the centres which, we are told, is the number of the Christ. There are eight centres if the spleen is counted, all of them are multiples of eight with the exception of the centre at the base of the spine which has four petals, one half of eight. In our day and in the Anglo Saxon mode of writing, the number eight is the basic symbol of all the centres, for the petals are really in form like a number of superimposed eights. The word petal is purely pictorial and a centre is formed on this pattern. First, a circle, O; then two circles, touching each other and making therefore an 8. Then, as the petals increase in number, it is simply a growth of these double circles, superimposed at differing angles one upon another until we arrive at the thousand-petalled lotus in the head.

These centres are, in the last analysis, twofold in function. They demonstrate the form building aspect of divinity and through their activity bring the outer form into manifestation; then towards the end of the evolutionary cycle—both in the macrocosm and the microcosm—they bring into expression the soul force and life and produce the incarnation of a fully revealed son of God, with all the powers and knowledge which divinity contains.

RULE FIFTEEN

The fires approach the shadow, yet burn it not. The fire sheath is completed. Let the magician chant the words that blend the fire and water.

The Esoteric Sense.
The Negation of the Great Illusion.
A Call to Service.
The New Age Groups and Training.

THE ESOTERIC SENSE

We come now to the consideration of the last rule for magic. As we cast our minds back over this long series of instructions certain basic lines of teaching stand out with exceptional clarity, casting lesser lines of instruction into the shade. Students would do well to remember that in the reading of any basic textbook (and this one is so regarded) a definite procedure should be adopted. The student should first of all read the textbook as a whole, in order to grasp its outstanding points, its main lines of teaching, and the three or four propositions upon which its entire structure is founded. Having grasped these, he can then begin to deal with, and to isolate, those subsidiary points which serve to elucidate and clarify the main essentials. After that, he can successfully deal with the details. Students therefore would find it of interest to review these instructions, and gather out of them the major points; then they can proceed to fill in the secondary teachings, and finally arrange the detailed data under the various heads which have emerged. This, when completed would constitute a synopsis of the book and would fix the knowledge it contains firmly in the student's memory.

One of the main teachings which can be seen most clearly in all instructions of a truly esoteric character, concerns the *attitude* of the student of the occult. He is supposed to be dealing with things subjective and esoteric; he aims to be a worker in white magic. As such, he must assume and consistently hold the position of the Observer, detached from the mechanism of observation and contact; he must recognise himself as essentially a spiritual entity, different in nature, objectives and methods of working from the bodies which he considers it wise to occupy temporarily and to employ. He must realise his unity and lines of contact with all similar workers and thus arrive at a conscious awareness of his position in the spiritual hierarchy of Beings. So much misinformation has been spread abroad and so much emphasis has been unwisely laid upon status and position in the so-called Hierarchy of souls, that sane and balanced disciples now seek to turn their thoughts elsewhere and to eliminate as far as may be all thought of grades and spheres of activity. It is possible, in the swing of the pendulum, to swing too far in the opposite direction and to discount these stages of activity. Do not misunderstand me however; I do not suggest that an attempt be made to place people and to decide where they stand upon the evolutionary ladder. This has been most foolishly done in the past, with much dishonour to the subject, so much so that, in the minds of the public, the whole matter has fallen into disrepute. If these stages are regarded sanely for what they are—states of extended consciousness, and grades of responsibility—then the danger of personality reaction to the terms "accepted disciple, initiate, adept, master" would be negligible and much trouble would be eliminated. It must ever be remembered that individual status is rigidly kept to oneself, and the point of evolution (which may be truthfully recognised as lying ahead of that of the average citizen) will be demonstrated by a life of active unselfish service and by the manifestation of an illumined vision which is ahead of the racial idea.

In the gathering together in the world at this time of the new Group of World Workers, true caution must be preserved. Each worker is responsible for himself and his service and for no one else. It is wise to gauge and approximate the evolutionary status, not upon claims made, but upon work accomplished and the love and wisdom shown. Judgment should be based upon an evidenced knowledge of the plan as it works out in the wise formulation of the nest step ahead for the human race; upon a *manifested esoteric sense*, and upon an influence or an auric power which is wide, constructive and inclusive.

You ask me to define more clearly what I mean by the words "esoteric sense". I mean essentially the power to live and to function subjectively, to possess a constant inner contact with the soul and the world in which it is found, and this must work out subjectively through love, actively shown; through wisdom, steadily outpoured; and through that capacity to include and to identify oneself with all that breathes and feels which is the outstanding characteristic of all truly functioning sons of God. I mean, therefore, an interiorly held attitude of mind which can orient itself at will in any direction. It can govern and control the emotional sensitiveness, not only of the disciple himself, but of all whom he may contact. By the strength of his silent thought, he can bring light and peace to all. Through that mental power, he can tune in on the world thought, and upon the realm of ideas and can discriminate between and choose those mental agencies and those concepts which will enable him, as a worker under the plan, to influence his environment and to clothe the new ideals in that thought matter which will enable them to be more easily recognised in the world of ordinary everyday thinking and living. This attitude of mind will enable the disciple also to orient himself to the world of souls and in that high place of inspiration and of light, discover his fellow-workers, communicate with them and—in union with them—collaborate in the working out of divine intentions.

This esoteric sense is the main need of the aspirant at this time of the world history. Until aspirants have somewhat grasped it and can use it, they can never form part of the New Group; they can never work as white magicians, and these Instructions will remain for them theoretical and mainly intellectual, instead of being practical and effective.

To cultivate this inner esoteric sense, meditation is needed, and continuous meditation, in the early stages of development. But as time elapses and a man grows spiritually, this daily meditation will perforce give way to a steady spiritual orientation and then meditation as now understood and needed will no longer be required. The detachment between a man and his usable forms will be so complete, that he will live ever in the "seat of the Observer", and from that point and attitude will direct the activities of the mind and of the emotions and of the energies which make physical expression possible and useful.

The first stage in this development and culture of the esoteric sense consists in the holding of the attitude of constant detached observation.

The new Group of World Workers might well be regarded in its outer ranks as a trained body of organised observers. I would divide the group into three divisions and I do so in order that aspirants and chelas all over the world may be guided in their knowledge as to where they stand individually and may, in sincerity and truth, begin to work with intelligence. They can be thus aided to place themselves.

First, there are the *Organised Observers*. These aspirants are learning to do two things. They are learning to practice that detachment which will enable them to live as souls in the world of daily affairs and to understand the real significance of the words: to work without attachment. They are also, secondly, those students of world affairs in one or other of the seven departments earlier referred to when I brought the new group to the attention of the world. They are studying the signs of the times. They investigate the great drama of history in order to discover its main trend and so express to the ordinary academic world and to the thinkers of the race what they see and understand.

Running all through human history is a triple thread and in the interplay of these three threads the story of evolution is to be found. One thread guides the thoughts of man as he deals with the development of the form aspect, with the racial trends, and it shows how undeviatingly the forms of races, of countries, and of the fauna and flora of our planetary life have kept pace with the needs of the slowly emerging sons of God. The second thread leads us to an understanding of the growth of consciousness, and indicates emergence from the instinctual stage into that of intellectual awareness, and on to that intuitional illumination which is the present goal of consciousness.

The third thread concerns the Plan itself and here we enter the realm of the truly unknown. What the plan is, and what the goal, is as yet totally unrealised except by the highest adept and the most exalted of the sons of God. Until the illumined mind and the power of intuitional response are developed in the human family, it is not possible for us to grasp the basic concepts which are to be found in the mind of God Himself. Until the highest point of the Mount of Initiation has been climbed, it is not possible to vision the Promised Land as it is. Until the limitations—the necessary limitations—of the three worlds have been surmounted and man can function as a free soul in the spiritual kingdom, that which lies beyond that kingdom must remain hid to man just as much as the human state of being and awareness remains a sealed book to the animal. This is a salutary and needed lesson which all disciples should grasp.

But observers of times and seasons can make rapid progress in intuitional growth if they persevere in their meditation, train their intellects, and endeavour always to think in terms of universals. Let them look at the historical retrospect as part of the emerging preparation which will inaugurate the future. Let them take heart of grace as they recognise the fact that the kingdom of souls is steadily becoming a physical plane phenomenon (do I speak paradoxically?) and will be known eventually as a kingdom of nature and considered so by the scientists before two centuries have passed away. These "Organised Observers" form the outer circle of the new group and their keynote is synthesis, the elimination of non-essentials and the organising of human knowledge. Working in the many fields of human awareness, they are distinguished by a non-sectarian spirit, and by an ability to deal with foundational essentials and to link up varying departments of human investigation into one organised and unified whole.

Second, the next group in the new Group of World Workers is that of the *telepathic communicators*. These are much fewer in number and are distinguished by their relatively close interrelation with each other. They are primarily a linking or a bridging group. They are gathered out of the more exoteric circle of the organised observers, but have a wider scope of service than they have, for they work in a more truly esoteric manner. They are in touch with each other, and with the organised observers, but they are likewise in touch with the group of men and women who stand at the very centre or heart of the world group. Their work is threefold and very difficult. Steadily they have to cultivate that detachment which characterises the soul which knows itself. Steadily they take the knowledge and information accumulated by the organised observers and adapt it to the need of the world, and give out the teaching. They work effectively but always from behind the scenes, and though they may be known in the world in this early stage of the work of the new group, and though they may be therefore recognised as teachers, writers and workers, later they will recede more and more into the background and will work through the outer circle. They will inspire them, and will place increasing responsibility upon their shoulders; they will nurture the growth of telepathic interplay in the world and thus weave those strands which will eventually bridge the present gap between the seen and the unseen and so make the new world possible—a world in which death as we know it will be abolished and a trained universal continuity of consciousness be established. That is why the emphasis is laid in training the members of this group in the new group, upon telepathic sensitivity. The members of this second circle of workers are taught to develop sensitiveness in three directions: to the thoughts of men in physical incarnation; to the minds of those who have passed over and who are still in mind bodies, and thirdly to the group of spiritual Beings who stand as the custodians of the evolutionary process and through whose hands the three threads of developing life steadily pass.

Their task is exceedingly hard, far harder than that of the first group and harder even than that of the last, for they lack as yet certain powers and needed experience. Their centre of consciousness is the intuition and not that of the synthesising intellect, and their state of awareness is wide and inclusive. They therefore can suffer more than the majority, and few there are who are not at this stage too sensitive for their own comfort and too responsive to vibrations emanating from the form aspect in all three worlds. Their state of detachment is not yet complete. They *bridge*, and therefore support infinite problems and respond to world pain. They see, if I may so express it, too much, for theirs is not yet the privilege of visioning with clarity the goal that lies two hundred years ahead. They sense the present need. They are responsive to the new tide of spiritual force which is flowing in. They carry the weight of humanity on their shoulders, and because they are somewhat coordinated, they live in all three worlds at once, and this few can do. They are aware of the urgency of the present opportunity and also of the apathy of the many and for these reasons they work under terrific pressure.

Third, the innermost group of all is that of the members of the Hierarchy itself. I care not the least whether these liberated souls are recognised as Elder Brethren of the race, as Masters of the Wisdom, as the Cloud of Witnesses, as the Christ and His Church, as Supermen or under any terms which the inherited tendencies of humanity or tradition may choose to call them. They themselves care less. The petty quarrels as to their personalities and names and status matter not at all. But they are the intelligent forces of the planet; they express, because of their state of expanded consciousness, the Mind of God; they embody the intelligent principle, immutable and unchanging, and through them flows the energy which we call the Will of God, for lack of better understanding. They know far more of the plan than do the two outer circles in the new Group of World Workers, for they see clearly just what is the next step which planetary evolution will guide the race to take during the next two hundred years. They do not occupy themselves with idle speculations as to the ultimate goal at the close of a world age. This may surprise you in view of the many speculations of the uninitiate. But so it is. They know that there is a time and a season for all things, and looking ahead and comprehending intuitively the goal for all kingdoms in the immediate future, all their united effort is bent to one end—the cultivating of the intuitional telepathic responsiveness of the Communicators who bridge the gap between them and the physical world. These latter in their turn seek to employ the Observers, Knowers, Communicators, and Observers—all working in a close if oft-times unrealised unity, and all responsive (according to their degree) to the impulsion of the Mind and Will of the Logos, the solar Deity.

Beyond this triple group stand the Thrones, Principalities, and Powers with whom we need not concern ourselves. On the other side stands humanity torn by the disasters of the past world war, bewildered by the social, religious and economic pressure of the present, sensitive and responsive to the influences and energies pouring in on the new tide of the Aquarian Age; unable to understand and explain, and conscious only of a longing for liberty of thought and of physical condition, snatching at every chance to gain knowledge and so providing a fertile field wherein this new group can work.

We have seen that the objective of all inner training is to develop the esoteric sense, and to unfold that inner sensitive awareness which will enable a man to function, not only as a Son of God in physical incarnation but as one who also possesses that continuity of consciousness which will enable him to be interiorly awake as well as exteriorly active. This is accomplished through developing the power to be a trained Observer. I commend these words to all aspirants. It is persistence in the attitude of right observation that brings about detachment from form, a subsequent power to use form at will and with the end in view of furthering hierarchical plans and consequent usefulness to humanity. When this power to observe has been somewhat brought about, we then have the aspirant joining that intermediate group of trained Communicators who stand between the aforementioned groups (the exoteric groups and the group of spiritual workers on the subjective plane), interpreting the one to the other. It is well to remember that even the members of the Hierarchy profit by the opinions and advice of those disinterested disciples who can be trusted to rightly recognise and interpret the need of the hour.

When this stage has been reached and a man is in conscious touch with the Plan then true magical work can begin. Men and women, who are beginning to live as souls, can undertake the magical work of the new age, and can inaugurate those changes and that rebuilding which will bring about the manifestation of the new heavens and the new earth, to which all the Scriptures of the world bear eloquent testimony. They can then work with forces in etheric matter and so bring into being those physical plane creations and organisations which will more adequately embody the life of God in the Aquarian Age which is now upon us. It is to this stage that Rule XV refers.

These words mark the consummation of the magical work, and are equally true of the magical work of a solar Logos, of a planetary Logos, of an incarnating soul, or of that advanced human being who has learnt to work as a white magician under the plan of the great White Lodge. It, of course, refers to the work of those who through intellectual achievement have learnt to work as magicians but on what is called the black side, for the same rules of magical work hold good for both groups, though the motivating impulse differs. But with the work of the black magician we have naught to do. That which they do is powerful in transient effect, using the word transient in its cyclic sense; but these effects must in due time cease, and be subordinated to the claims and the work of the bringers of light and of life.

The shadow stage is the dim and uncertain period which is found prior to dense and concrete manifestation. It does not here refer to the shadow as the counterpart in physical manifestation of the soul. It refers to one of the intermediate stages in the creative process. It is technically called the "stage of the waxing and the waning of the nebulae", and this stage precedes the appearance of the more stabilised and relatively static exoteric form. In the formation of a solar system, this is recognised as a preliminary period and can be seen going on in the starry heavens. It indicates the stage wherein the Great Magician is only in process of carrying forward His work; He has not yet finally chanted those mystic words or those spiritual sounds which will produce concretion and the tangible appearance of form.

The Secret Doctrine refers to the three fires, and these are of ancient usage; the Vishnu Purana gives these fires exactly the same nomenclature as does H.P.B. who borrowed the terms from the ancient Scripture. Electric Fire, Solar Fire and Fire by Friction, when brought into conjunction, produce the manifested macrocosm and microcosm, and to this conjunction my earlier Treatise on Cosmic Fire referred. These fires are esoterically one fire but this fire produces, according to the witnessing consciousness (itself at varying stages of evolutionary development) the effect of differentiated fiery essence. This fiery essence can be known as Life itself, or as the "Self-shining Light," or it can be known as the active form inherent in the one substance which underlies all phenomena. In this final rule for magic the fires which are considered are those of matter itself which approach the shadow and (as the Old Commentary symbolically expresses it) "rise up from the second darkness at the call of the spirit of light and meet in their appointed place that which will absorb them and raise them to the fiery point from whence the fires of living light and radiant life have come."

THE NEGATION OF THE GREAT ILLUSION

The phrase in Rule XV which says "that blend the fire and water" has reference to the effect produced at the point of condensation, after the great words bringing about that effect have been pronounced. This rule is almost incapable of explanation and it is not permitted to me to give to you the words that effect this process. Only some hints may be given which will serve to encourage the true aspirant to think and may, alas, only irritate the casual thinker who seeks easy and quick methods and formulas through which to work. Heat and moisture are present in the production of all forms of life, but the great mystery (and almost the final mystery to be explained to the adept) is how the merging of three fires can produce moisture or the watery element. This problem and this phenomenon constitute the basis of the Great Illusion to which the ancient books refer; through the agency of the combination, the enveloping maya is produced. There is, in reality, no such thing as water; the watery sphere, the astral plane, is, could you but realise it, an illusory effect and has no real existence. Yet—in time and space and to the understanding of the witnessing consciousness—it is more real than that which it hides and conceals. I cannot make this clearer in words. It is only possible to suggest to the intelligent student that the light of his soul (reflected in his mind) and the energy of form (as expressed in his etheric body) are for him, in the realm of temporary duality , his two basic realities. The watery nature of his astral experience in which these two aspects of divinity seem (again illusion, be it noted) to meet and work is but a glamorous phenomenon and in an occult sense is not based on fact. Any true aspirant knows that his spiritual progress can be gauged in terms of his freedom from this illusion and of his release into the clear air and pure light of his spiritual consciousness. In its consciousness, the animal kingdom works with the second of these two basic realities, and for it the life of the etheric body and the force which governs the animal or material nature are the prime expression of truth. Yet the animal is beginning to sense dimly the world of illusion and possesses certain psychic powers and senses which recognise yet fail to interpret the astral plane. The veil of illusion is beginning to fail before the eyes of the animal but it knows it not. The human being has wandered for ages in the world of illusion, for it is of his own creating. Yet man in his turn, from the standpoint of consciousness, has contact with both the realities and learns little by little to dissipate the illusion by the steady growth of the radiant light of the soul. May I pause here to remind you that duality is only a stage on the evolutionary arc, leading eventually to the realisation of unity.

The veil of illusion resembles the moment before dawn when the world of familiar things is seen through the fogs and the streamers of mist which veil the world form and also veil the rising sun. Then we have that half-time, that mysterious and vague period when the real is hidden by the unreal; then we have that weird and distorted condition when forms are not seen as they truly are but lose their shape and colour and perspective. True vision is then impossible. The astral stage and the vast cycle of time in which the great illusion holds sway can therefore be judged, from the above symbolic approach, to be but temporary and transient. It is not the stage of a definitely divine manifestation; it is not the stage of pure undimmed awareness; it is not the stage of the perfected work. It is that period of time wherein the half-Gods walk; it is the time wherein truth is only dimly sensed, the vision only vaguely and occasionally seen; it is the stage of the half-realised Plan, and when one works on partial knowledge, difficulty and mistakes are bound to supervene. It is also the stage of distortion and of constant mutability: whilst it is in evidence we have the apparently ceaseless pulling hither and thither by forces, working blindly and seemingly without purpose. As far as humanity is concerned, it is the time wherein man is enveloped in mist and fog, and lost in the miasmas arising out of the ground (symbol of the foundational nature of the animal kingdom). Yet at times this stage is seen to be unreal as the dawning light of the spiritual consciousness pierces through the surrounding darkness. It is the interlude between the dominance of the animal consciousness and that of the spiritual, and this interlude of astral illusion is only known in the human family. There is no astral plane except in the consciousness of the fourth kingdom in nature, for man is "under illusion" in a sense different to the conscious awareness of any other kingdom—subhuman or superhuman.

I despair in making my meaning clear. How can one who is subject to the illusions of the senses, as are all human creatures, conceive of the state of consciousness of those who have freed themselves from the illusions of the astral plane or realise the state of awareness of those forms of life which have not yet developed astral consciousness? It is the dual nature of the mind which causes this illusion, for the mind of man presents to him the keys of the kingdom of heaven or locks upon him the door of entrance into the world of spiritual realities. It is the concretising unprincipled mind which brings about all the troubles of humanity. It is the sense of I-ness and the spirit of separative individuality which has brought humanity to its present condition, and yet even that is a part of the great developing process. It is the consciousness of duality, and the subjectively realised and synchronously acknowledged sense of "I am God" and "I am form" which has plunged mankind into the great illusion.

Yet it is this very illusion which renders up to man eventually the secret password into the kingdom of God and brings about his release. It is this maya itself which serves to guide him into truth and knowledge; it is on the plane of the astral that the heresy of separateness has to be overcome, and it is on the field of Kurukshetra that the individual aspiring Arjuna, and the cosmic Arjuna learn the lesson that the knower and the known are one. The secret science of the Master of the Wisdom is the secret of how to dissipate the fogs and mist and darkness and gloom which are produced by the union of the fires in the early stages. The secret of the Master is the discovery that there is no astral plane; he finds that the astral plane is a figment of the imagination and has been created through the uncontrolled use of the creative imagination and the misuse of the magical powers. The work of the hierarchy is primarily to bring to an end the shadows and to dispel the moisture; the aim of the Masters is to let in the light of the soul and to show that spirit and matter are the two realities which constitute the units and that it is only in time and in space and through the cyclic misuse of the magical and psychic powers that the astral plane of the great illusion has come into being and is now so real a thing that it is—in a certain sense—more real (to man) than the kingdom of light and the kingdom of form. In one most interesting sense it is true that because the human being is a soul and because the light of the soul is found within him and is gradually growing into fuller radiance this itself produces the illusion. Because of this illusion, the magical work has been carried forward along wrong lines and has been based on wrong motives and fitted into a scheme which is stronger than the average worker, for *the whole force of the world illusion is against all the efforts of the beginner in white magic.*

The rules therefore end with the statement that the magician chants the words that "blend the fire and water"—but these are the rules for the aspirant. The rules for initiates of a paralleling kind end with the words: "Let the initiate sound the note that unifies the fires". This is significant and of much encouragement to the beginner in the magical work. He is still perforce working on the astral plane and he cannot possibly avoid so doing for much time. The mark of growth for him is the steady withdrawal of his consciousness from that plane and his attainment of mental poise and of mental awareness, followed by creative work on the mental plane. There is an interesting and ancient proclamation found in the archives of the adepts which covers some of the stages in the magical work, couched of course in symbolic form:

"Let the magician stand within the great world sea. Let him immerse himself in water and there let him stand his ground. Let him look down into the watery depths. Nothing is seen in form correct. Nothing appears but water. Beneath his feet it moves, around him, and above his head. He cannot speak; he cannot see. Truth disappears in water.

"Let the magician stand within the stream. Around him water flows. His feet stand firm on land and rock, but all the forms he sees are lost in the grey immensity of mist. The water is around his neck, but, feet on rock and head in air, he maketh progress. All is distortion still. He knows he stands, but where to go and how to go he knows not, nor understands. He sounds the words of magic, but muffled, dim and lost, the mist returns them to him, and no true note sounds forth. Around him are the many sounds of many forms, which swallow up his sound.

"Let the magician stand in watery mist, free of the running stream. Some outlines dim appear. He sees a little distance on the Path. Flickers of light break through the clouds of mist and fog. He hears his voice; its note is clearer and more true. The forms of other pilgrims can be seen. Behind him is the sea. Beneath his feet is seen the stream. Around him mist and fog. Above his head no sky is seen nor sun.

"Let the magician stand on higher ground, but in the rain. The drops pour down upon him; the thunder breaks; the lightning flashes in the sky. But as the rain pours down, it dissipates the mist, it washes clean the form and clears the atmosphere.

"Thus forms are seen and sounds are heard, though dim as yet, for loud the thunder roars and heavy is the sound of failing rain. But now the sky is seen; the sun breaks forth and in between the drifting

clouds, expanses of the blue of heaven cheer the tired eyes of the disciple.
"Let the magician stand upon the mountain top. Beneath him in the valleys and the plains, water and streams and clouds are seen. Above him is the blue of heaven, the radiance of the rising sun, the pureness of the mountain air. Each sound is clear. The silence speaks with sound."

Then come the highly significant phrases which give the picture of the consummation:

"Let the magician stand within the sun, looking from thence upon the ball of earth. From that high point of peace serene let him sound forth the words that will create the forms, build worlds and universes and give his life to that which he has made. Let him project the forms created on the mountain top in such a way that they can cleave the clouds which circle round the ball of earth, and carry light and power. These shall dispel the veil of forms which hide the true abode of earth from the eye of the beholder."

Such is the end of the magical work. It involves the discovery that the astral plane and the astral light so-called are but the cinematographs created by man himself. What man has created he can also destroy.

More as to the magical work I may not at this time give. The words that blend may not under any circumstances be given except under the oath of secrecy which governs automatically the pledged disciple; these oaths are given to no man but are rendered by the aspirant to his own soul when that soul has conveyed to him the words. He finds them for himself as the result of tireless effort and endeavour. He knows that these formulas are the prerogative of all souls and can only be known and safely used by those who have realised the Self as One. He therefore pledges himself never to reveal these words to any one who is not functioning as a soul or who is wandering blinded in the vale of illusion. From this automatic response to knowledge by the knowers of the race, the Hierarchy of Adepts has gathered its personnel.

A CALL TO SERVICE

In closing this treatise on the magical work of the individual aspirant I seek to do two things:

1. Indicate the immediate goal for students in this century, and summarise time steps that they must take.
2. Indicate the things which must be eliminated and overcome and the penalties which overtake the probationer and the disciple when mistakes are made and faults are condoned.

First of all, the immediate goal must be well recognised, if lost effort is to be avoided and real progress achieved. Many well-intentioned aspirants are prone to give undue time to their registered aspirations, and to the formulation of their plans for service. The world aspiration is now so strong and humanity is now so potently orienting itself towards the Path that sensitive people everywhere are being swept into a vortex of spiritual desire, and ardently long for the life of liberation, of spiritual undertakings and of recorded soul consciousness. Their recognition of their own latent possibilities is now so strong that they over-estimate themselves; they give much time to picturing themselves as the ideal mystic or in deploring their lack of spiritual achievement or their failure to achieve a sphere of service. Thus they become lost, on the one hand, in the vague and misty realms of a beautiful idealism, of colourful hypotheses, and of delightful theories; on the other hand, they become engulfed in a dramatisation of themselves as centres of power in a field of fruitful service; they draw up, mentally, plans for world endeavour to see themselves as the pivotal point around which that service will move; they frequently make an effort to work out these plans and produce an organisation, for instance on the physical plane, which is potentially valuable but equally potentially useless, even if not dangerous. They fail to realise that the motivating impulse is primarily due to what the Hindu teachers call a "sense of I-ness", and that their work is founded on a subjective egoism which must—and will—be eliminated before true service can be rendered.

This tendency to aspiration and to service is right and good and should be seen as forming part of the coming universal consciousness and equipment of the race as a whole. It is steadily coming to the surface owing to the growing strength of the Aquarian influence which (from about the year A.D. 1640) has been gaining in potency and is producing two effects: it is breaking down the crystallised old forms of the Piscean age, and is stimulating the creative faculties, as they express themselves in group concepts, and group plans. As all of you well know, this is the cause of the present disturbed conditions, and these conditions can be summed up in the words: *impersonalization* wherein the state, group or groups are regarded as of more importance than the individual and his rights; *amalgamation*, which is the tendency to fuse, blend, and cohere and to produce that interrelation which must eventually mark the intercourse of humanity and produce that "synthesis of all the single men", which Browning so truly remarks is the goal of the evolutionary process and marks the conclusion of the journey of the divine prodigal; and sensitive *intercommunication* between units, groups and combinations of groups, both on the subjective and objective sides of manifestation. In these three words—impersonalization, amalgamation, and intercommunication—you have summed up for you the outstanding phenomena which are appearing among us at this time. Students are urged to consider the plan as it is thus expressing itself, and to study these growing tendencies in human affairs. The fact that they are so prominent will appear, if the student will take the trouble to consider the panorama of history; he will then note that even the history of five hundred years ago will reveal to him the fact that at that time great individuals were the prominent factors, and that history is concerned largely with the doings of powerful personalities who cast their spell over their time and age; then isolation and separateness governed human affairs and every man fought for his own land and every man forgot his brother and lived selfishly; then there was little interrelation between different races or between human families, and there was no real means of communication, except that of personal contact, which was frequently impossible.

Students should therefore ponder on these words which will be found to become of increasing importance during the next fifty years. This is far enough ahead for the average student to look and to plan, and in their recognition of this phase of the working out of the divine Purpose, they would do well to study their individual life expression and to ask themselves the following questions:

1. Are they wasting time in mystical dreams, or are they occupied in a practical application of the sensed spiritual truths, thus making them part of their daily experience?

2. Do they find that their reaction to the growing impersonality of the age is one of resentment, or do they find that this relatively new attitude of personal detachment is tending to solve their own personal problems?

3. Can they register an increasing ability to sense the thoughts and ideas of others, and do they find that they are becoming more sensitive and therefore more able to swing into the great tide of intercommunication?

4. How much is the faculty of dramatisation governing their daily life? Do they find that they are the centre of the universe, which revolves automatically around them, or are they working at the problem of decentralising themselves and at absorption in the whole?

These and other questions which will arise may serve to indicate the responsiveness of the aspirant to the coming in of the new age.

In this treatise on individual development and on astral control, a vision has been given and a rule of life expounded which holds in it the needed instruction for the interlude between the two great ages—the Piscean and the Aquarian. A part of the underlying purpose has been expressed in words—a purpose which is recognised by many all over the world and which is working out in practically every department of human life. It is subconsciously registered and intuitively followed by many who know nothing of the technicalities of the plan. Those who guide the human race are not particularly concerned as to the success of the emerging new conditions. That is most definitely assured, and the growth of human realisation and of the spiritual consciousness of non-separateness cannot be arrested. The problem is what means to continue to employ to bring these desired ends about in such a way that the form nature can be keyed up and prepared to handle its new responsibilities, and deal with its new knowledges without undue suffering and those painful cleavages and hours of agony which attract more attention than the more subtle and successful growth of divine awareness. Every time there is a tendency towards synthesis and understanding in the world, every time the lesser is merged in the greater and the unit is blended in the whole, every time great and universal concepts make their impact upon the minds of the masses, there is a subsequent disaster and cataclysm and breaking down of the form aspect and of that which might prevent those concepts becoming physical plane facts. This is therefore the problem of the hierarchical workers:—how to avert the dreaded suffering and carry man along whilst the tidal wave of this spiritual realisation sweeps over the world and does its needed work. Hence the present call to service which is sounding like a trumpet in the ear of all attentive disciples.

This call to service usually meets with a response, but that response is coloured by the personality of the aspirant and tinctured with his pride, and his ambition. Need is truly realised. The desire to meet the need is genuine and sincere; the longing to serve and lift is real. Steps are taken which are intended by the aspirant to enable him to fit in with the plan. But the trouble with which we on the inner side have perforce to deal is, that though there is no question as to willingness and desire to serve, the characters and temperaments are such that well nigh insuperable difficulties are presented. Through these aspirants we have to work, and the material they present gives us much trouble frequently.

These latent characteristics often do not make their appearance until after the service has been undertaken. That they are there, the watching guides may suspect, but even they have not the right to withhold opportunity. When there is this delayed appearance the tragedy is that many others suffer besides the aspirant concerned. As the human fabric makes itself felt and stands out of the mist of idealism, of lovely plans and much talk and arranging, many are in the meantime attracted by synchronous idealism, and gather around the server. When the hidden weaknesses appear, they suffer as well as he. The method of the Great Ones, which is to seek out those who have trained themselves somewhat in sensitive response and to work through them, carries with it certain dangers. The ordinary well-meaning aspirant is not in such danger as the more advanced and active disciple. He is in danger in three directions and can be swept off his feet in three ways:

1. His whole nature is under undue stimulation on account of his inner contacts and the spiritual forces

with which he is in touch, and this carries with it real danger, for he hardly knows as yet how to handle himself, and is scarcely aware of the risk entailed.

2. The people with whom he is working, in their turn, make his problem. Their greed, their adulation, and praise, and their criticism tend to becloud his way. Because he is not sufficiently detached and spiritually advanced, he walks bemused in a cloud of thoughtforms, and knows it not. Thus he loses his way and wanders from the original intent and again he knows it not.

3. His latent weaknesses must emerge under the pressure of the work, and inevitably he will show signs of cracking at times, if I may use such a word. The personality faults become strengthened as he seeks to carry his particular form of service to the world. I refer to that service which is self sought and formulated on a background of personal ambition and love of power, even if only partially recognised or not recognised at all. He is under strain naturally, and—like a man carrying a heavy load up a steep hill—he discovers points of strain, and evinces a tendency to break down physically, or to lower his ideal so as to conform to weaknesses.

To all this must be added the strain of the period itself, and the general condition of unhappy humanity. This subconsciously has its effect on all disciples, and upon all who are now working in the world. Some are showing signs of physical pressure, though the inner life remains poised and normal, sane and rightly oriented. Others are breaking up emotionally and this produces two effects according to the point of development of the aspirant to service. He is either, through the strain, learning detachment, and this curiously enough is what might be called the "defense mechanism" of the soul in this present period of world unfoldment, or he is becoming increasingly nervous and is on the way to become a neurotic. Others, again, are feeling the pressure in the mental body. They become bewildered in some cases and no clear truth appears. They then work on without inspiration, and because they know it to be right and they also have the rhythm of work. Others are grasping opportunity as they see it and, to do so, fall back on innate self-assertion (which is the outstanding fault of the mental types) and build up a structure around their service, and construct a form which in reality embodies what they desire, what they think to be right, but which is separative and the child of their minds and not the child of their souls. Some, in their turn, more potent and more coordinated, feel the pressure of the entire personality; the versatile psychic nature responds both to need and to the theory of the plan; they realise their truly valuable assets and know they have somewhat to contribute. They are still, however, so full of what is called *personality* that their service is gradually and steadily stepped down to the level of that personality, and is consequently coloured by their personality reactions, their likes and dislikes, and their individual life tendencies and habits. These eventually assert themselves and there is then a worker, doing good work but spoiling it all by this unrealised separateness and individual methods. This means that such a worker gathers to himself only those whom he can subordinate and govern. His group is not coloured by the impulses of the new age, but by the separative instincts of the worker at the centre. The danger here is so subtle that much care must be taken by a disciple in self-analysis. It is so easy to be glamoured by the beauty of one's own ideals and vision, and by the supposed rectitude of one's own position, and yet all the time be influenced subjectively by love of personal power, individual ambition, jealousy of other workers, and the many traps which catch the feet of the unwary disciple.

But if true impersonality is cultivated, if the power to stand steady is developed, if every situation is handled in a spirit of love and if there is a refusal to take hasty action and to permit separation to creep in, then there will be the growth of a group of true servers, and the gathering out of those who can materialise the plan and bring to birth the new age and its attendant wonders.

To do this, there must be courage of the rarest kind. Fear holds the world in thrall, and no one is exempt from its influence. For the aspirant and for the disciple are two kinds of fear which require to be especially considered. The fears that we dealt with in the earlier part of the treatise, and the fears that are inherent, as you know, in existence itself are familiar to all of us. They have their root in the instinctual nature (economic fears, fears arising out of the sex life, physical fear and terror, fear of the unknown, with that dominating fear of death which colours so many lives) and have been the subject of much psychological investigation. With them I do not seek to deal. They are to be overcome by the life of the soul as it permeates and transforms the daily life, and by the refusal of the aspirant to accord them any recognition. The first method builds towards future strength of character, and prevents the coming in of any new fears. They cannot exist when the soul is consciously controlling life and its situations. The second negatives the old thought forms and brings about eventually their destruction through lack of nourishment. A dual process is therefore carried forward, producing a genuine manifestation of the qualities of the spiritual man and a growing freedom from the thralldom of age-old fear concepts. The student finds himself becoming steadily detached from the prime governing instincts which have hitherto served to weld him into the general scheme of the elementary planetary life. It might be valuable here to point out that all the major instincts have their roots in that peculiar quality of the planetary life,—fear reactions, leading to activity of some kind. As you know the psychologists list five main and dominant instincts, and we will very briefly touch upon them.

The *instinct of self-preservation* has its roots in an innate fear of death; through the presence of this fear, the race has fought its way to its present point of longevity and endurance. The sciences which concern themselves with the preservation of life, the medical knowledge of the day, and the achievements of civilised comfort have all grown out of this basic fear. All has tended to the persistence of the individual, and to his preserved condition of being. Humanity persists, as a race and as a kingdom in nature, as a result of this fear tendency, this instinctual reaction of the human unit to self-perpetuation.

The *instinct of sex* has its main root in the fear of separateness and of isolation, and in a revolt against separative unity on the physical plane, against aloneness; and it has resulted in the carrying forward of the race and the persistence and propagation of the forms through which the race can come into manifestation.

The *herd instinct* can easily be seen to have its root in a similar reaction; for the sense of safety and for convinced assured security—based on numerical aggregations—men have always sought their own kind and herded themselves together for defense and for economic stability. Out of this instinctual reaction of the race as a whole, our modern civilisation is the result; its vast centres, its huge cities and its massed tenements have emerged, and we have modern herding, carried to the nth degree.

The fourth great instinct, that *of self-assertion*, is also based on fear; it connotes the fear of the individual that he will fail of recognition and thus lose much that would otherwise be his. As time has progressed, the selfishness of the race has thus grown; its sense of acquisitiveness has developed and the power to grasp has emerged (the "will to power" in some form or another) until today we have the intense individualism and the positive sense of importance which have produced much of the modern economic and national troubles. We have fostered self-determination, self-assertion and self-interest until we are presented with a well-nigh insuperable problem. But out of it all, much good has come and will come, for no individual is of value until he realises that value for himself, and then with definiteness sacrifices the acquired values for the good of the whole.

The *instinct to enquire* in its turn is based on fear of the unknown, but out of this fear has emerged-—as a result of age-long enquiry—our present educational and cultural systems and the entire structure of scientific investigation.

These tendencies, based on fear have (because man is divine) acted as a tremendous stimulation of his entire nature, and have carried him forward to his present point of wide comprehension and usefulness; they have produced our modern civilisation with all its defects and yet with all its indicated divinity. Out of these instincts carried forward into infinity, and out of the process of their transmutation into their higher correspondences the full flower of soul expression will emerge. I would like to point out the following:

The instinct of self-presentation finds its consummation in assured immortality, and of this the work undertaken by the spiritualists and psychic investigators right down the ages is the mode of approach and the inevitable guarantee.

The sex instinct has worked out and finds its logical consummation in the relationship-—consciously realised-—of the soul and the body. This is the keynote of mysticism and religion, which is today, as ever, the expression of the Law of Attraction, not as it expresses itself through physical plane marriage, but as it finds its consummation (for man) in the sublime marriage carried forward with conscious intent between the positive soul and the negative and receptive form.

The herd instinct finds its divine consummation in an awakened group consciousness, which is evidenced today in the general tendency towards amalgamations, and the widespread fusing and blending which are going on everywhere. It demonstrates in the ability to think in terms of internationalism, of universal concepts, which will eventually result in the establishing of universal brotherhood.

The instinct of self-assertion, in its turn, has given to our modern civilisation its intense individualism, the cult of the personality, and the production of ancestor and hero-worship. It is leading, however, to the assertion of the Self, of the divine inner Ruler, and out of our newest science, psychology, will emerge a knowledge of the assertive and dominant spiritual Self, and lead finally to the manifestation of the kingdom of souls on earth.

And what of the instinct to enquire? Transmuted into divine investigation and transformed by the application of the light of the soul in the realm of enquiry, we shall have humanity carried forward into the Hall of Wisdom and thus man will leave behind the experiences of the Hall of Knowledge. Our great educational centres will become schools for the development of intuitive perception and of spiritual awareness.

The following table should be carefully studied by the student:

Instinct	Correspondence	Mode
1. Self-preservation	Immortality	Spiritualistic Research.
2. Sex	Spiritual union	Religion.
	At-one-ment	Mysticism.
3. Herd	Group consciousness	Brotherhood.
4. Self-Assertion	Assertion of the Self	Psychology.

5. Enquiry---------------- Intuition----------------------- Education.

Thus the fears which beset humanity, having their roots in instincts, seem nevertheless to be divine characteristics, misapplied and misused. When, however, they are rightly understood and used, and transmuted by the knowing soul, they produce awareness and are the source of growth and that which conveys to the dormant soul——in time and space——the needed impulse, impetus and urge to progress which have carried man forward from the caveman stage and the prehistoric cycle, through the long period of history, and can be trusted today to carry him forward with increasing rapidity, as he now arrives at intellectual comprehension and can apply himself to the problem of progress in full awareness.

Students need to realise more deeply that the whole process is a divine one, and that evil, so-called, is but an illusion and an inherent part of duality, giving place in time and out of time to a divine unity. Evil is due to wrong perception and erroneous interpretation of that which is perceived. The achievement of true vision, plus right understanding, brings about freedom from the instinctual reactions and evokes that inner detachment which enables a man to walk at liberty in the kingdom of God.

But what of the two fears with which the aspirant has peculiar concern? What of the fear of public opinion, and fear of failure? These are two potent factors in the life of service, and hinder many.

Those who are beginning to work in cooperation with the plan and are learning the significance of service are prone to fear that what they do will be criticised and misjudged, or fall a victim to the reverse idea that what they do will not be sufficiently liked, appreciated and understood. They demand liking and praise. They gauge success by numbers and by response. They dislike to have their motives impugned and misjudged, and rush violently into explanation; they are unhappy if their methods, the personnel of their group, and the way in which their service is rendered comes under the tongue of criticism. The false objectives of numbers, of power or of a formulated doctrine control them. Unless what they do measures up to the standards or conforms to the technique of the group of minds which surrounds them or appeals the most to them, they are unhappy and consequently frequently change their plans, alter their viewpoint, and lower their standard until it conforms to their immediate mass psychology, or their chosen counsellors.

The true disciple sees the vision. He then seeks to keep so closely in touch with his soul that he can stand with steadiness whilst he endeavours to make that vision a reality; he aims to achieve what, from the standpoint of the world seems to be impossible, knowing that the vision is not materialised through expediency and undue adaptation of the suggested ideas of worldly or intellectual counsellors. Public opinion and the advice of those who are Piscean in their tendencies and not Aquarian are carefully considered but not unduly so, and when advice is found to be separative and tends to eliminate harmony, and produces a lack of brotherly love and understanding, it is discarded at once. When there is evidenced a constantly critical attitude towards other workers in the field of world service and where there is a capacity to see only selfishness and fault and to impute wrong motives and to believe evil, then the true aspirant refuses to be swayed and goes serenely on his way.

In the coming cycle I emphatically tell you that the true work will be carried forward (the work of spiritually welding the world into a synthesis and the production of a recognised brotherhood of souls) only by those who refuse to be separative and whose words are watched so that no evil is spoken; these are the workers who see the divine in all and refuse to think evil and impute evil; they work with sealed lips; they deal not with their brothers affairs, nor reveal that which concerns them; their lives are coloured by understanding and by love; their minds are characterised by a trained spiritual perception and that spiritual awareness which employs a keen intellect as the corollary of a loving spirit.

May I repeat in other words this theme, for its importance is vital and the effect of the work of these instruments on the world is immense. These men and women whose mission it is to inaugurate the New Age have learned the secret of silence; they are animated ceaselessly by a spirit of inclusive love; their tongues lead them not astray into the field of ordinary criticism, and they permit no condemnation of others; they are animated by the spirit of protection. To them will be committed the work of fostering the life of the New Age.

To those who have not yet reached this point in evolution and whose vision is not so clear, nor their natures so disciplined, there remains the important work, on a lower level, of working with their kind. Their attributes and qualities bring to them those who resemble them; they do not work in such loneliness and their work is more outwardly successful, though not always so.

It must be remembered that all work, in the sight of the Great Ones, is of equal importance. For those souls who are at the stage where a home or office provides sufficient experience, that is for them the supreme effort; their attempt to work is—on its own level—as great an achievement as to fulfill the destiny of a Christ or a Napoleon. Forget this not and seek to see life truly and not with its distinctions-—men-made and dangerous. A disciple who has not yet the fuller vision of a more trained worker and who is only just learning the ABC of public work may, with all his failures and dense stupidities, be doing as well as an older disciple with his wider knowledge and experience.

THE NEW AGE GROUPS AND TRAINING

To those of us who are working on the inner side, the workers in the world fall into three groups:

1. Those, few and far between, who are true Aquarians. These work under real difficulties, for their vision is beyond the grasp of the majority, and they meet often lack of understanding, frequent disappointment in their fellow workers, and much loneliness.

2. Those who are straight Pisceans. These work with much greater facility and find a more rapid response from those around them. Their work is more doctrinal, less inclusive and coloured by the spirit of separation. They include the mass of world workers in all the various departments of human thought and welfare.

3. Those Pisceans who are enough developed to respond to the Aquarian message, but who-—as yet-— cannot trust themselves to employ the real Aquarian methods of work and message.

For instance, they have in the political field, a sense of internationalism, but they cannot apply it when it comes to the understanding of others. They think they have a universal consciousness, but when it comes to a test, they discriminate and eliminate. They constitute a much smaller group than the true Pisceans and are doing good work and filling a much needed place. The problem they present however to the Aquarian worker lies in the fact that though they respond to the ideal and regard themselves as of the new age, they are not truly so. They see a bit of the vision and have grasped the theory but cannot express it in action.

Thus we have these three groups doing much needed work and reaching through their united undertakings the mass of people and fulfilling thus their dharma. One group works necessarily under the glamour of public opinion. The intermediate group has a most difficult task to perform, for where there is no clear vision the voice of their chosen environment and the voice of the inner group of world Knowers are often in conflict and they are pulled hither and thither as they respond first to one and then to the other. The group of those who respond more fully to the incoming Aquarian vibration register the voices of the leaders of the other two groups, but the voice of the guiding Masters and the voice of the group of world Masters serve to guide them unerringly forward.

I have sought to explain the above modes and methods of work, for the times are hard and clarity of thought is needed if the work is to go forward as desired. Even such triple distinctions as exist between the groups are themselves of a separative tincture, and it is yet impossible to preserve any idea in its true and synthetic relation. It is a gain when the many thousands of separative groups can be grouped into three comprehensive ones and the mind of the disciple be thus freed from the detailed analysis of the world situation among the workers with the Plan.

The second great test of the sensitive disciple is fear of failure. This is based on past experience (for all have failed), on a realisation of the immediate need and opportunity, and on an acute appreciation of individual limitation and deficiency. It is the result oft times of a response to the lowered spiritual and physical vitality of the race today. Never before has there been a time when fear of failure has more widely haunted the human family. Another cause of this reaction is to be found in the fact that mankind *as a whole* and for the first time in the history of the race, senses the vision and has therefore a truer sense of relative values than ever before. Men know themselves to be divine, and this is becoming increasingly a universal realisation. Hence the present unrest and revolt from tramelling conditions. It is however a serious waste of time for a disciple to ponder upon a failure or to fear failing. There is no such thing as failure; there can only be loss of time. That in itself is serious in these days of dire world need, but the disciple must inevitably some day make good and retrieve his past failures. I need not point out that we learn by failure, for that is a well known truth, and is known as such by all who are attempting to live as souls. Nor need the disciple sorrow over the failures, apparent or real, of his fellow disciples. The *sense of time* produces glamour and disappointment, whereas the work goes truly forward, and a lesson learnt by failure acts as a safeguard for the future. Thus it leads to rapid growth. An honest disciple may be momentarily glamoured, but in the long run nothing can really deter him. What are a few brief years in a comparative cycle of aeons? What is a second of time in a span of man's allotted seventy years? To the individual disciple they appear most important; to the onlooking soul, they seem as nothing at all. For the world perhaps, a temporary failure may connote delay in expected help, but that again is brief, and help will come from other sources, for the Plan goes unerringly forward.

May I in all earnest offer to you the paradoxical injunction to work with utter earnestness, and yet at the same time to refuse to work with such earnestness, and not to take yourself so earnestly? Those who stand on the inner side and study the work of the world aspirants today see an almost pitiful distress of individual deficiency, a sustained and strenuous effort on their part to "make themselves what they ought to be", and yet at the same time a distressing lack of proportion, and no sense of humour whatsoever. I urge upon you to cultivate both these qualities. Do not take yourself so seriously, and you will find that you will release yourself for freer and more potent work. Take the Plan seriously and the call to serve, but waste not time in constant self-analysis.

Therefore the immediate goal for all aspiring disciples at this time can be seen to be as follows:

1. An achievement of clarity of thought as to their own personal and immediate problems and primarily the problem as to their objective in service. This is to be done through meditation.

2. The development of sensitivity to the new impulses which are flooding the world at this time. This is to be brought about by loving all men more and through love and understanding contacting them with greater facility. Love reveals.

3. The rendering of service with complete impersonality. This is done by eliminating personal ambition and love of power.

4. The refusal to pay attention to public opinion or to failure. This is done by the application of strict attention to the voice of the soul, and by an endeavour to dwell ever in the secret place of the Most High.

We have merged our first point as to the immediate goal and the steps to be taken to reach it with our second point as to conduct and the factors which must be eliminated. It only remains therefore to point out the penalties which will overtake the probationary disciple and the trained worker should he give way to the glamour and to the faults inherent in his nature and permit them to hinder his work and come between him and the visioned goal.

It might be pointed out that there are three main points of danger in the life of service. I am not here dealing with the individual training of the disciple but with his life of service, and with the activities in which he is engaged as a worker. His temperament, equipment of characteristics (physical, emotional, and mental) do have a potent effect on his environment and on the people he seeks to help, and also his family background, his world training and his speech.

The first point of danger is his physical condition. On this I cannot enlarge beyond begging all disciples to act with wisdom to give themselves sufficient sleep, right food (which must vary for each individual), and those surroundings, if possible, which will enable them to work with the greatest facility. The penalty for the infringing of these suggestions works out in lack of power in service and in the growing thralldom of the physical body. Where the physical body is in poor condition, the disciple has to add the liabilities incident upon the bringing in of force which he finds himself unable to handle.

The second point of danger is to be found in the astral illusion in which all humanity lives, and its power to glamour even experienced workers. I have considered this at length in this treatise, which is, as you know, a treatise on the control of the astral body and a right understanding of its laws. Only mental control, plus true spiritual perception, will suffice to pierce this illusory astral miasma, and reveal to the man that he is a spiritual entity in incarnation and in touch—through his mind—with the Universal Mind. The penalty which overtakes the disciple who persistently permits himself to be glamoured is obvious. His vision becomes fogged and misty and he "loses the sense of touch" as it is called in the old commentaries. He wanders "down the lanes of life and misses that straight highway which will lead him to his goal."

The third danger (and one that is very prevalent at this time) is that of mental pride and consequent inability to work in group formation. The penalty for this is often a temporary success and an enforced working with a group, which has been devitalised of its best elements and which has in it only those people who feed the personality of the head of the group. Because of the emphasis upon his own ideas and his own methods of working, a disciple finds that his group lacks those factors and those people who would have rounded it out, who would have balanced his endeavour, and given to his undertaking those qualities which he himself lacks. This is, in itself, a sufficient punishment, and quickly brings the honest disciple to his senses. Let a disciple who is intelligent, honest and basically true so err, and in time he will awaken to the fact that the group he has gathered around him are moulded by him or he is moulded by them; they are oft embodiments of himself and repeat him. The law works rapidly in the case of a disciple, and thus adjustments are speedily made.

I would like to point out to the student that, having with steadfastness gone forward he will discover that the exoteric and esoteric linking of the outer schools and inner school or rank of knowers of truth is so close that not one earnest student goes totally unrecognised. In the press of the work and in the burden and toil of the day's labours it is an encouragement to know that there are those who watch, and that every loving deed, every aspiring thought and every unselfish reaction is noted and known. Bear in mind, however, that it comes to the recognition of the Helpers through the increased vibration of the aspirant and not through a specific knowledge of the deed accomplished or the thought sent out. Those who teach are occupied with principles of truth, with vibratory rates and with the quality of the light to be seen. They are not aware of, nor have they the time to consider, specific deeds, words and conditions, and the sooner students grasp this and put out of their minds any hope of contacting a phenomenal individual whom they call a Master, with so much leisure, of such developed powers that he can occupy himself with their trivial affairs in time and space, the more rapidly will they progress.

Where, however, there is steady growth, an application to occult principles so that definite changes are produced in the bodies used, and an increasing radiatory light, it is known and recorded, and the aspirant is rewarded by increased opportunity to serve his fellowmen. They do not reward by commendation, by patting on the head, or by expressing their pleasure in words. They are occupied in making knowers and masters out of everyday men and women by:

1. Teaching them to know themselves.

2. Setting them free from authority by awakening interest and enquiry in their minds, and then indicating (not more than that) the direction in which the answer should be sought.

3. Giving them those conditions which will force them to stand on their own feet and rely on their own souls and not on any human being, be he a beloved friend, teacher, or a Master of the Wisdom.

I seek not to repeat myself. Most of the points that concern the work of the aspirant today I have considered earlier in this treatise. It remains now for all of you to study it with care. I close with an appeal to all who read these instructions to rally their forces, to renew their vows of dedication to the service of humanity, to subordinate their own ideas and wishes to the group good, to take their eyes off themselves and fix them anew upon the vision, to guard their tongues from idle speech and criticism, from gossip and inuendo, and to read and study so that the work may go intelligently forward. Let all students make up their minds in this day of emergency and of rapid unfolding opportunity to sacrifice all they have to the helping of humanity. Now is the need and the demand. The urgency of the hour is upon us, and I call upon all of you whom I am seeking to help, to join the strenuous effort of the Great Ones. They are working day and night in an effort to relieve humanity and to offset those evils and disasters which are immanent in the present situation. I offer to you opportunity and I tell you that you are needed—even the very least of you. I assure you that groups of students, working in unison and with deep and unfaltering love for each other, can achieve significant results.

That each of you may so work, and that each of you may lose sight of self in the realisation of world need, is the earnest prayer and deepest aspiration of your brother, THE TIBETAN.

www.ingramcontent.com/pod-product-compliance
Lightning Source LLC
Chambersburg PA
CBHW041926260326
41914CB00009B/1182